Early in the summer, I got hooked on Starbucks' DMOF (Dark Mocha & Orange Frappuccino) and I drank one every day. But since they've discontinued them, I've drastically curtailed my trips to Starbucks. My current trend is ice-azuki from Toraya. I'm getting a craving for it even as I write this...

Wait, was this volume coming out in the fall?

-Tite Kubo

BLEACH is author Tite Kubo's second title. Kubo made his debut with ZOMBIEPOWDER., a four-volume series for WEEKLY SHONEN JUMP. To date, BLEACH has been translated into numerous languages and has also inspired an animated TV series that began airing in the U.S. in 2006. Beginning its serialization in 2001, BLEACH is still a mainstay in the pages of WEEKLY SHONEN JUMP. In 2005, BLEACH was awarded the prestigious Shogakukan Manga Award in the *shonen* (boys) category.

BLEACH
Vol. 47: END OF THE CHRYSALIS AGE
SHONEN JUMP Manga Edition

STORY AND ART BY
TITE KUBO

English Adaptation/Lance Caselman
Translation/Joe Yamazaki
Touch-up Art & Lettering/Mark McMurray
Design/Yukiko Whitley, Kam Li
Editor/Alexis Kirsch

BLEACH © 2001 by Tite Kubo. All rights reserved. First published
in Japan in 2001 by SHUEISHA Inc., Tokyo. English translation rights
arranged by SHUEISHA Inc.

Printed in the U.S.A.

Published by VIZ Media, LLC
P.O. Box 77010
San Francisco, CA 94107

10 9 8 7 6 5 4 3 2 1
First printing, September 2012

PARENTAL ADVISORY
BLEACH is rated T for Teen and is recommended
for ages 13 and up. This volume contains
fantasy violence.
ratings.viz.com

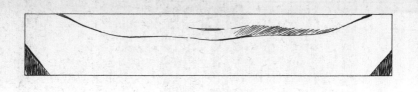

If you became a snake tomorrow
And began devouring people,
If you roared your love for me
With that mouth you use to devour people
Could I still say that I love you
As I do today?

BLEACH 47
END OF THE CHRYSALIS AGE

STARS AND

Isshin Kurosaki

Kisuke Urahara

Ichigo Kurosaki

plot

When high school student Ichigo Kurosaki meets Soul Reaper Rukia Kuchiki his life is changed forever. Soon Ichigo is a soul-cleansing Soul Reaper too, and he finds himself having adventures, as well as problems, that he never would have imagined. Now Ichigo and his friends must stop renegade Soul Reaper Aizen and his army of Arrancars from destroying the Soul Society and wiping out Karakura as well.

After a fierce battle in Las Noches to save Orihime, Ichigo heads to Karakura Town for the final battle! As he faces Aizen, the villain reveals that he has been manipulating Ichigo like a puppet ever since he first met Rukia. But before Ichigo can come to grips with this, his father Isshin appears wearing a Soul Reaper uniform! Isshin clashes with Aizen while Ichigo fights Gin, and Urahara and Yoruichi join the battle as well. But Aizen soon assumes a strange and deadly new form!

BLEACH ALL

藍染惣右介
Sôsuke Aizen

Gin Ichimaru

松本乱菊
Rangiku Matsumoto

市丸ギン

STORIES

BLEACH 47

END OF THE CHRYSALIS AGE

Contents

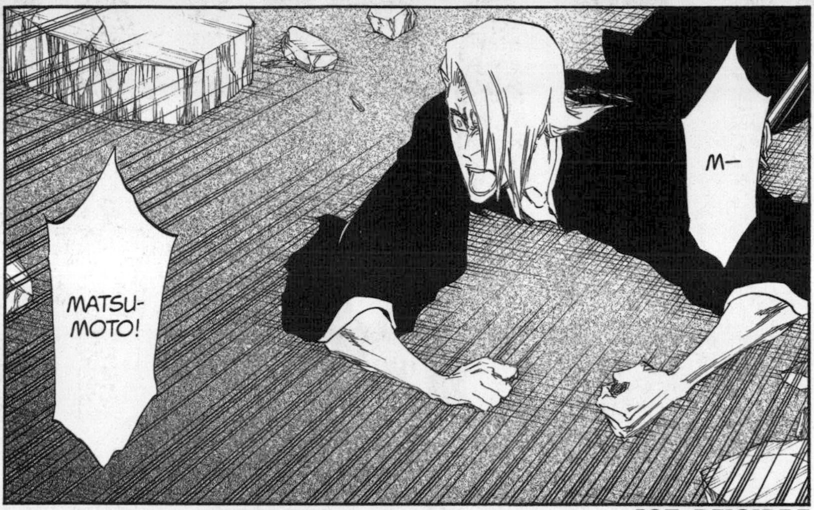
M—
MATSU-MOTO!

405. DEICIDE 7

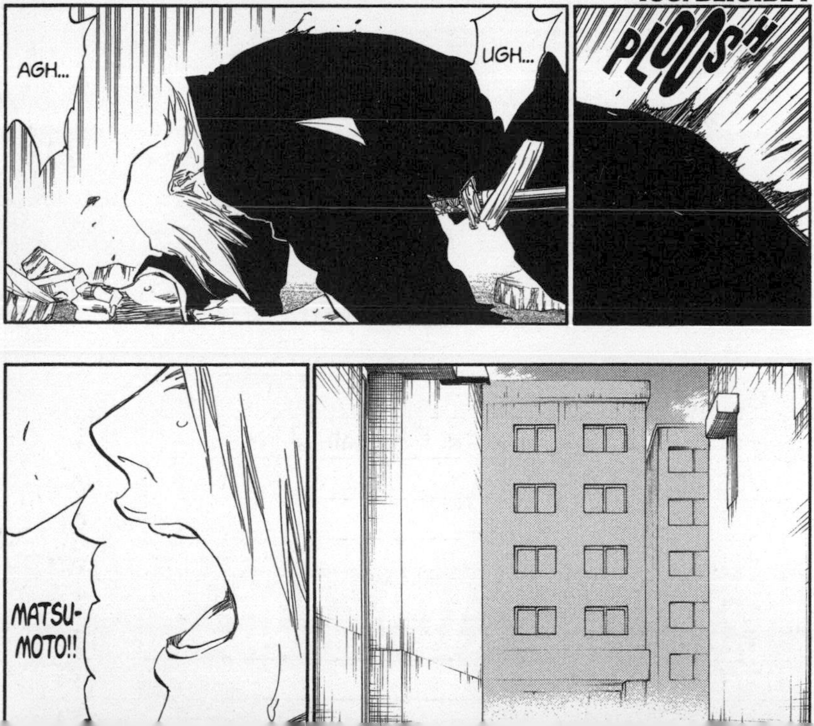
PLOOSH
UGH...
AGH...
MATSU-MOTO!!

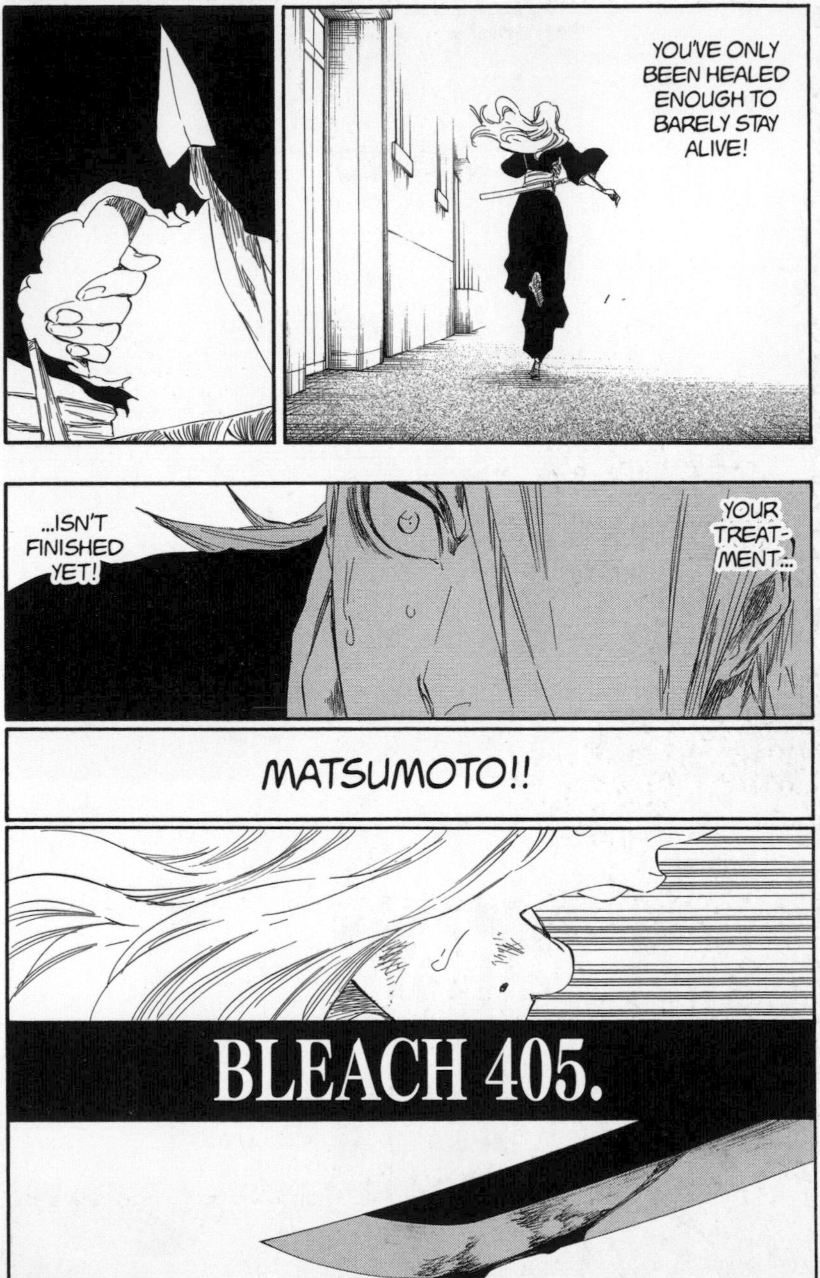
YOU'VE ONLY BEEN HEALED ENOUGH TO BARELY STAY ALIVE!
YOUR TREAT-MENT...
...ISN'T FINISHED YET!
MATSUMOTO!!
BLEACH 405.

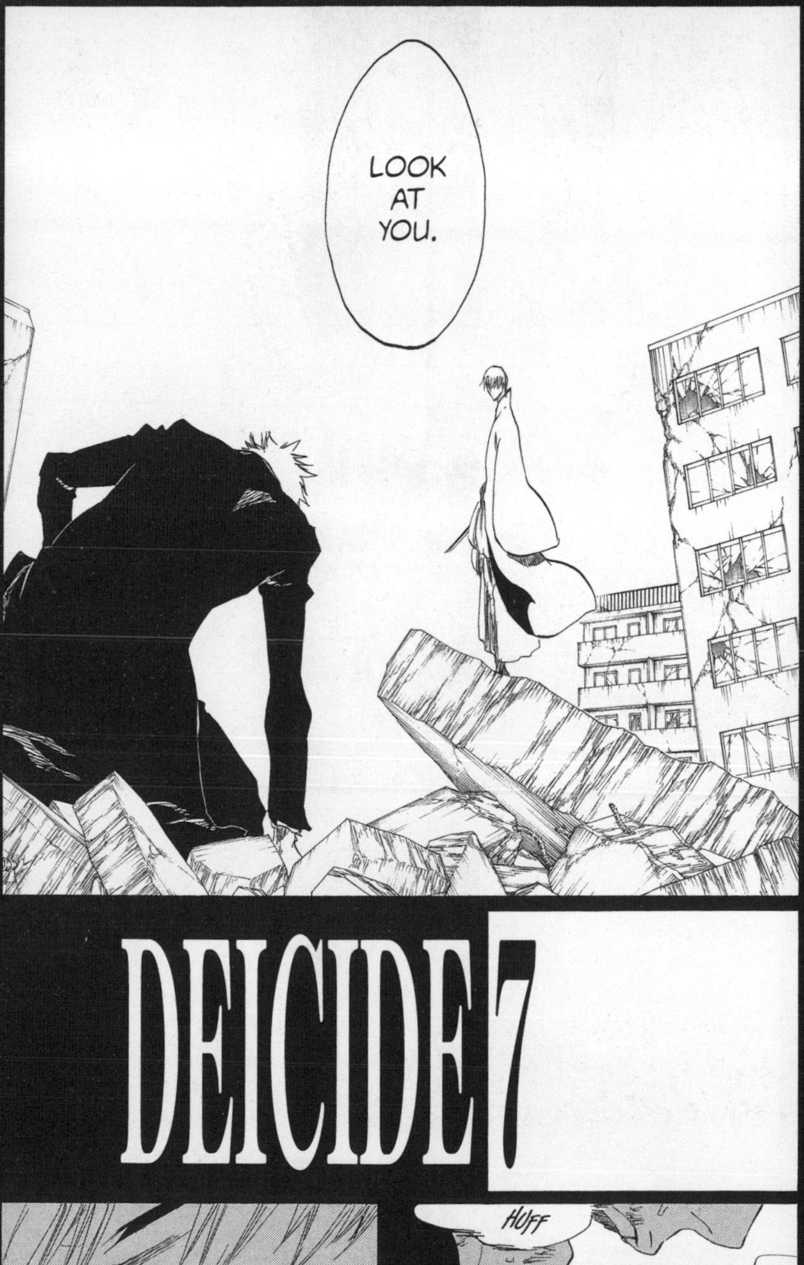
LOOK AT YOU.
DEICIDE 7
HUFF
HUFF

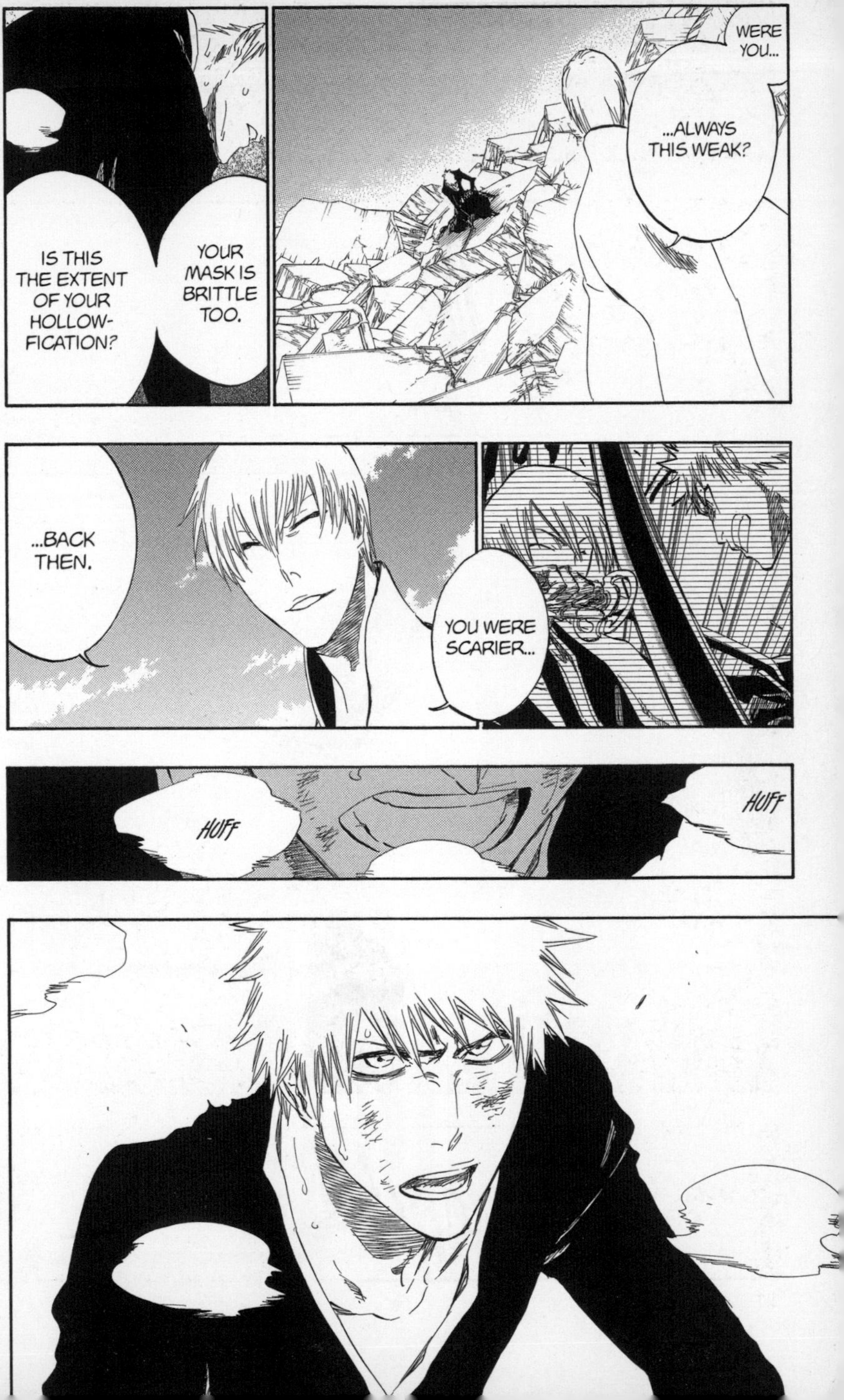
WERE YOU...
...ALWAYS THIS WEAK?
YOUR MASK IS BRITTLE TOO.
IS THIS THE EXTENT OF YOUR HOLLOW-FICATION?
YOU WERE SCARIER...
...BACK THEN.
HUFF
HUFF

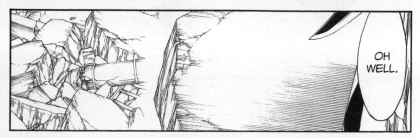

OH WELL.

JUST...

...RUN AWAY.

WHAT ?!

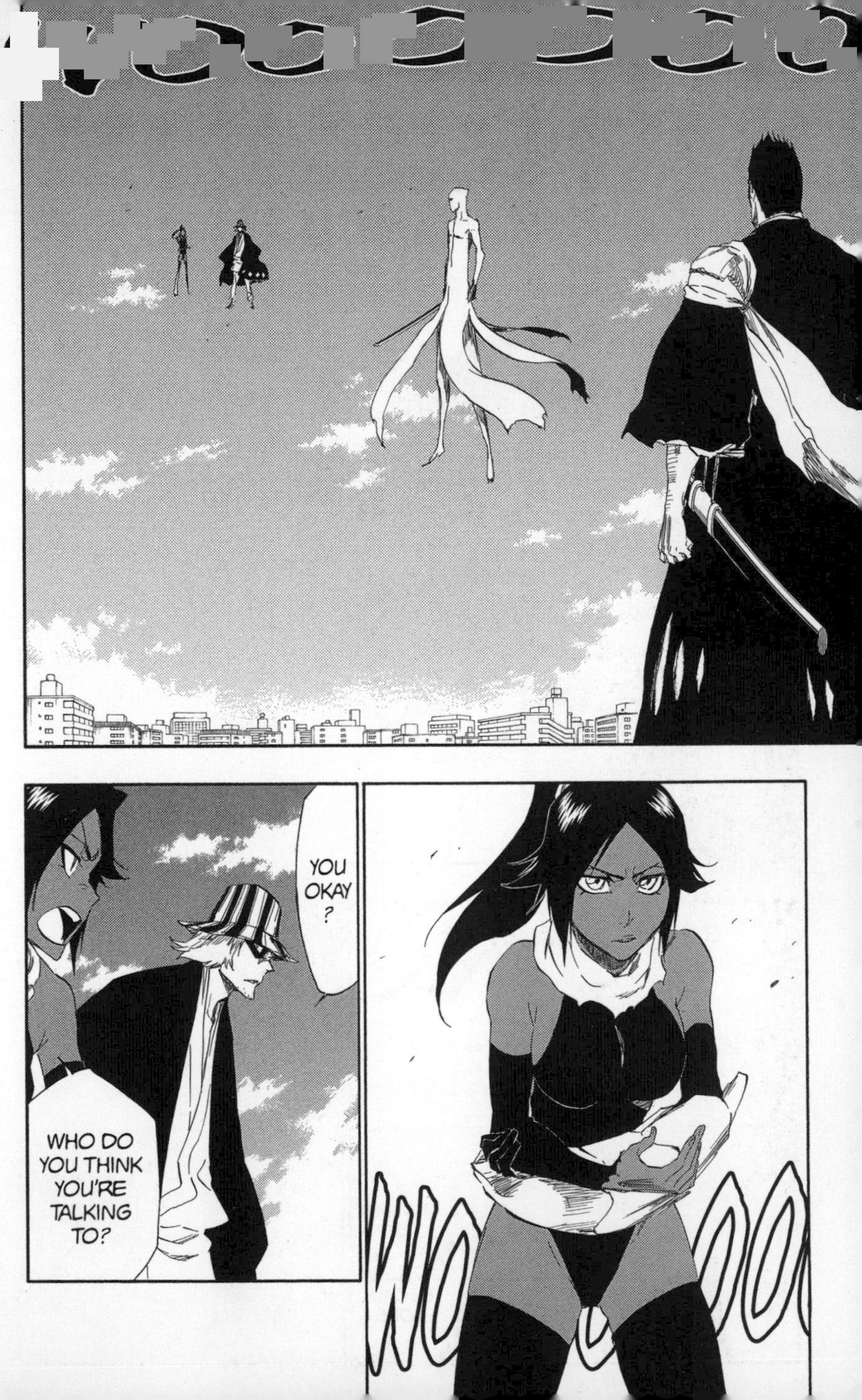
YOU OKAY?
WHO DO YOU THINK YOU'RE TALKING TO?

READ THIS WAY

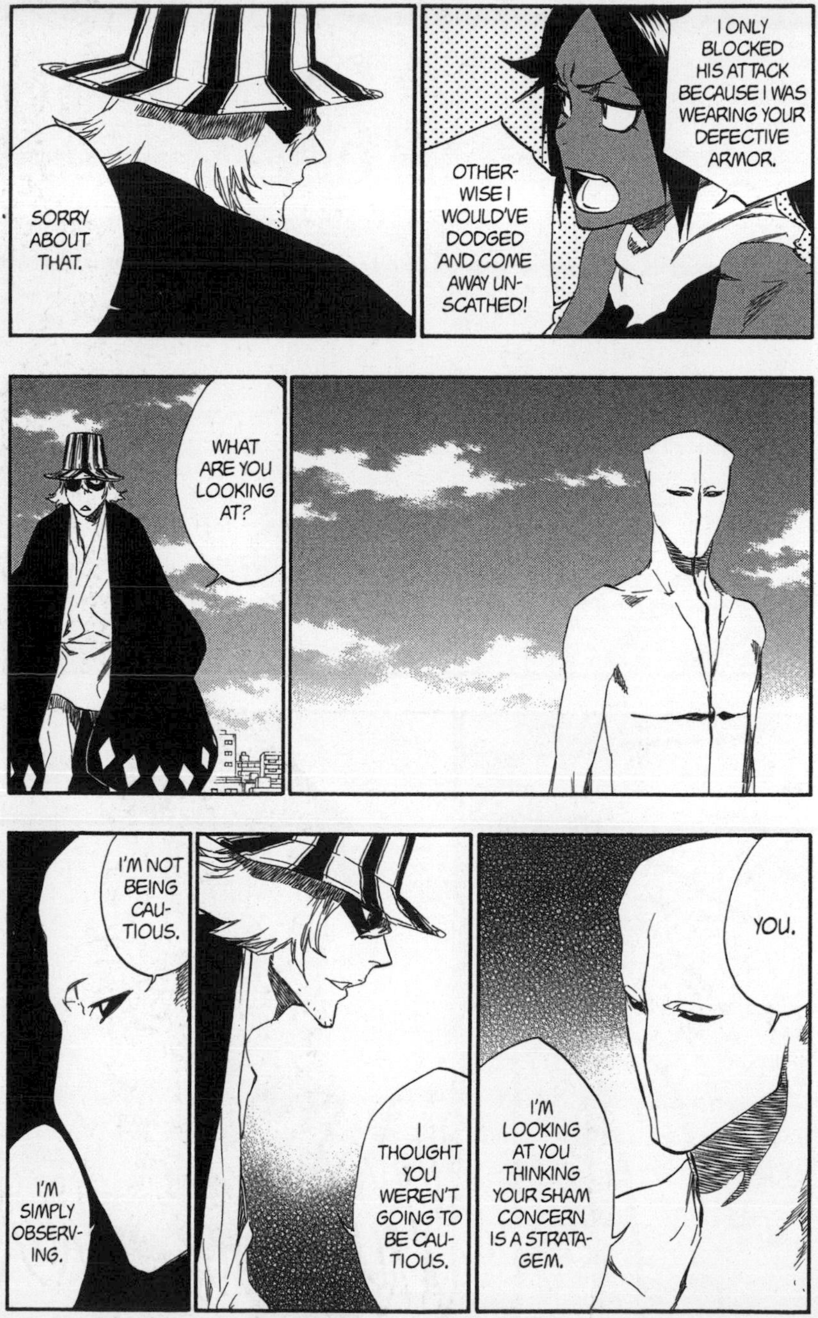

I ONLY BLOCKED HIS ATTACK BECAUSE I WAS WEARING YOUR DEFECTIVE ARMOR.
OTHERWISE I WOULD'VE DODGED AND COME AWAY UNSCATHED!
SORRY ABOUT THAT.
WHAT ARE YOU LOOKING AT?
YOU.
I'M LOOKING AT YOU THINKING YOUR SHAM CONCERN IS A STRATAGEM.
I THOUGHT YOU WEREN'T GOING TO BE CAUTIOUS.
I'M NOT BEING CAUTIOUS.
I'M SIMPLY OBSERVING.

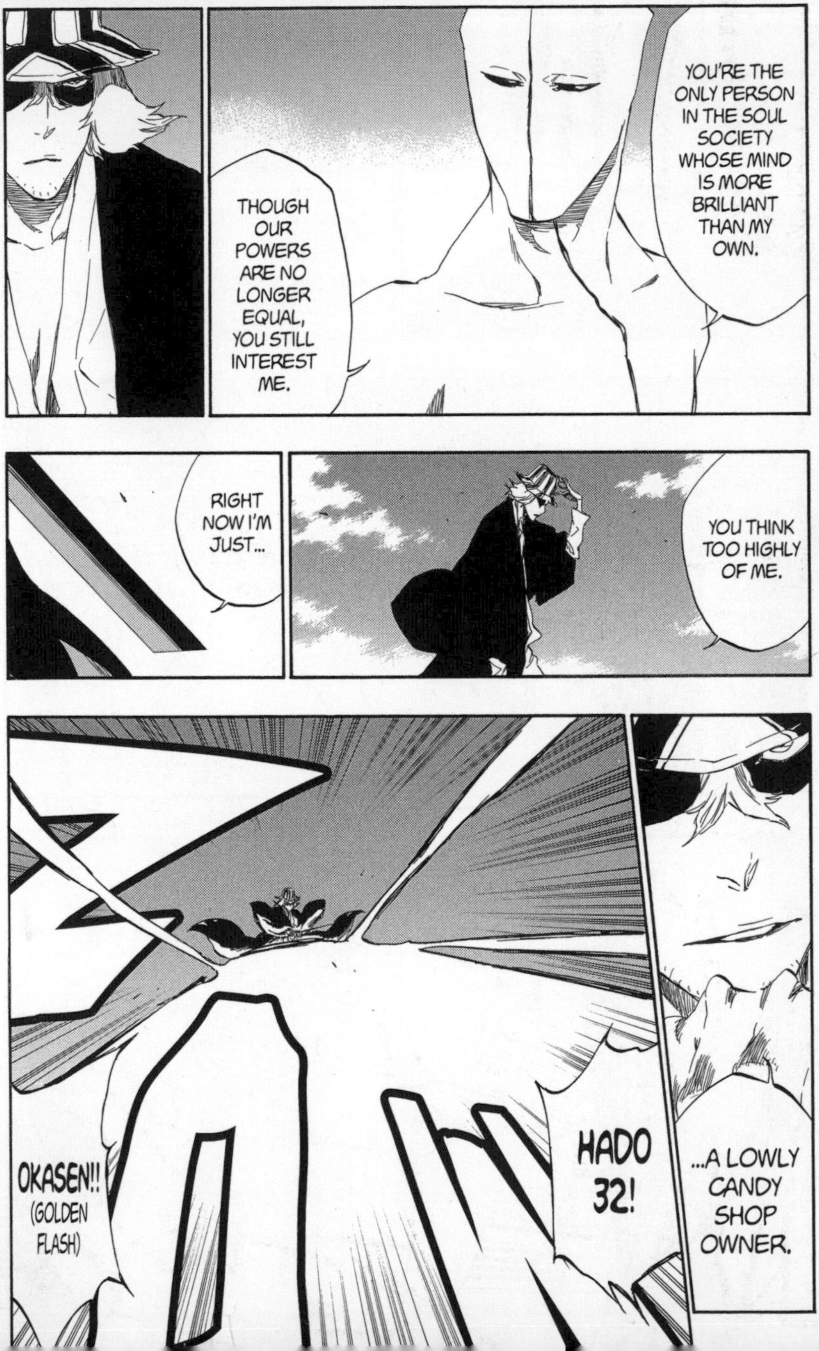
YOU'RE THE ONLY PERSON IN THE SOUL SOCIETY WHOSE MIND IS MORE BRILLIANT THAN MY OWN.
THOUGH OUR POWERS ARE NO LONGER EQUAL, YOU STILL INTEREST ME.
YOU THINK TOO HIGHLY OF ME.
RIGHT NOW I'M JUST...
...A LOWLY CANDY SHOP OWNER.
HADO 32!
OKASEN!!
(GOLDEN FLASH)

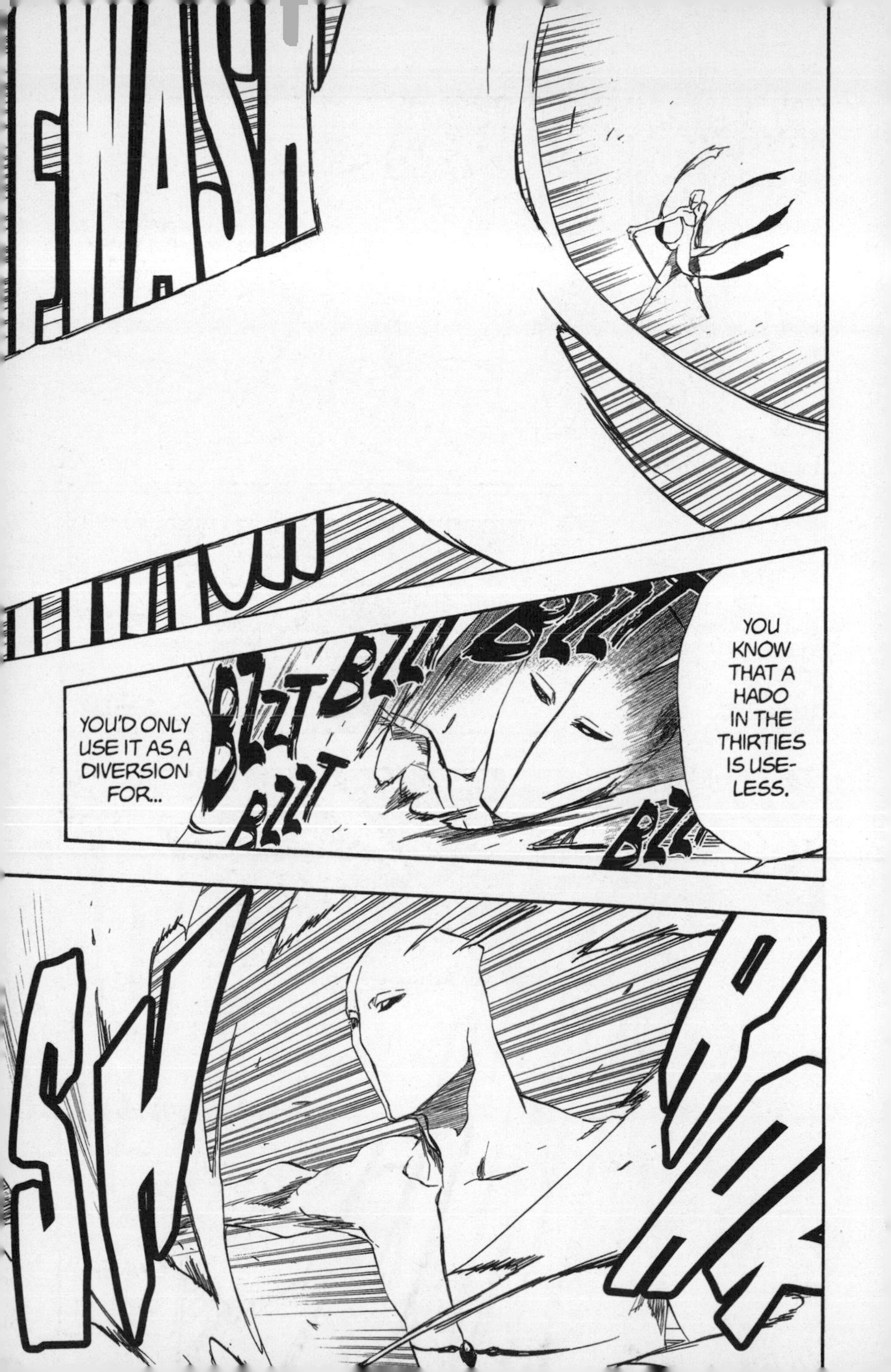
SWASH
YOU KNOW THAT A HADO IN THE THIRTIES IS USE-LESS.
BZZT
YOU'D ONLY USE IT AS A DIVERSION FOR...
BZZT
BZZT

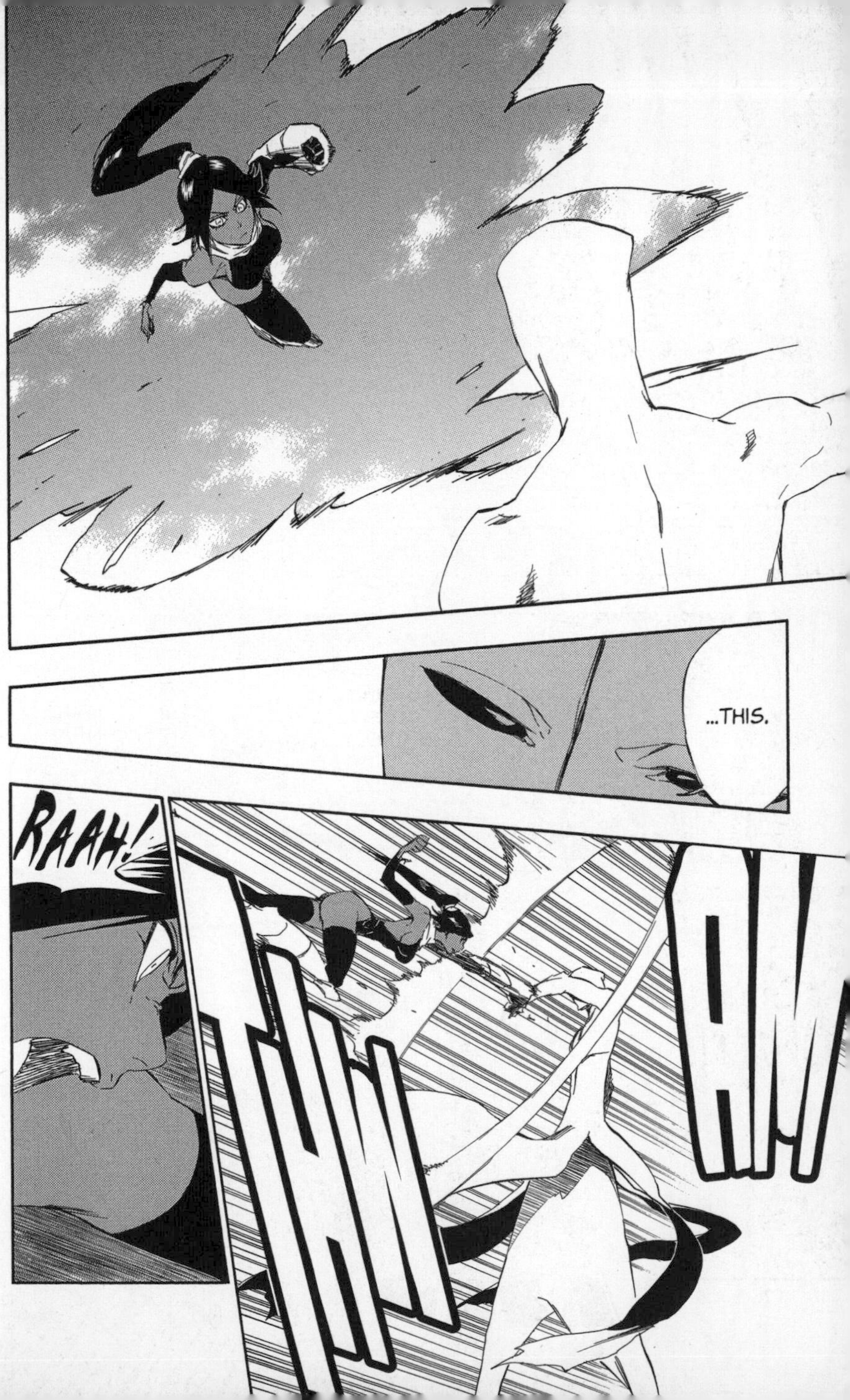
...THIS.
THWAM
RAAH!

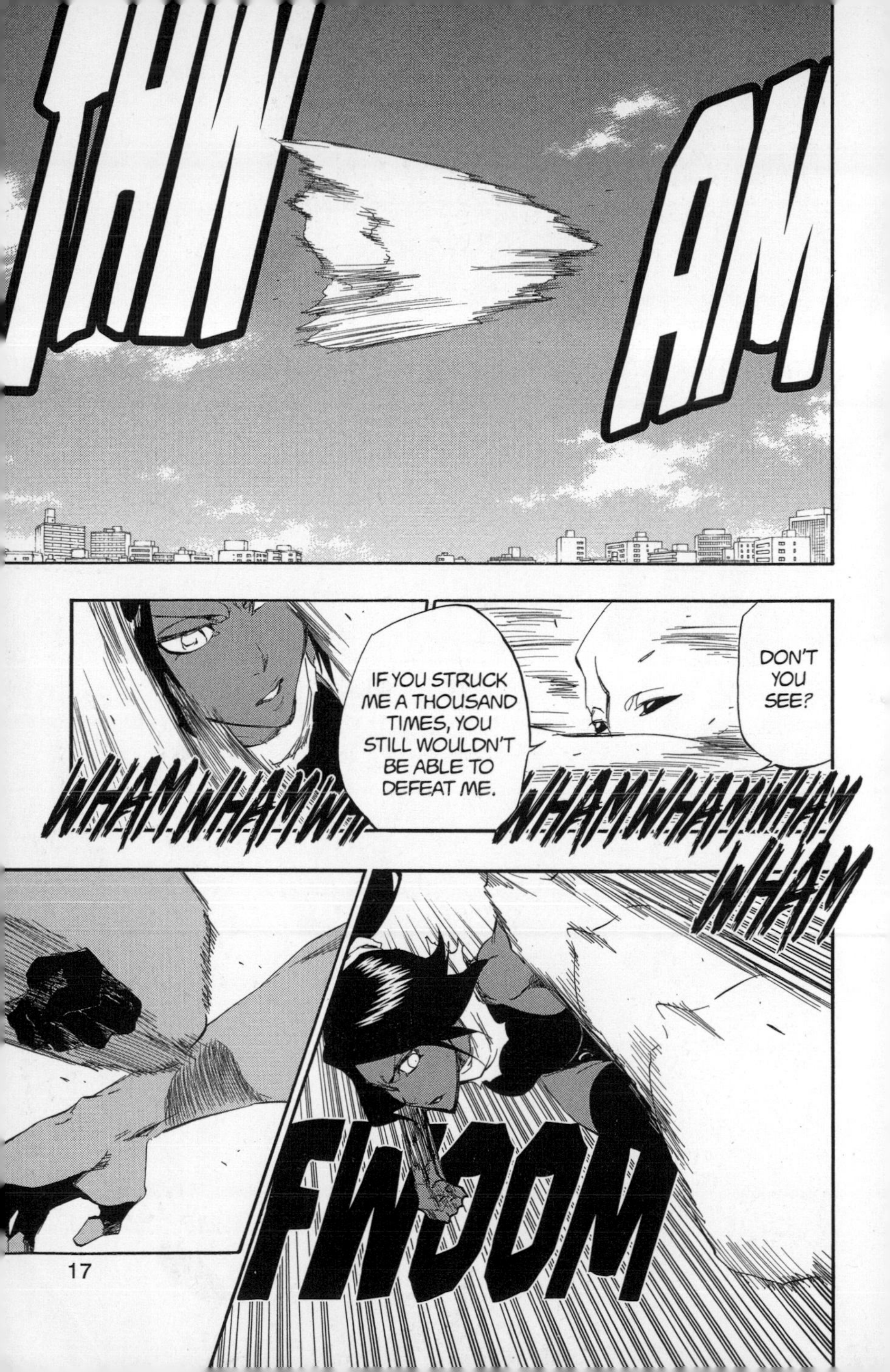
THWAM
DON'T YOU SEE?
IF YOU STRUCK ME A THOUSAND TIMES, YOU STILL WOULDN'T BE ABLE TO DEFEAT ME.
WHAM WHAM WHAM
WHAM
WHAM WHAM WH
FWOOM

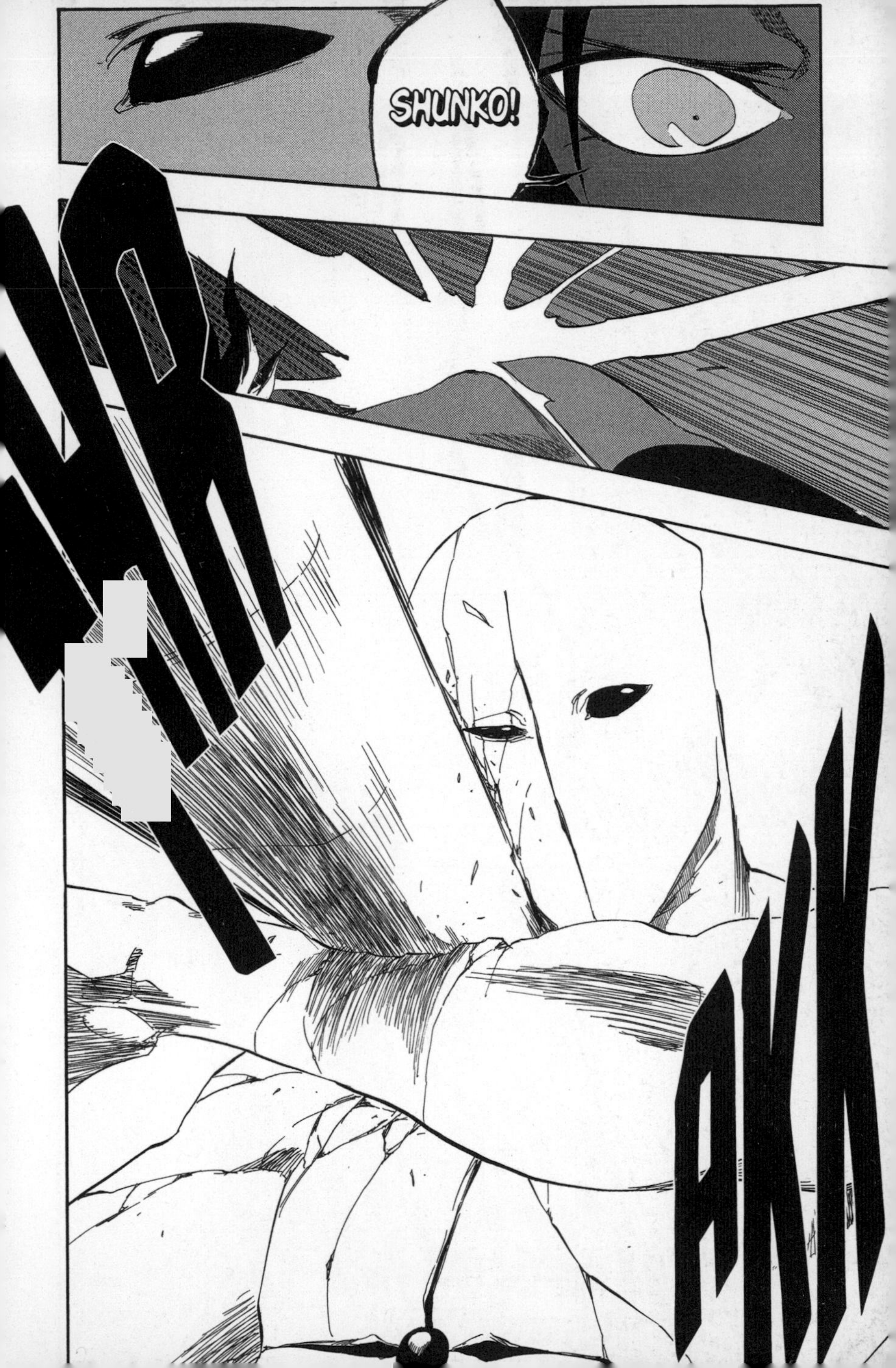
SHUNKO!

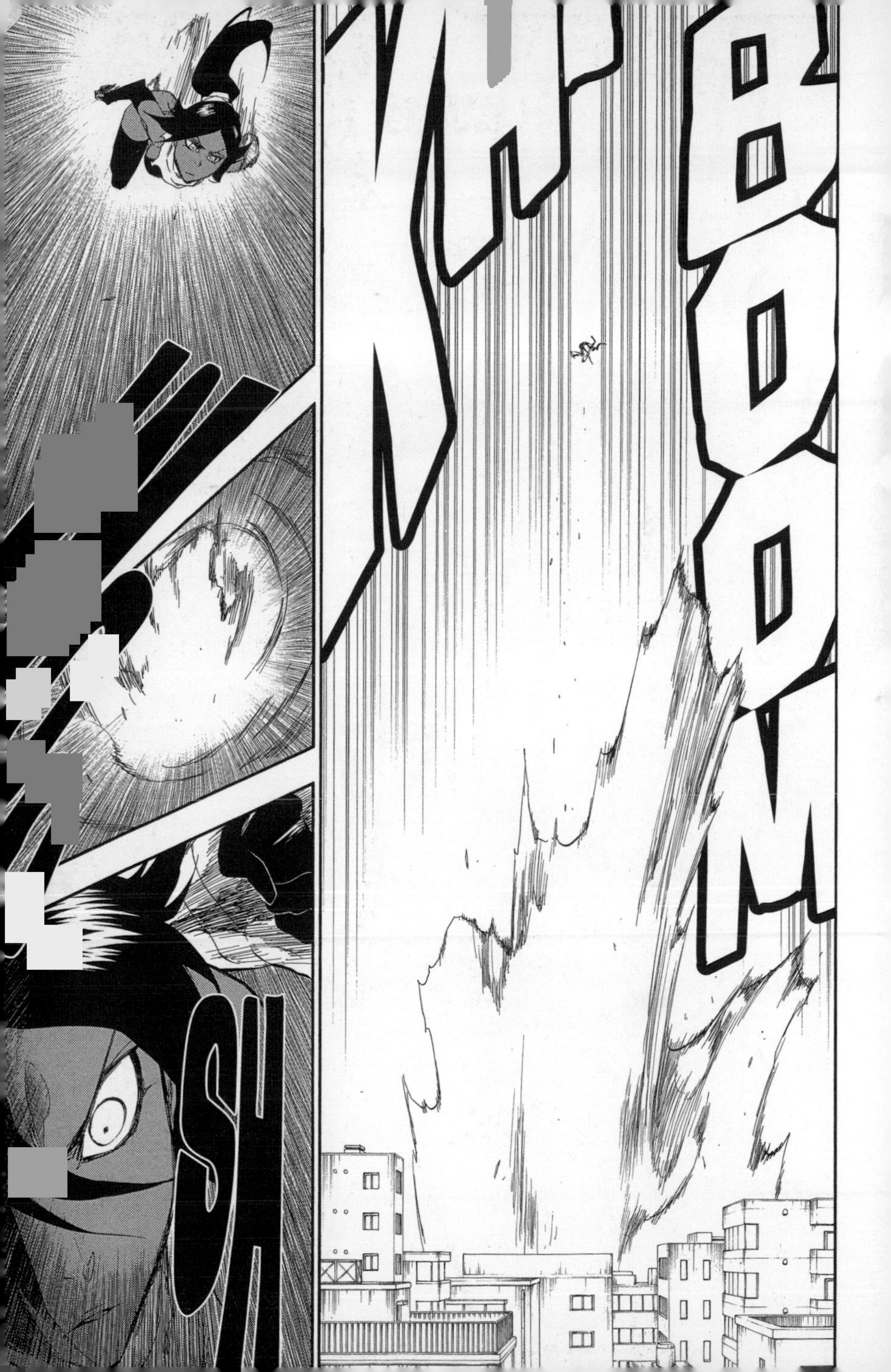

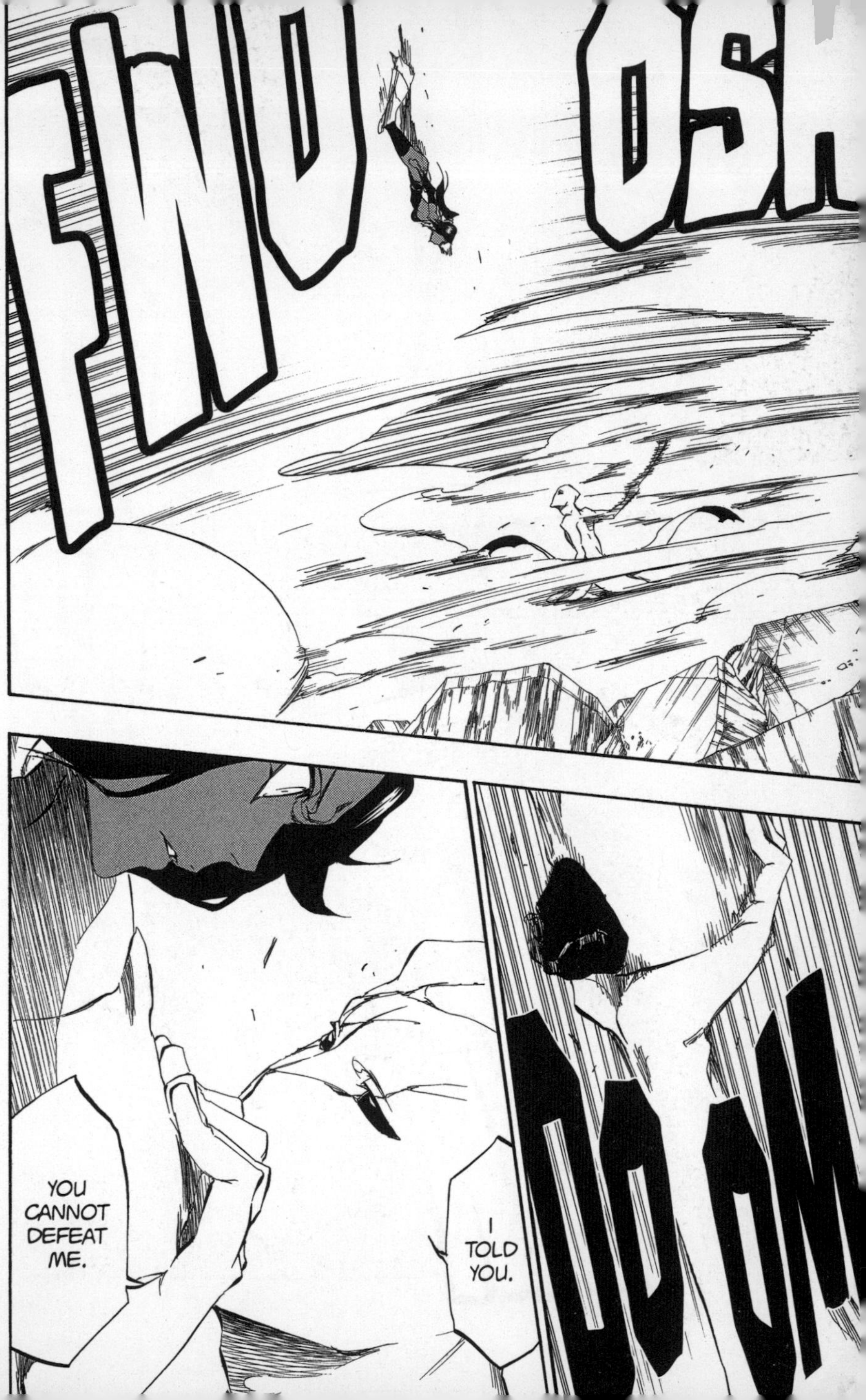
I TOLD YOU.
YOU CANNOT DEFEAT ME.

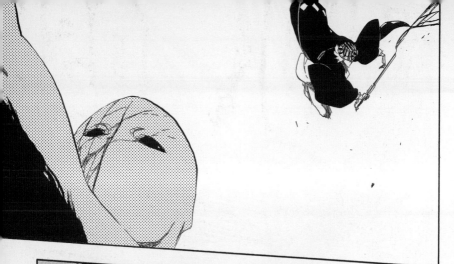

SHIBARI BENIHIME.
(BINDING RED PRINCESS)

DID YOU REALLY THINK YOU COULD BIND ME WITH...

THWAP

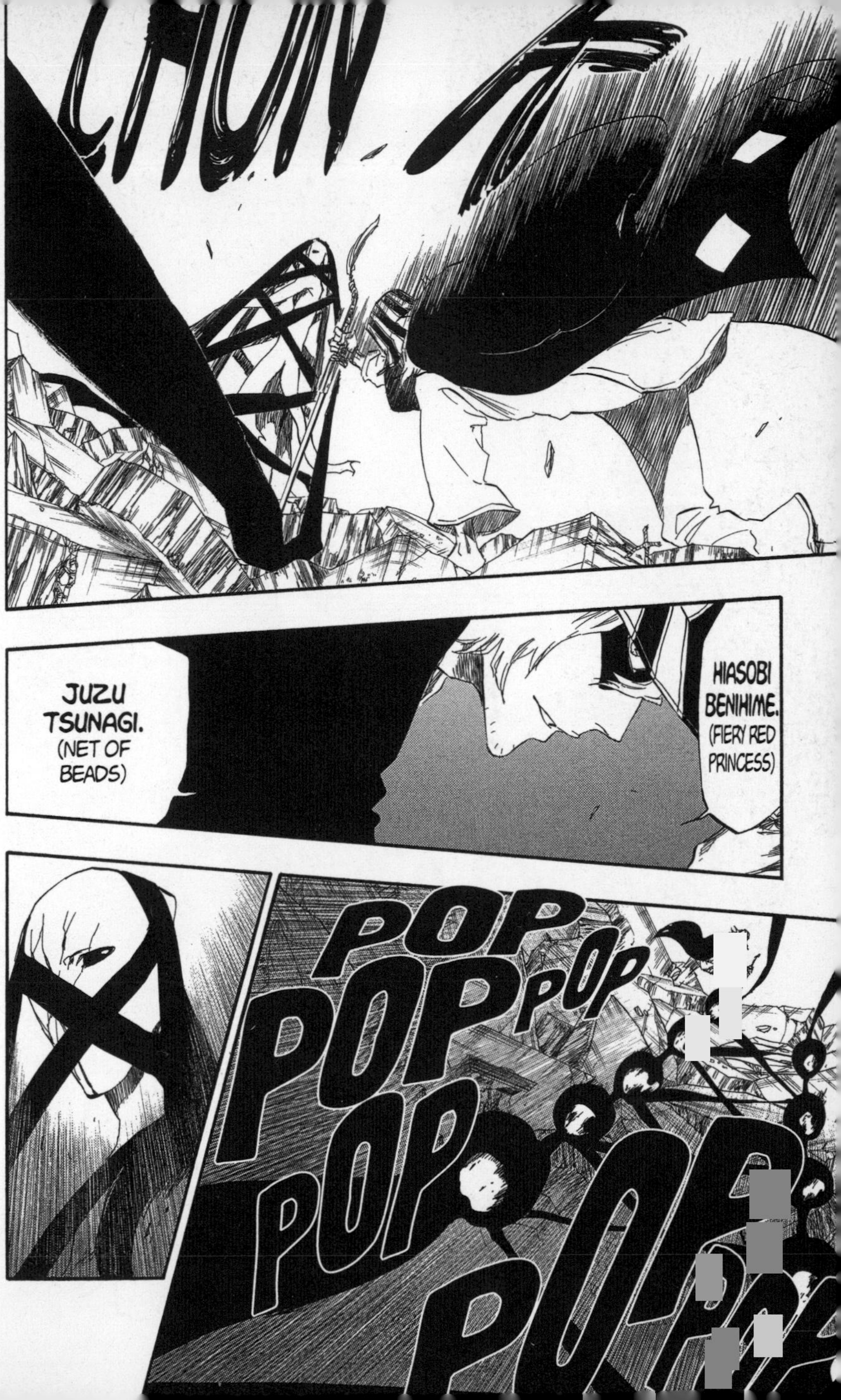
CHUN
HIASOBI BENIHIME.
(FIERY RED PRINCESS)
JUZU TSUNAGI.
(NET OF BEADS)
POP
POP
POP
POP
POP

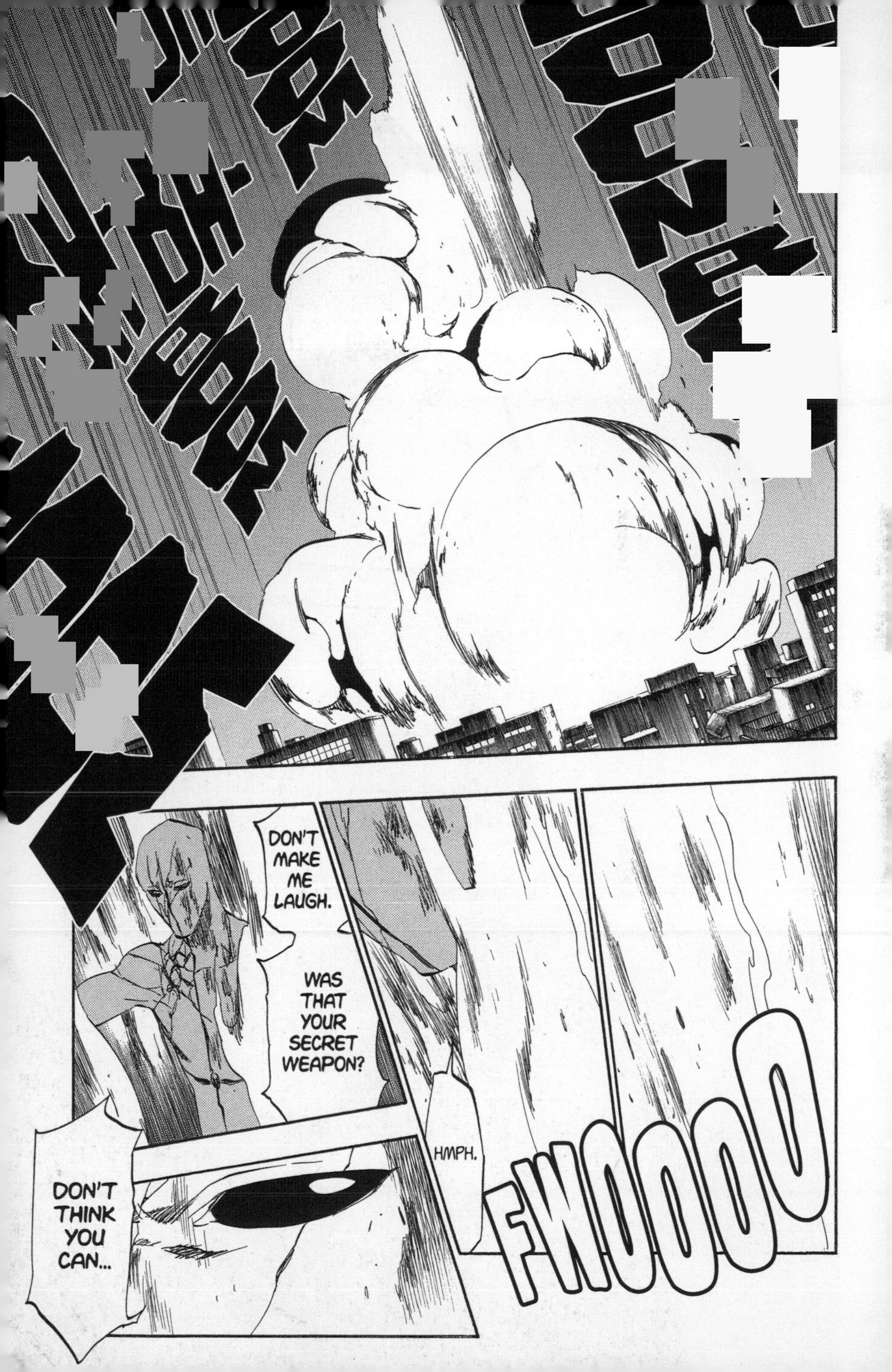
FWOOOO
HMPH.
DON'T MAKE ME LAUGH.
WAS THAT YOUR SECRET WEAPON?
DON'T THINK YOU CAN...

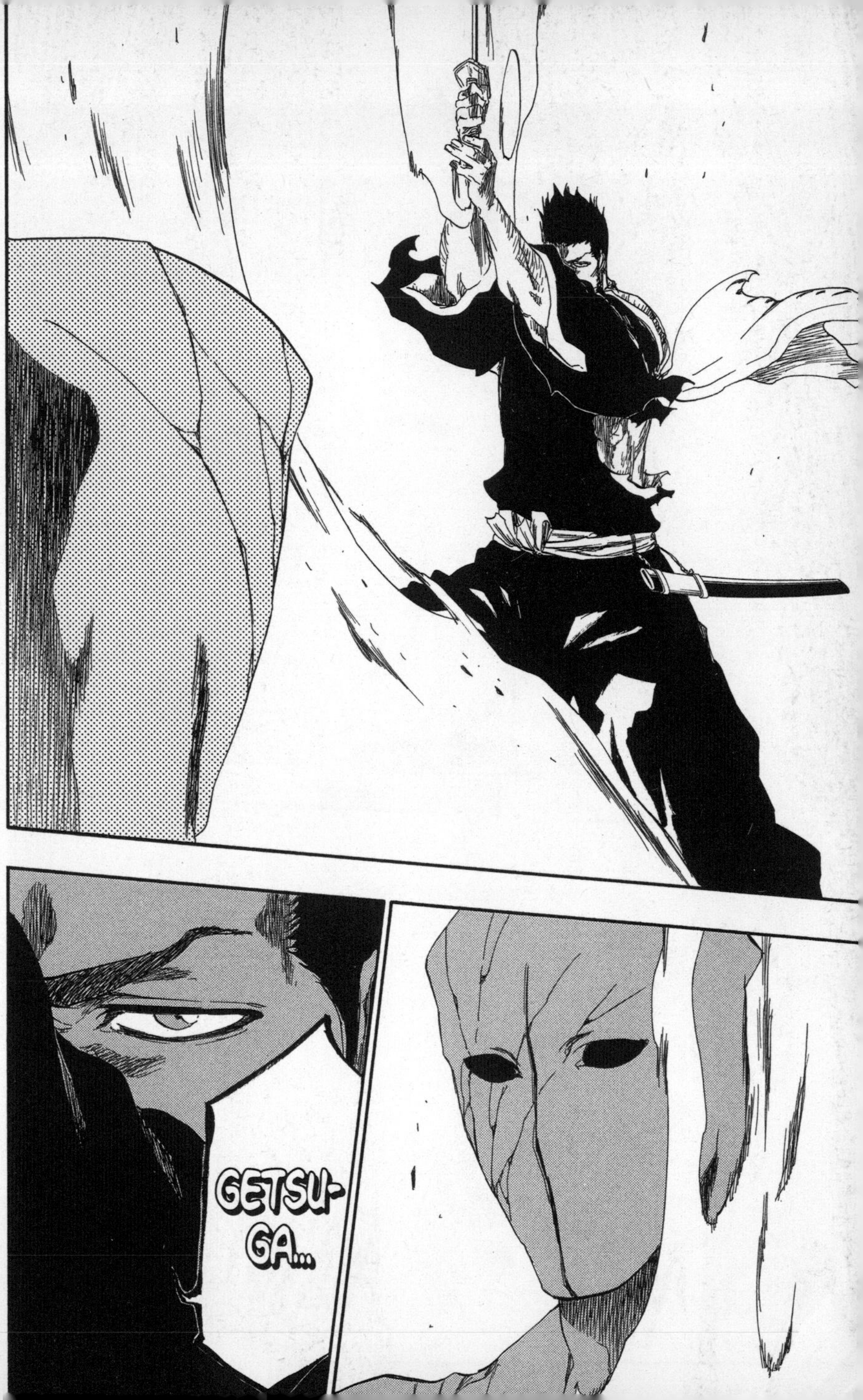
GETSU-
GA...

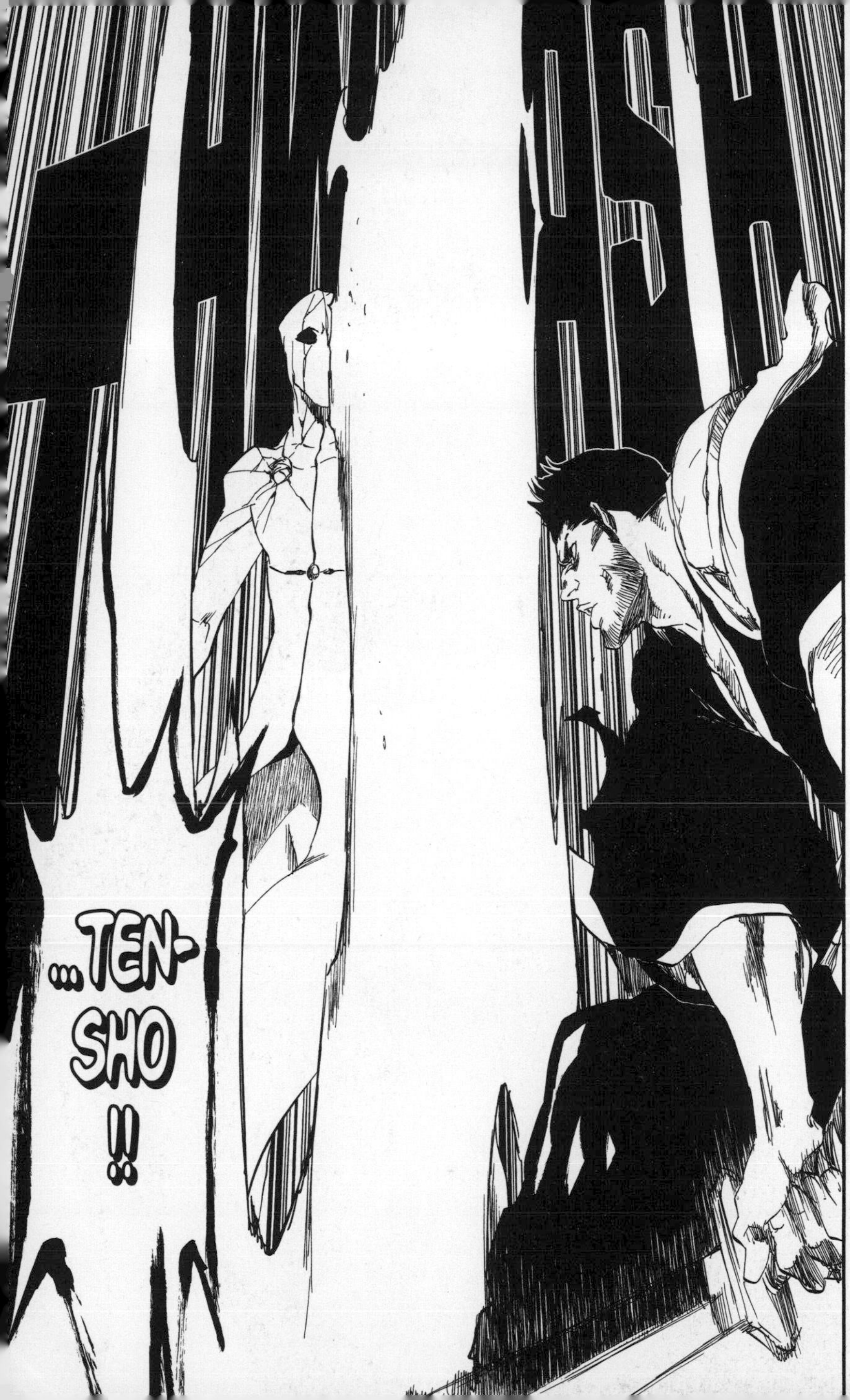
...TEN-SHO!!

406. DEICIDE 8 end of the Chrysalis Age

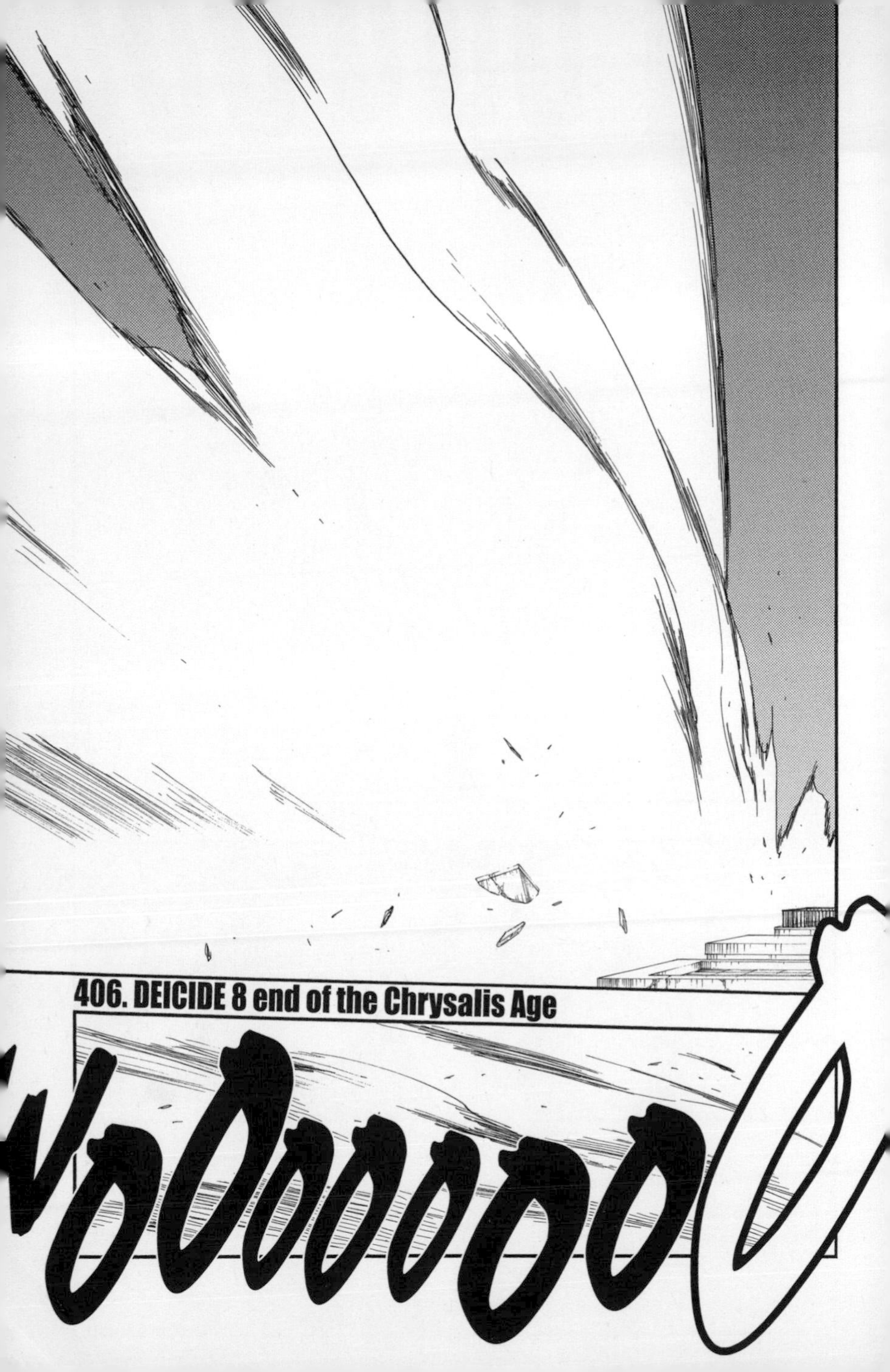

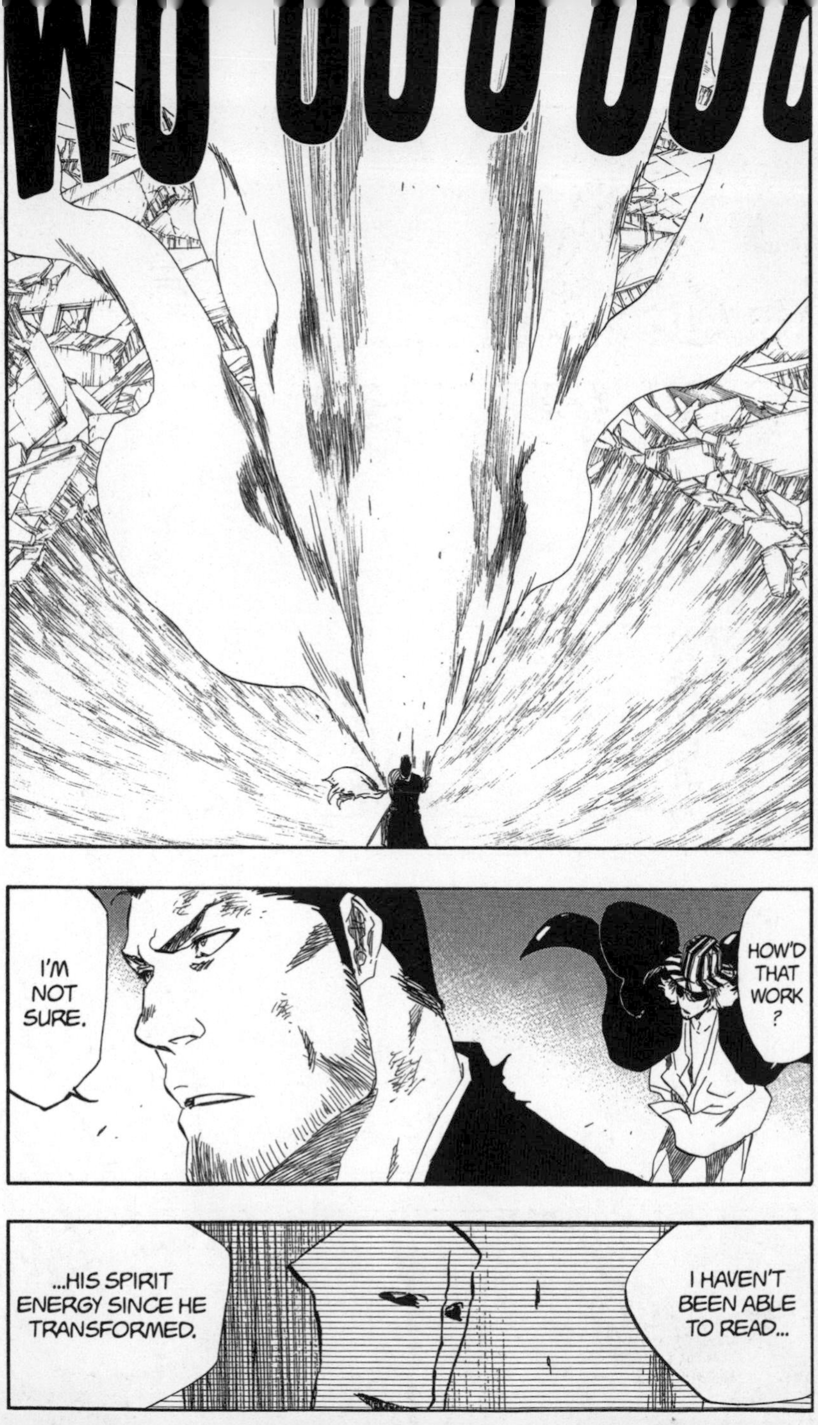
WOOOOOOO
HOW'D THAT WORK?
I'M NOT SURE.
I HAVEN'T BEEN ABLE TO READ...
...HIS SPIRIT ENERGY SINCE HE TRANSFORMED.

READ THIS WAY

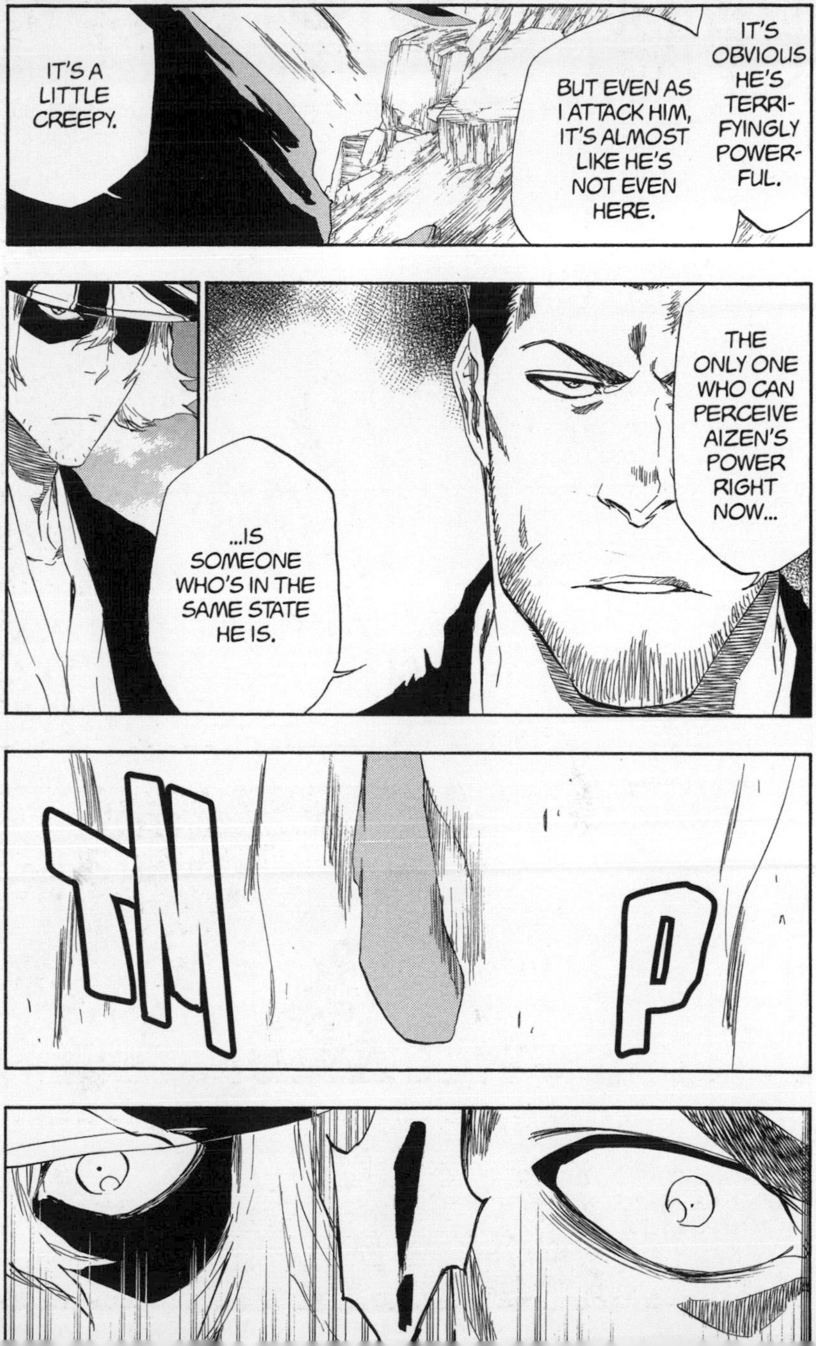

IT'S OBVIOUS HE'S TERRI-FYINGLY POWER-FUL.
BUT EVEN AS I ATTACK HIM, IT'S ALMOST LIKE HE'S NOT EVEN HERE.
IT'S A LITTLE CREEPY.
THE ONLY ONE WHO CAN PERCEIVE AIZEN'S POWER RIGHT NOW...
...IS SOMEONE WHO'S IN THE SAME STATE HE IS.
TMP

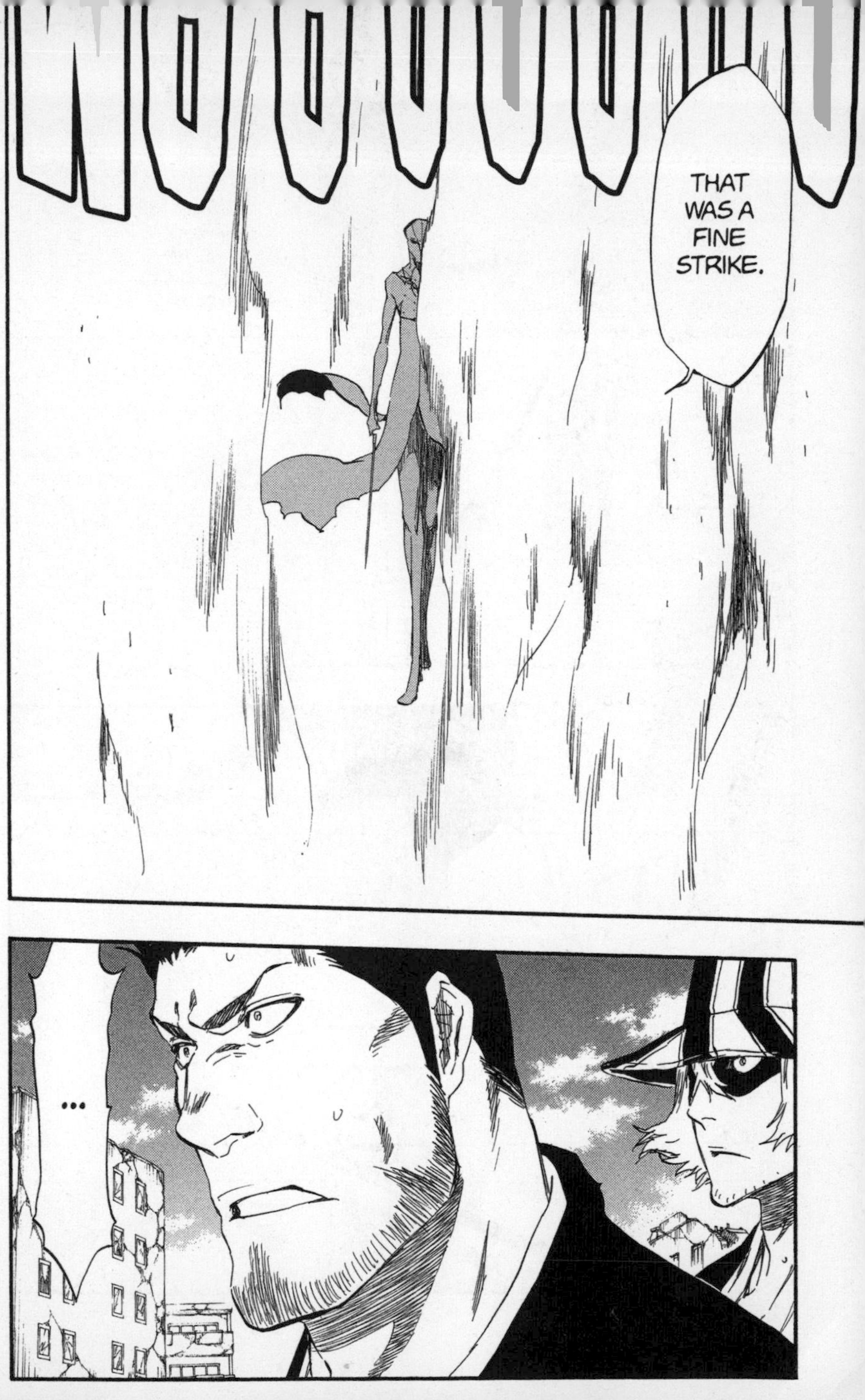
THAT WAS A FINE STRIKE.
...

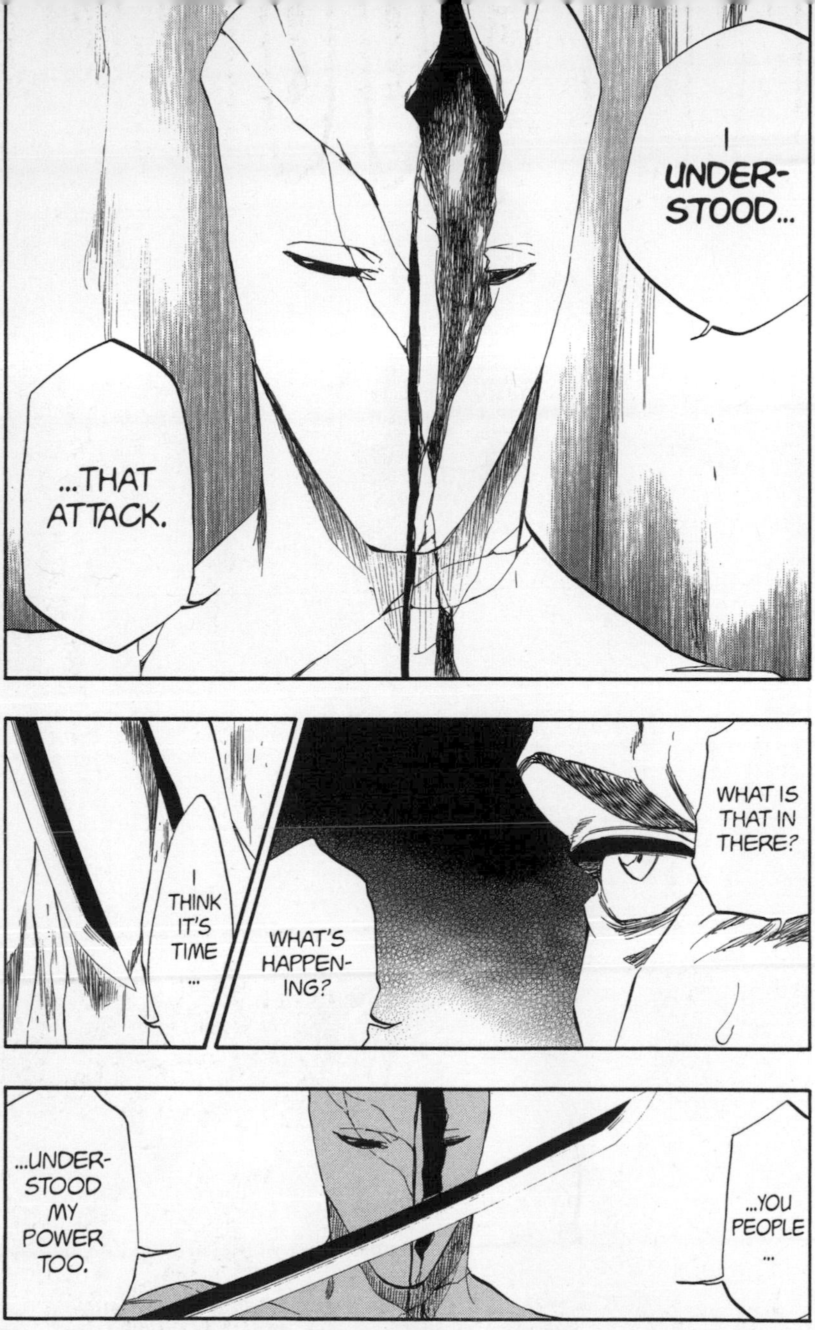
I UNDER-STOOD...
...THAT ATTACK.
WHAT IS THAT IN THERE?
WHAT'S HAPPEN-ING?
I THINK IT'S TIME ...
...YOU PEOPLE ...
...UNDER-STOOD MY POWER TOO.

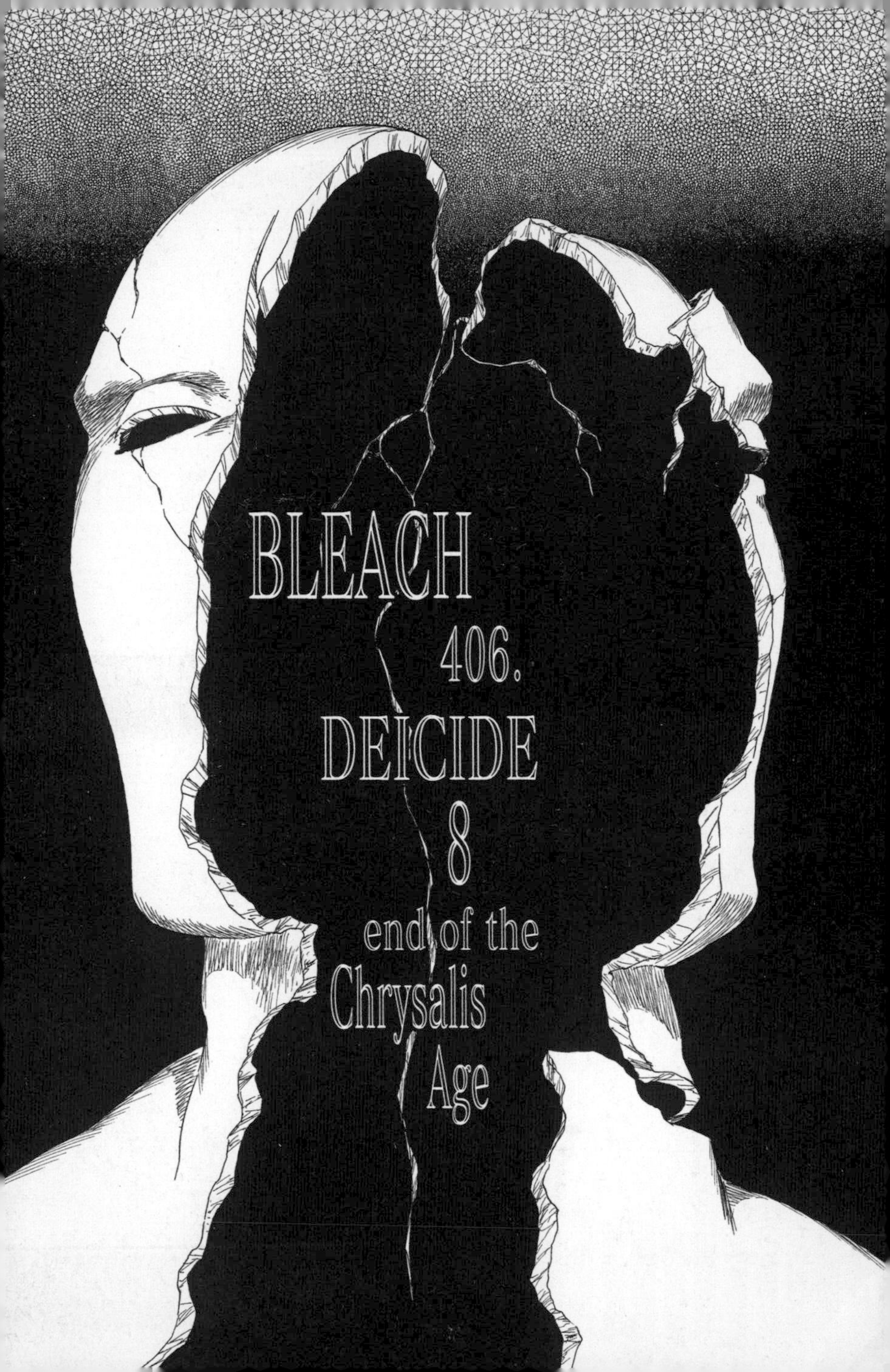
BLEACH
406.
DEICIDE
8
end of the
Chrysalis
Age

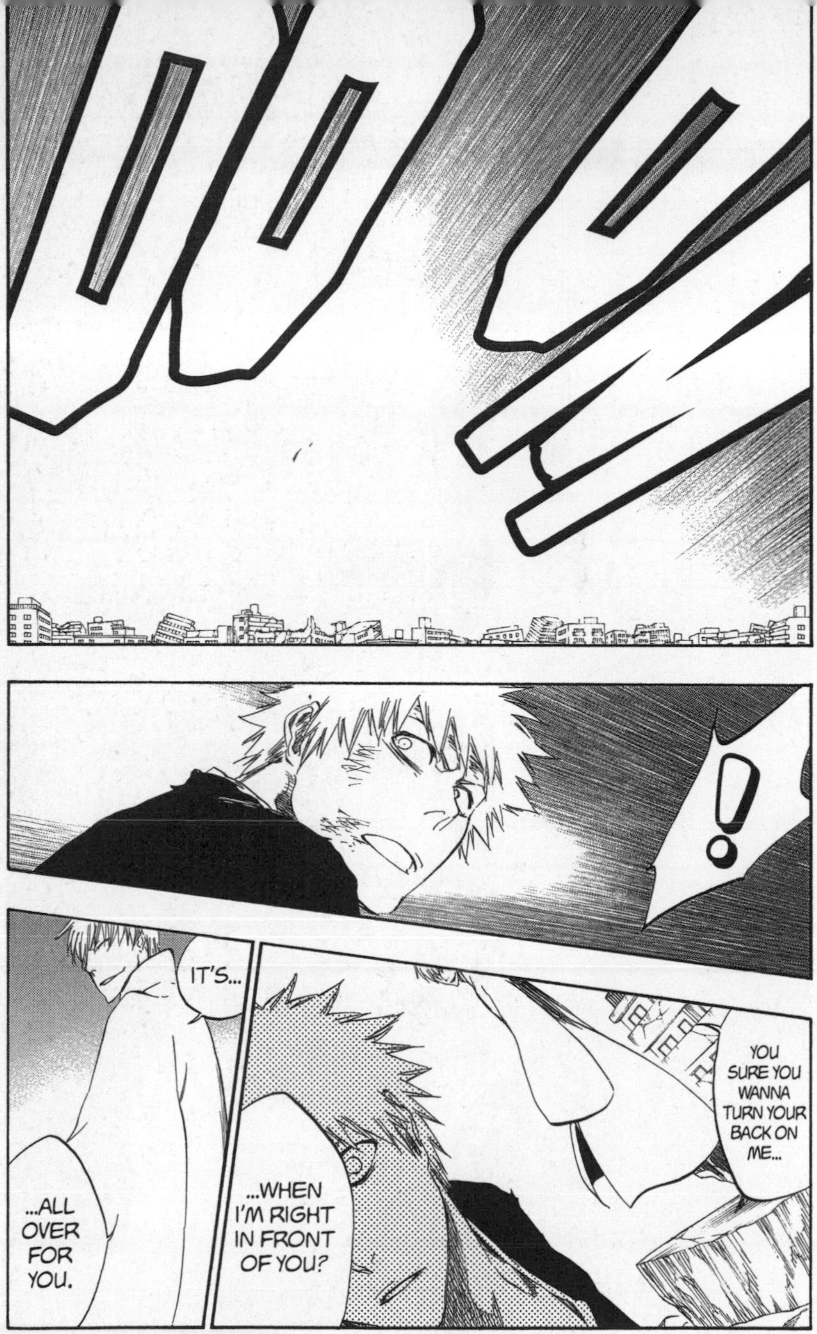
!
YOU SURE YOU WANNA TURN YOUR BACK ON ME...
...WHEN I'M RIGHT IN FRONT OF YOU?
IT'S...
...ALL OVER FOR YOU.

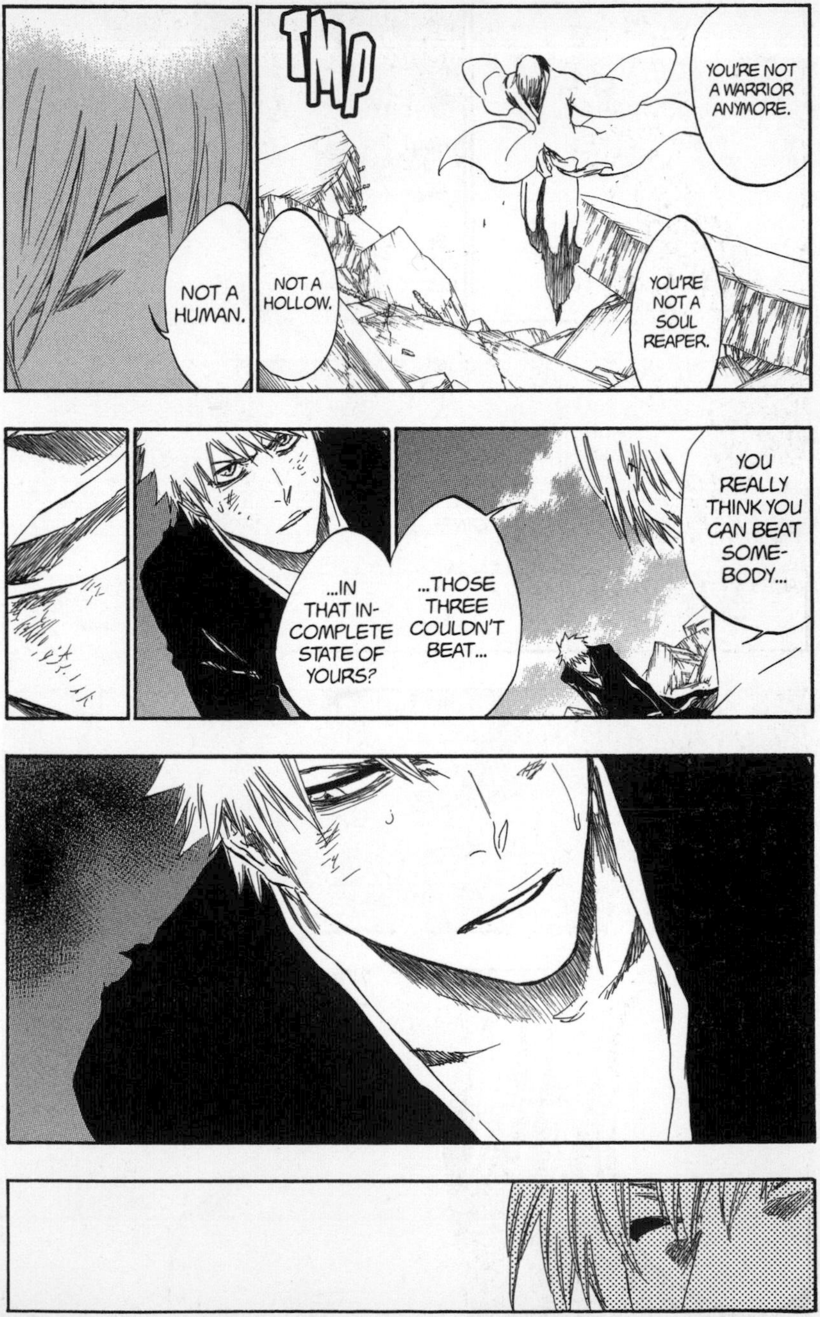
YOU'RE NOT A WARRIOR ANYMORE.
TMP
YOU'RE NOT A SOUL REAPER.
NOT A HOLLOW.
NOT A HUMAN.
YOU REALLY THINK YOU CAN BEAT SOME-BODY...
...THOSE THREE COULDN'T BEAT...
...IN THAT IN-COMPLETE STATE OF YOURS?

READ THIS WAY

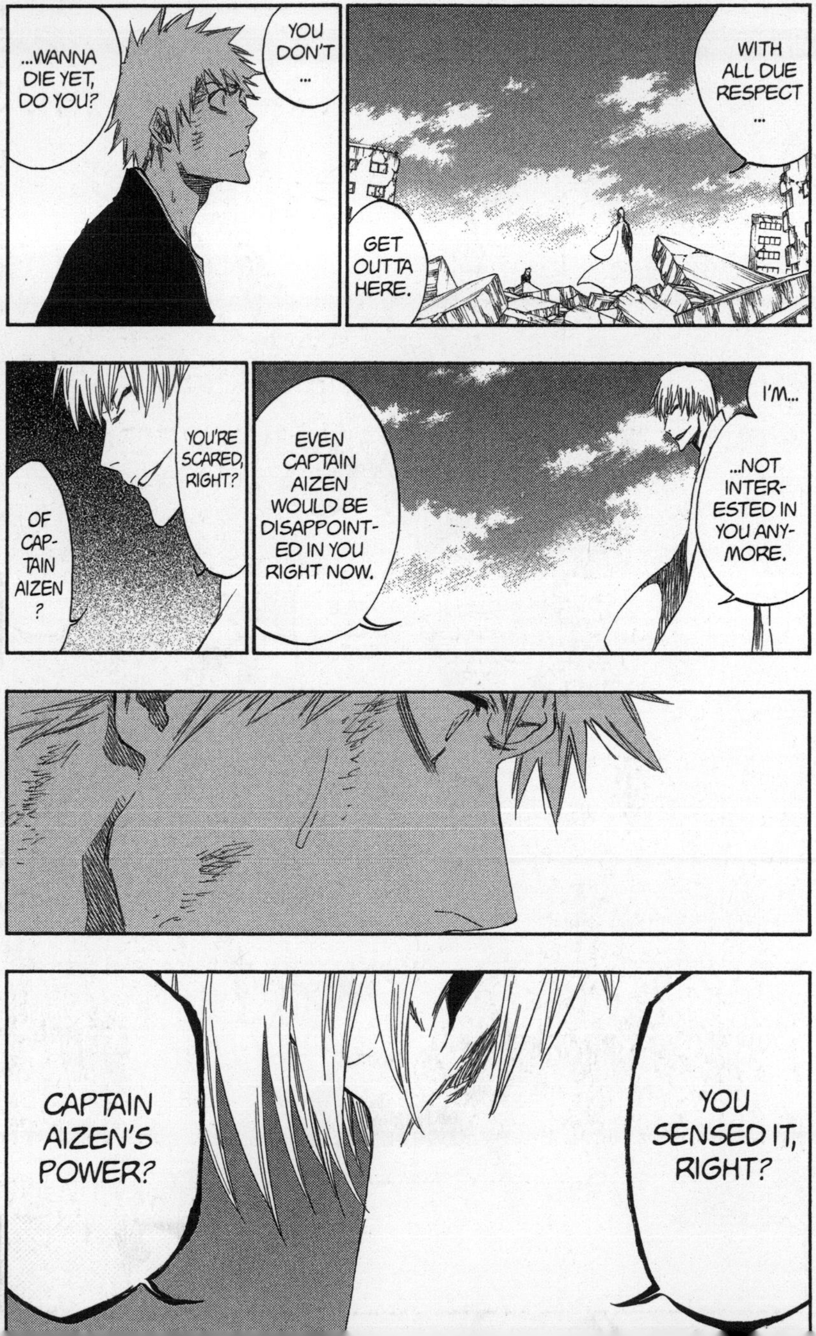
WITH ALL DUE RESPECT ...
GET OUTTA HERE.
YOU DON'T ...
...WANNA DIE YET, DO YOU?
I'M...
...NOT INTERESTED IN YOU ANYMORE.
EVEN CAPTAIN AIZEN WOULD BE DISAPPOINTED IN YOU RIGHT NOW.
YOU'RE SCARED, RIGHT?
OF CAPTAIN AIZEN?
YOU SENSED IT, RIGHT?
CAPTAIN AIZEN'S POWER?

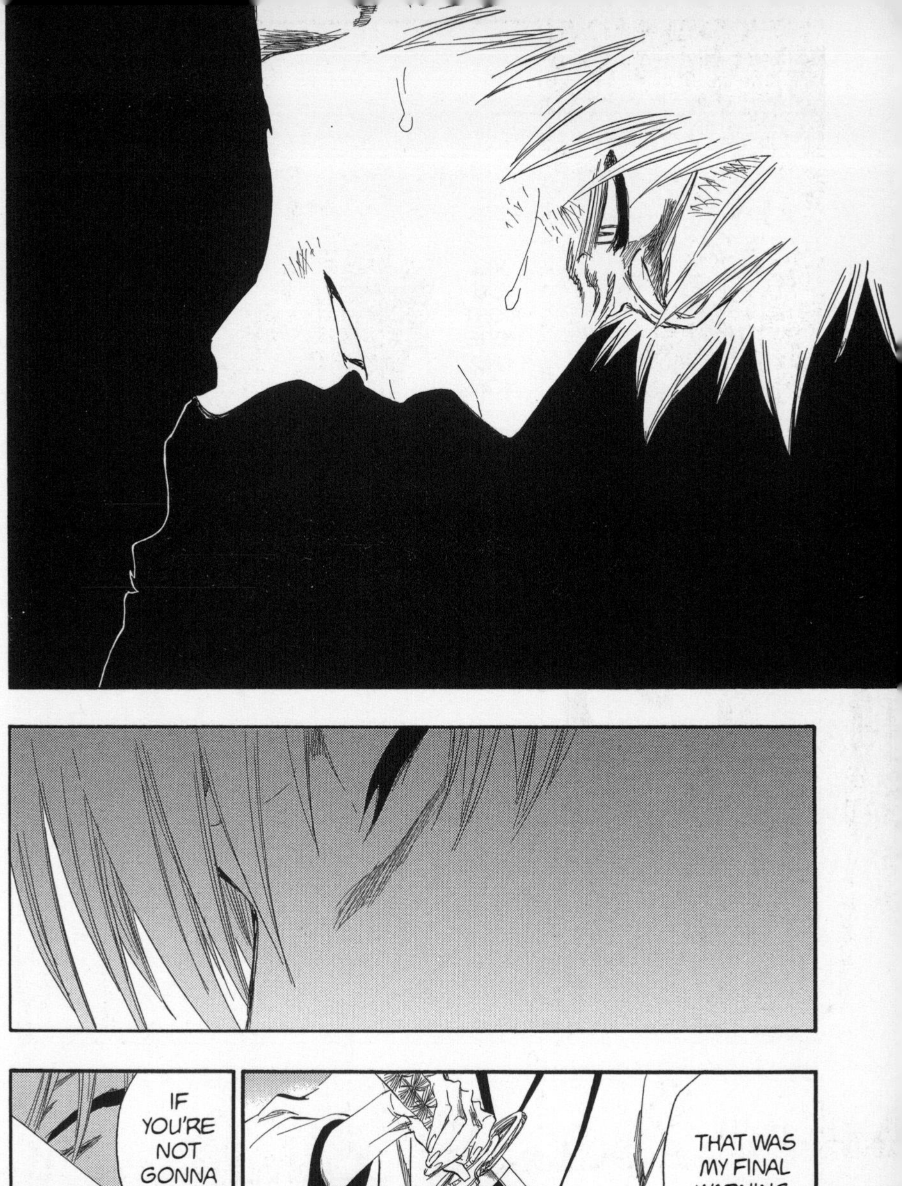
THAT WAS MY FINAL WARNING.
IF YOU'RE NOT GONNA RUN...

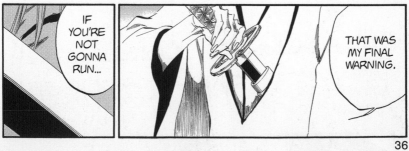

...I'LL...

...KILL YOU RIGHT HERE AND NOW.

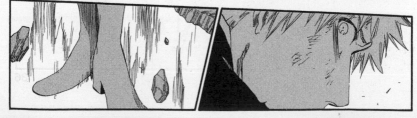

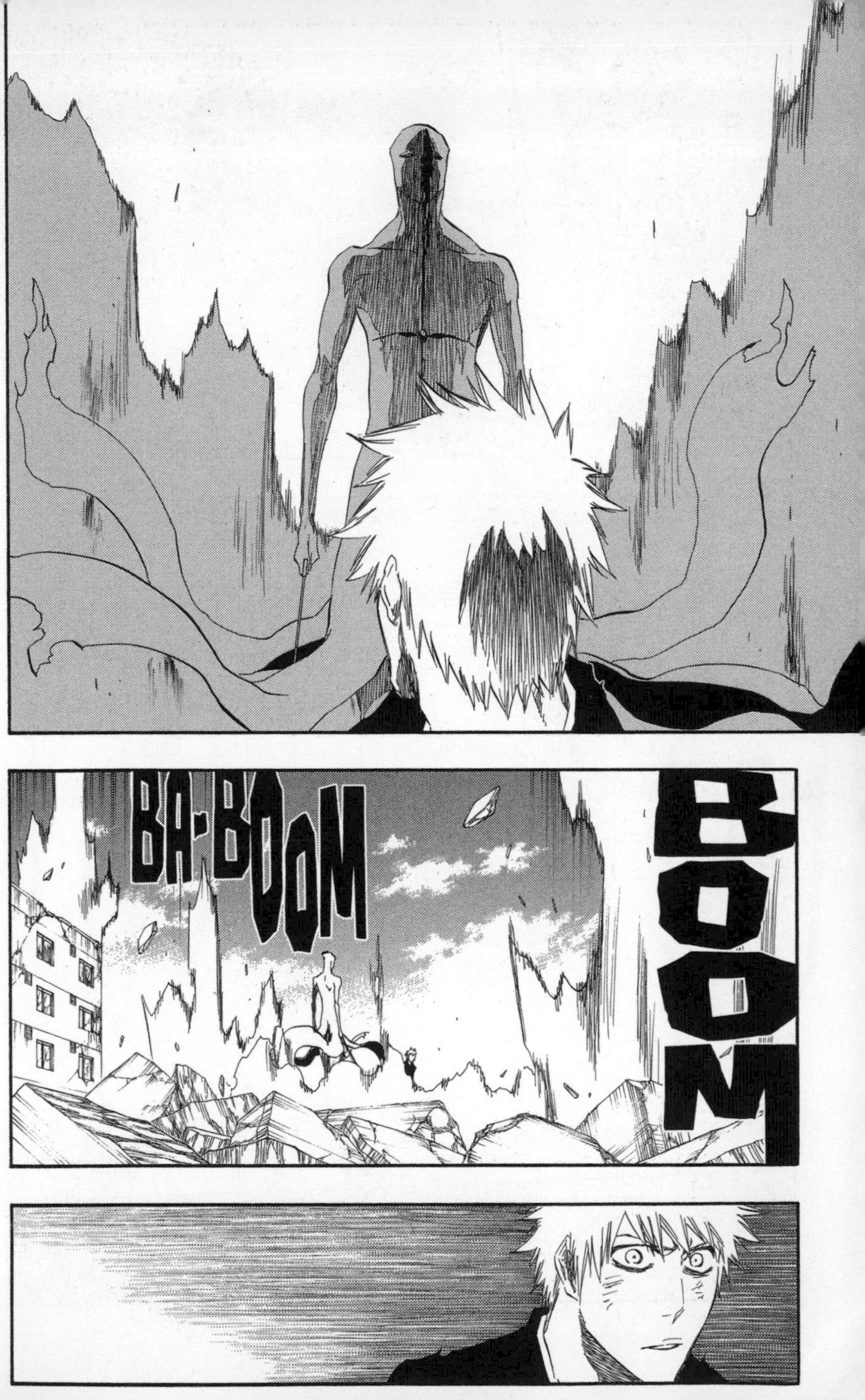
BOOM
BA-BOOM

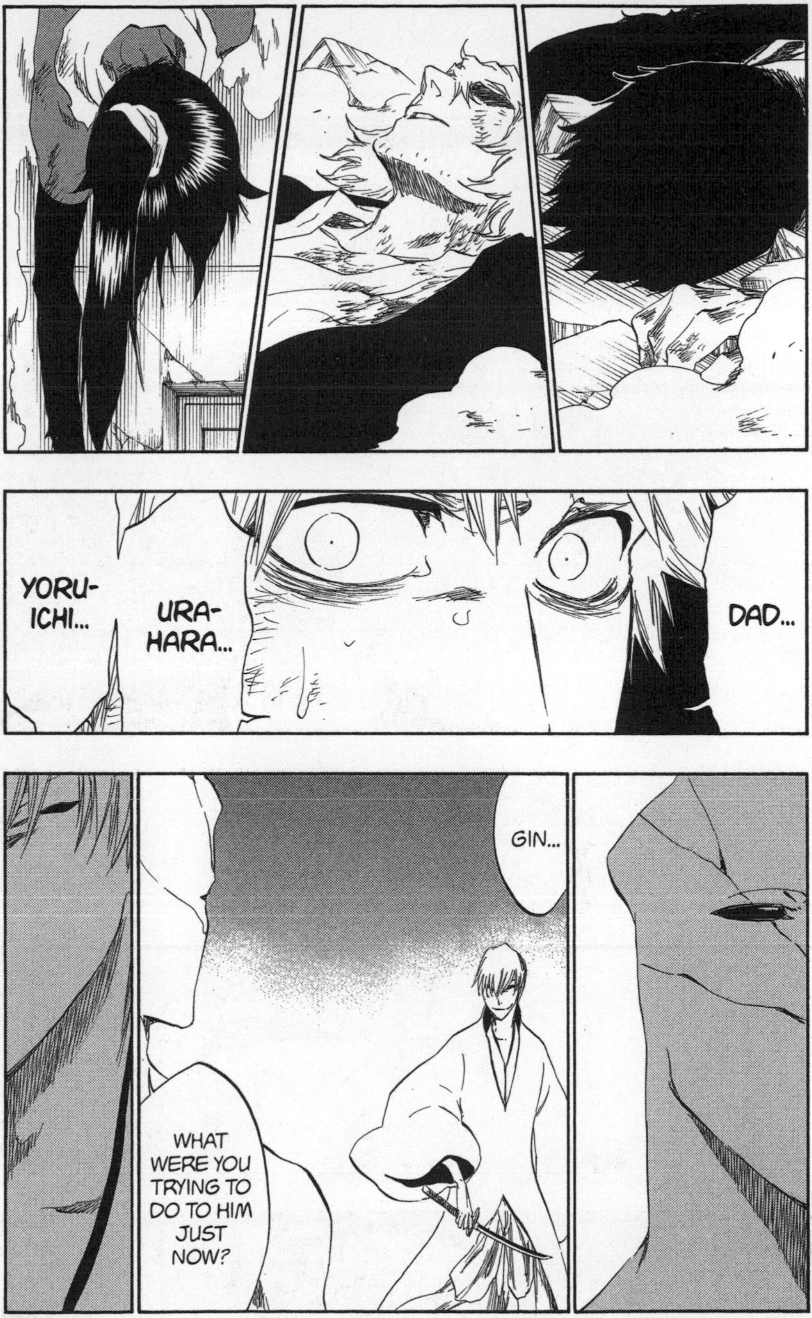
DAD...
URA-HARA...
YORU-ICHI...
GIN...
WHAT WERE YOU TRYING TO DO TO HIM JUST NOW?

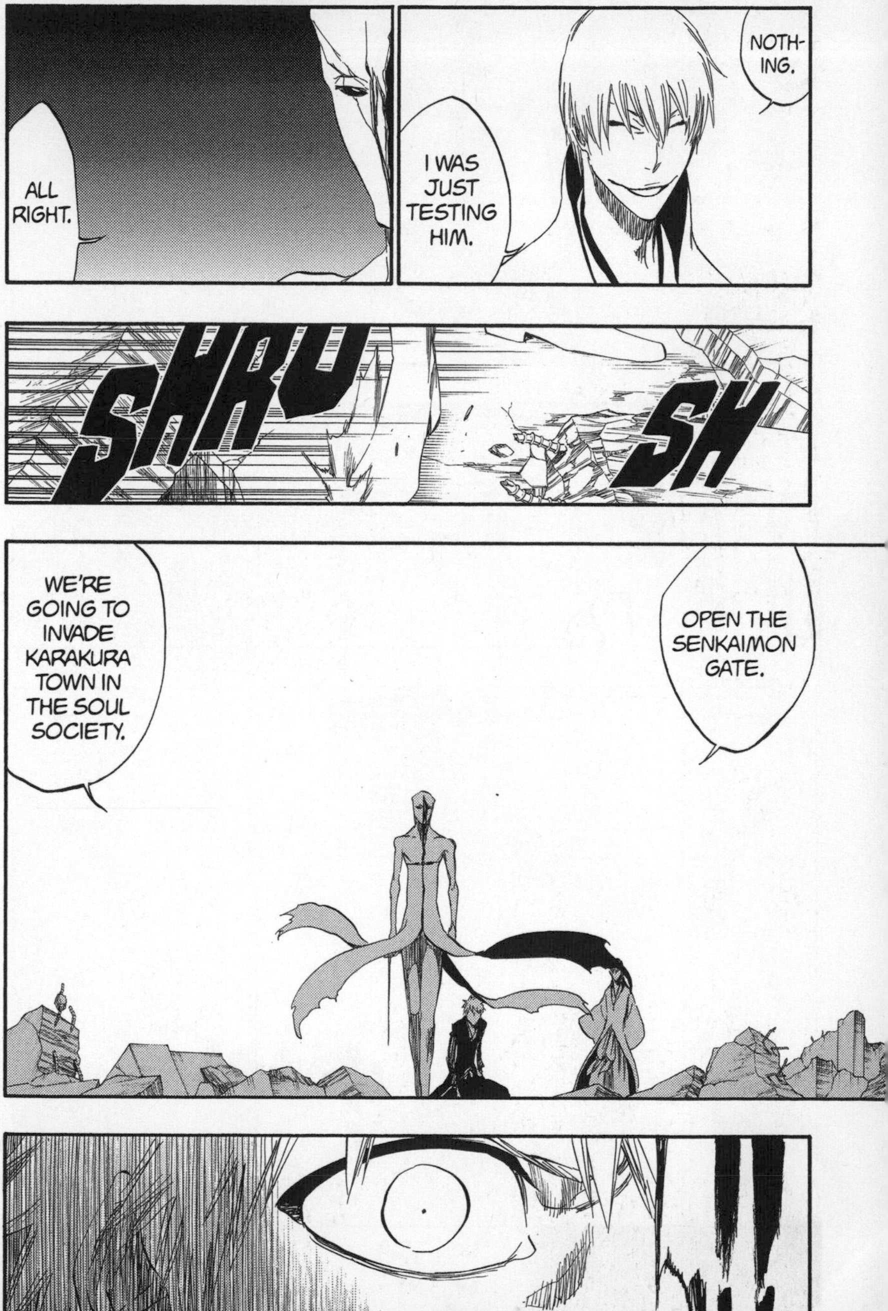
NOTH-ING.
I WAS JUST TESTING HIM.
ALL RIGHT.
SHRO
SH
OPEN THE SENKAIMON GATE.
WE'RE GOING TO INVADE KARAKURA TOWN IN THE SOUL SOCIETY.

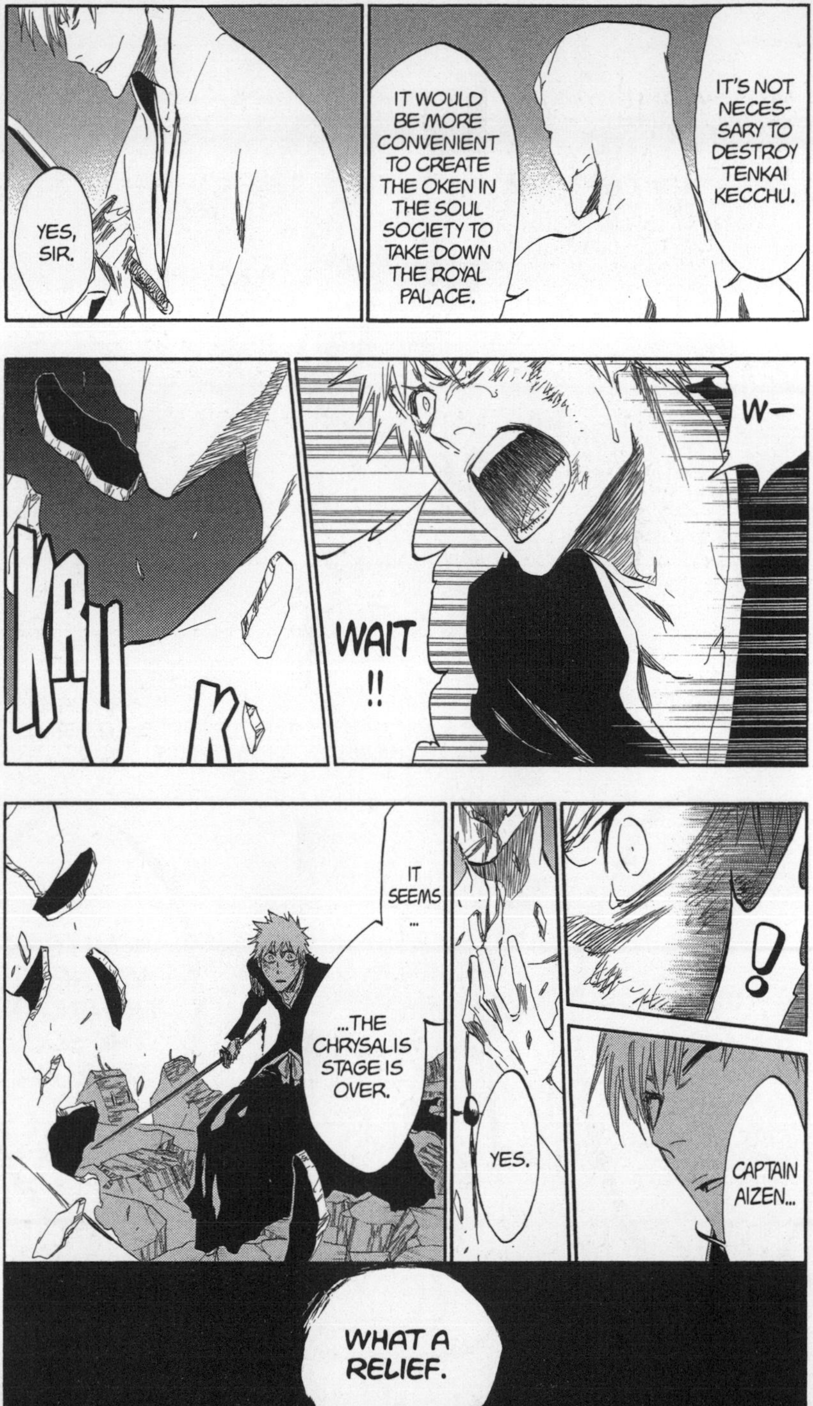
IT'S NOT NECES-SARY TO DESTROY TENKAI KECCHU.
IT WOULD BE MORE CONVENIENT TO CREATE THE OKEN IN THE SOUL SOCIETY TO TAKE DOWN THE ROYAL PALACE.
YES, SIR.
W—
WAIT !!
KRU
K
!
CAPTAIN AIZEN...
YES.
IT SEEMS ...
...THE CHRYSALIS STAGE IS OVER.
WHAT A RELIEF.

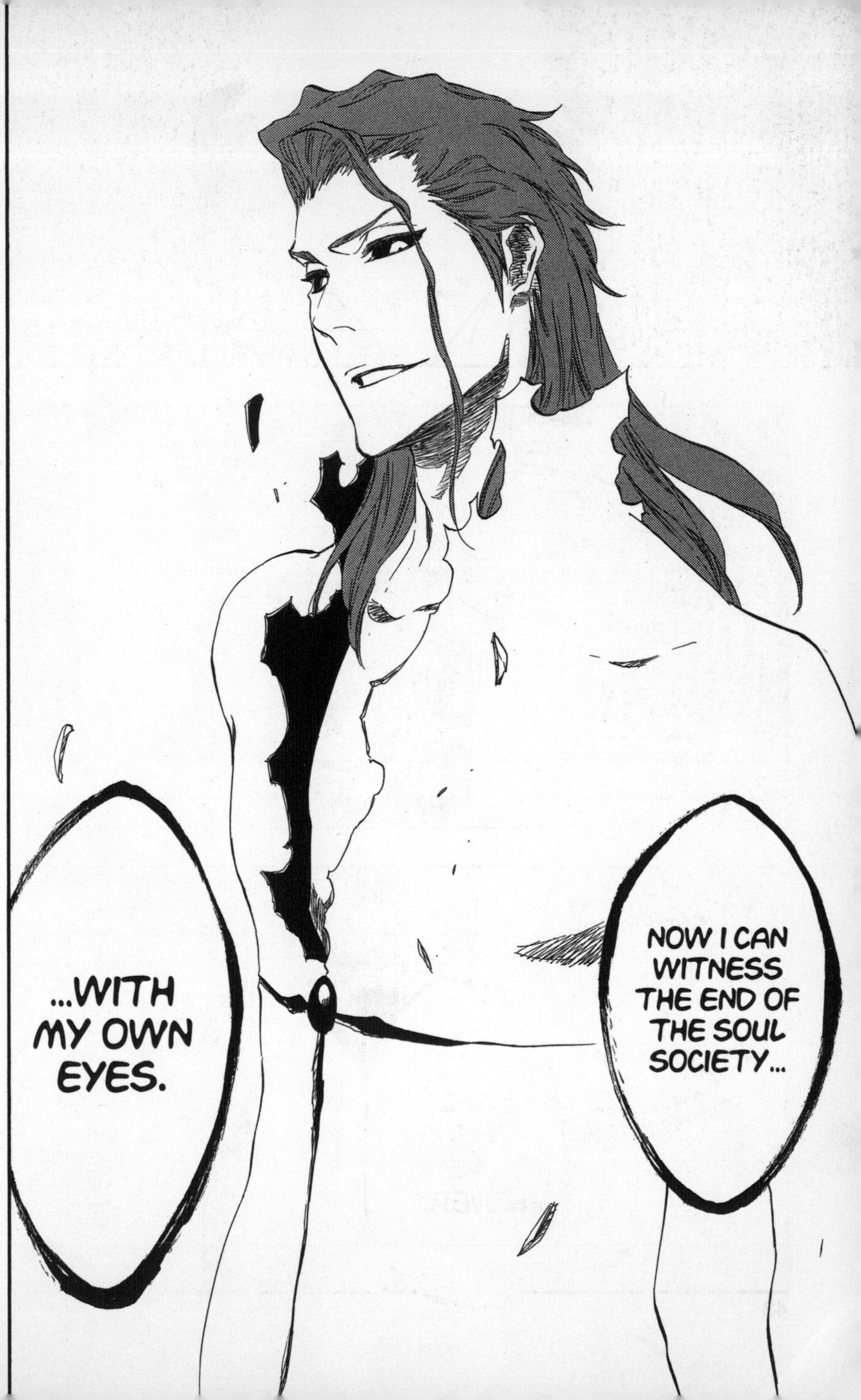
NOW I CAN WITNESS THE END OF THE SOUL SOCIETY...
...WITH MY OWN EYES.

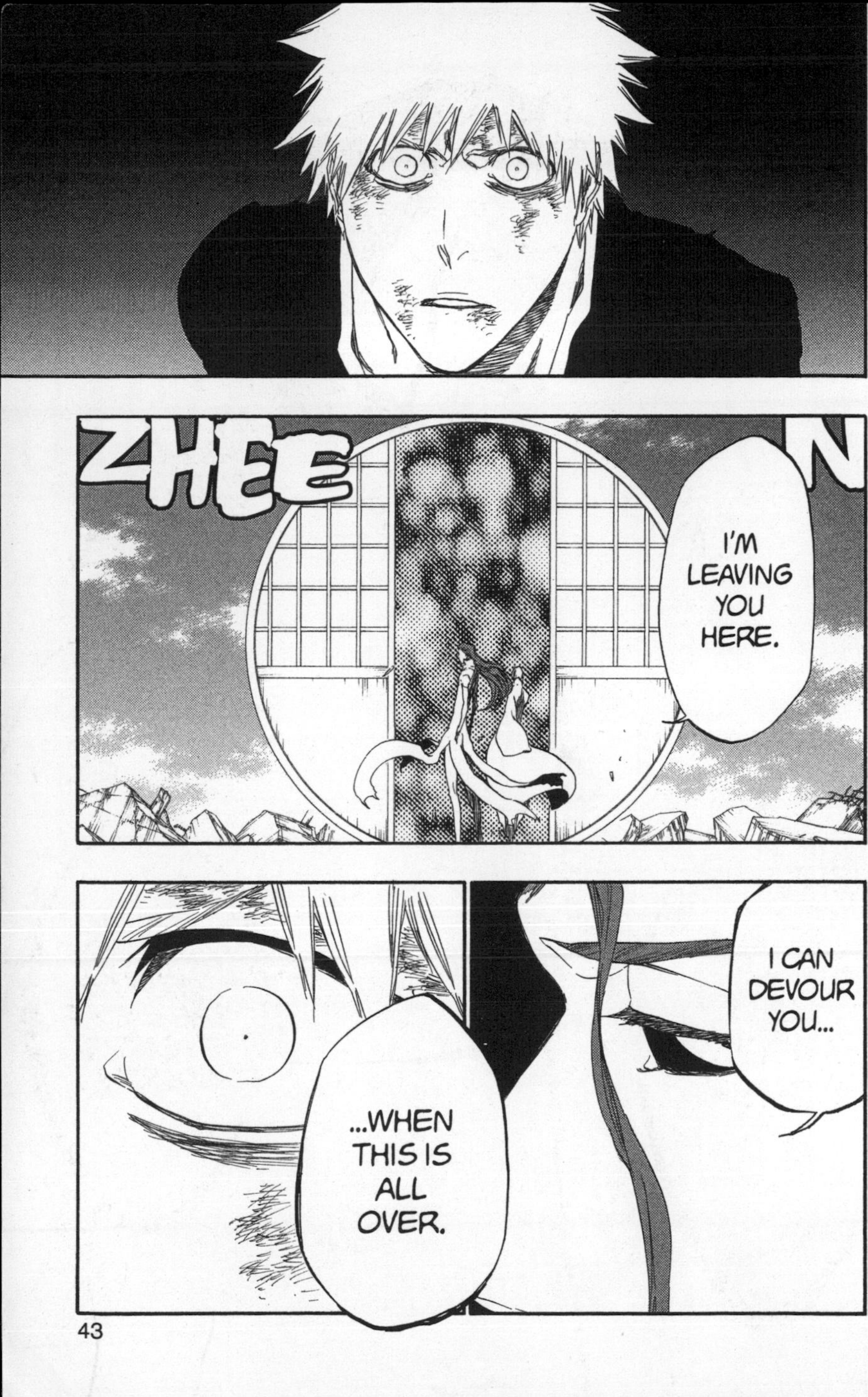
ZHEE N
I'M LEAVING YOU HERE.
I CAN DEVOUR YOU...
...WHEN THIS IS ALL OVER.

WHAT
THE...

WHAT'S
GOING...

DON'T
JUST
STAND
THERE!

OPEN
THE SEN-
KAIMON!

ICHIGO
!!

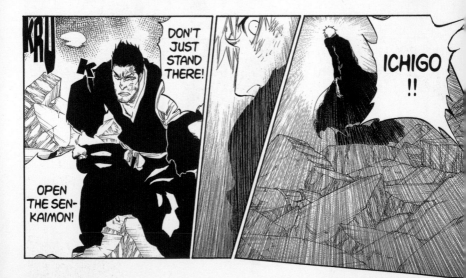

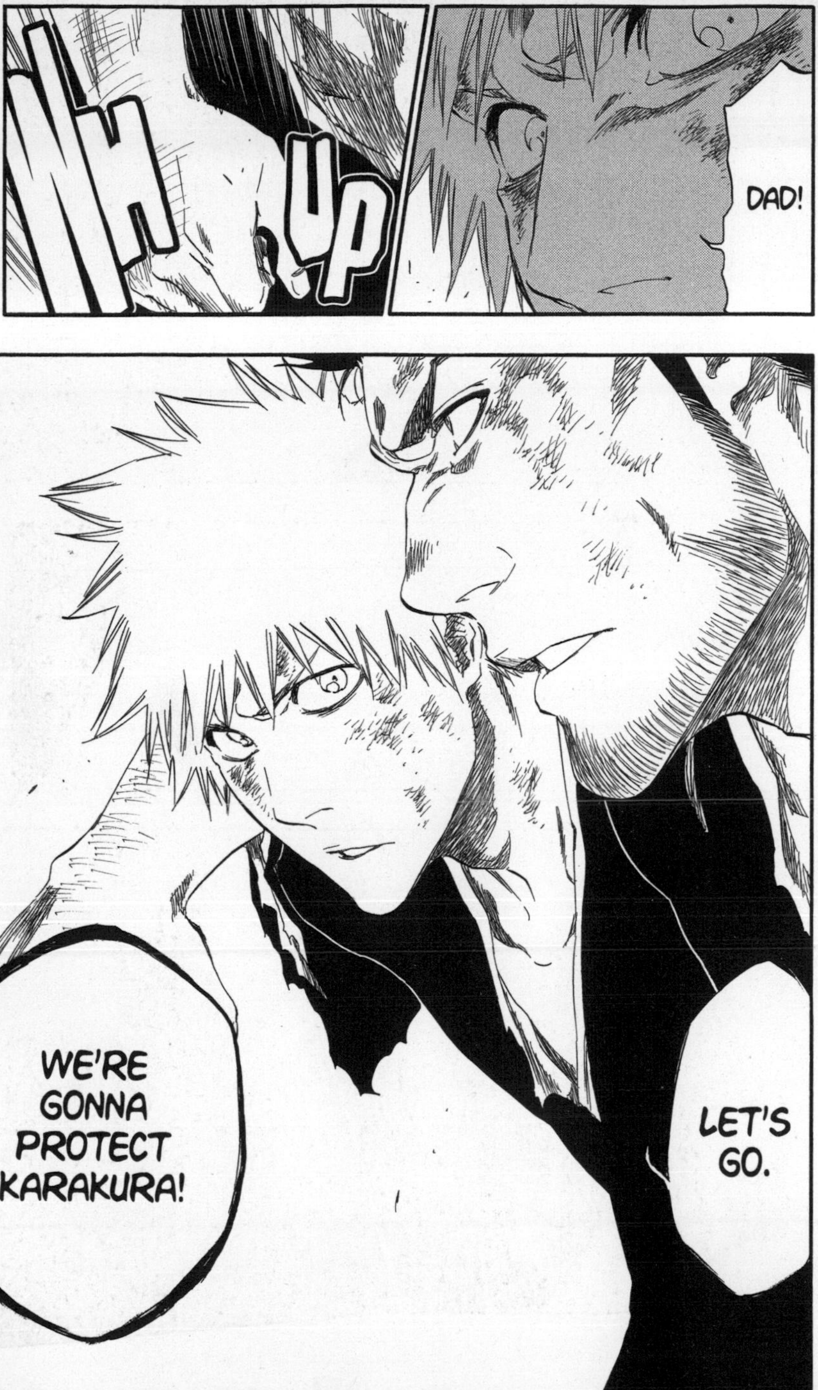
DAD!
WHUP
LET'S GO.
WE'RE GONNA PROTECT KARAKURA!

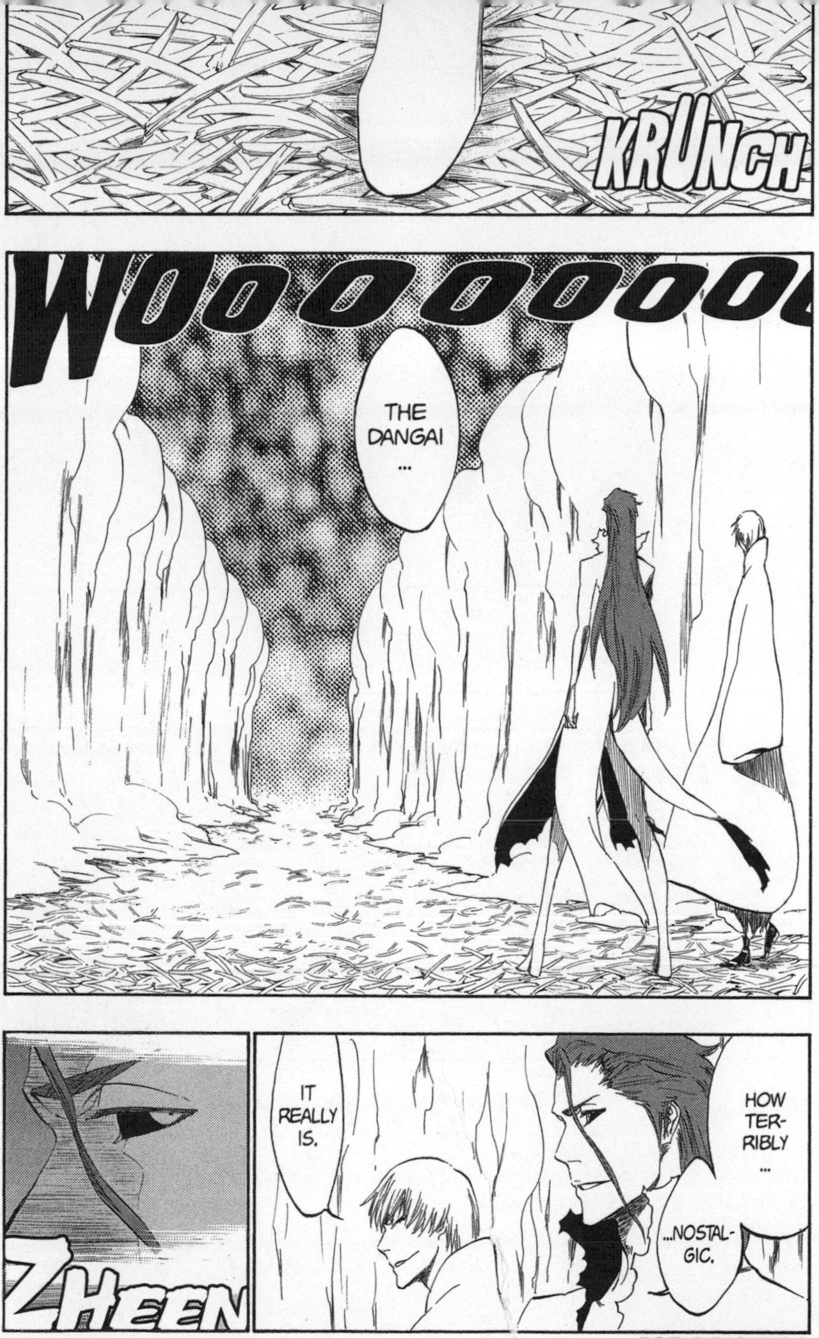
KRUNCH
WOOOOOOOO
THE DANGAI ...
HOW TERRIBLY ...
...NOSTALGIC.
IT REALLY IS.
ZHEEN

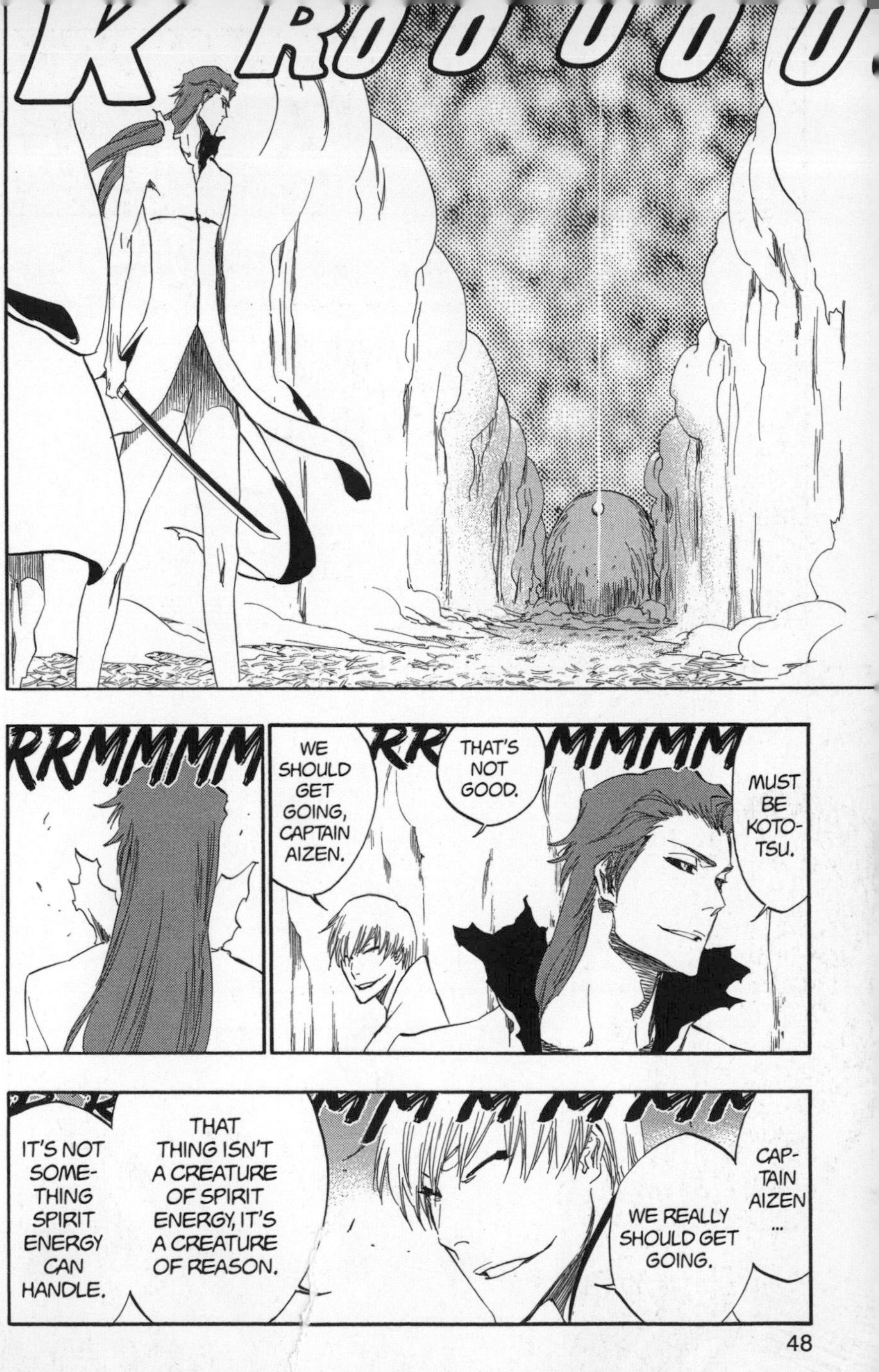
KROOOOOO
RRMMMM
MUST BE KOTO-TSU.
THAT'S NOT GOOD.
WE SHOULD GET GOING, CAPTAIN AIZEN.
RRMMMM
CAPTAIN AIZEN...
WE REALLY SHOULD GET GOING.
THAT THING ISN'T A CREATURE OF SPIRIT ENERGY, IT'S A CREATURE OF REASON.
IT'S NOT SOMETHING SPIRIT ENERGY CAN HANDLE.

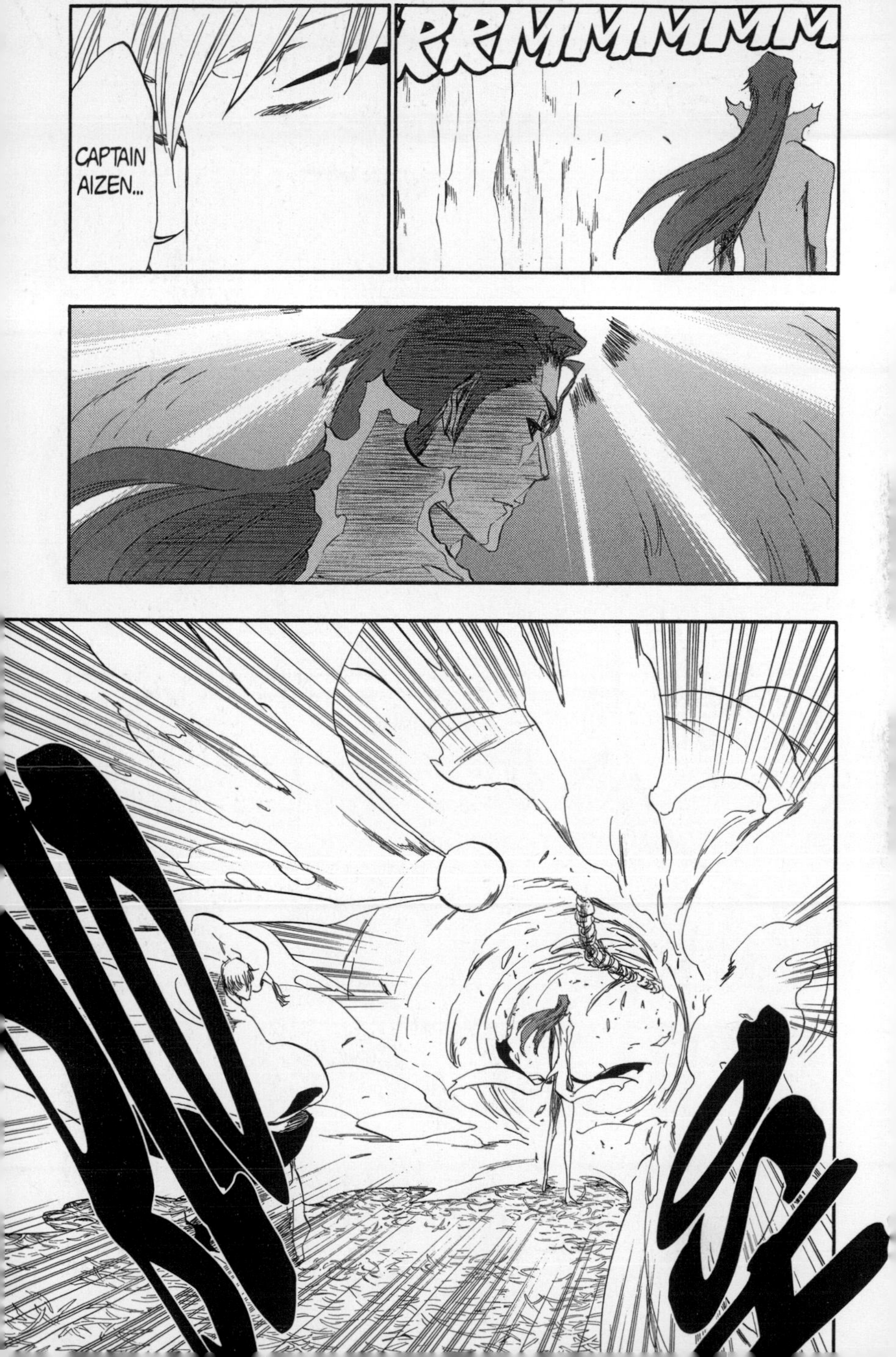
RRMMMMMM
CAPTAIN AIZEN...

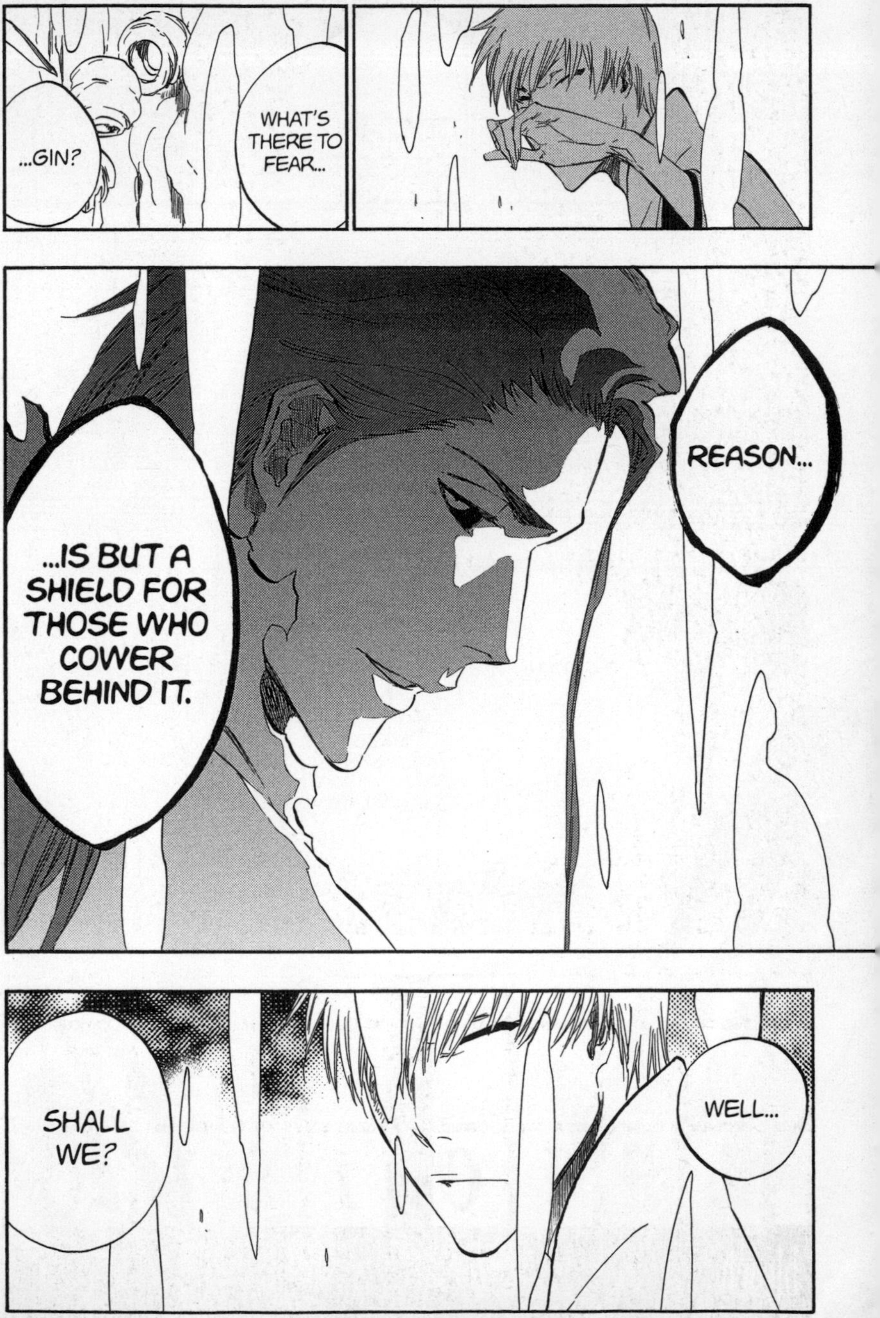
WHAT'S THERE TO FEAR...
...GIN?
REASON...
...IS BUT A SHIELD FOR THOSE WHO COWER BEHIND IT.
WELL...
SHALL WE?

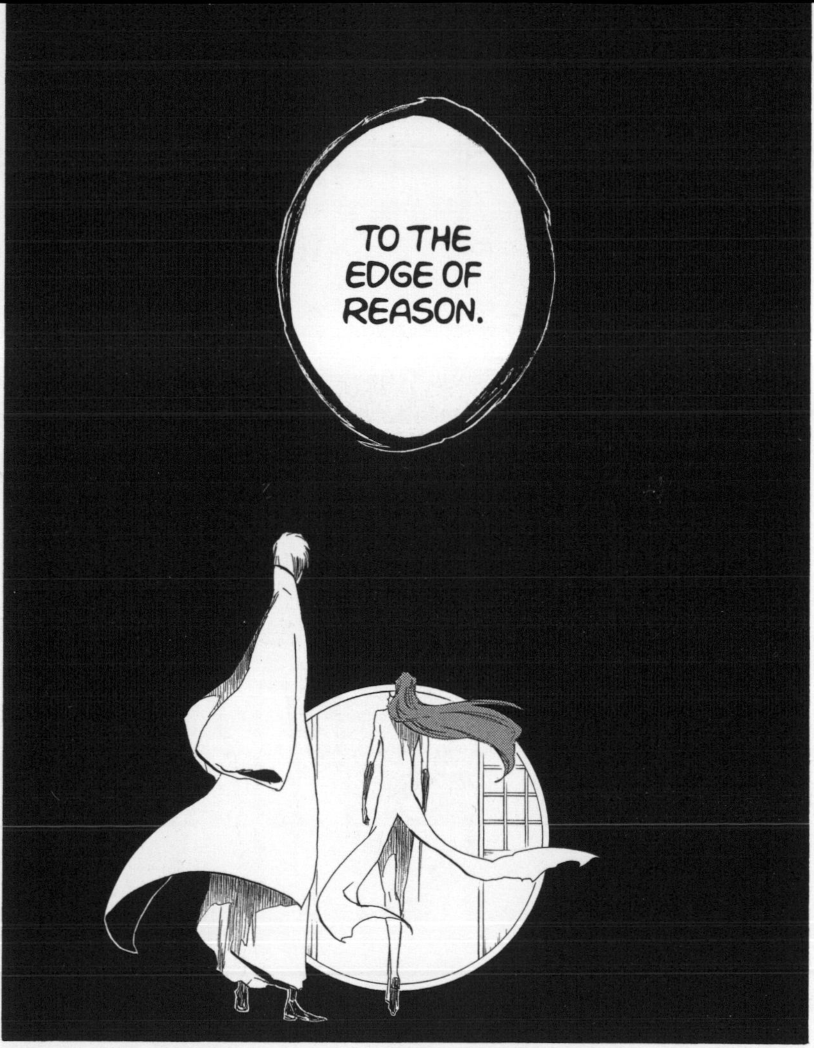
TO THE EDGE OF REASON.

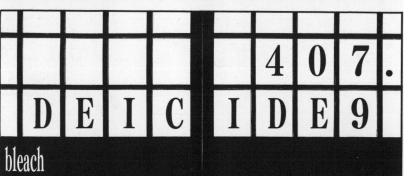

407. DEICIDE 9

bleach

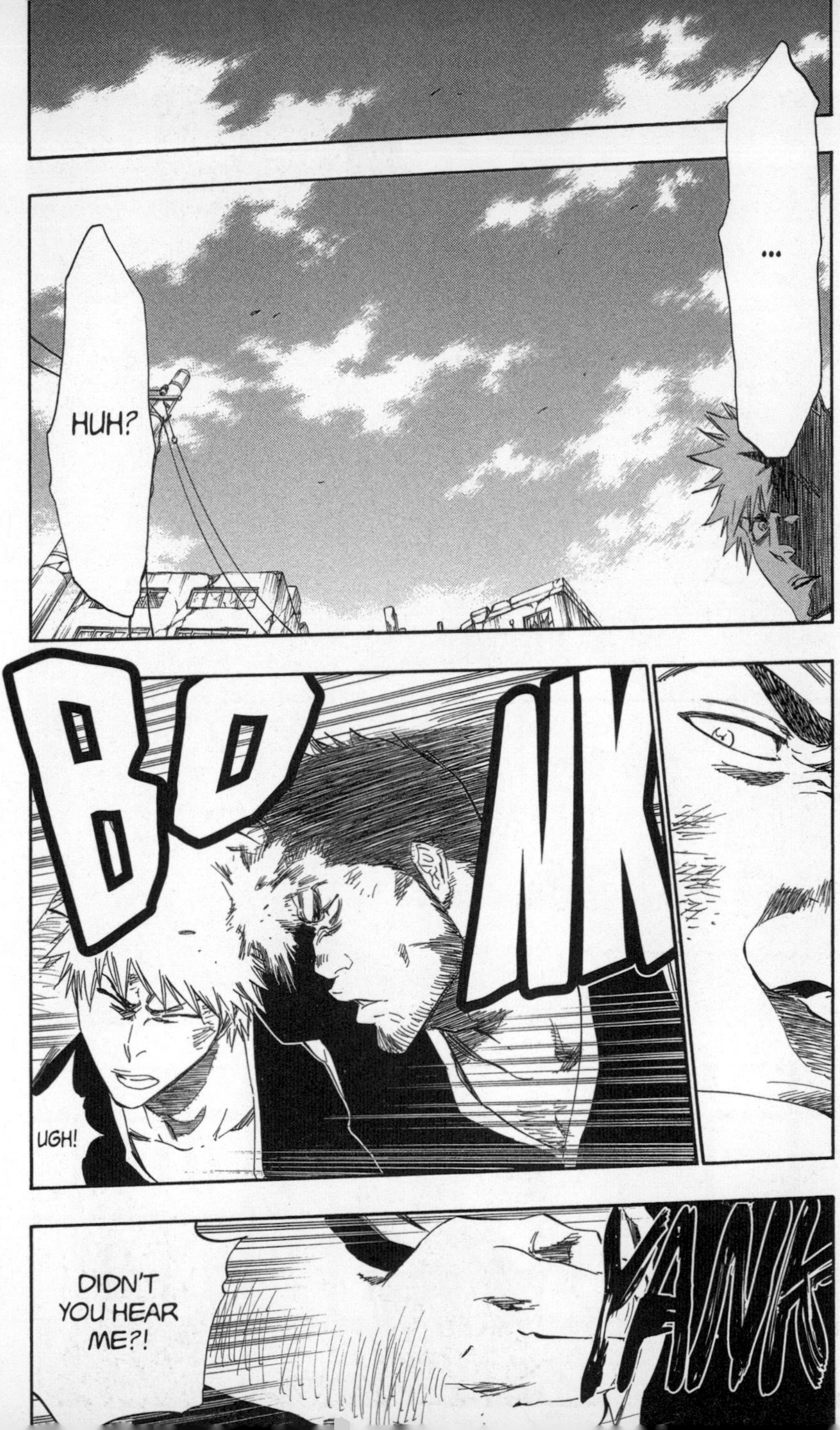
...
HUH?
BOMK
UGH!
YANK
DIDN'T YOU HEAR ME?!

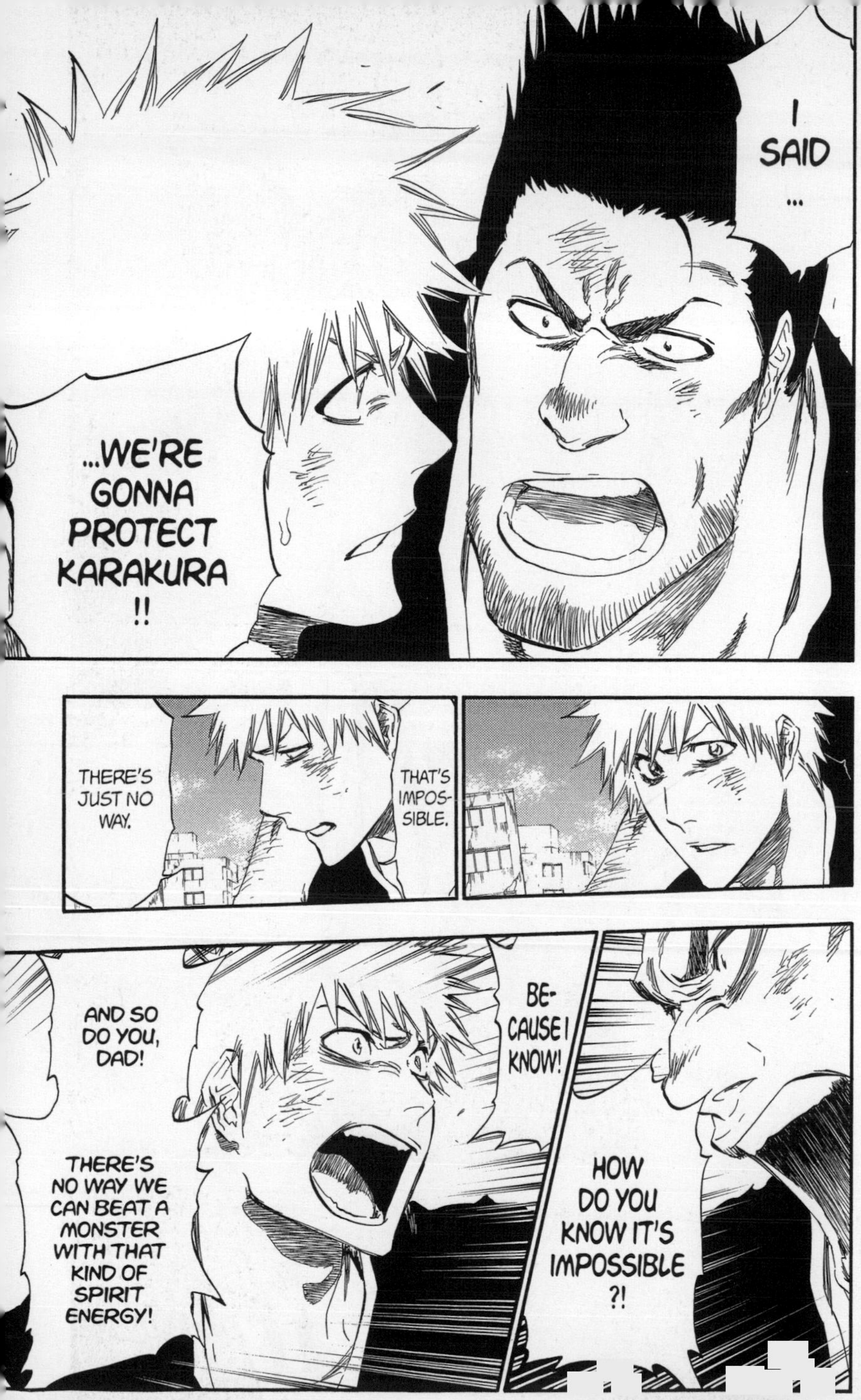
I SAID ...
...WE'RE GONNA PROTECT KARAKURA !!
THAT'S IMPOS-SIBLE.
THERE'S JUST NO WAY.
HOW DO YOU KNOW IT'S IMPOSSIBLE ?!
BE-CAUSE I KNOW!
AND SO DO YOU, DAD!
THERE'S NO WAY WE CAN BEAT A MONSTER WITH THAT KIND OF SPIRIT ENERGY!

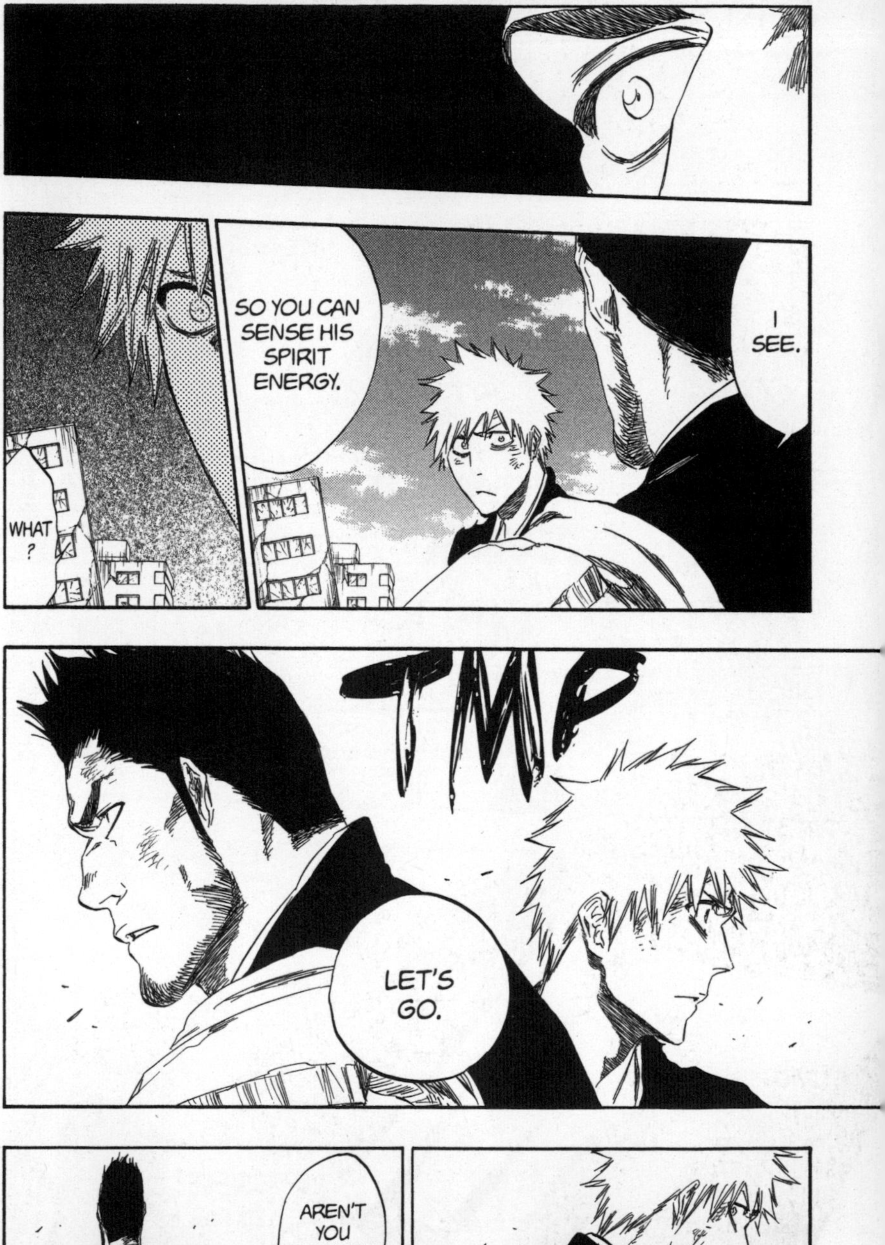
I SEE.
SO YOU CAN SENSE HIS SPIRIT ENERGY.
WHAT?
TMP
LET'S GO.
AREN'T YOU COMING?

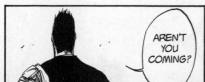

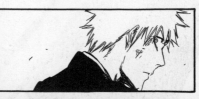

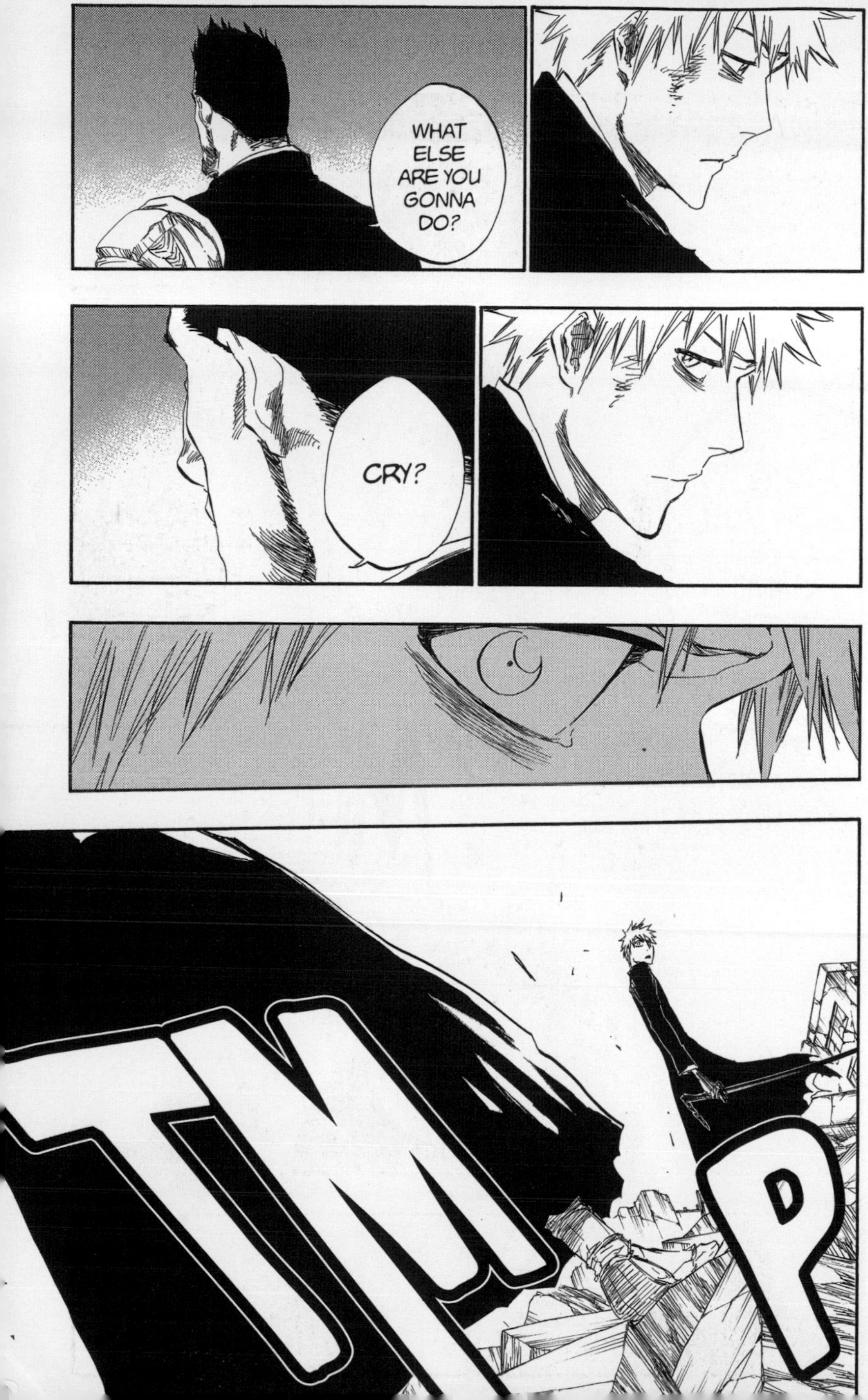
WHAT ELSE ARE YOU GONNA DO?
CRY?

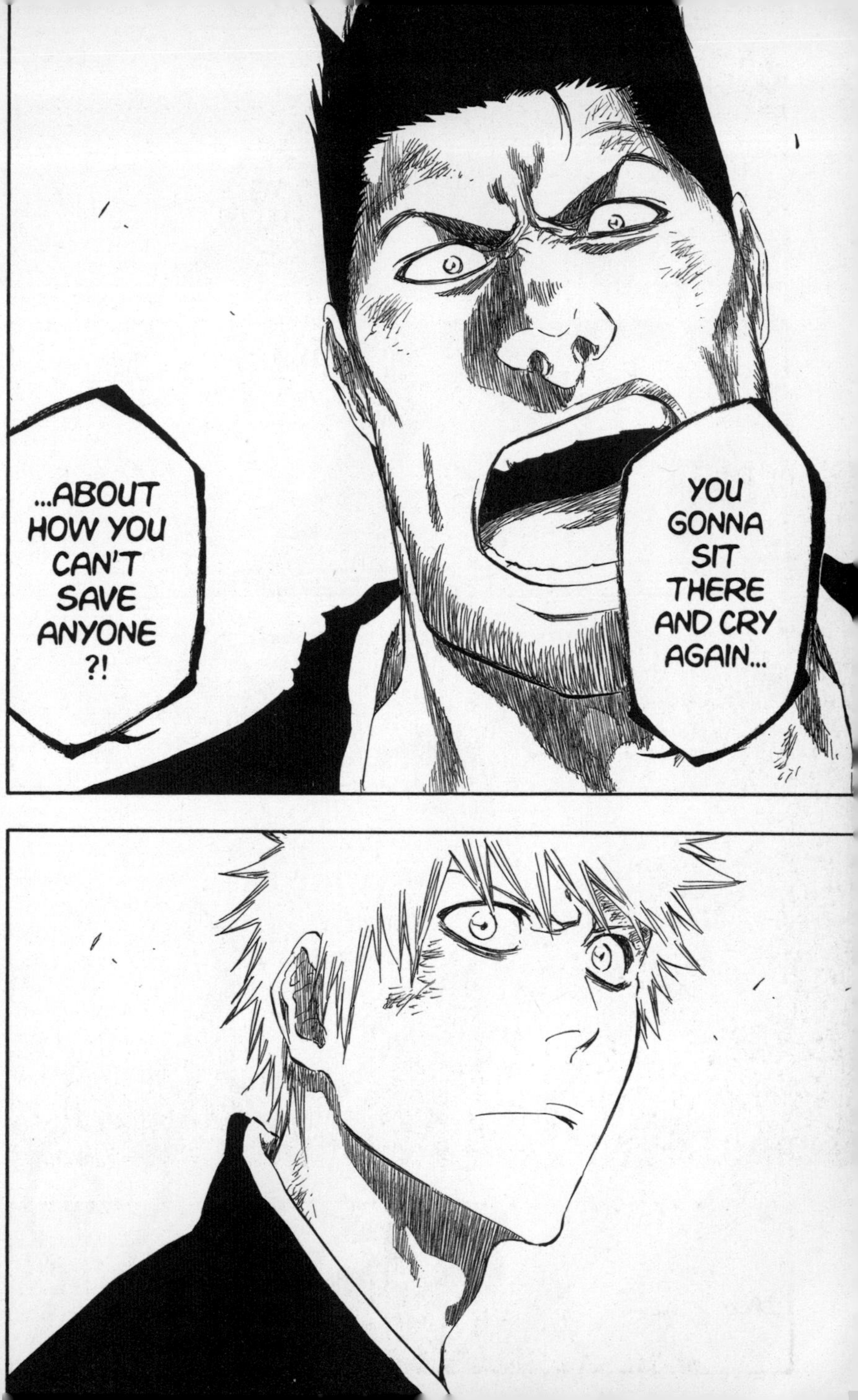
YOU GONNA SIT THERE AND CRY AGAIN...
...ABOUT HOW YOU CAN'T SAVE ANYONE ?!

READ THIS WAY

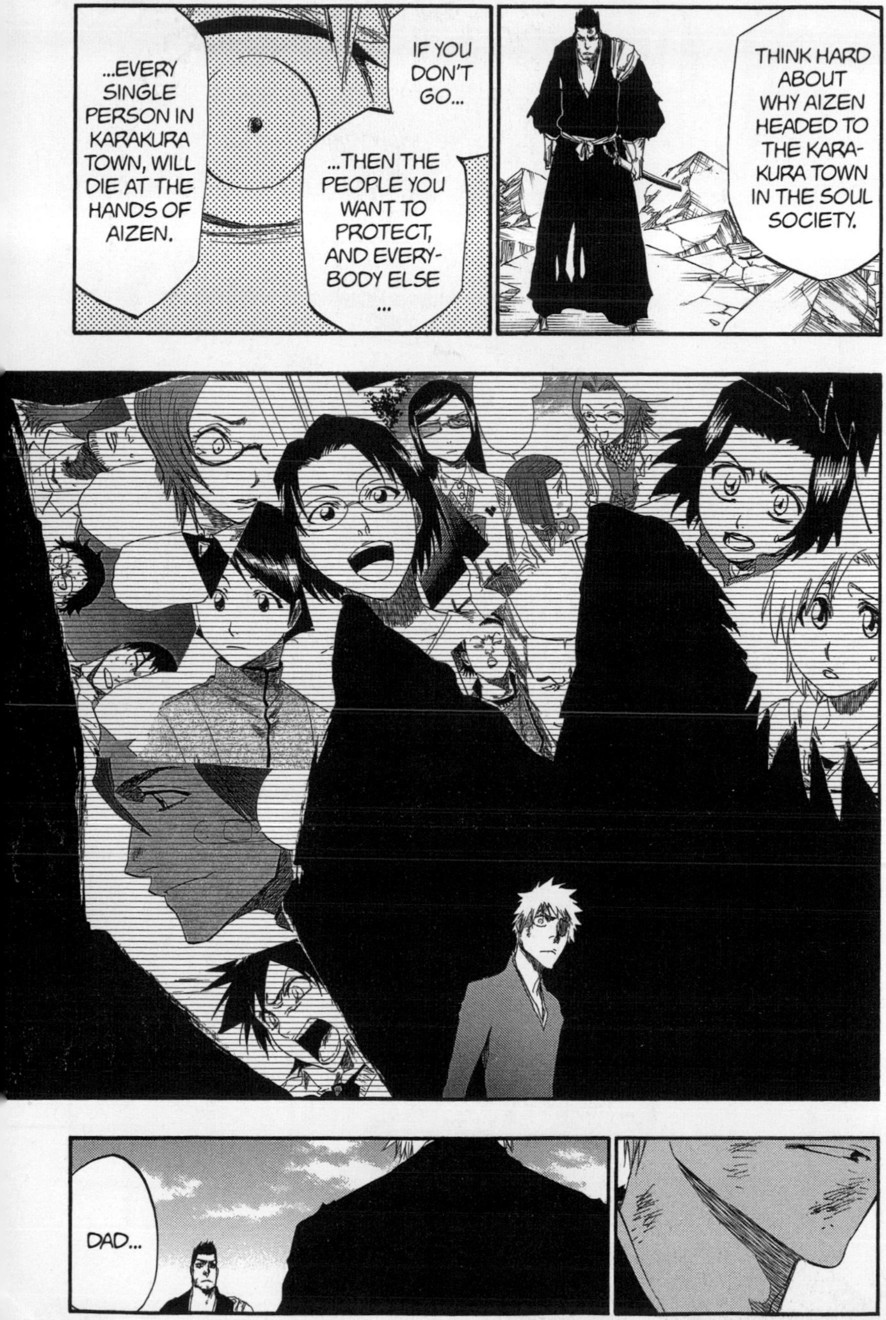

THINK HARD ABOUT WHY AIZEN HEADED TO THE KARA-KURA TOWN IN THE SOUL SOCIETY.
IF YOU DON'T GO...
...THEN THE PEOPLE YOU WANT TO PROTECT, AND EVERY-BODY ELSE ...
...EVERY SINGLE PERSON IN KARAKURA TOWN, WILL DIE AT THE HANDS OF AIZEN.
DAD...

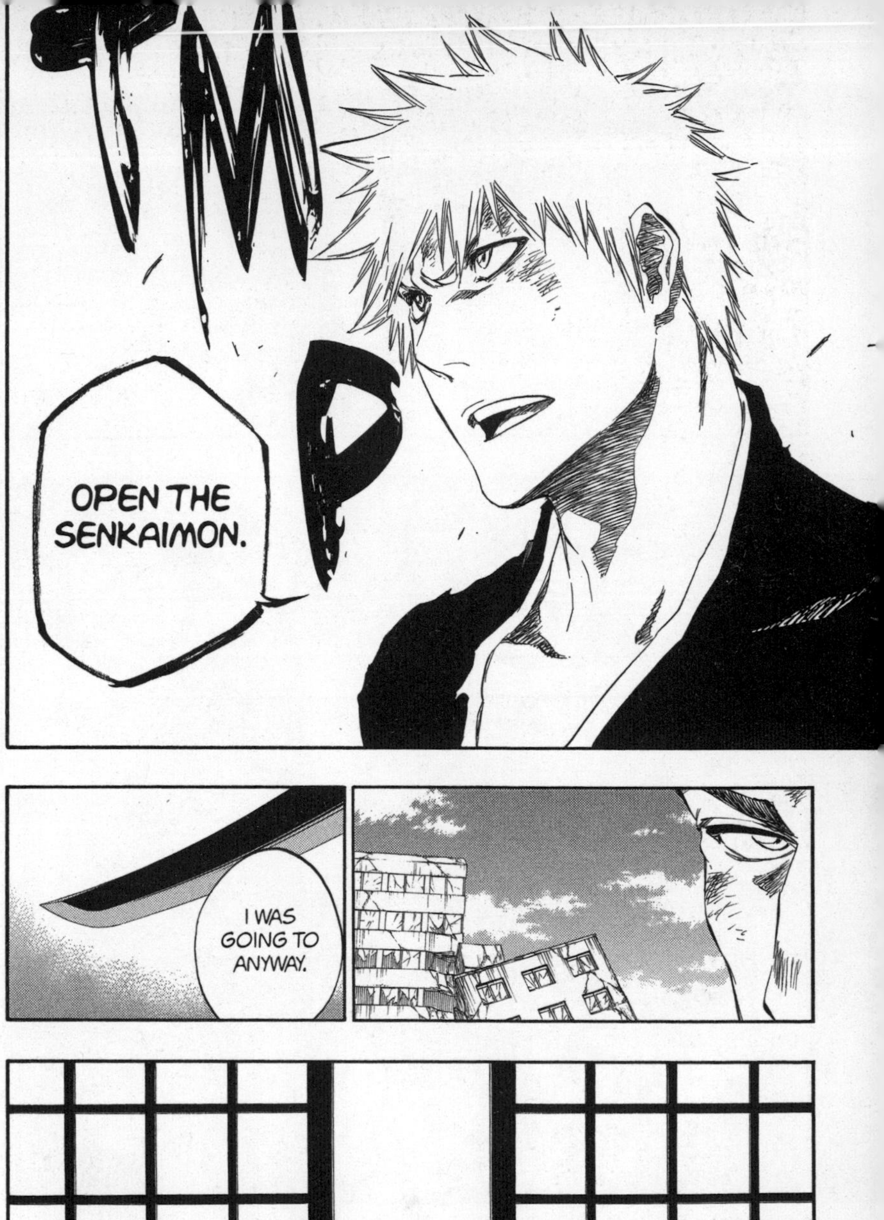
OPEN THE SENKAIMON.
I WAS GOING TO ANYWAY.

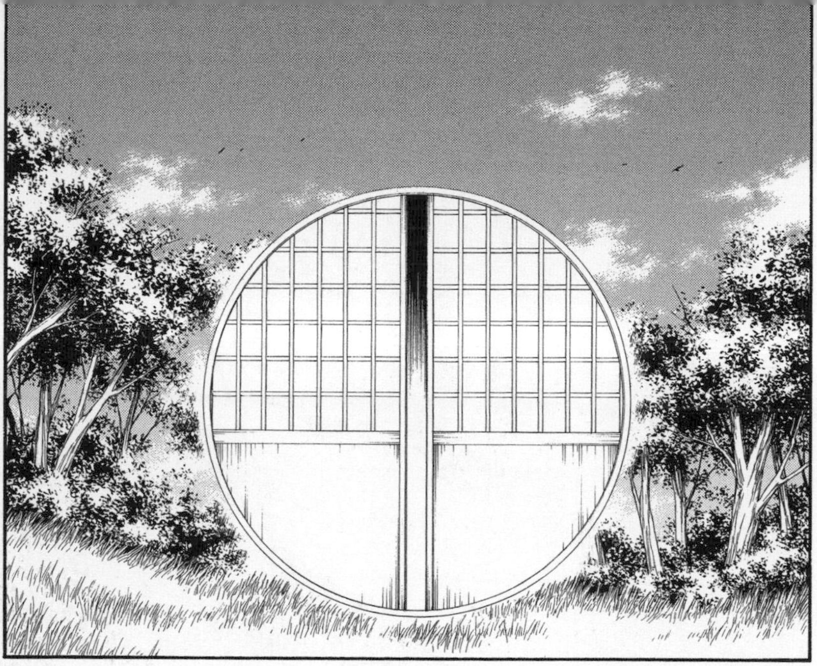

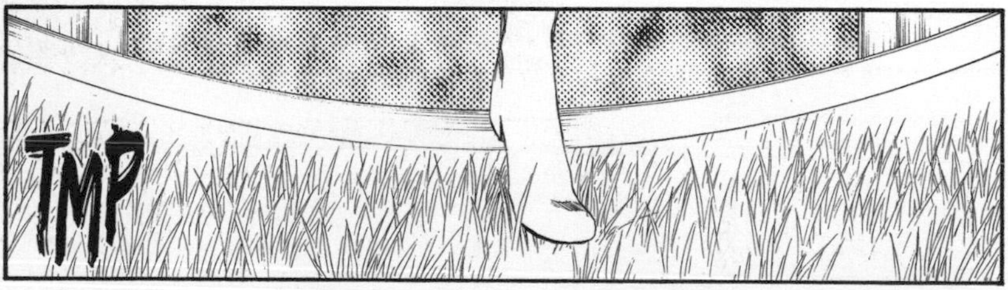
TMP

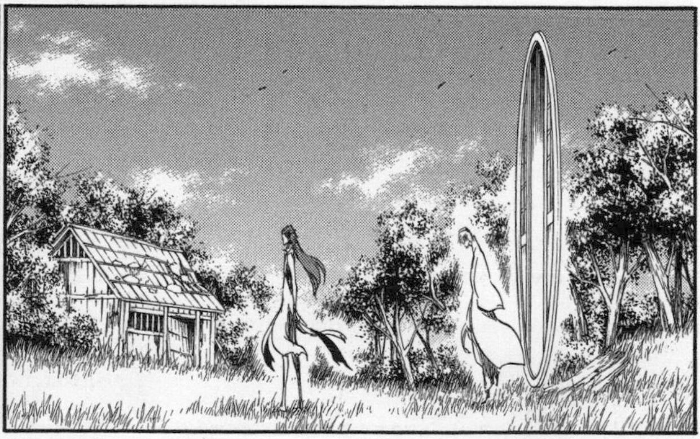

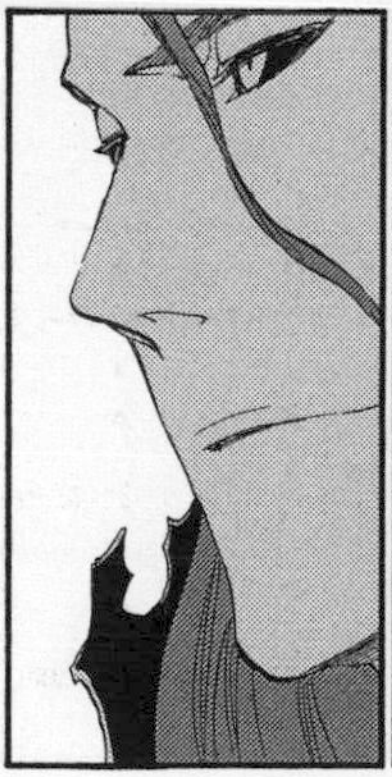

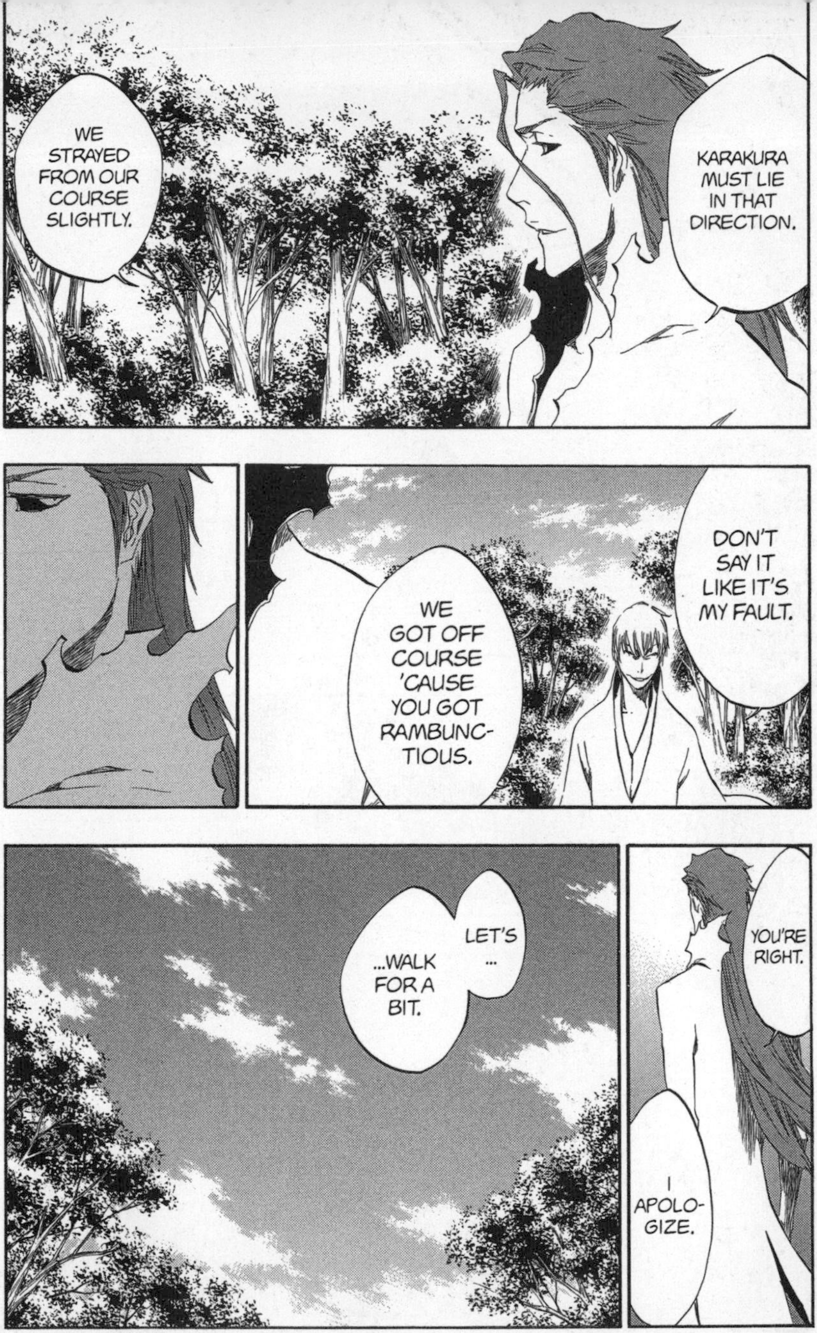
KARAKURA MUST LIE IN THAT DIRECTION.
WE STRAYED FROM OUR COURSE SLIGHTLY.
DON'T SAY IT LIKE IT'S MY FAULT.
WE GOT OFF COURSE 'CAUSE YOU GOT RAMBUNC-TIOUS.
YOU'RE RIGHT.
I APOLO-GIZE.
LET'S ...
...WALK FOR A BIT.

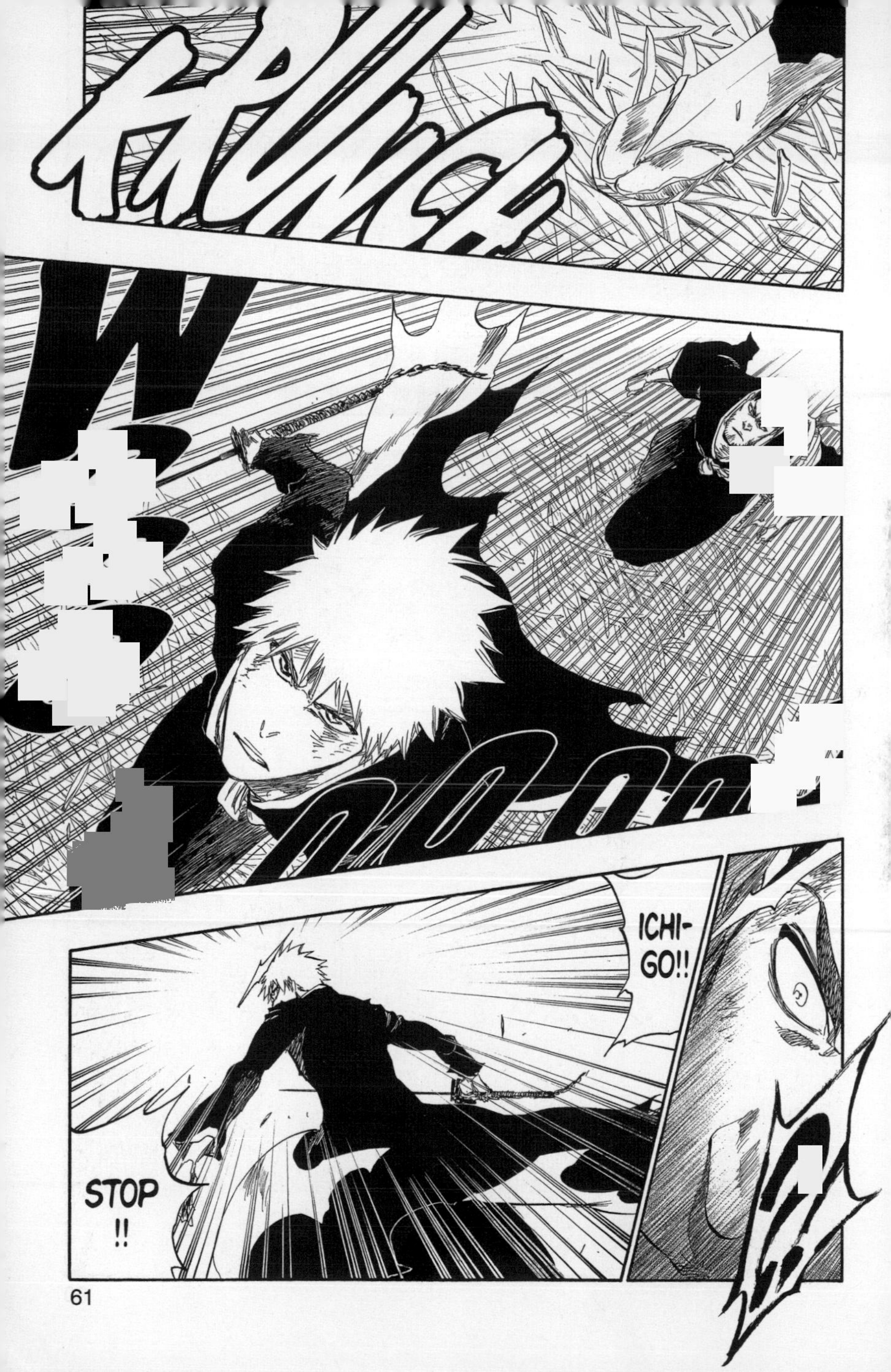
ICHI-
GO!!
STOP
!!

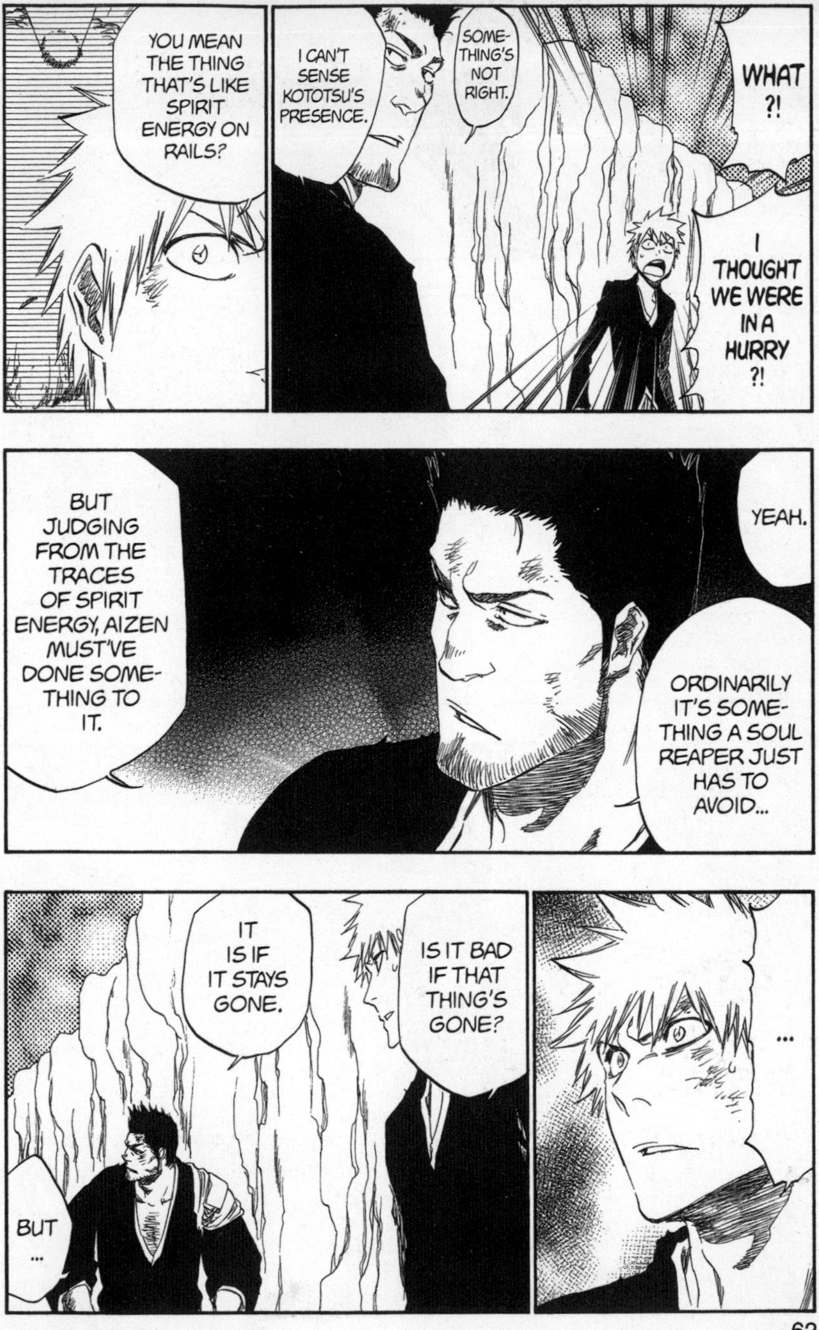
WHAT ?!
I THOUGHT WE WERE IN A HURRY ?!
SOME-THING'S NOT RIGHT.
I CAN'T SENSE KOTOTSU'S PRESENCE.
YOU MEAN THE THING THAT'S LIKE SPIRIT ENERGY ON RAILS?
YEAH.
ORDINARILY IT'S SOME-THING A SOUL REAPER JUST HAS TO AVOID...
BUT JUDGING FROM THE TRACES OF SPIRIT ENERGY, AIZEN MUST'VE DONE SOME-THING TO IT.
...
IS IT BAD IF THAT THING'S GONE?
IT IS IF IT STAYS GONE.
BUT ...

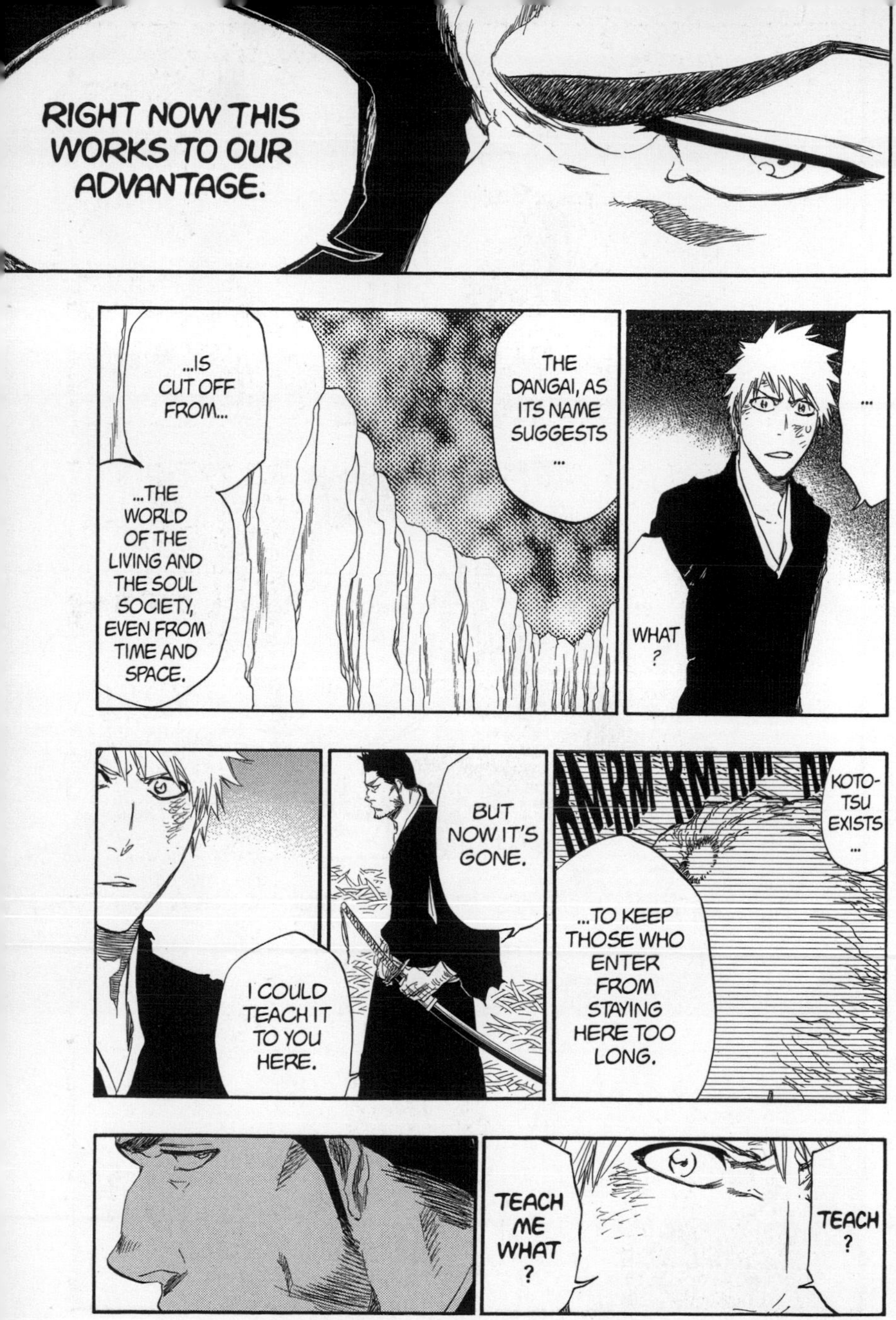
RIGHT NOW THIS WORKS TO OUR ADVANTAGE.
...
WHAT?
THE DANGAI, AS ITS NAME SUGGESTS...
...IS CUT OFF FROM...
...THE WORLD OF THE LIVING AND THE SOUL SOCIETY, EVEN FROM TIME AND SPACE.
RMRM
KOTO-TSU EXISTS...
...TO KEEP THOSE WHO ENTER FROM STAYING HERE TOO LONG.
BUT NOW IT'S GONE.
I COULD TEACH IT TO YOU HERE.
TEACH?
TEACH ME WHAT?

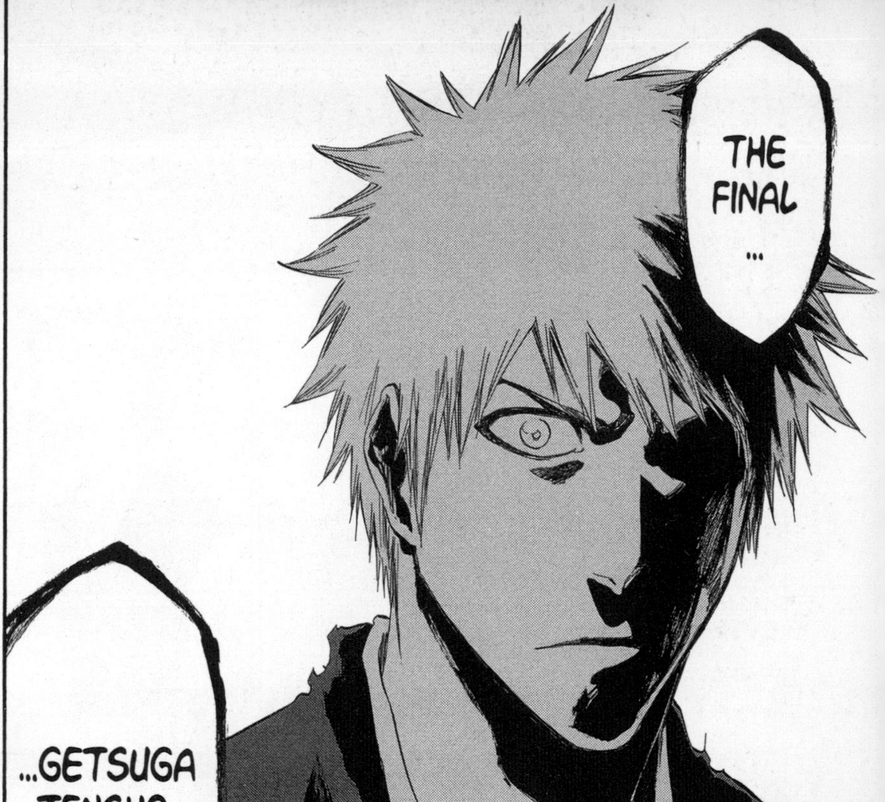
THE FINAL ...
...GETSUGA TENSHO.
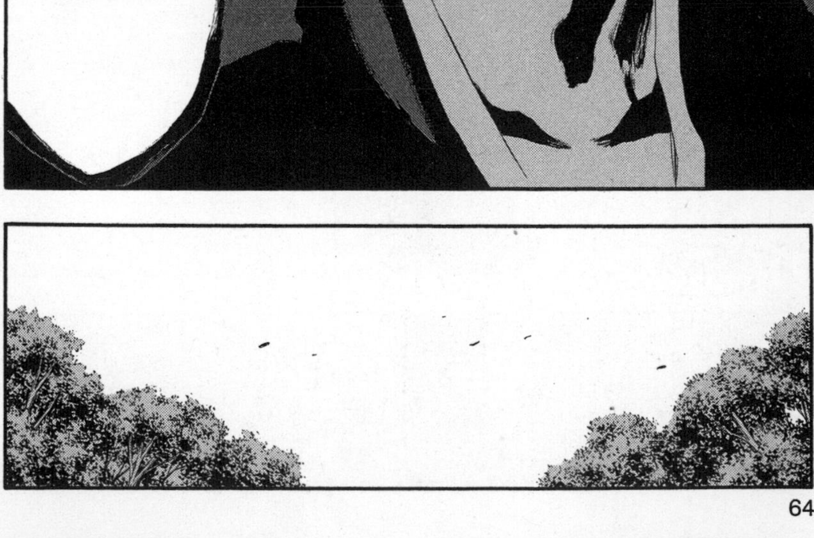

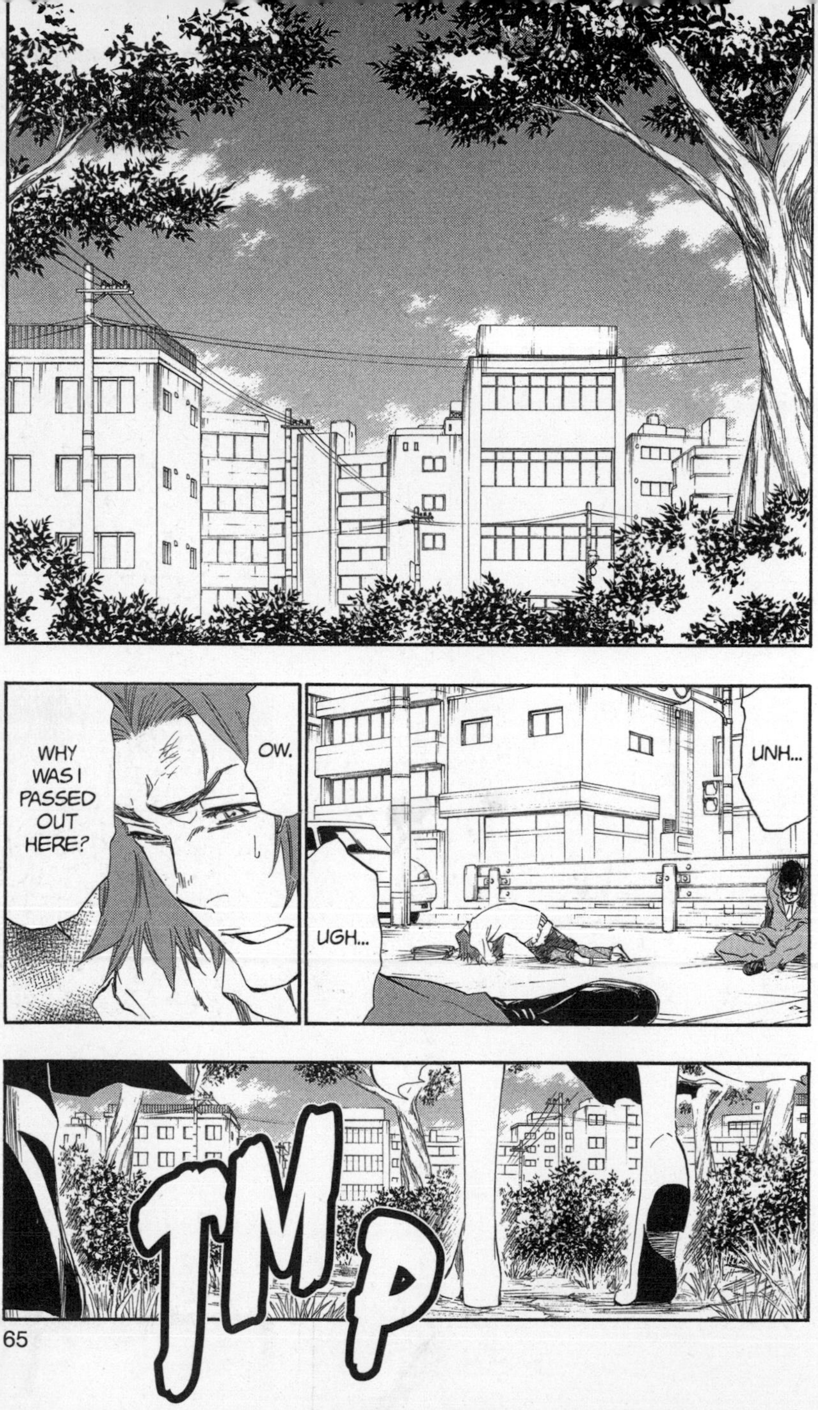
UNH...
UGH...
OW.
WHY WAS I PASSED OUT HERE?
TMP

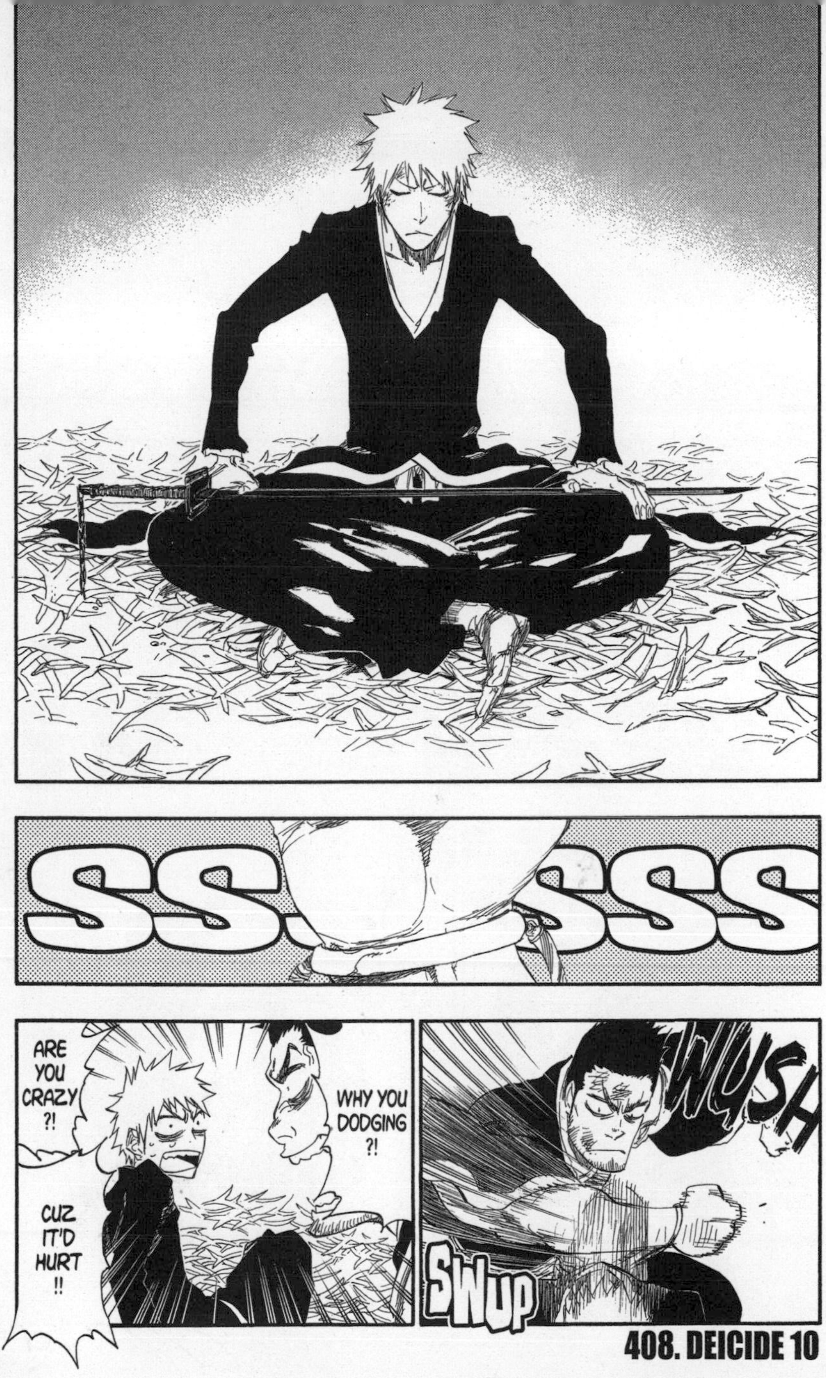
SS
SSS
WUSH
SWUP
WHY YOU DODGING?!
ARE YOU CRAZY?!
CUZ IT'D HURT!!

408. DEICIDE 10

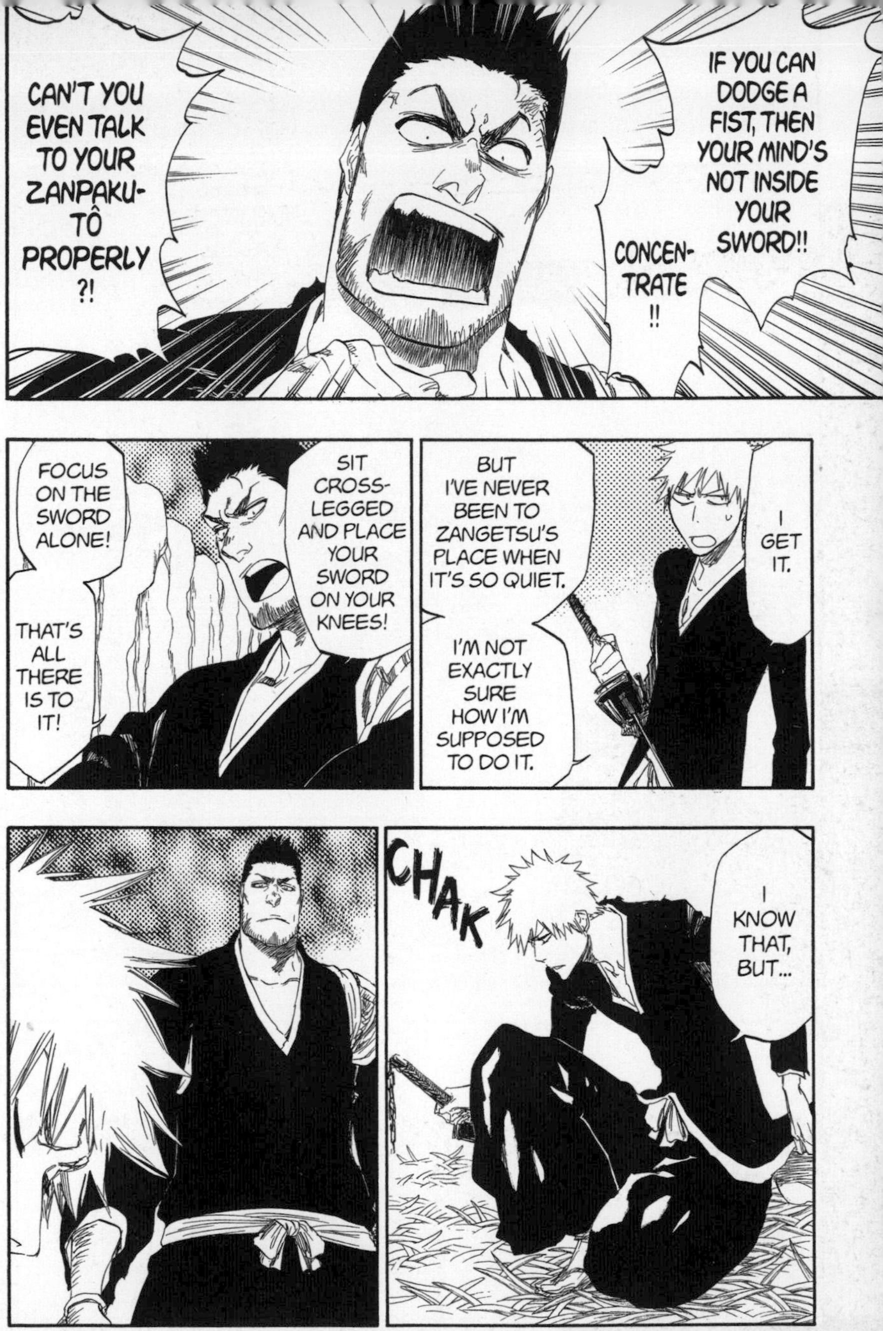
IF YOU CAN DODGE A FIST, THEN YOUR MIND'S NOT INSIDE YOUR SWORD!!
CONCEN-TRATE!!
CAN'T YOU EVEN TALK TO YOUR ZANPAKU-TÔ PROPERLY?!
I GET IT.
BUT I'VE NEVER BEEN TO ZANGETSU'S PLACE WHEN IT'S SO QUIET.
I'M NOT EXACTLY SURE HOW I'M SUPPOSED TO DO IT.
SIT CROSS-LEGGED AND PLACE YOUR SWORD ON YOUR KNEES!
FOCUS ON THE SWORD ALONE!
THAT'S ALL THERE IS TO IT!
I KNOW THAT, BUT...
CHAK

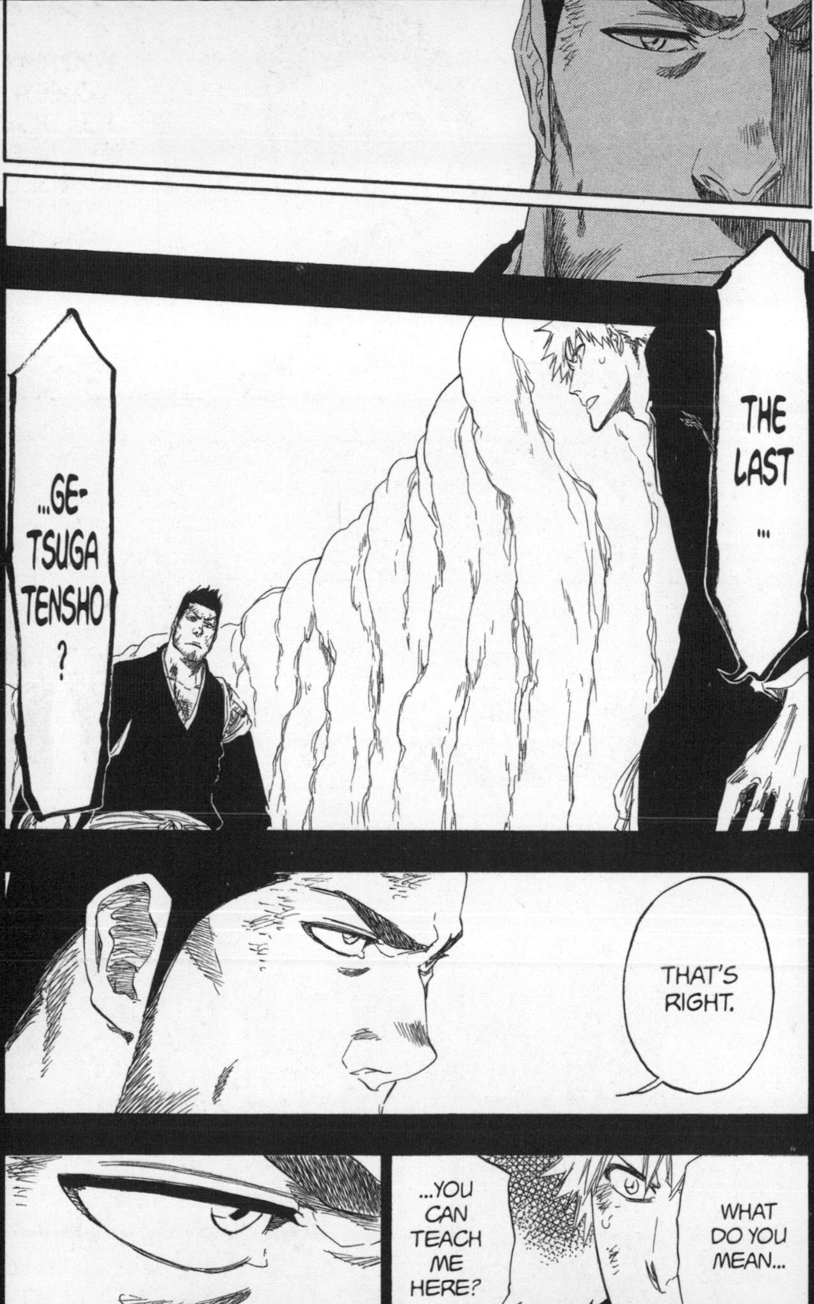
THE LAST ...
...GE-TSUGA TENSHO ?
THAT'S RIGHT.
WHAT DO YOU MEAN...
...YOU CAN TEACH ME HERE?

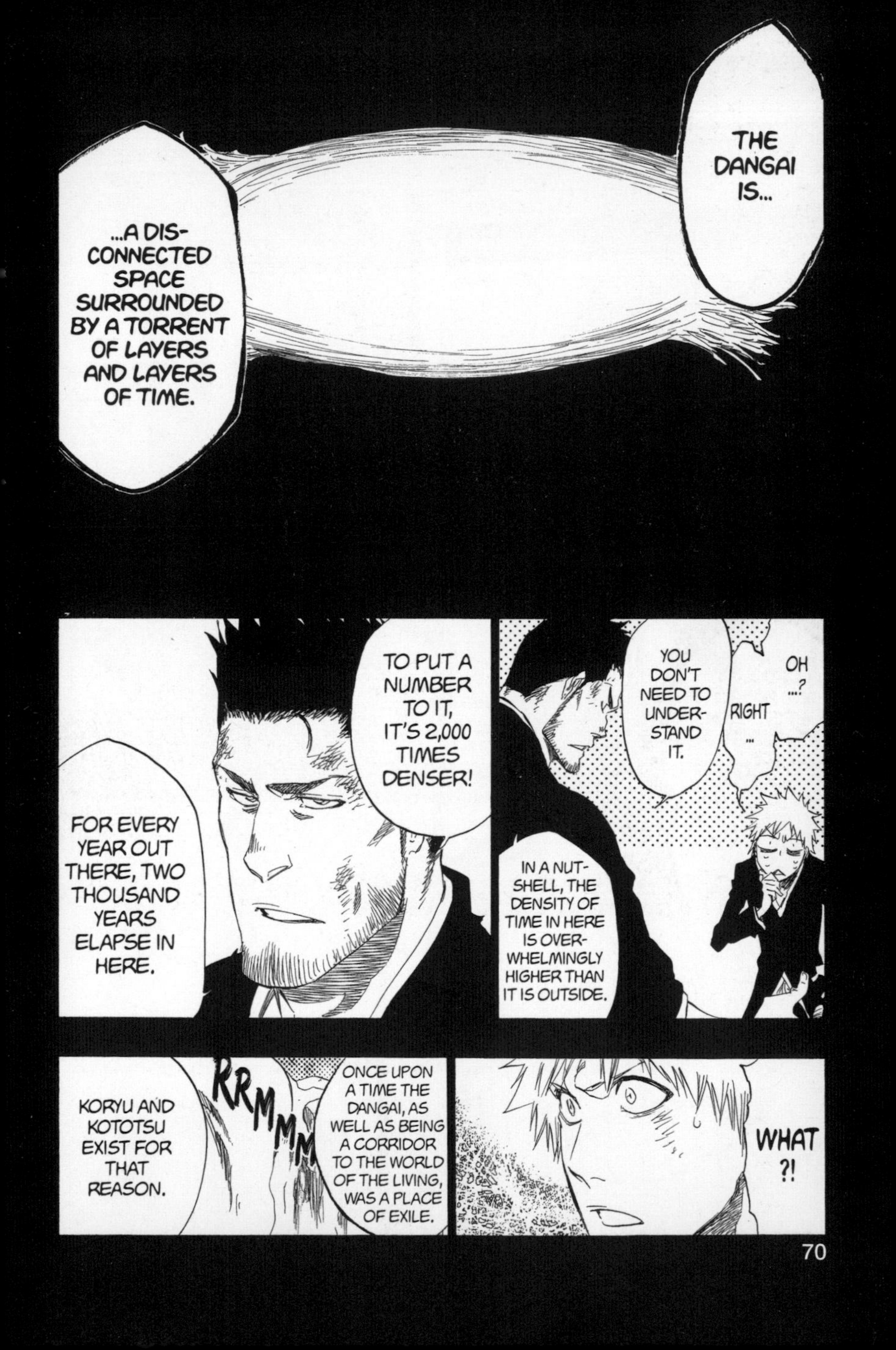
THE DANGAI IS...
...A DISCONNECTED SPACE SURROUNDED BY A TORRENT OF LAYERS AND LAYERS OF TIME.
OH ...?
RIGHT ...
YOU DON'T NEED TO UNDERSTAND IT.
IN A NUTSHELL, THE DENSITY OF TIME IN HERE IS OVERWHELMINGLY HIGHER THAN IT IS OUTSIDE.
TO PUT A NUMBER TO IT, IT'S 2,000 TIMES DENSER!
FOR EVERY YEAR OUT THERE, TWO THOUSAND YEARS ELAPSE IN HERE.
WHAT ?!
ONCE UPON A TIME THE DANGAI, AS WELL AS BEING A CORRIDOR TO THE WORLD OF THE LIVING, WAS A PLACE OF EXILE.
RRMMMM
KORYU AND KOTOTSU EXIST FOR THAT REASON.

READ THIS WAY

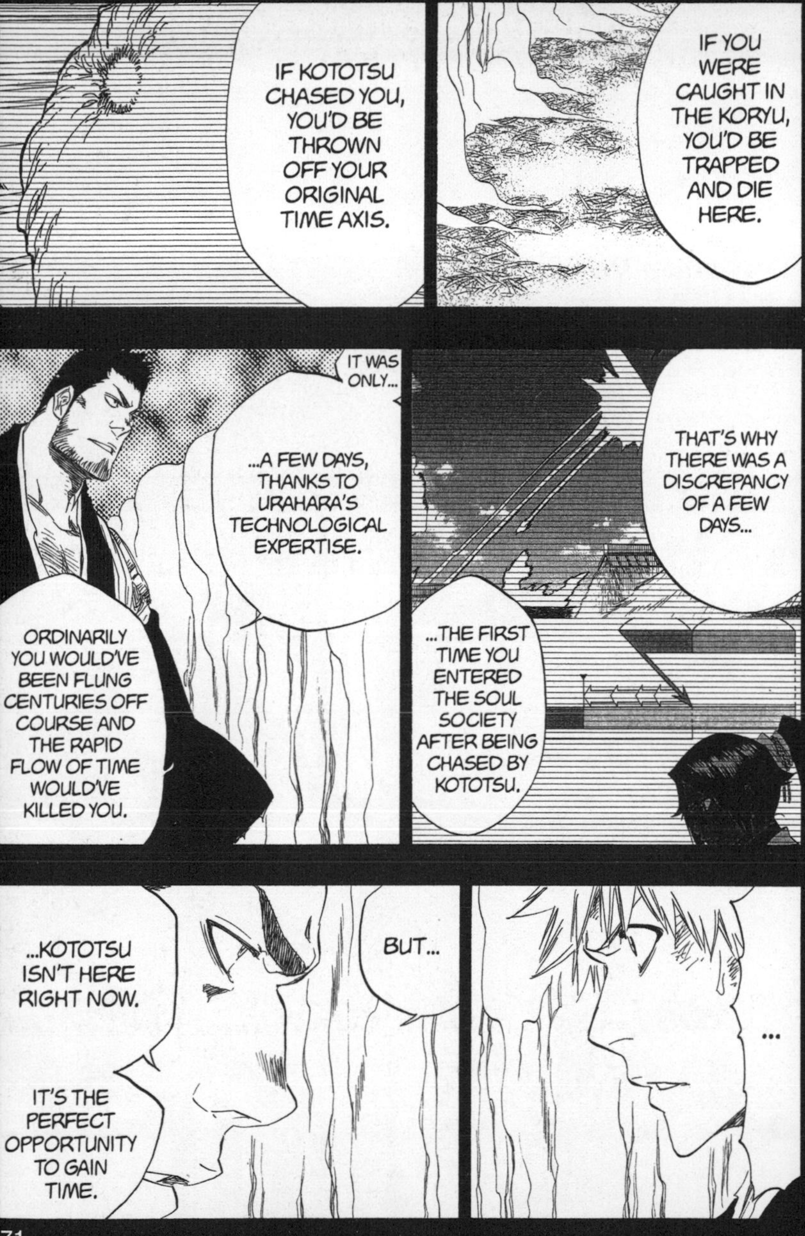
IF YOU WERE CAUGHT IN THE KORYU, YOU'D BE TRAPPED AND DIE HERE.
IF KOTOTSU CHASED YOU, YOU'D BE THROWN OFF YOUR ORIGINAL TIME AXIS.
THAT'S WHY THERE WAS A DISCREPANCY OF A FEW DAYS...
...THE FIRST TIME YOU ENTERED THE SOUL SOCIETY AFTER BEING CHASED BY KOTOTSU.
IT WAS ONLY...
...A FEW DAYS, THANKS TO URAHARA'S TECHNOLOGICAL EXPERTISE.
ORDINARILY YOU WOULD'VE BEEN FLUNG CENTURIES OFF COURSE AND THE RAPID FLOW OF TIME WOULD'VE KILLED YOU.
...
BUT...
...KOTOTSU ISN'T HERE RIGHT NOW.
IT'S THE PERFECT OPPORTUNITY TO GAIN TIME.

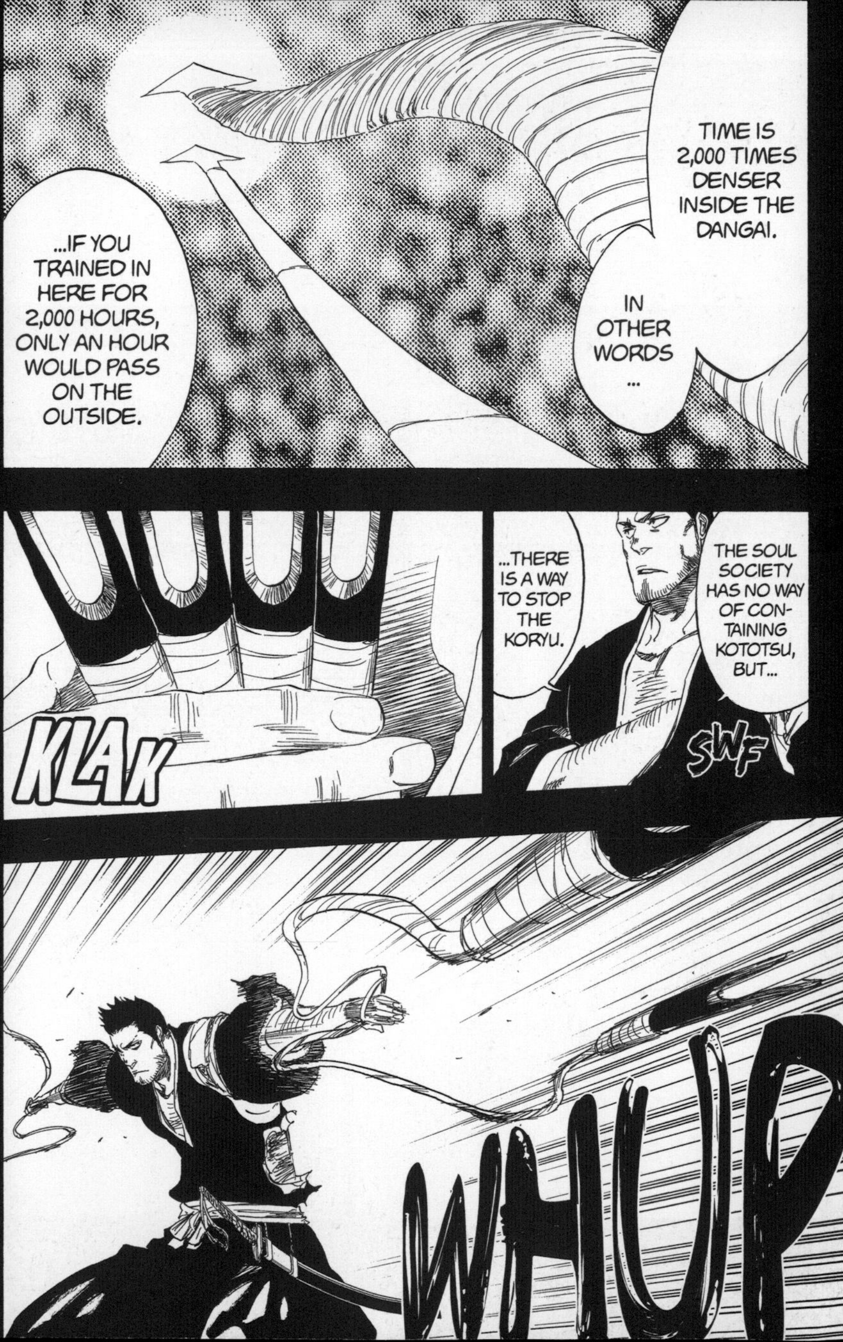
TIME IS 2,000 TIMES DENSER INSIDE THE DANGAI.
IN OTHER WORDS...
...IF YOU TRAINED IN HERE FOR 2,000 HOURS, ONLY AN HOUR WOULD PASS ON THE OUTSIDE.
THE SOUL SOCIETY HAS NO WAY OF CON-TAINING KOTOTSU, BUT...
...THERE IS A WAY TO STOP THE KORYU.
SWF
KLAK
WHUP

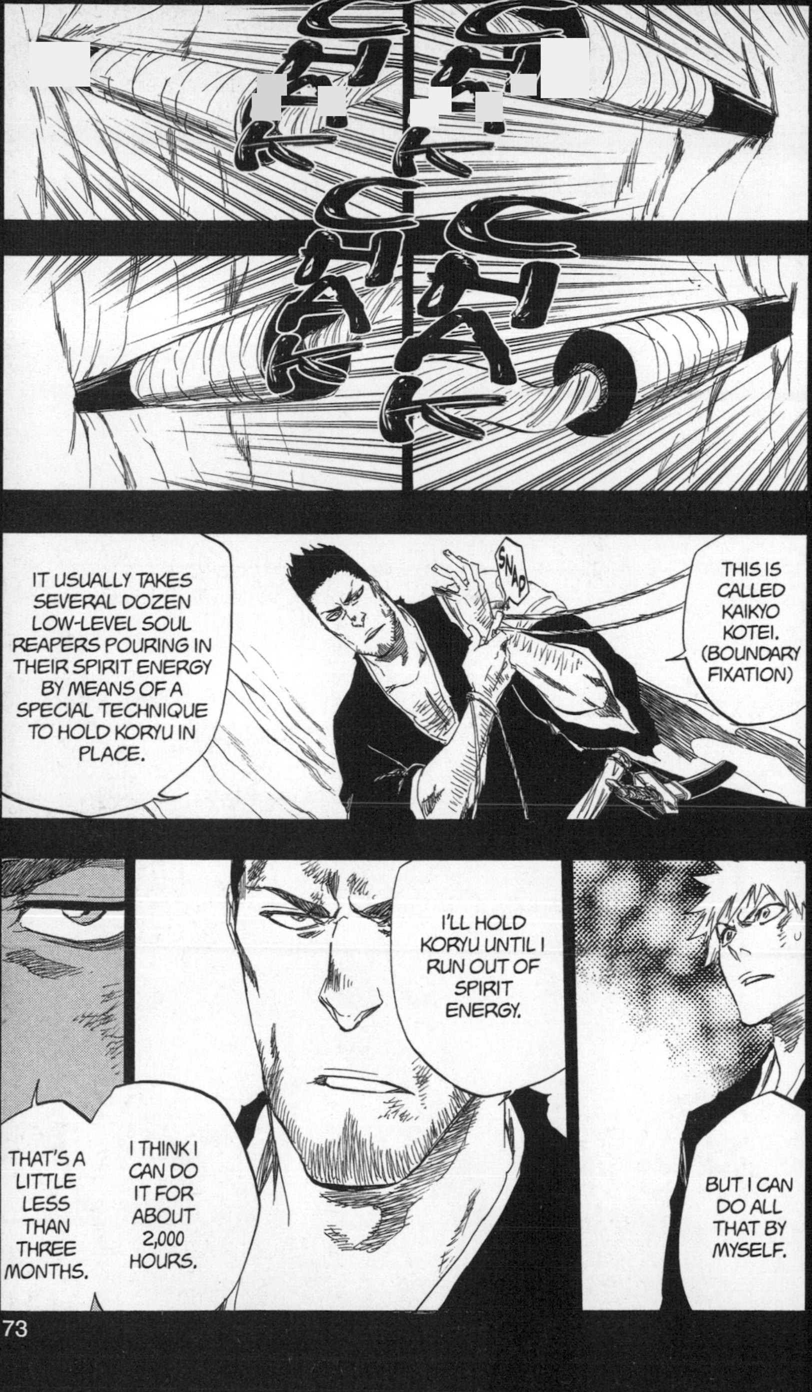
CHAK
CHAK
CHAK
CHAK
THIS IS CALLED KAIKYO KOTEI. (BOUNDARY FIXATION)
SNAP
IT USUALLY TAKES SEVERAL DOZEN LOW-LEVEL SOUL REAPERS POURING IN THEIR SPIRIT ENERGY BY MEANS OF A SPECIAL TECHNIQUE TO HOLD KORYU IN PLACE.
BUT I CAN DO ALL THAT BY MYSELF.
I'LL HOLD KORYU UNTIL I RUN OUT OF SPIRIT ENERGY.
I THINK I CAN DO IT FOR ABOUT 2,000 HOURS.
THAT'S A LITTLE LESS THAN THREE MONTHS.

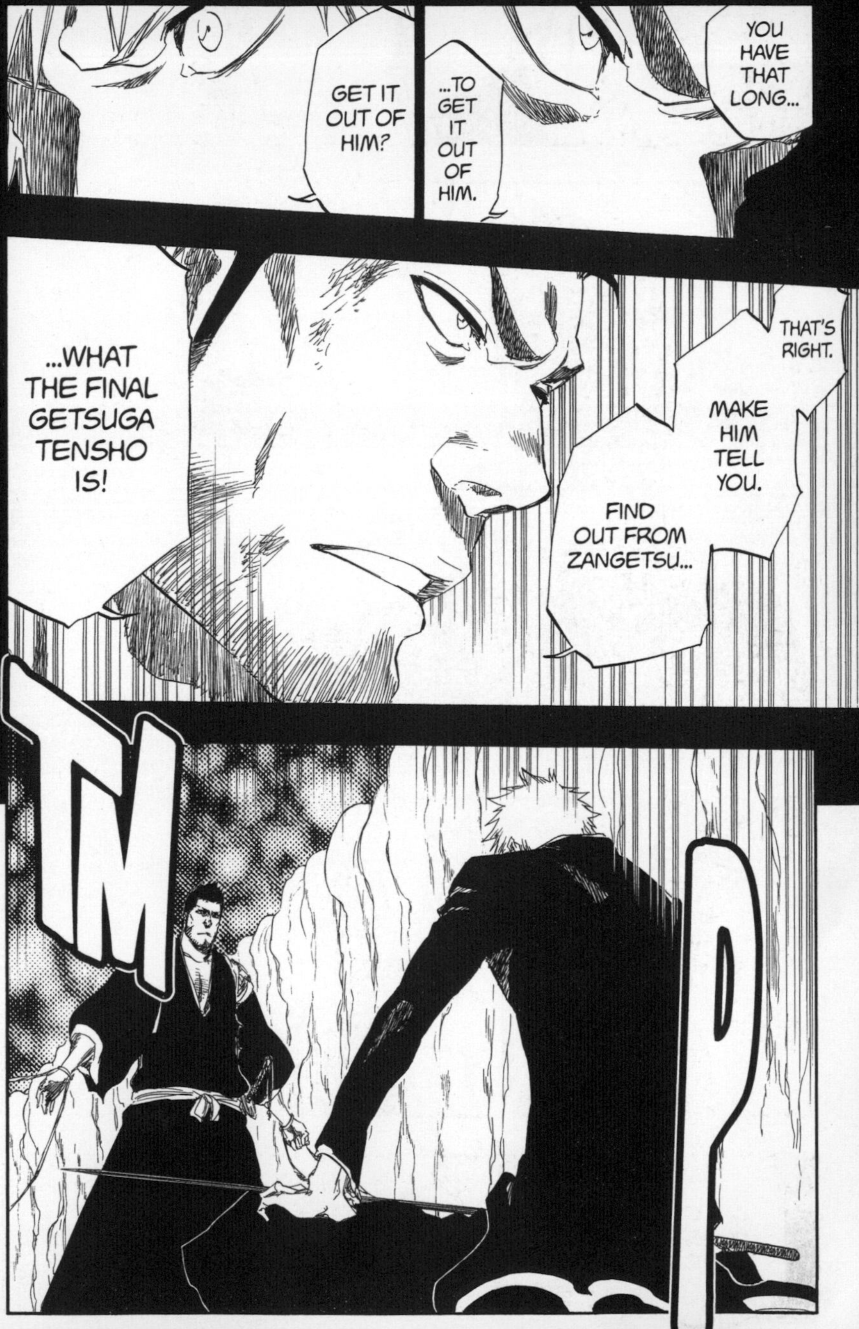

YOU HAVE THAT LONG...
...TO GET IT OUT OF HIM.
GET IT OUT OF HIM?
THAT'S RIGHT.
MAKE HIM TELL YOU.
FIND OUT FROM ZANGETSU...
...WHAT THE FINAL GETSUGA TENSHO IS!
TMP

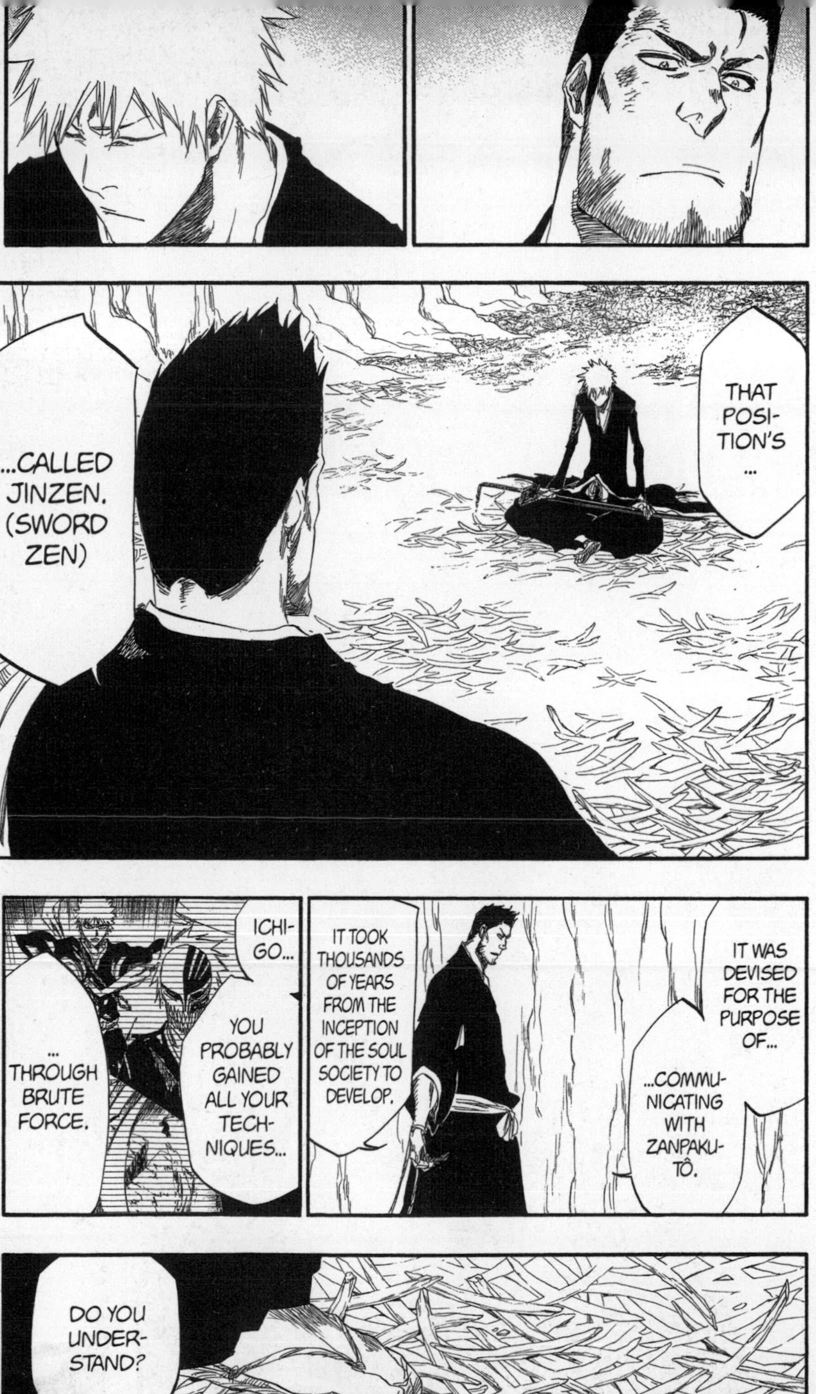
THAT POSITION'S ...
...CALLED JINZEN. (SWORD ZEN)
IT WAS DEVISED FOR THE PURPOSE OF...
...COMMUNICATING WITH ZANPAKUTÔ.
IT TOOK THOUSANDS OF YEARS FROM THE INCEPTION OF THE SOUL SOCIETY TO DEVELOP.
ICHIGO...
YOU PROBABLY GAINED ALL YOUR TECHNIQUES...
...THROUGH BRUTE FORCE.
DO YOU UNDERSTAND?

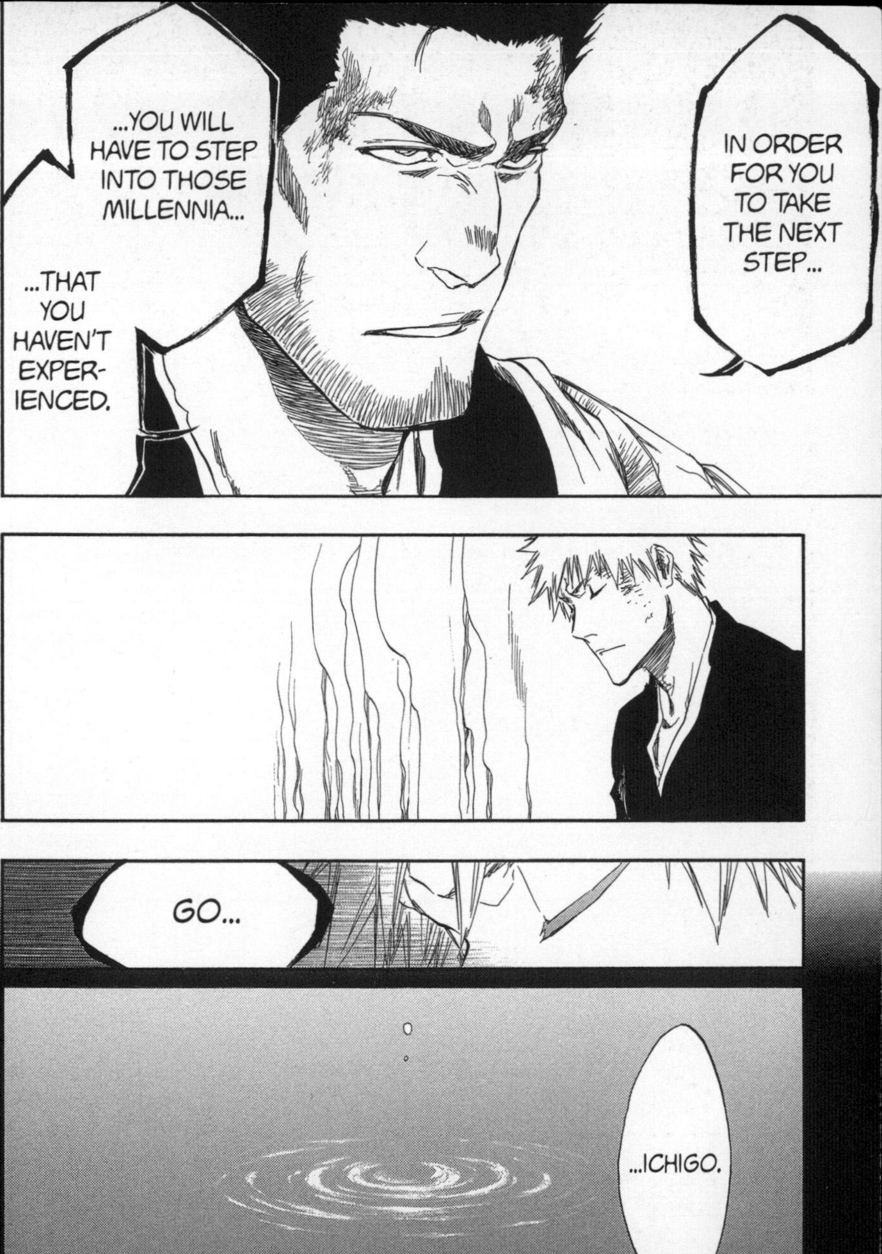
IN ORDER FOR YOU TO TAKE THE NEXT STEP...
...YOU WILL HAVE TO STEP INTO THOSE MILLENNIA...
...THAT YOU HAVEN'T EXPER-IENCED.
GO...
...ICHIGO.

DEICIDE 10

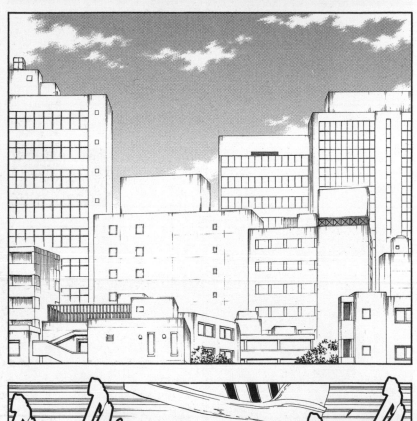

TMP TMP TMP TMP TMP

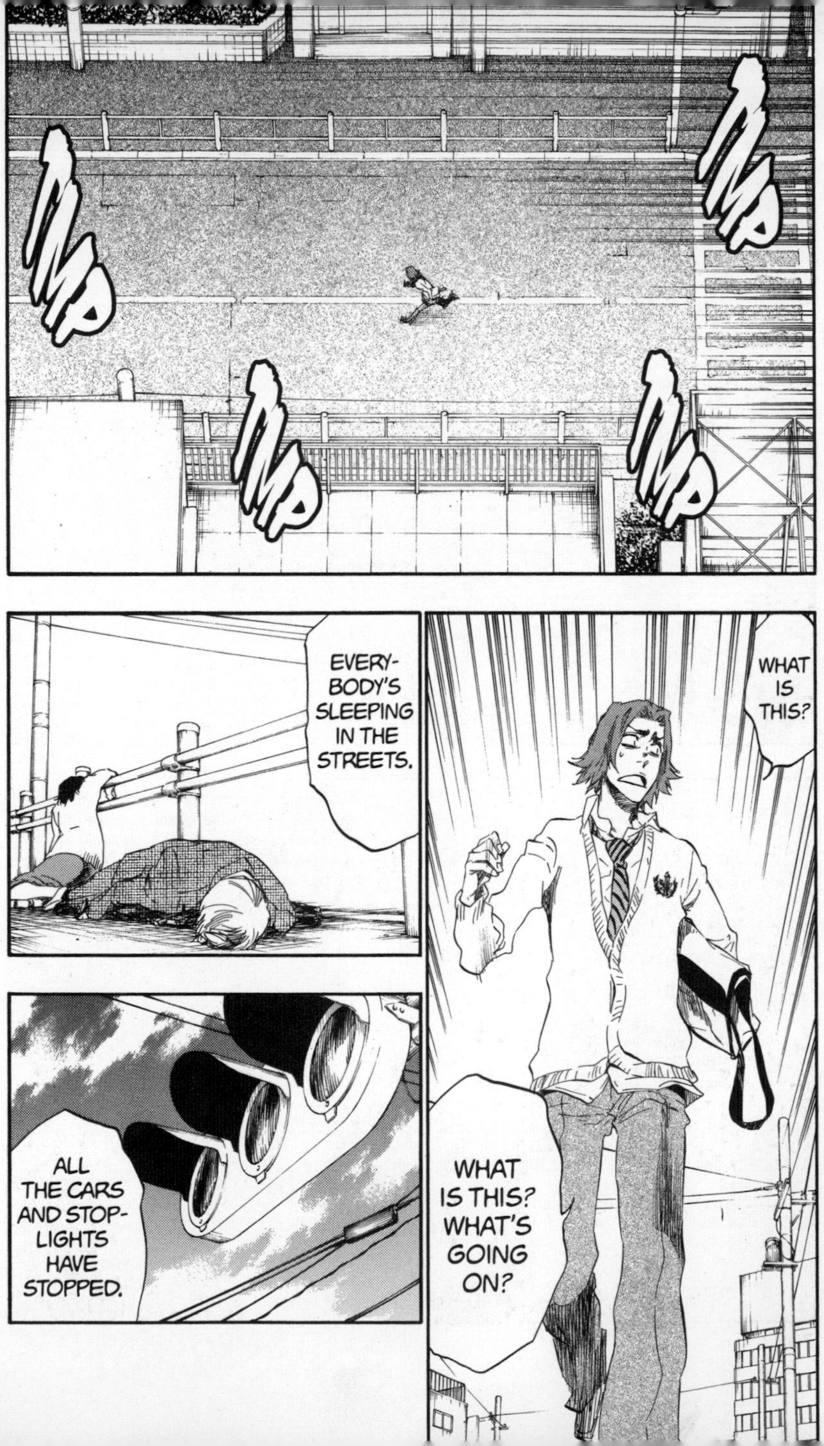
TMP
TMP
TMP
TMP
WHAT IS THIS?
WHAT IS THIS? WHAT'S GOING ON?
EVERY-BODY'S SLEEPING IN THE STREETS.
ALL THE CARS AND STOP-LIGHTS HAVE STOPPED.

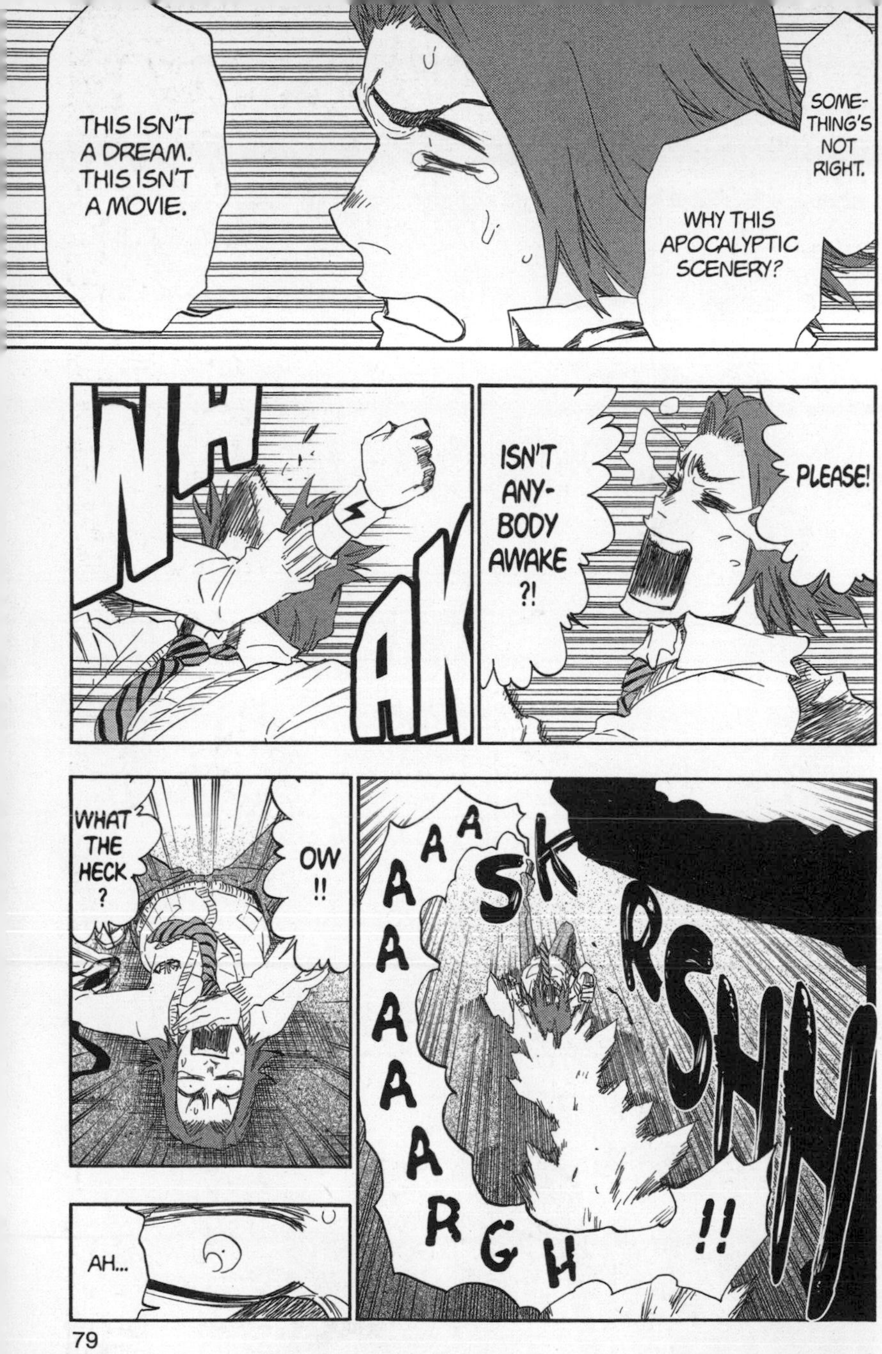
SOME-THING'S NOT RIGHT.
WHY THIS APOCALYPTIC SCENERY?
THIS ISN'T A DREAM. THIS ISN'T A MOVIE.
PLEASE!
ISN'T ANY-BODY AWAKE ?!
WH
AK
SKRRSHH!!
AAAAAAAAARGH
OW !!
WHAT THE HECK ?
AH...

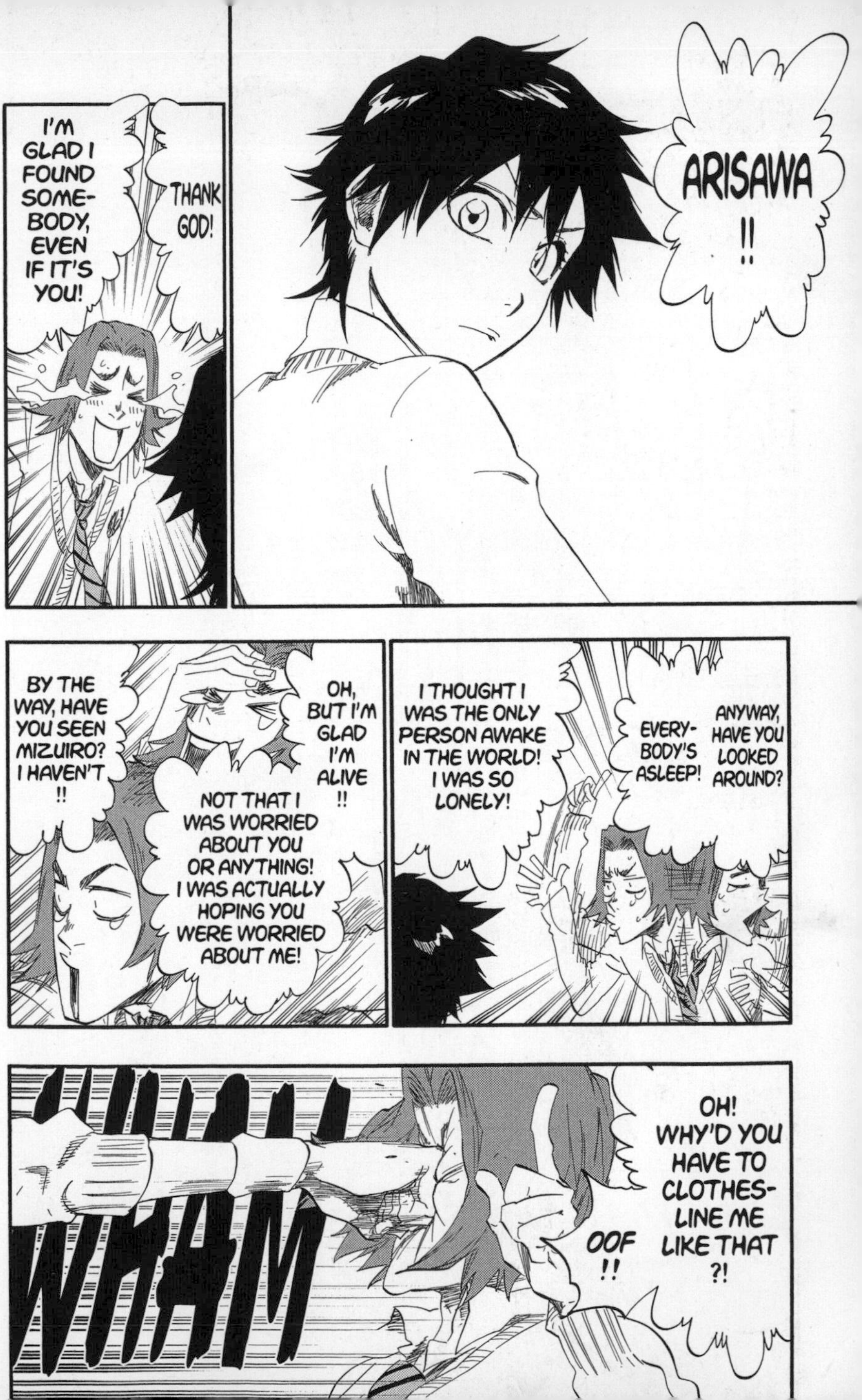
ARISAWA!!
THANK GOD!
I'M GLAD I FOUND SOMEBODY, EVEN IF IT'S YOU!
ANYWAY, HAVE YOU LOOKED AROUND?
EVERYBODY'S ASLEEP!
I THOUGHT I WAS THE ONLY PERSON AWAKE IN THE WORLD! I WAS SO LONELY!
OH, BUT I'M GLAD I'M ALIVE!!
BY THE WAY, HAVE YOU SEEN MIZUIRO? I HAVEN'T!!
NOT THAT I WAS WORRIED ABOUT YOU OR ANYTHING! I WAS ACTUALLY HOPING YOU WERE WORRIED ABOUT ME!
OH! WHY'D YOU HAVE TO CLOTHESLINE ME LIKE THAT?!
OOF!!
WHAM

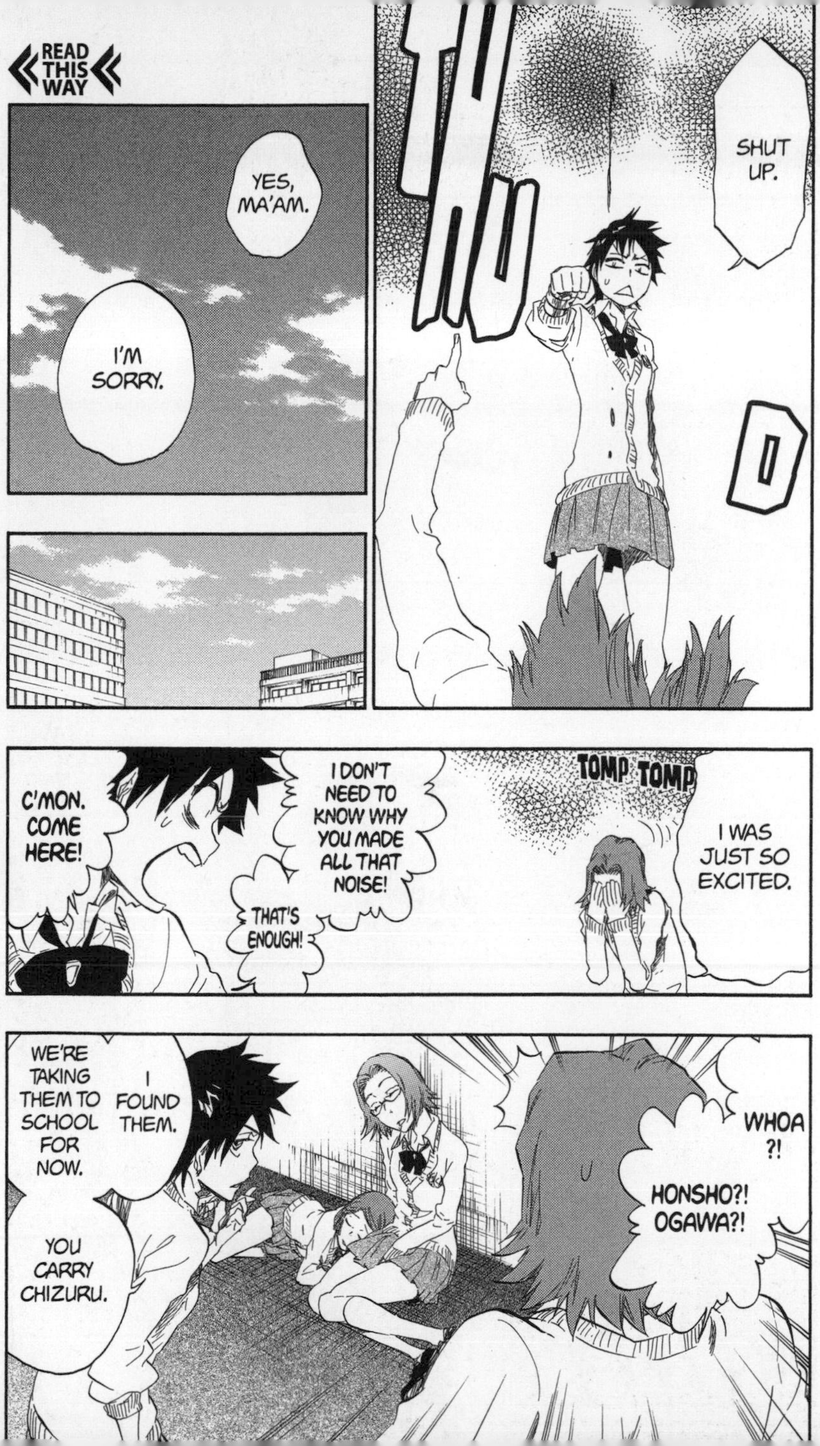
READ THIS WAY
SHUT UP.
THUD
YES, MA'AM.
I'M SORRY.
TOMP TOMP
I WAS JUST SO EXCITED.
I DON'T NEED TO KNOW WHY YOU MADE ALL THAT NOISE!
THAT'S ENOUGH!
C'MON. COME HERE!
WHOA?!
HONSHO?! OGAWA?!
I FOUND THEM.
WE'RE TAKING THEM TO SCHOOL FOR NOW.
YOU CARRY CHIZURU.

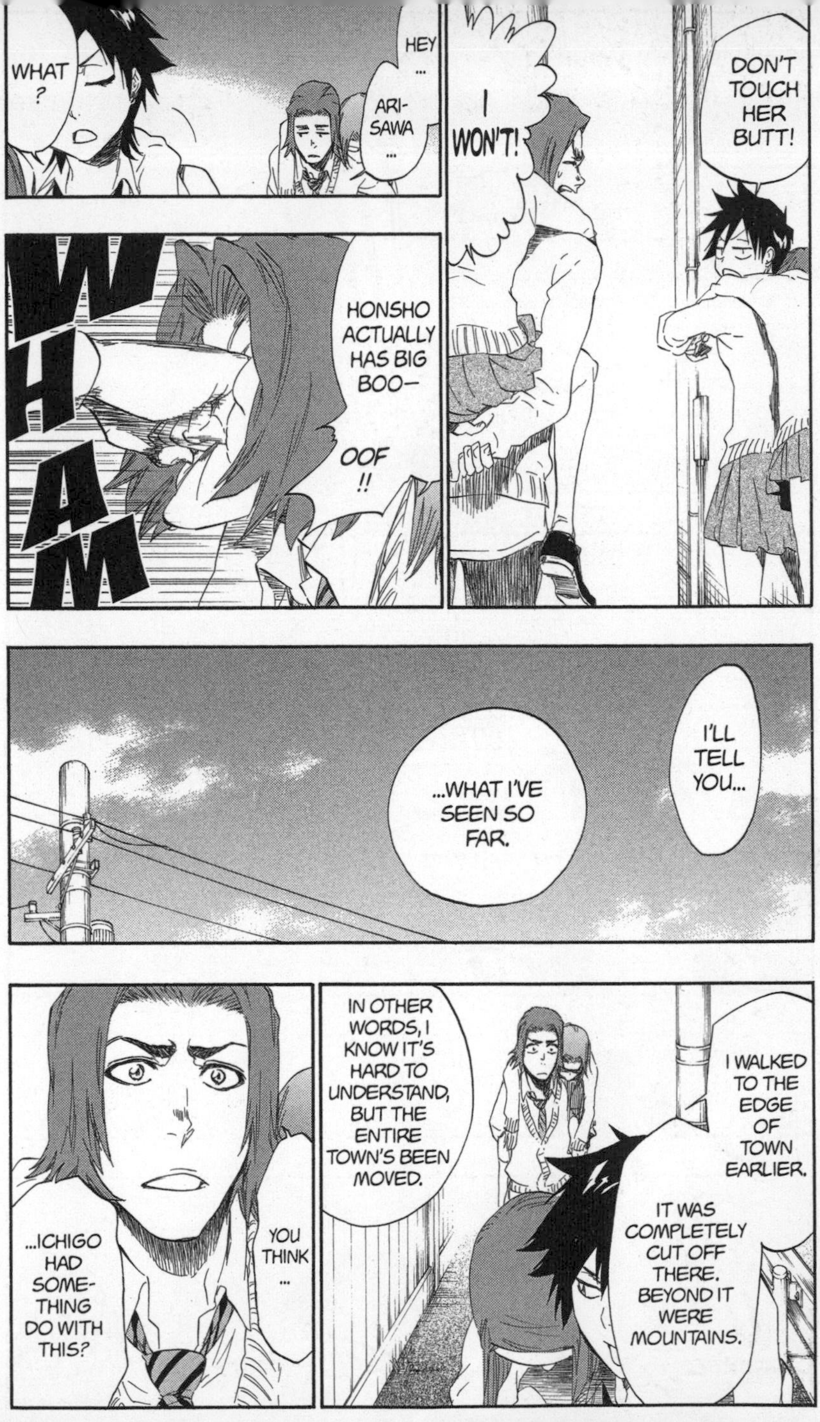
DON'T TOUCH HER BUTT!
I WON'T!
HEY ... ARISAWA ...
WHAT ?
HONSHO ACTUALLY HAS BIG BOO—
OOF !!
WHAM
I'LL TELL YOU...
...WHAT I'VE SEEN SO FAR.
I WALKED TO THE EDGE OF TOWN EARLIER.
IT WAS COMPLETELY CUT OFF THERE. BEYOND IT WERE MOUNTAINS.
IN OTHER WORDS, I KNOW IT'S HARD TO UNDERSTAND, BUT THE ENTIRE TOWN'S BEEN MOVED.
YOU THINK ...
...ICHIGO HAD SOMETHING DO WITH THIS?

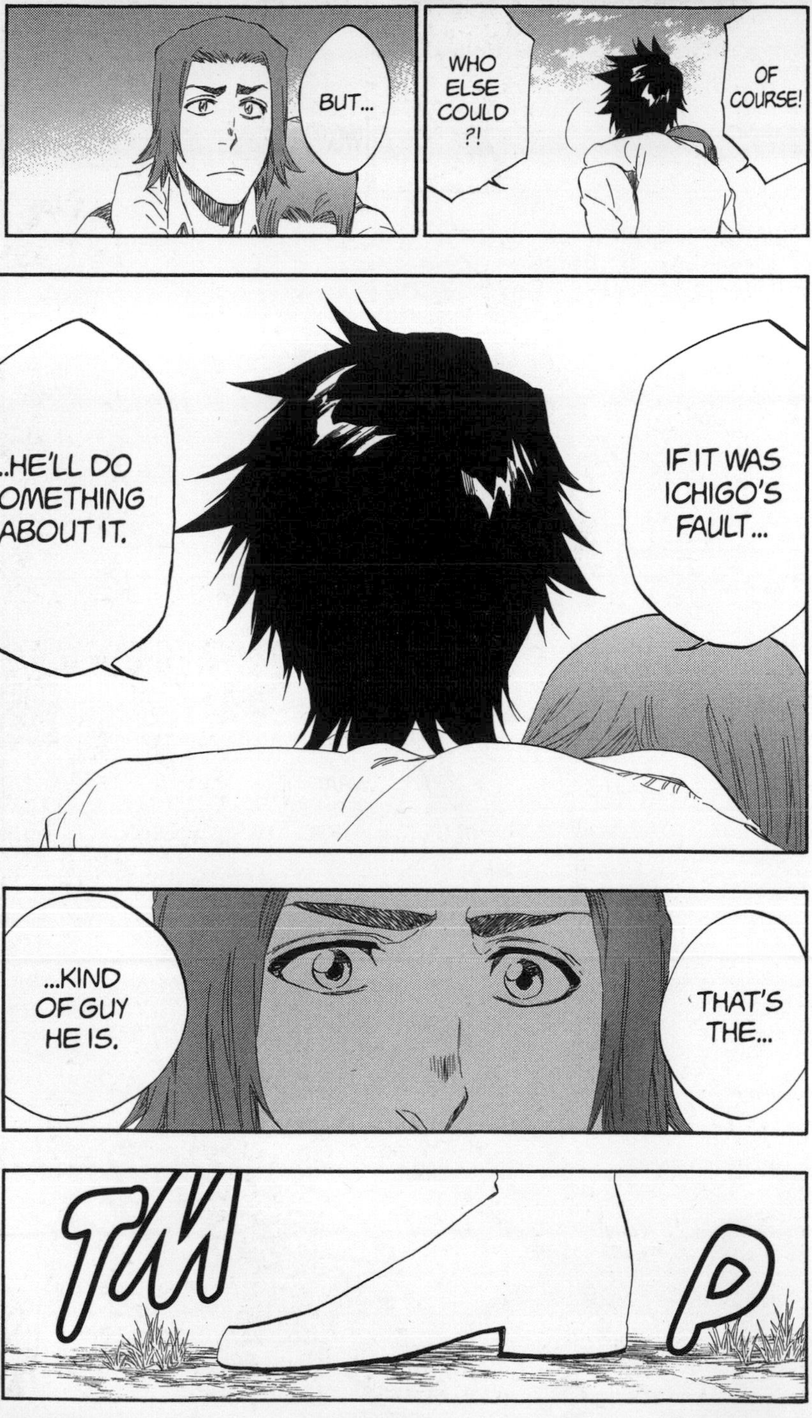
OF COURSE!
WHO ELSE COULD ?!
BUT...
IF IT WAS ICHIGO'S FAULT...
...HE'LL DO SOMETHING ABOUT IT.
THAT'S THE...
...KIND OF GUY HE IS.
TMP

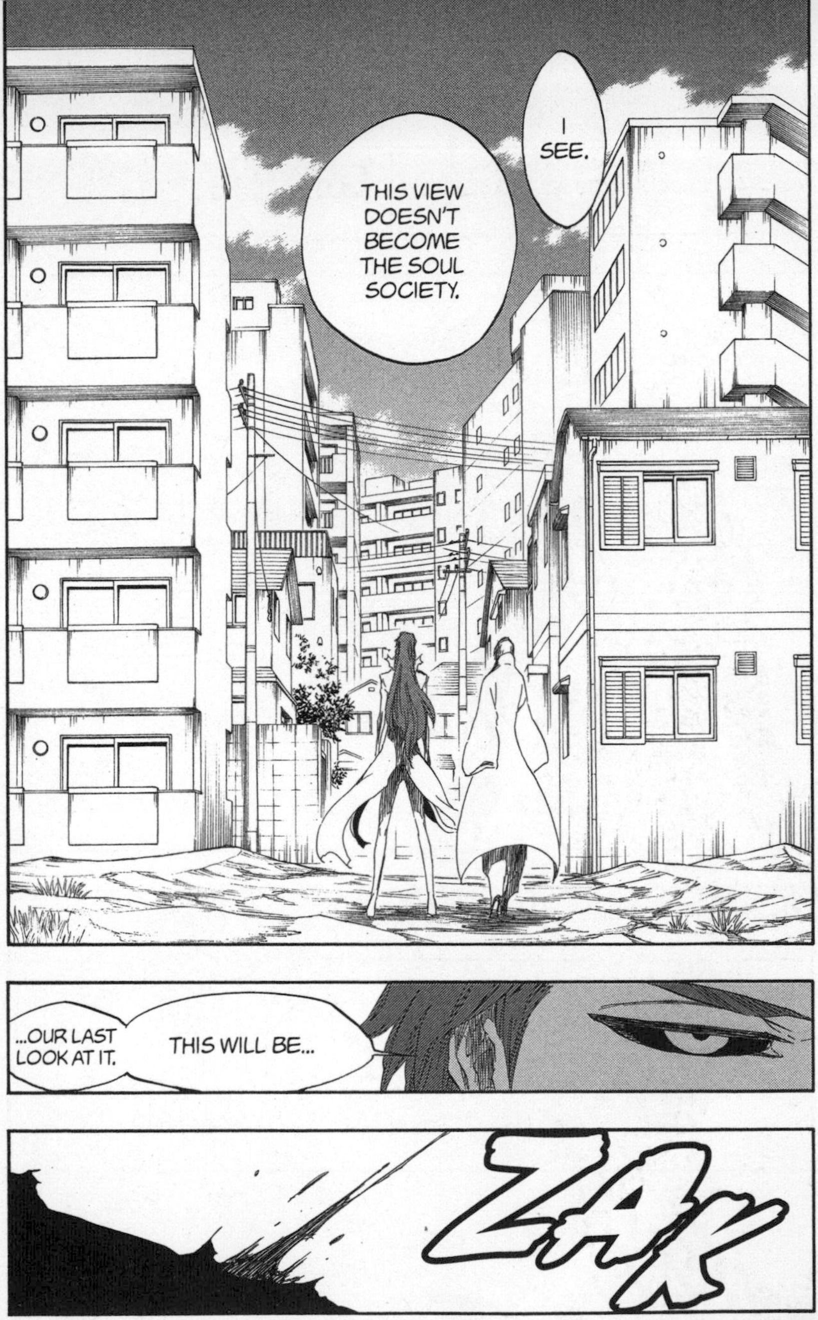
I SEE.
THIS VIEW DOESN'T BECOME THE SOUL SOCIETY.
THIS WILL BE...
...OUR LAST LOOK AT IT.
ZAK

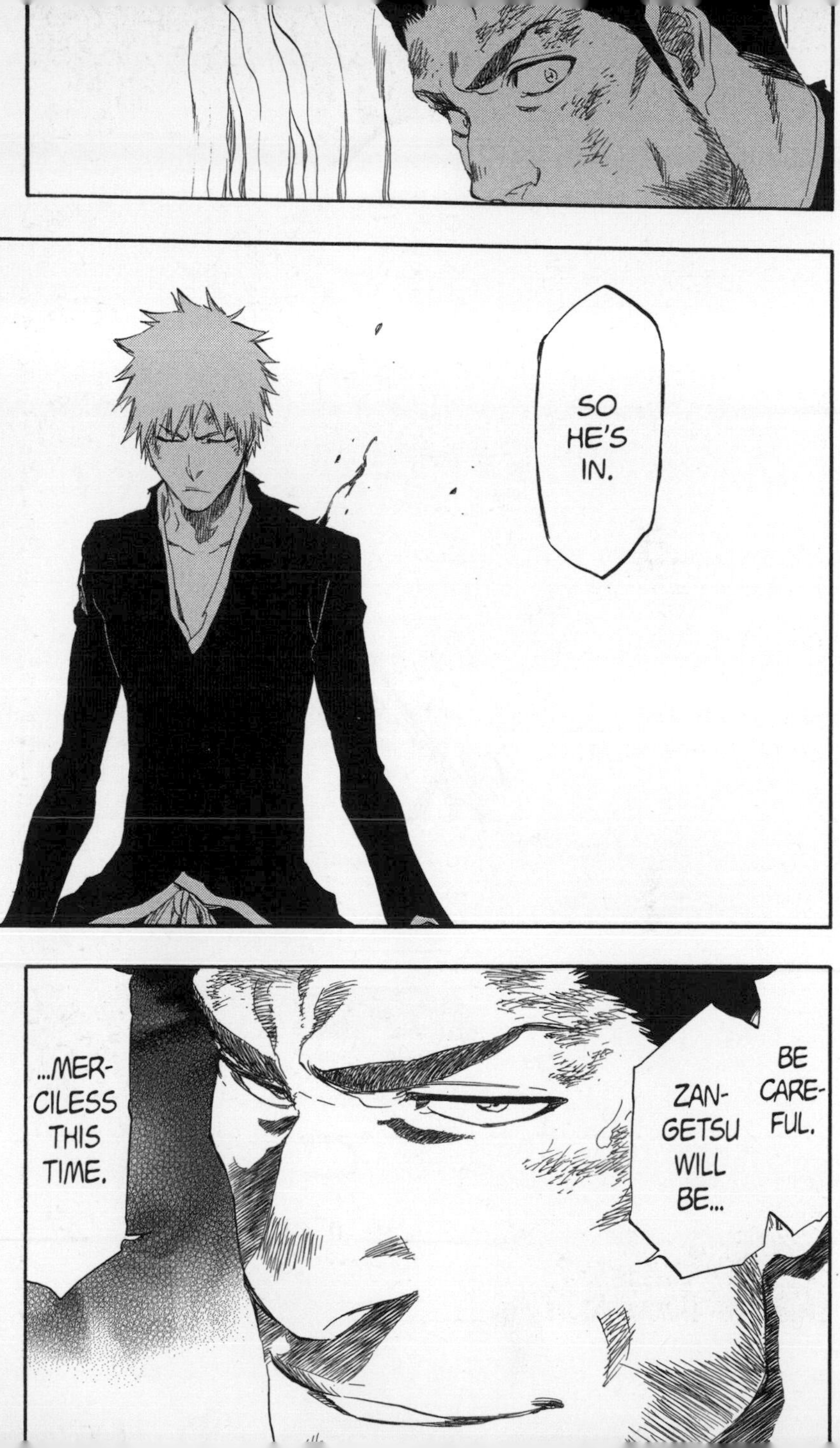
SO HE'S IN.
BE CAREFUL.
ZANGETSU WILL BE...
...MERCILESS THIS TIME.

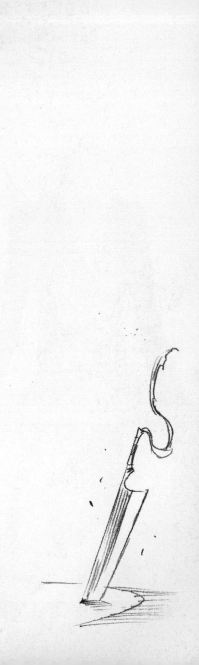

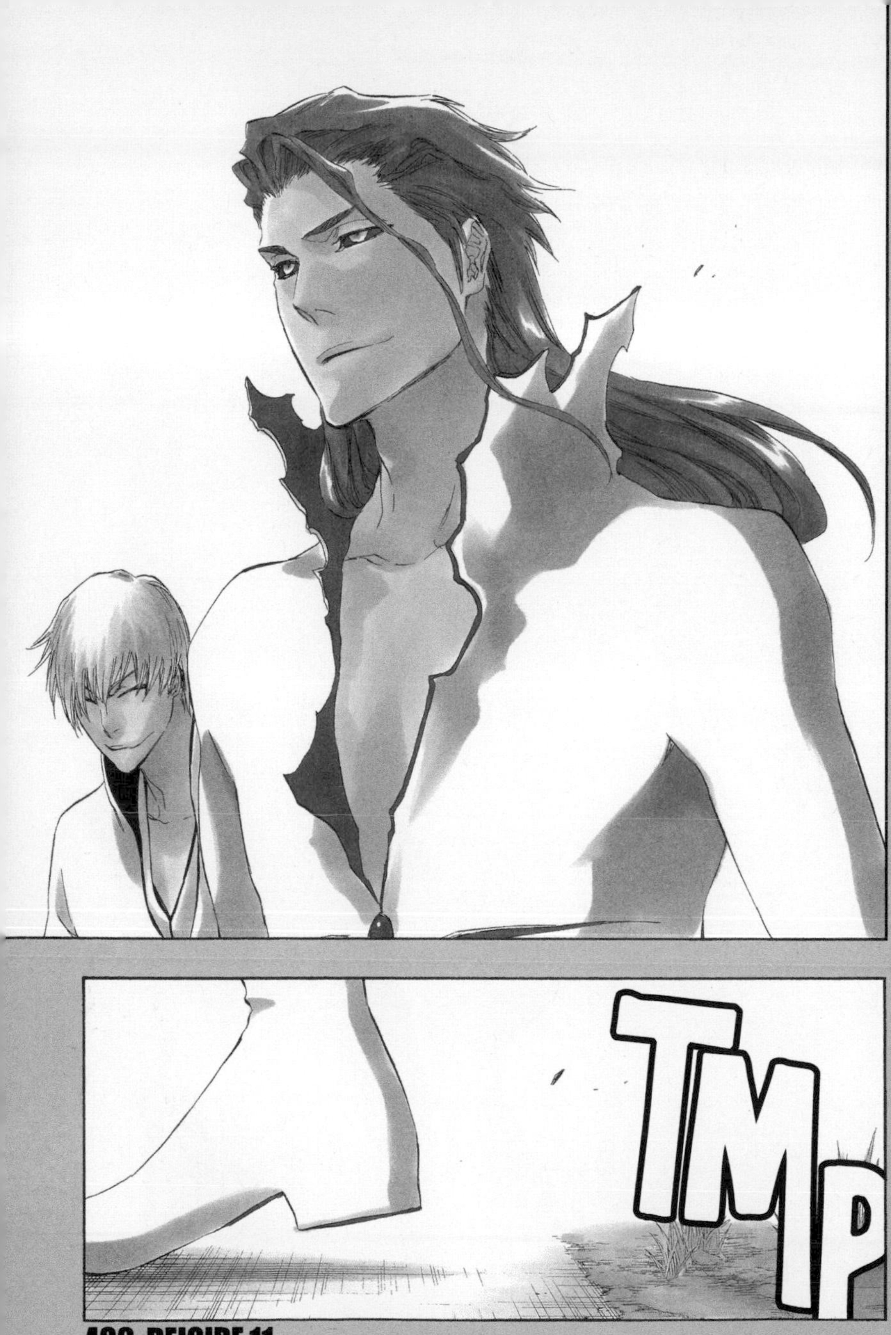
TMP

409. DEICIDE 11

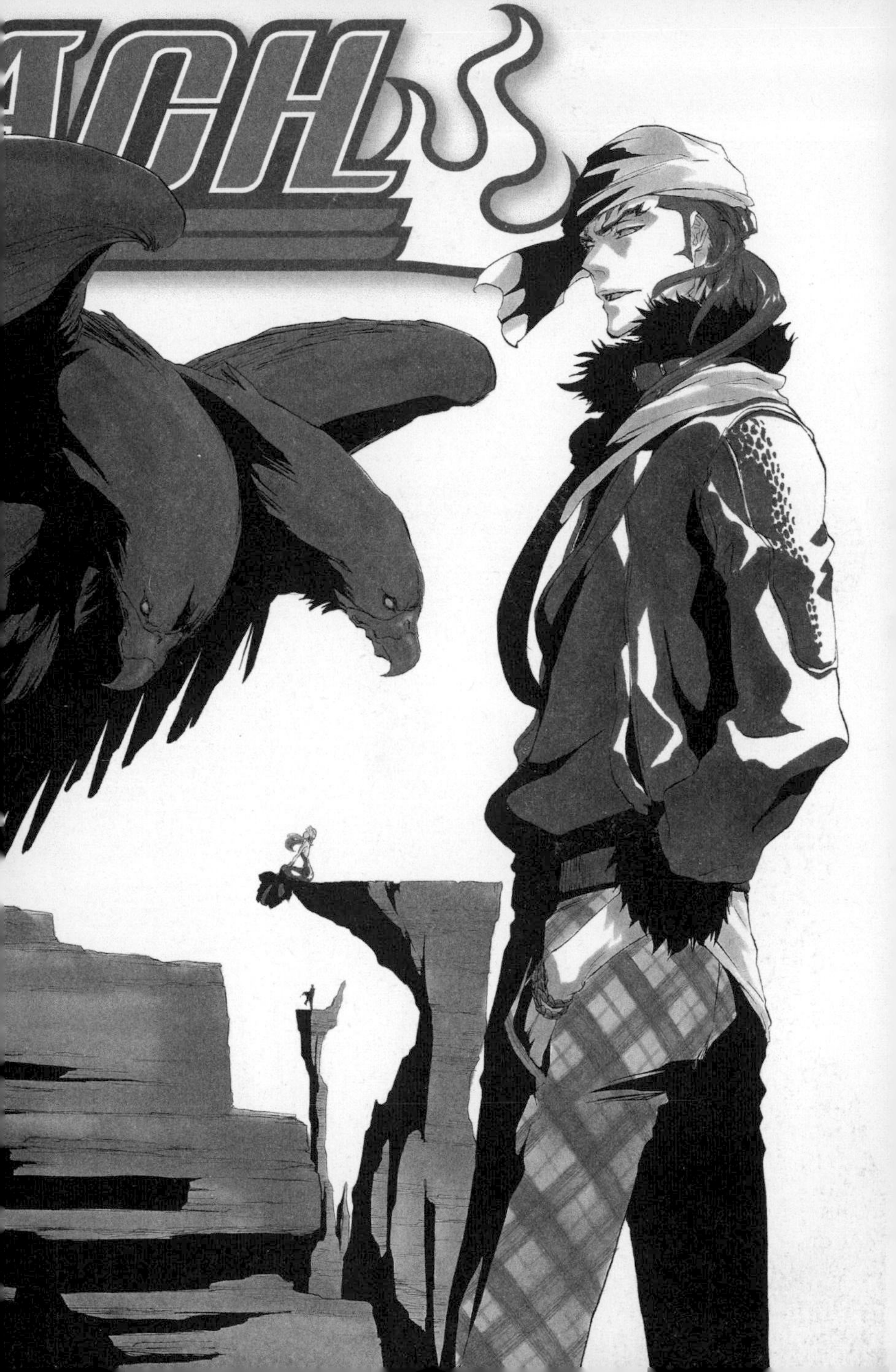
ACH

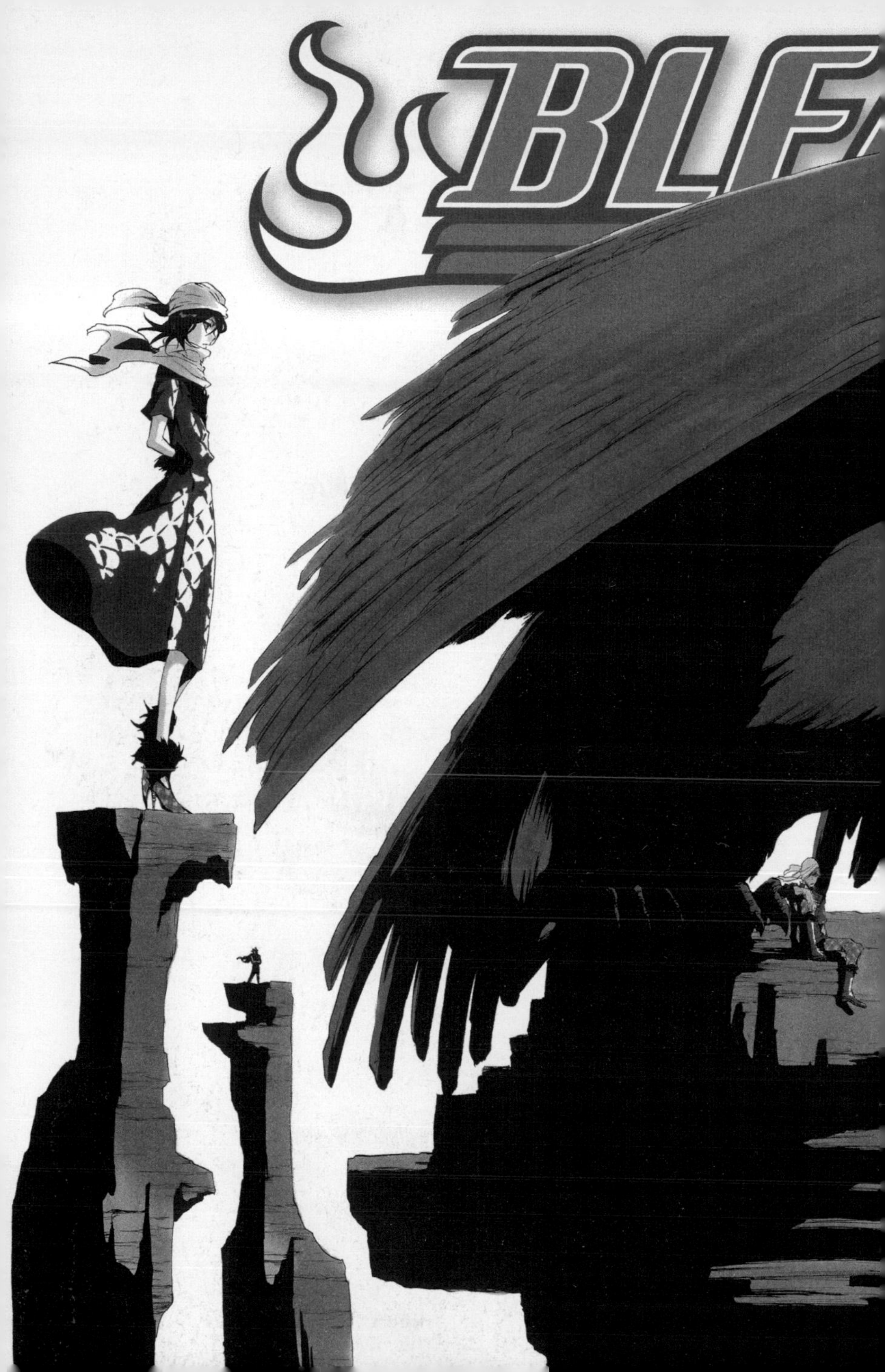

BLEACH
ブリーチ

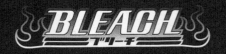

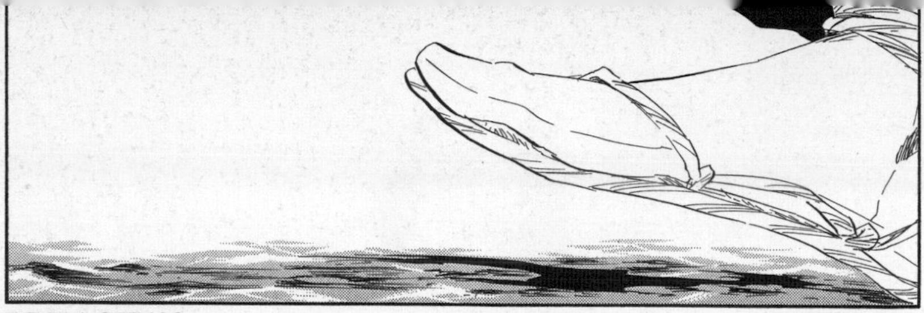

BLEACH409. DEICIDE11

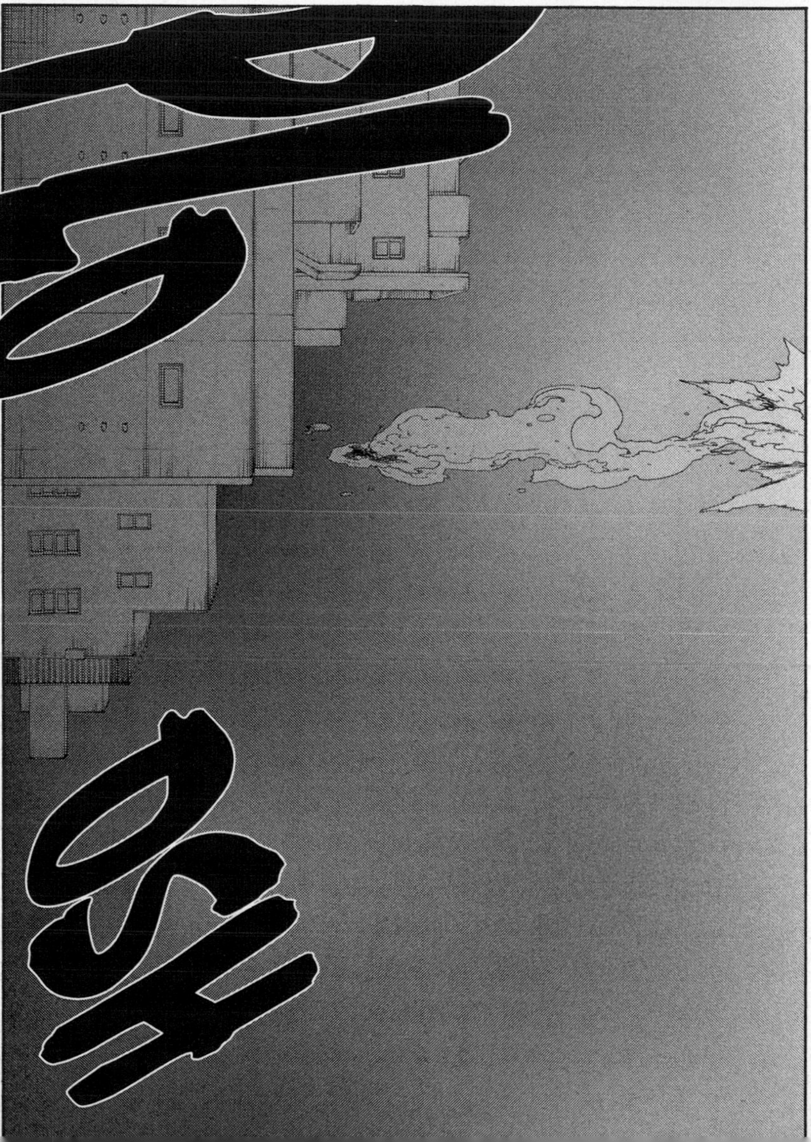

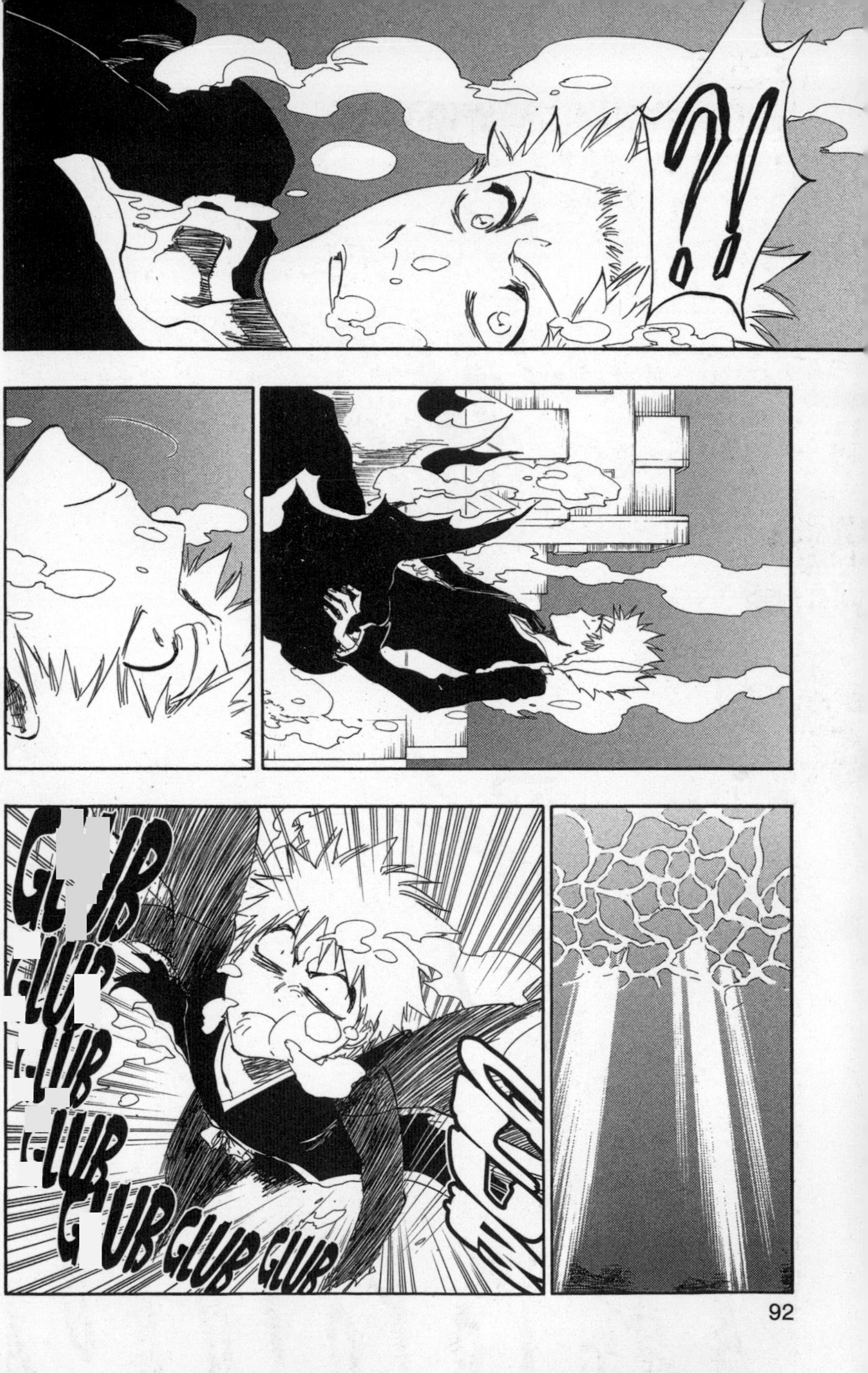
?!
GLUB GLUB

WHUP

KRAK

WOO

GLUB GLUB GLUB

SH

N

WOOOOO

RELAX.

93

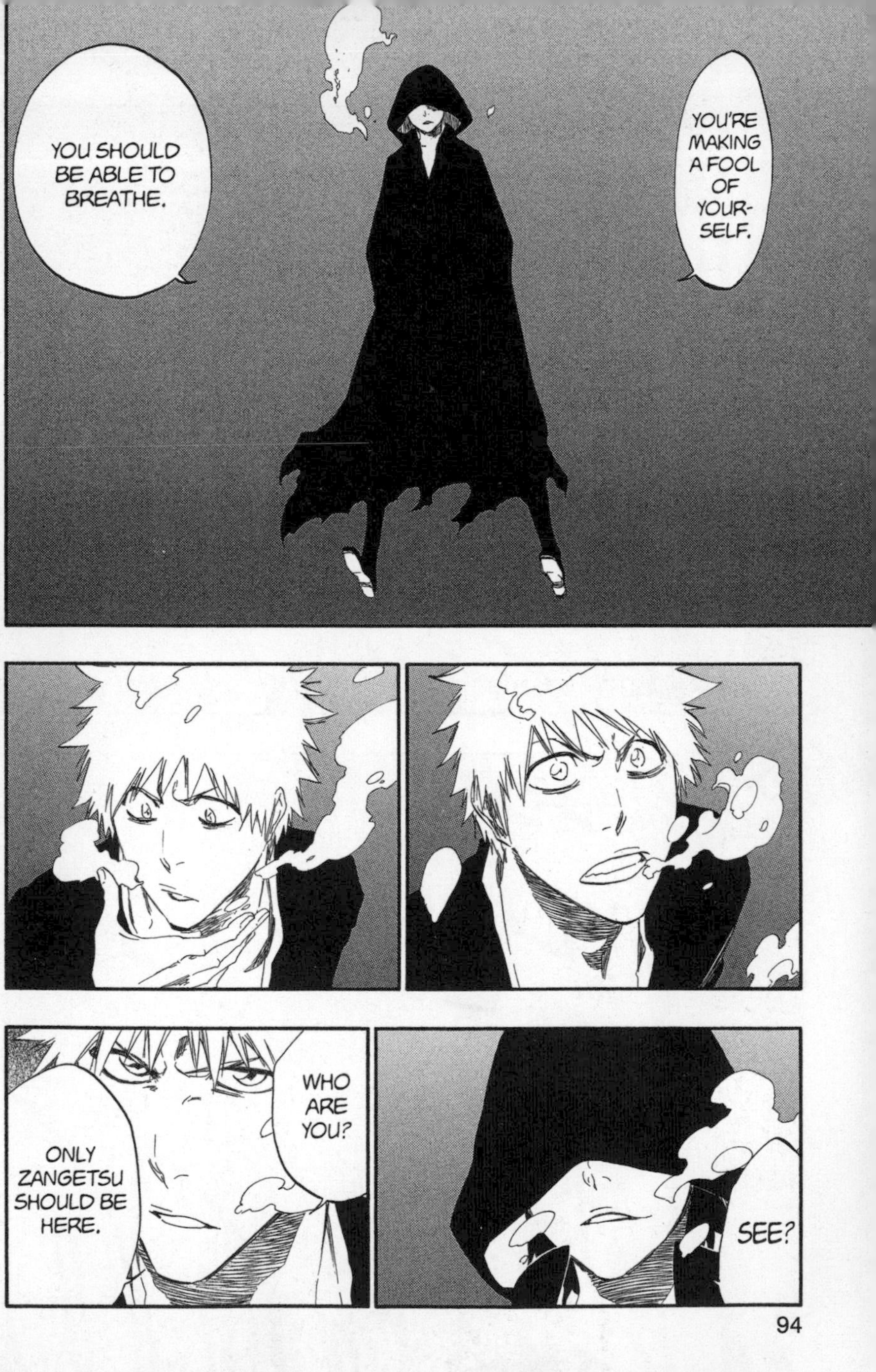
YOU'RE MAKING A FOOL OF YOUR-SELF.
YOU SHOULD BE ABLE TO BREATHE.
SEE?
WHO ARE YOU?
ONLY ZANGETSU SHOULD BE HERE.

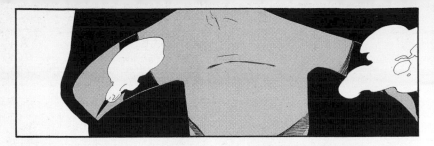

WMM

NOW IS THAT ANY WAY...

...TO SPEAK TO THE PERSON WHO TAUGHT YOU HOW TO BREATHE?

WHUP

!!

TENSA ZANGE-TSU?

FWUP

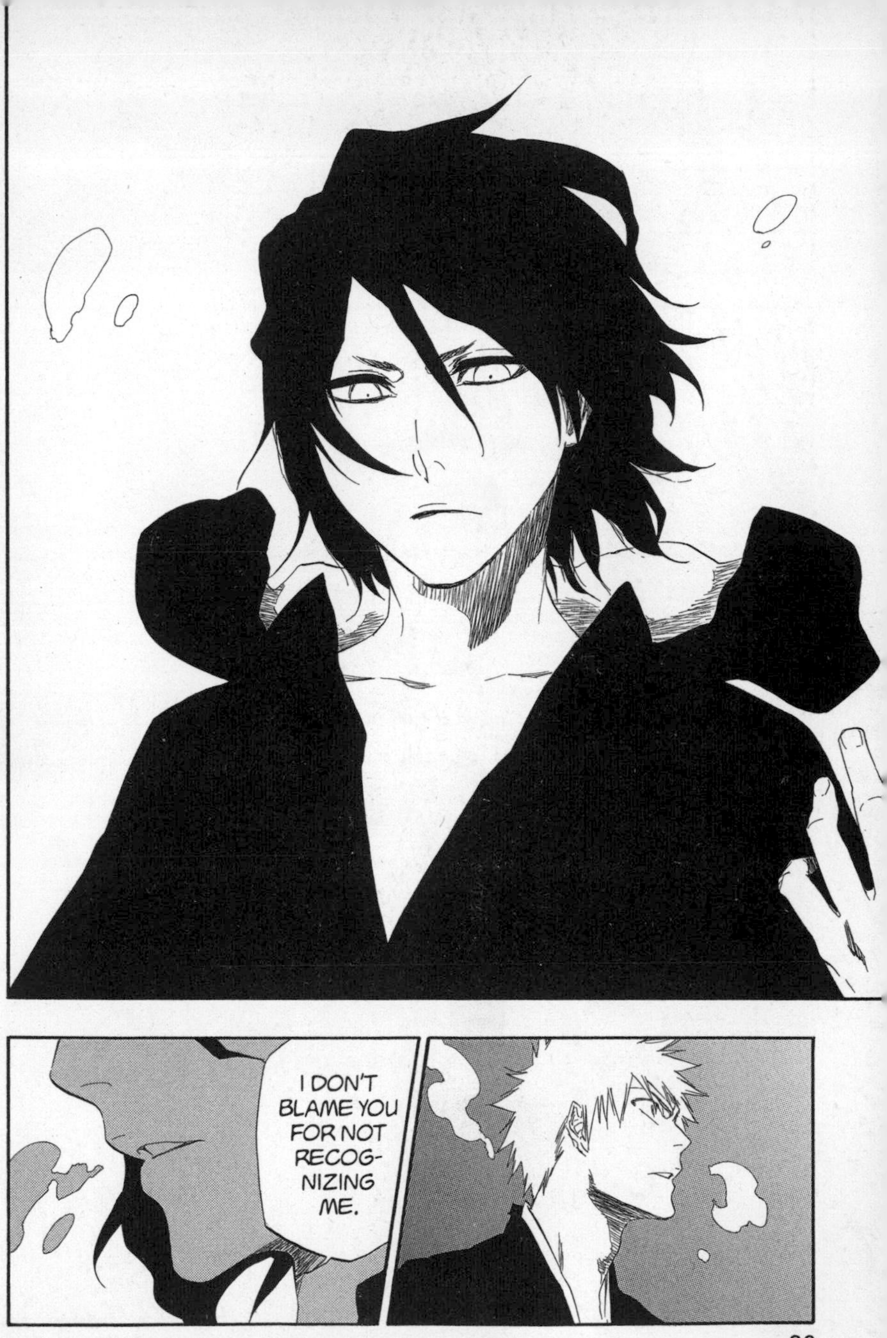
I DON'T BLAME YOU FOR NOT RECOG-NIZING ME.

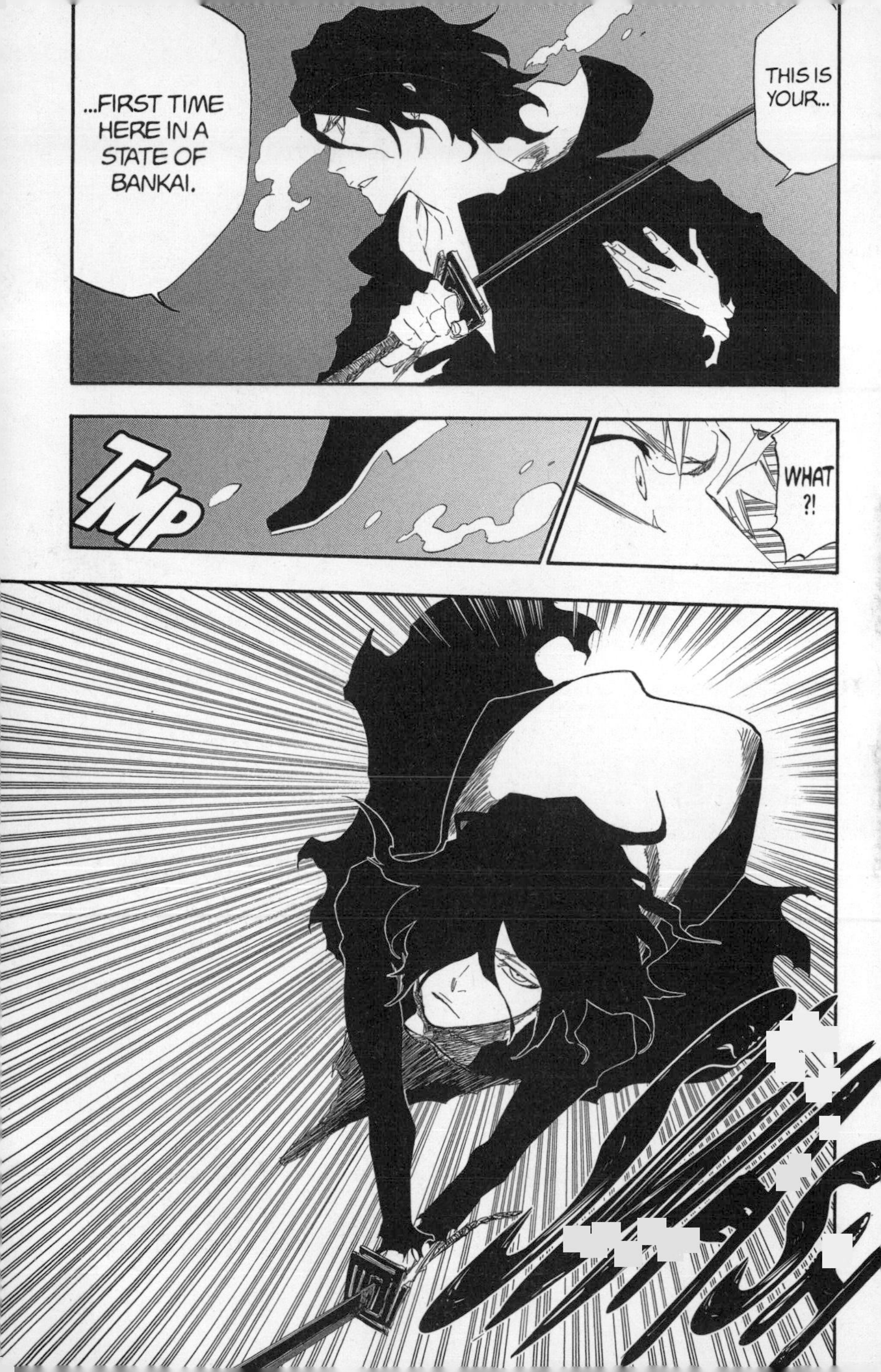
THIS IS YOUR...
...FIRST TIME HERE IN A STATE OF BANKAI.
WHAT ?!
TMP

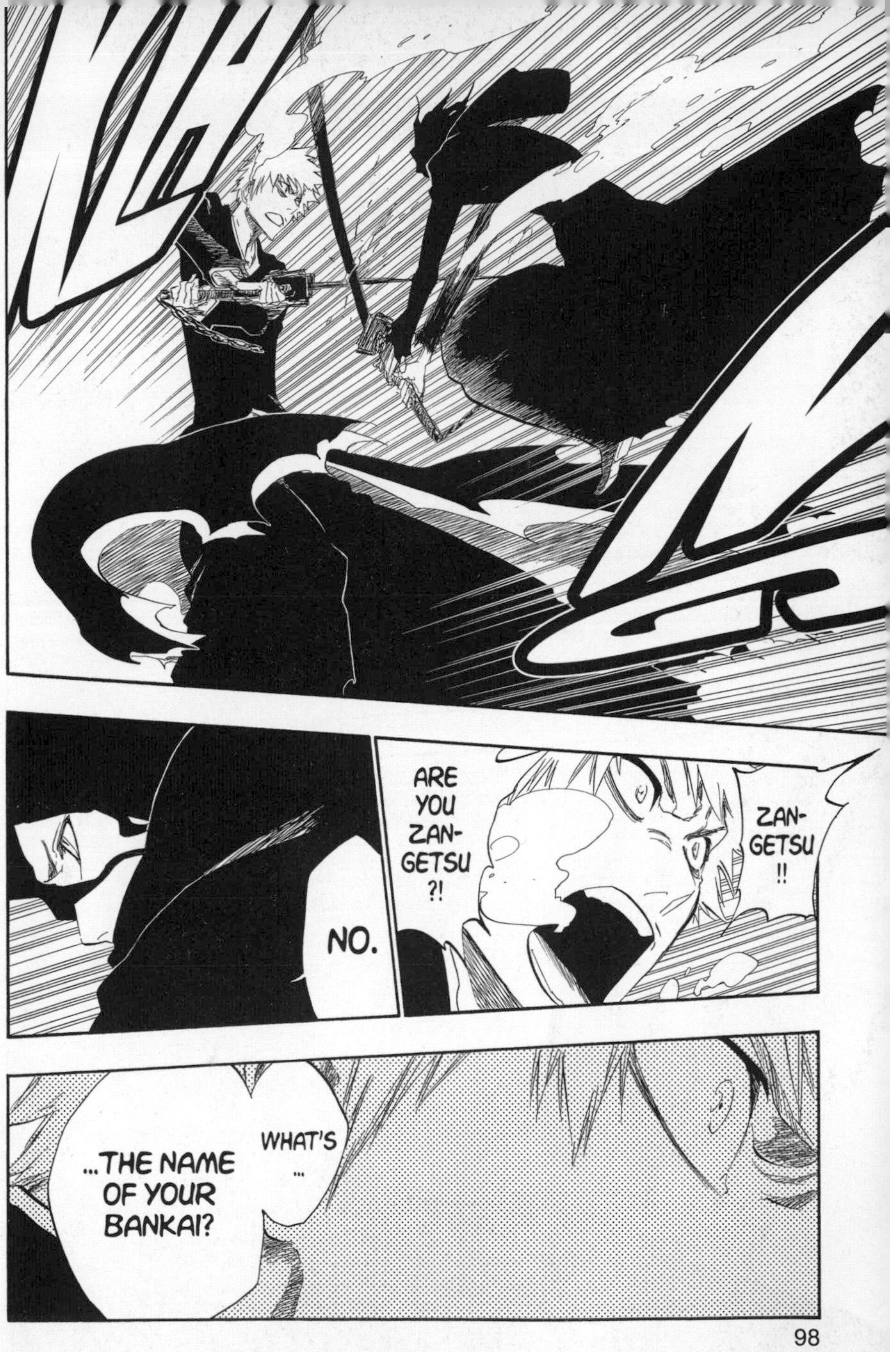
ZAN-GETSU!!
ARE YOU ZAN-GETSU?!
NO.
WHAT'S...
...THE NAME OF YOUR BANKAI?

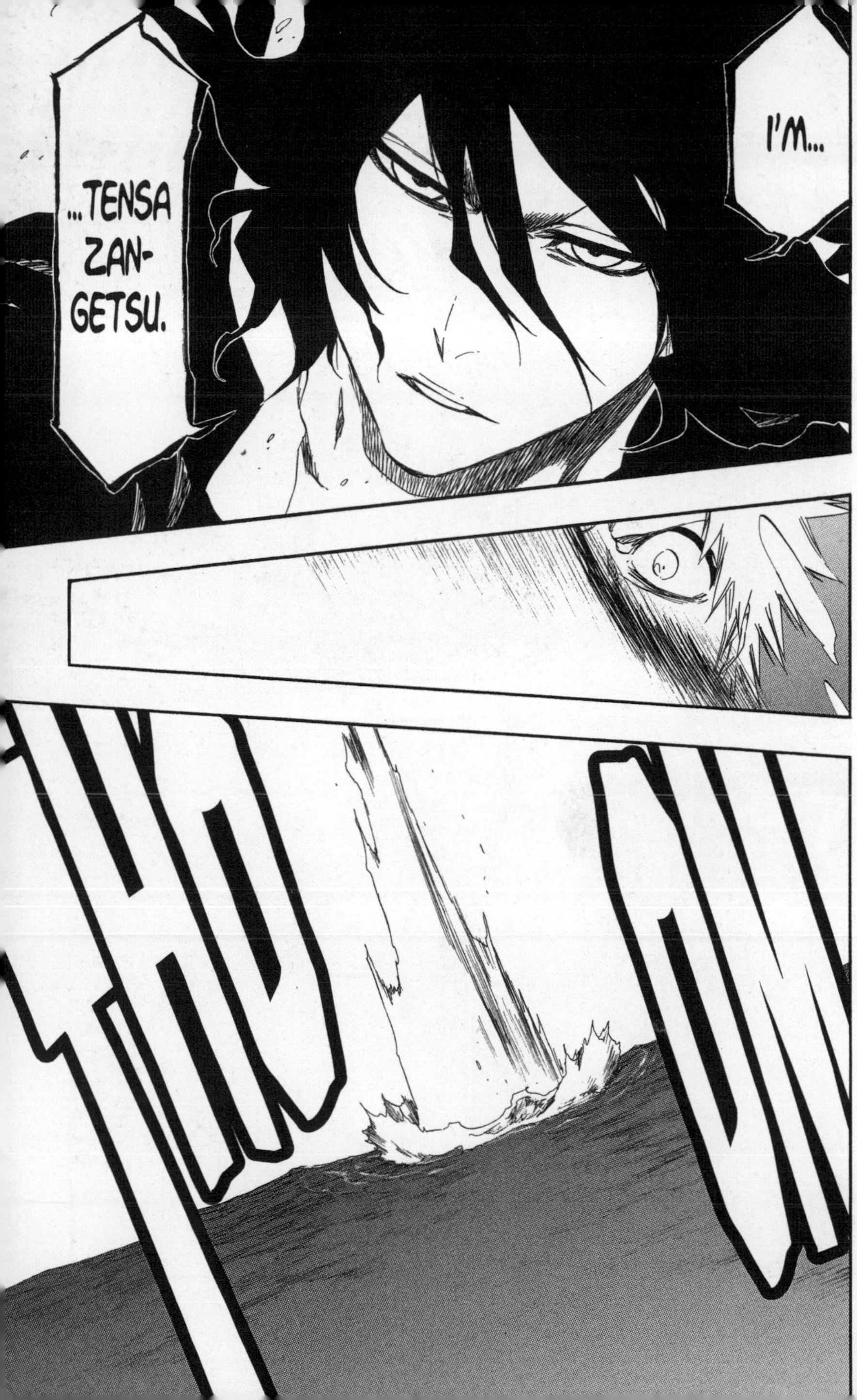
I'M...
...TENSA ZAN-GETSU.
THOOM

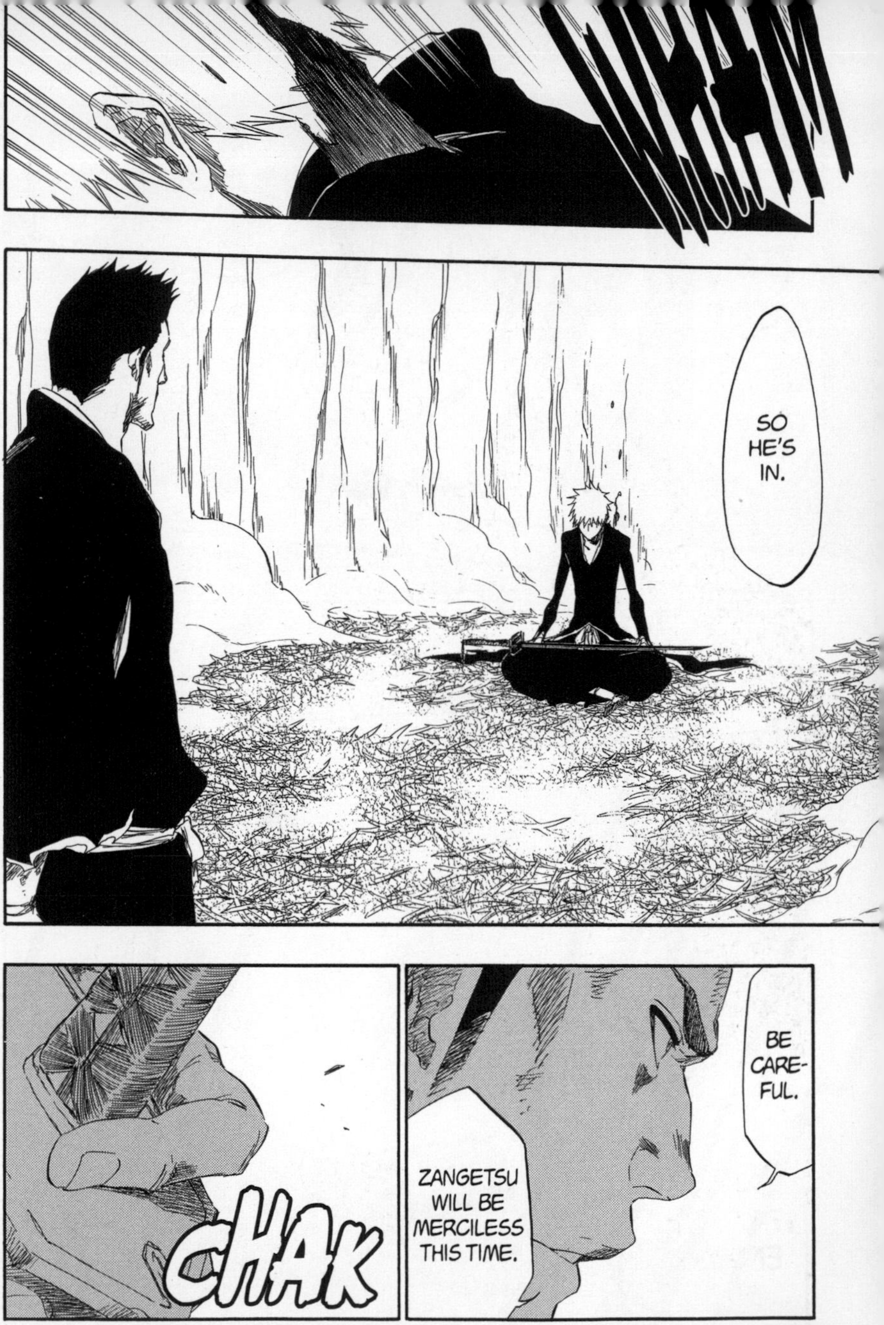
WHAM
SO HE'S IN.
BE CAREFUL.
ZANGETSU WILL BE MERCILESS THIS TIME.
CHAK

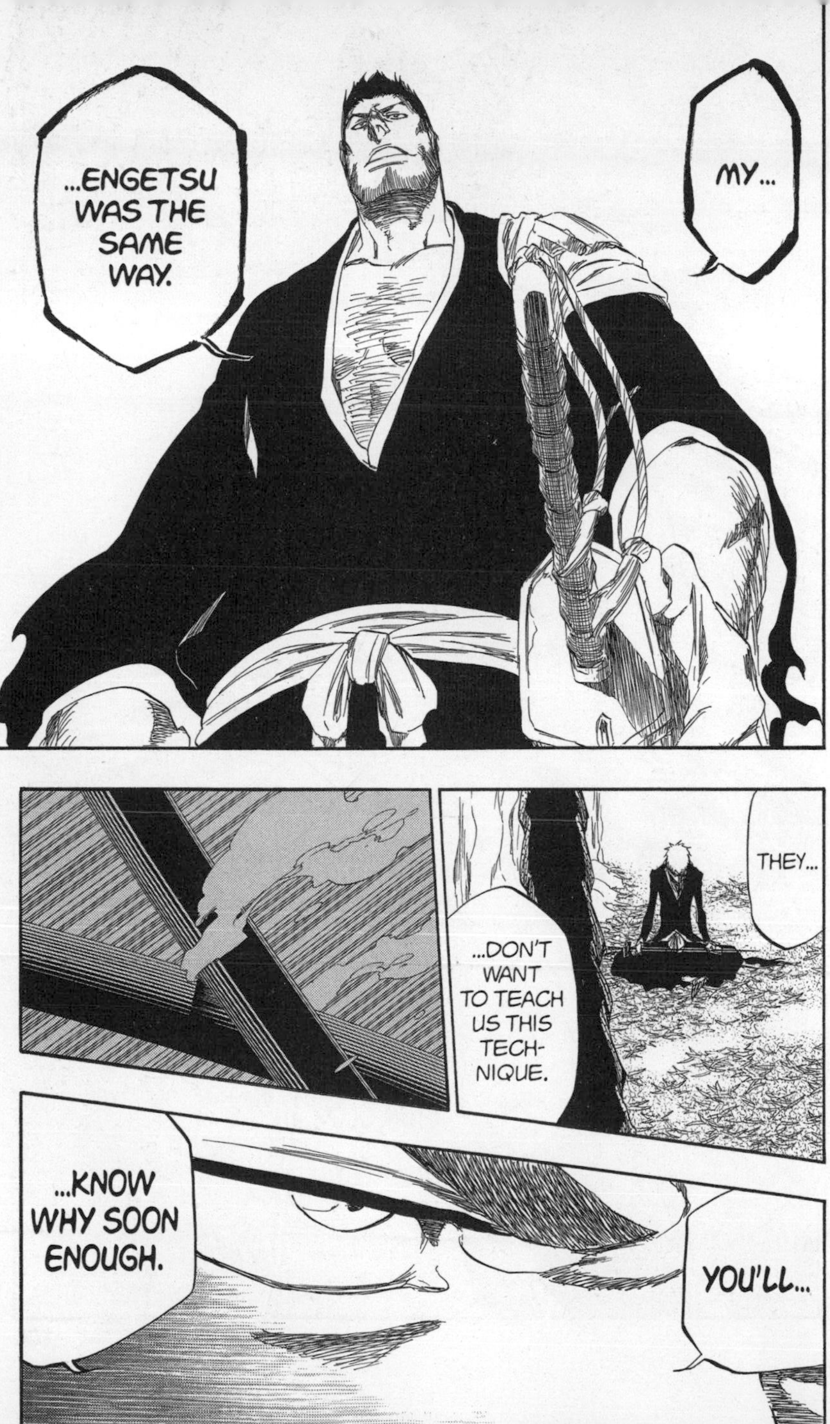
MY...
...ENGETSU WAS THE SAME WAY.
THEY...
...DON'T WANT TO TEACH US THIS TECH-NIQUE.
YOU'LL...
...KNOW WHY SOON ENOUGH.

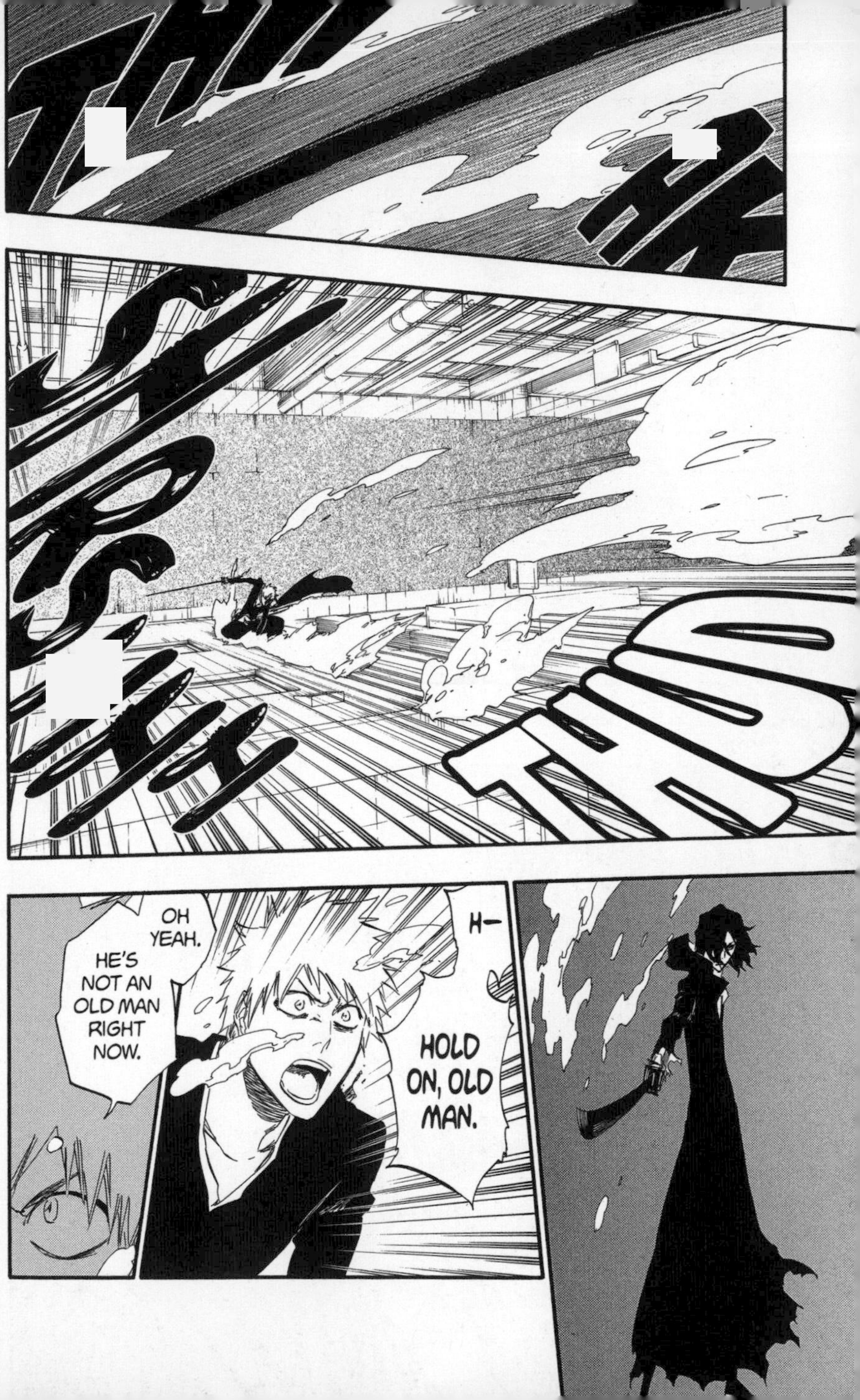
H—
HOLD ON, OLD MAN.
OH YEAH. HE'S NOT AN OLD MAN RIGHT NOW.

READ THIS WAY

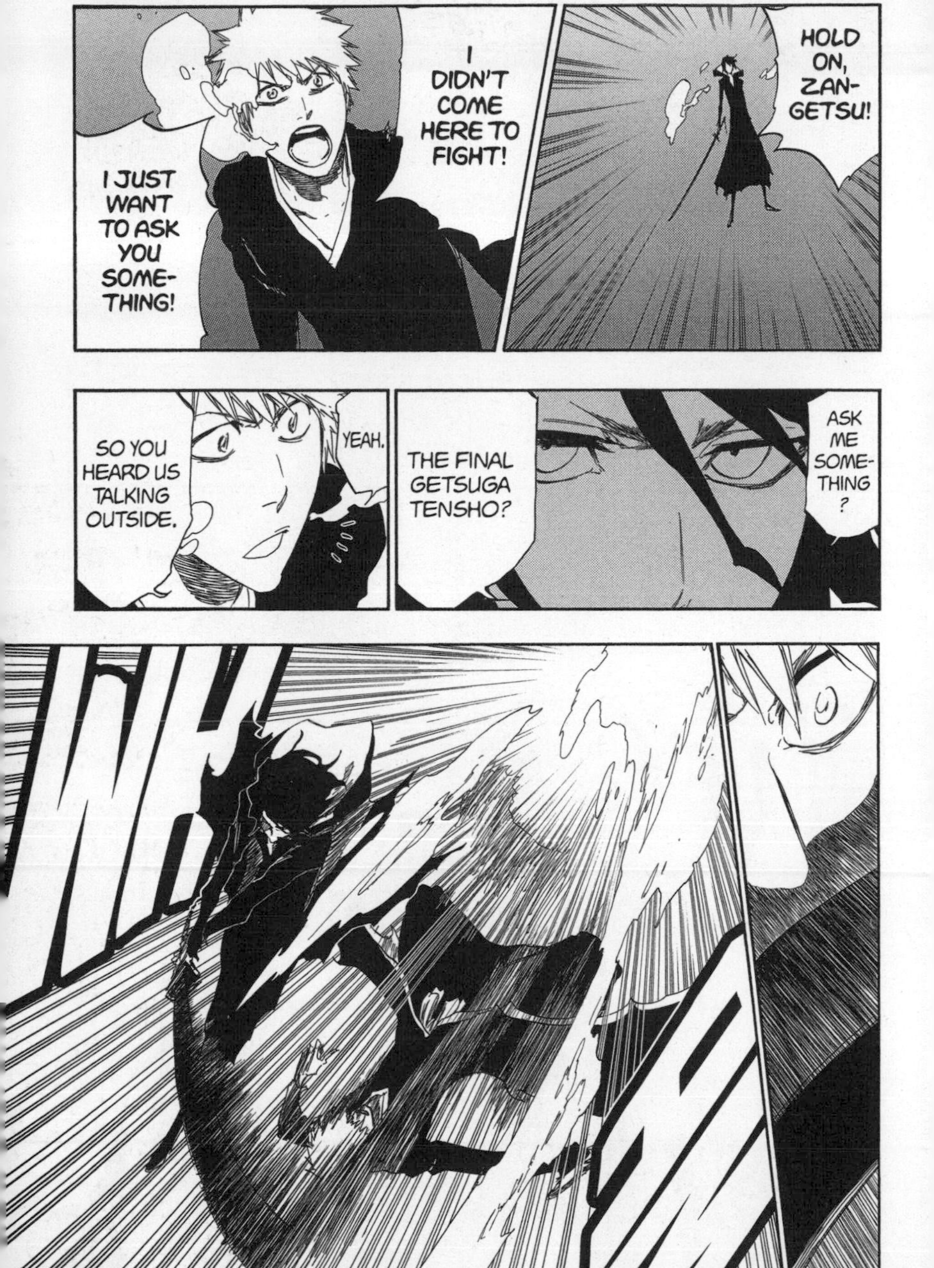
HOLD ON, ZAN-GETSU!
I DIDN'T COME HERE TO FIGHT!
I JUST WANT TO ASK YOU SOME-THING!
ASK ME SOME-THING?
THE FINAL GETSUGA TENSHO?
YEAH.
SO YOU HEARD US TALKING OUTSIDE.

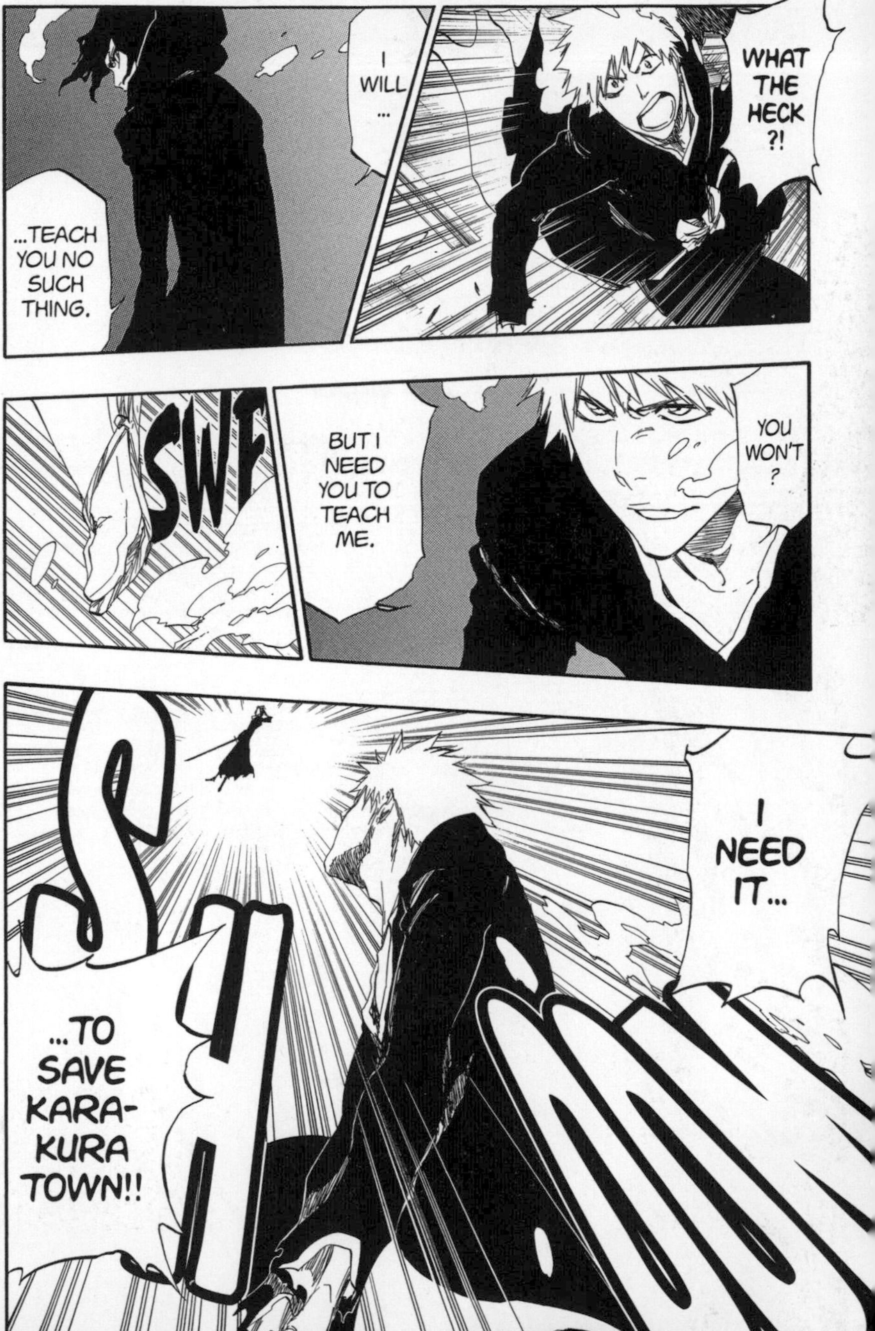
WHAT THE HECK?!
I WILL...
...TEACH YOU NO SUCH THING.
YOU WON'T?
BUT I NEED YOU TO TEACH ME.
SWF
I NEED IT...
...TO SAVE KARAKURA TOWN!!

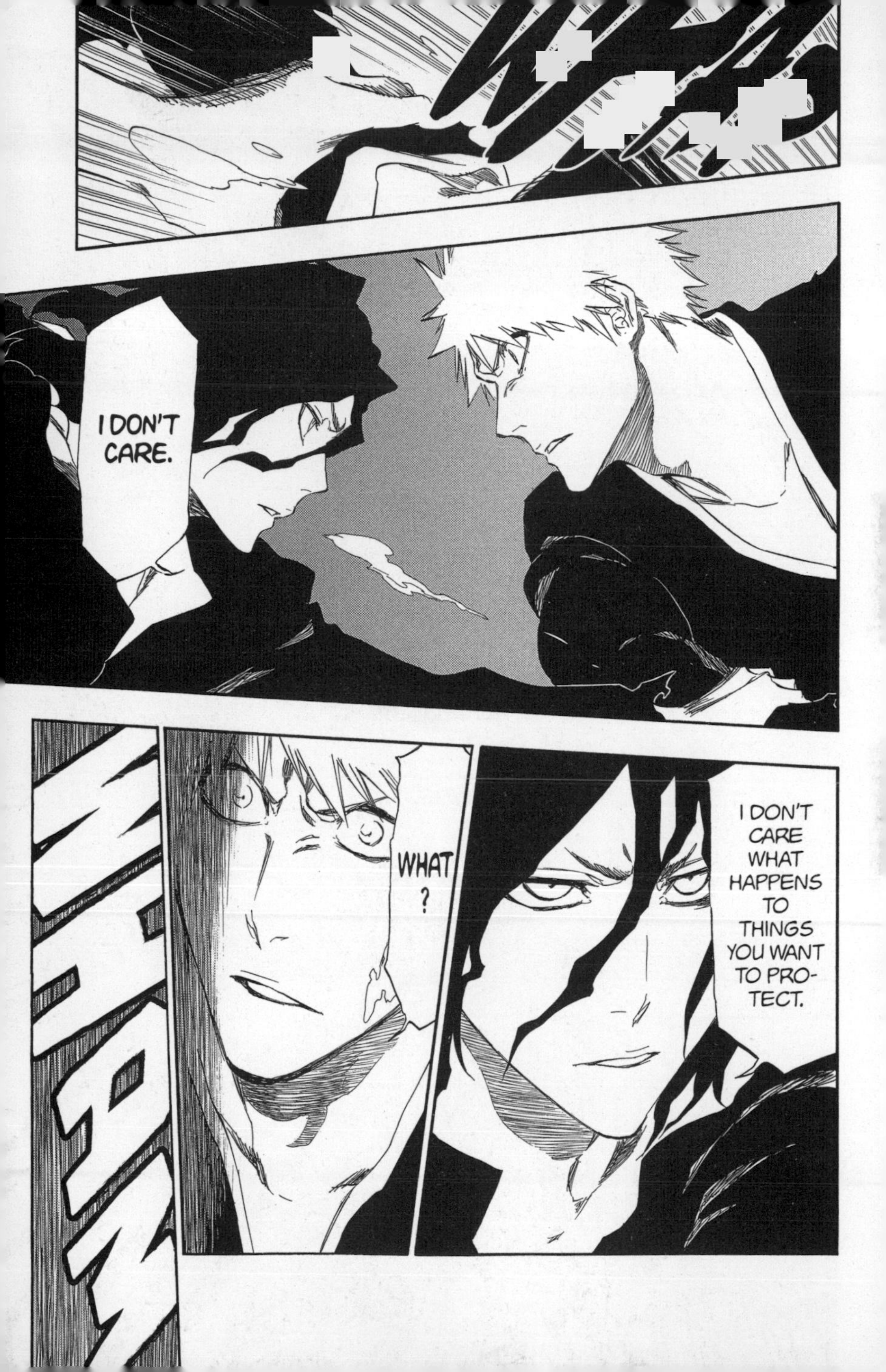
I DON'T CARE.
I DON'T CARE WHAT HAPPENS TO THINGS YOU WANT TO PROTECT.
WHAT?

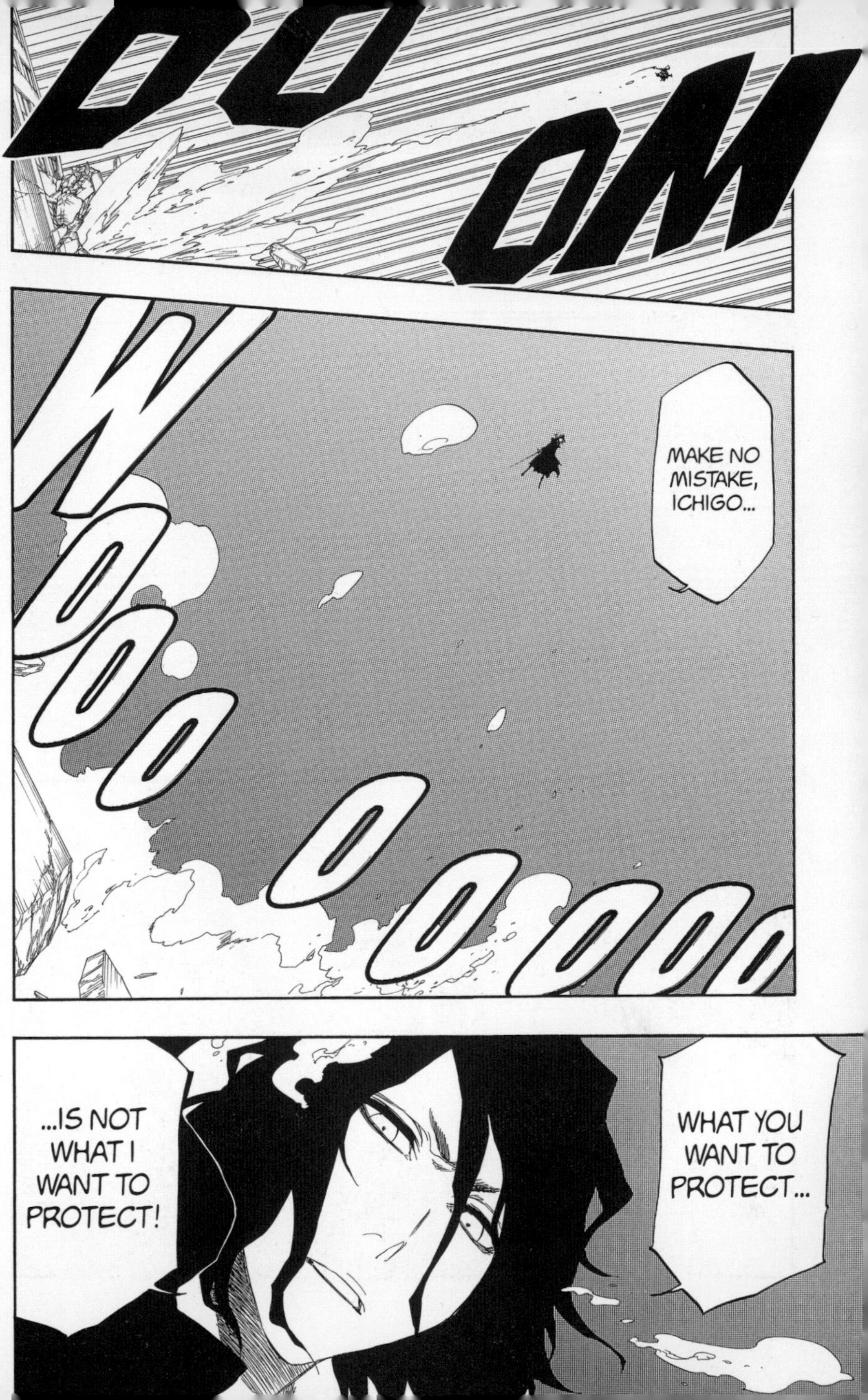
DOOOM
WOOOOOOOOO
MAKE NO MISTAKE, ICHIGO...
WHAT YOU WANT TO PROTECT...
...IS NOT WHAT I WANT TO PROTECT!

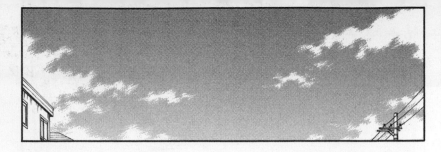

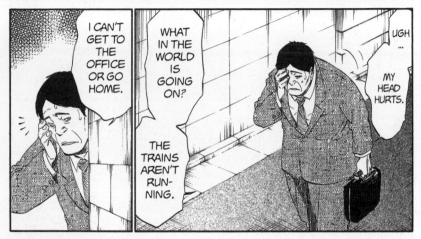

UGH ... MY HEAD HURTS.
WHAT IN THE WORLD IS GOING ON?
THE TRAINS AREN'T RUN-NING.
I CAN'T GET TO THE OFFICE OR GO HOME.
OH...
YOU'RE ...
THANK GOD SOME-BODY ELSE IS AWAKE.
DO YOU KNOW WHAT'S HAPPEN-ING?
DON'T COME NEAR ME.

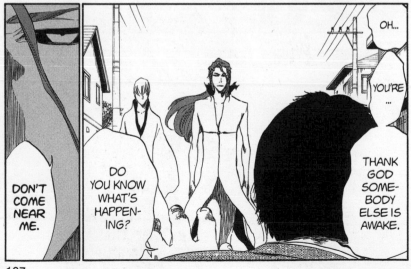

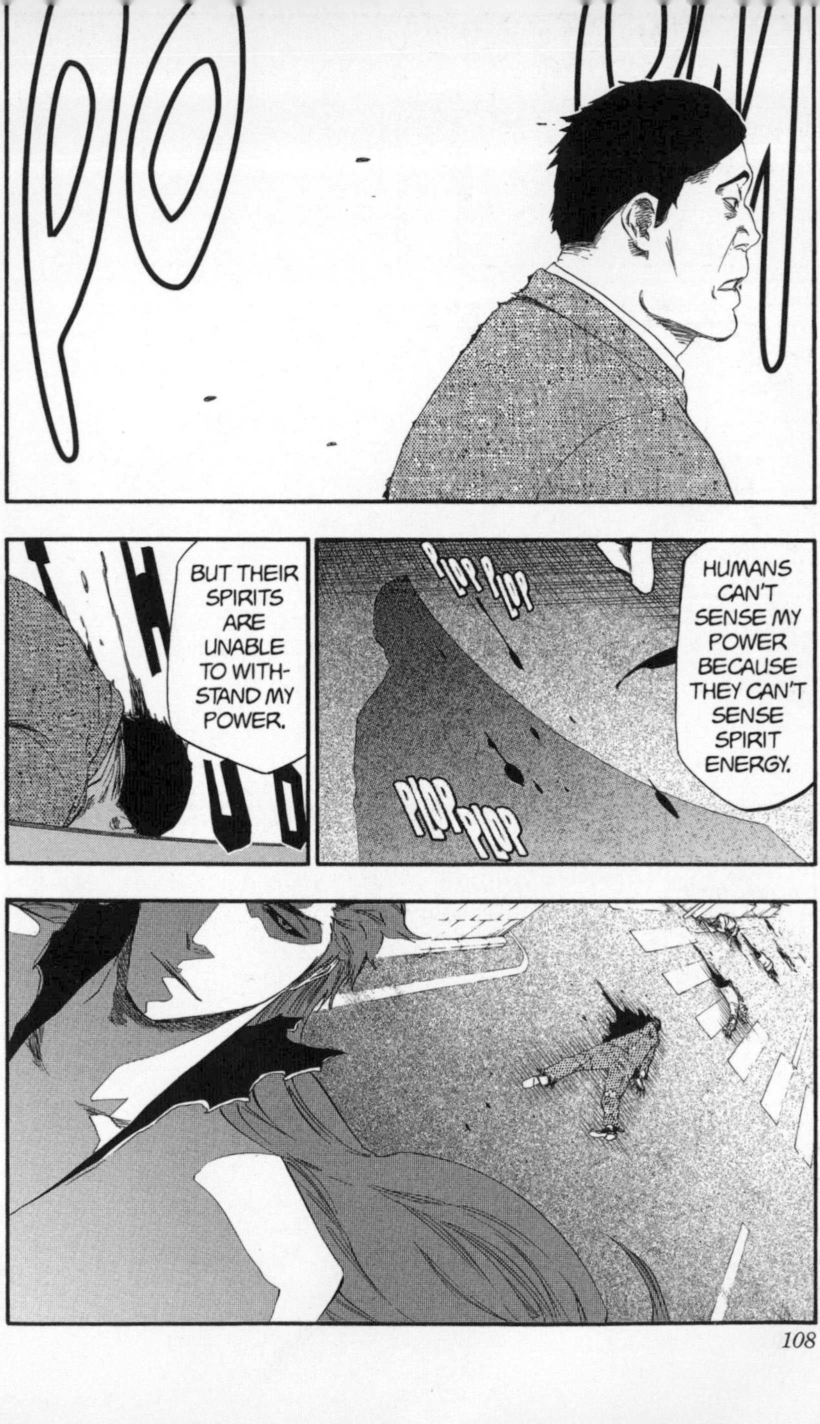
PLOP PLOP
HUMANS CAN'T SENSE MY POWER BECAUSE THEY CAN'T SENSE SPIRIT ENERGY.
PLOP PLOP
BUT THEIR SPIRITS ARE UNABLE TO WITH-STAND MY POWER.

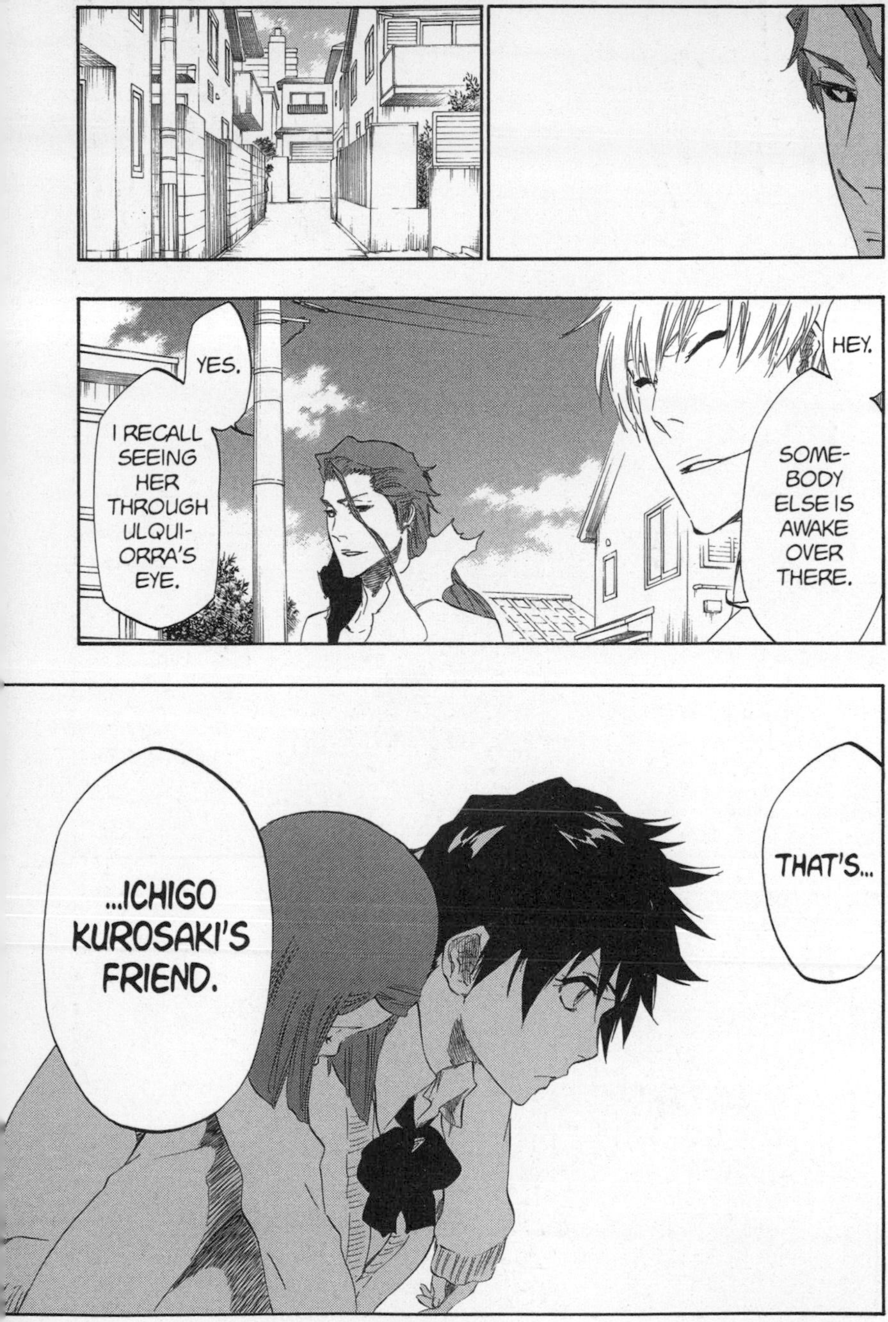
HEY.
SOME-BODY ELSE IS AWAKE OVER THERE.
YES.
I RECALL SEEING HER THROUGH ULQUI-ORRA'S EYE.
THAT'S...
...ICHIGO KUROSAKI'S FRIEND.

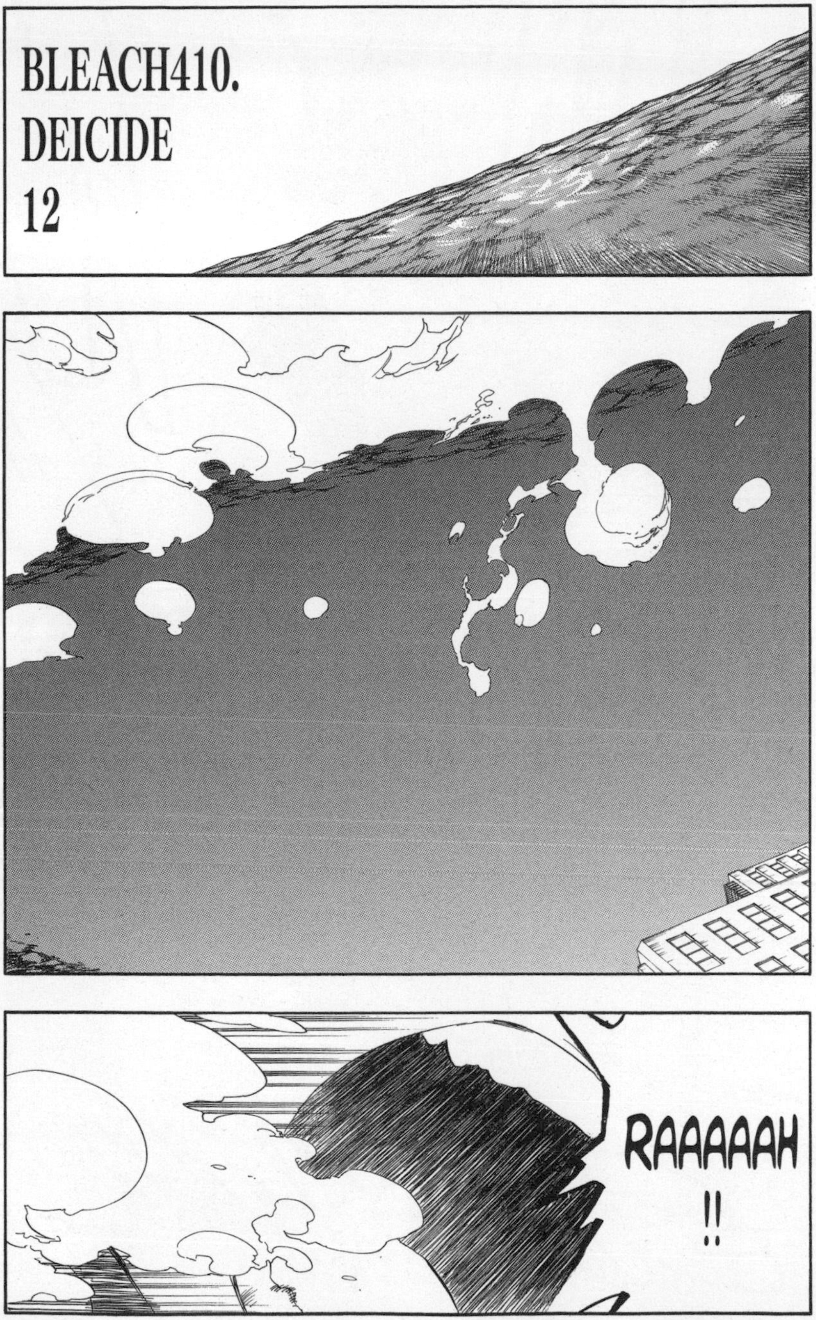
BLEACH410.
DEICIDE
12
RAAAAAH
!!

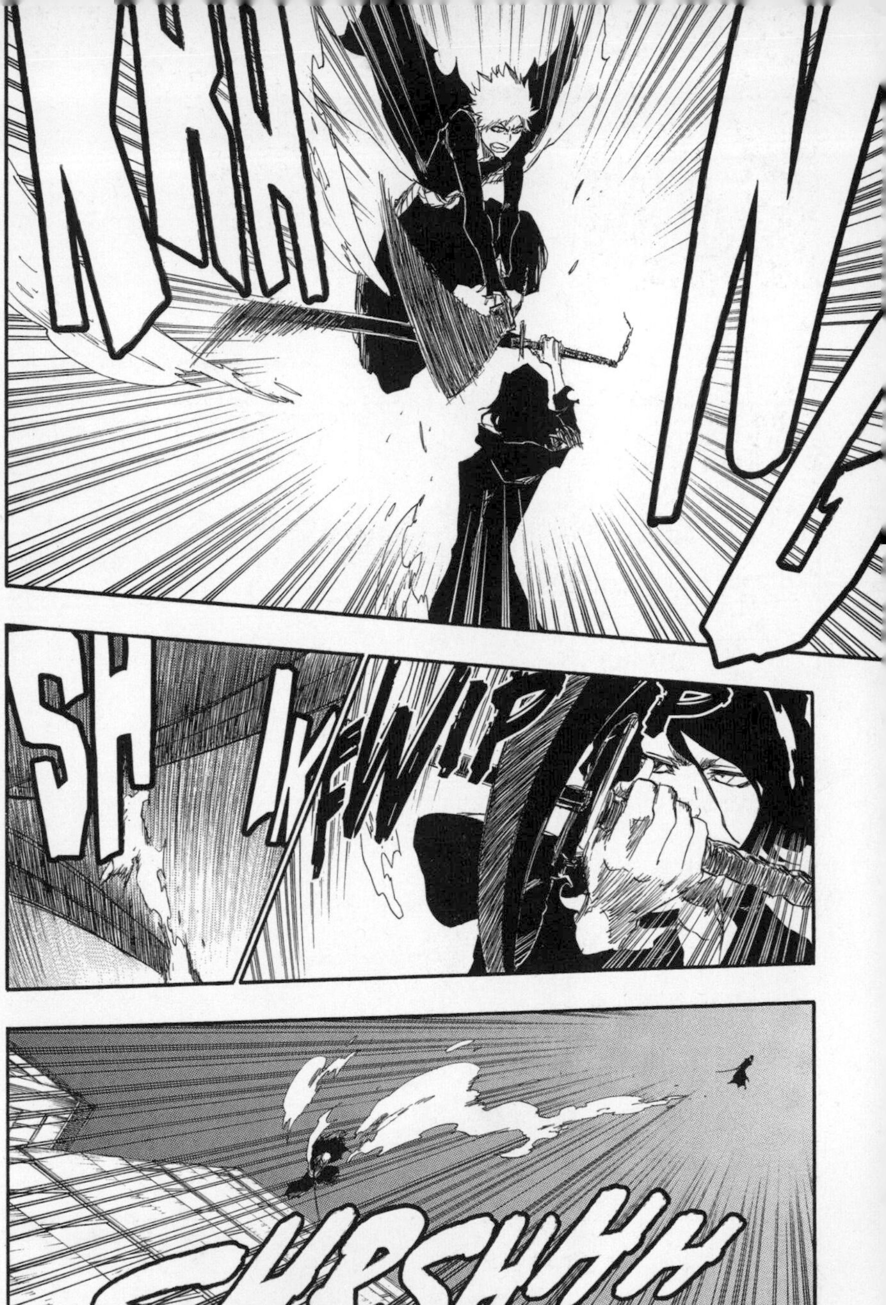
KWIP
SHRSHHH

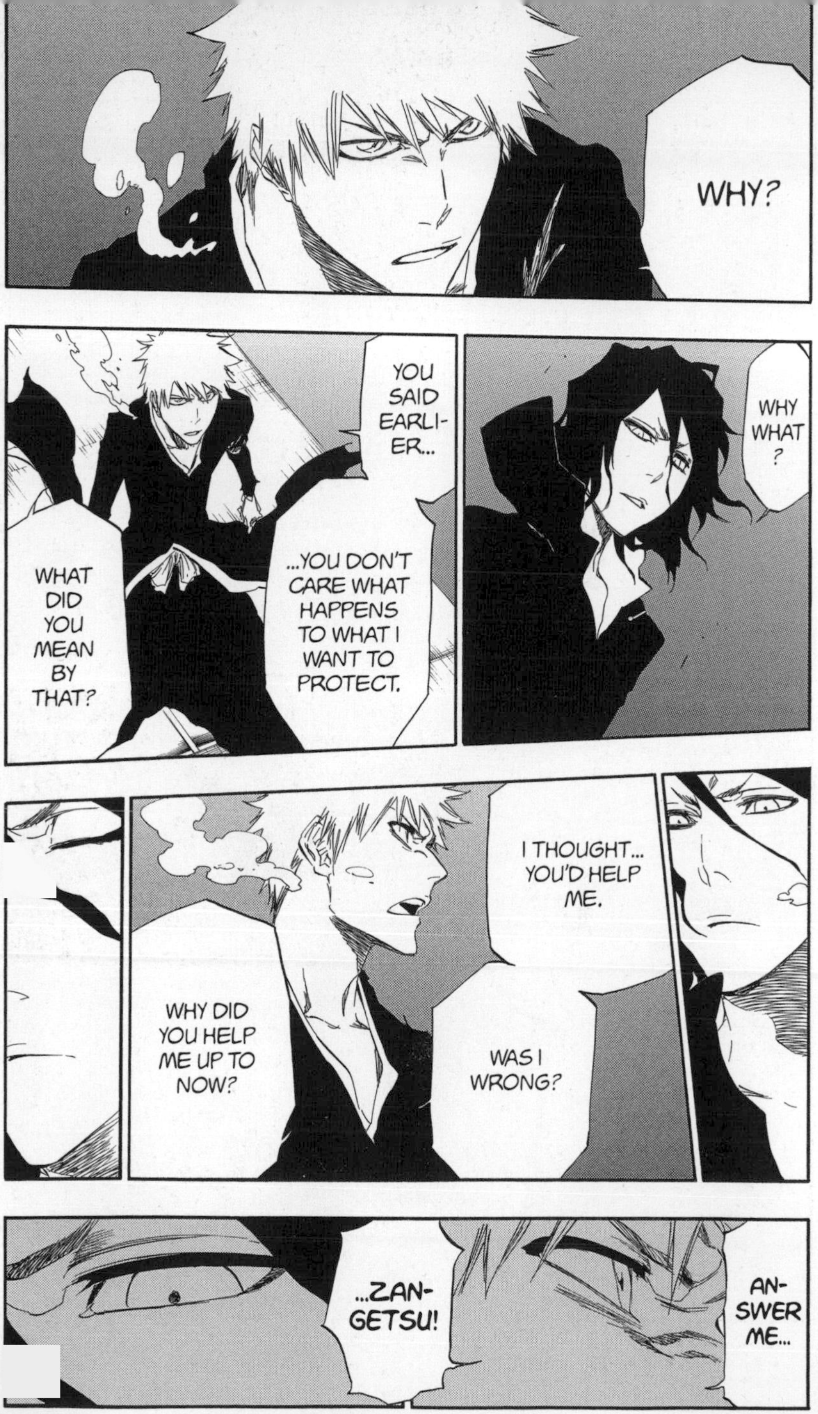
WHY?
WHY WHAT?
YOU SAID EARLIER...
...YOU DON'T CARE WHAT HAPPENS TO WHAT I WANT TO PROTECT.
WHAT DID YOU MEAN BY THAT?
I THOUGHT... YOU'D HELP ME.
WAS I WRONG?
WHY DID YOU HELP ME UP TO NOW?
ANSWER ME...
...ZANGETSU!

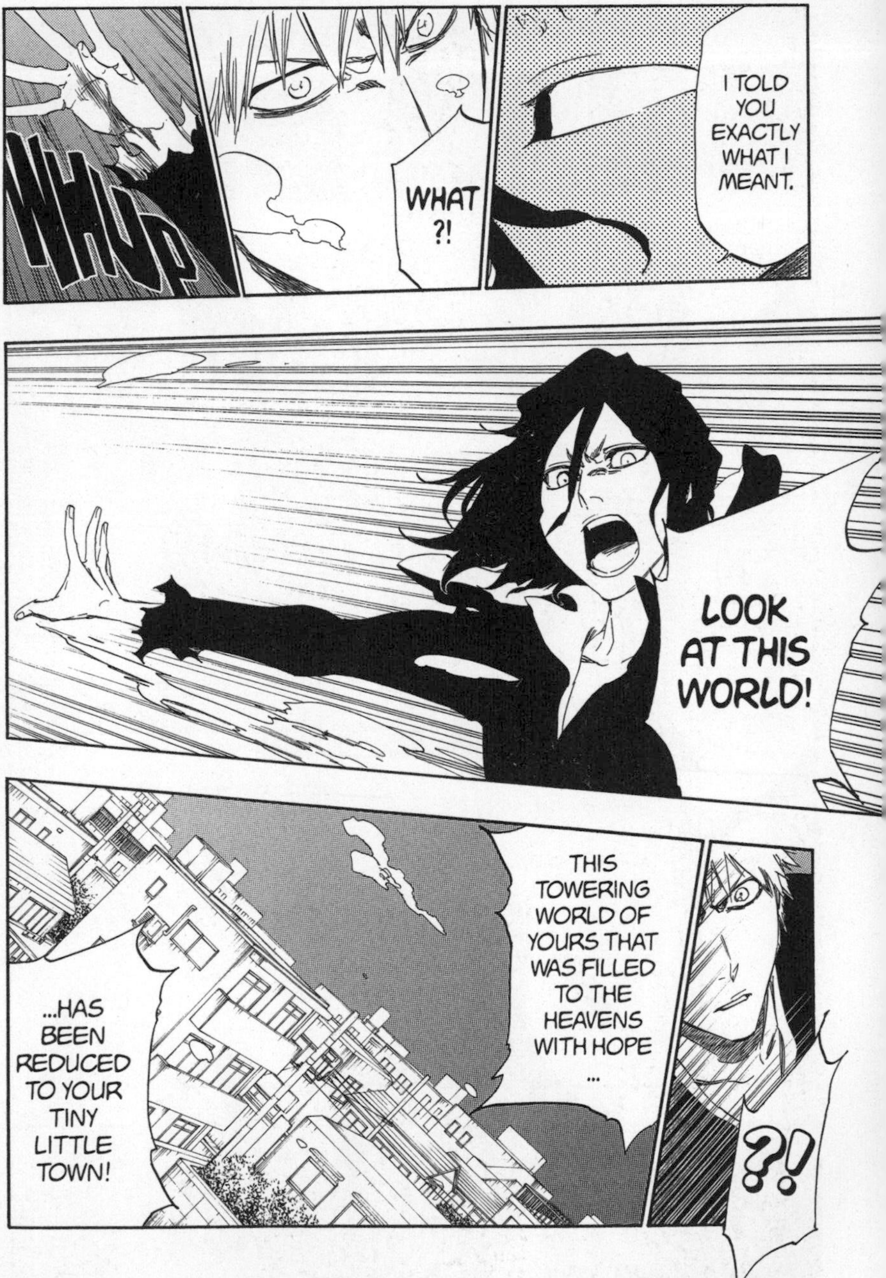
I TOLD YOU EXACTLY WHAT I MEANT.
WHAT ?!
WHUP
LOOK AT THIS WORLD!
?!
THIS TOWERING WORLD OF YOURS THAT WAS FILLED TO THE HEAVENS WITH HOPE ...
...HAS BEEN REDUCED TO YOUR TINY LITTLE TOWN!

READ THIS WAY

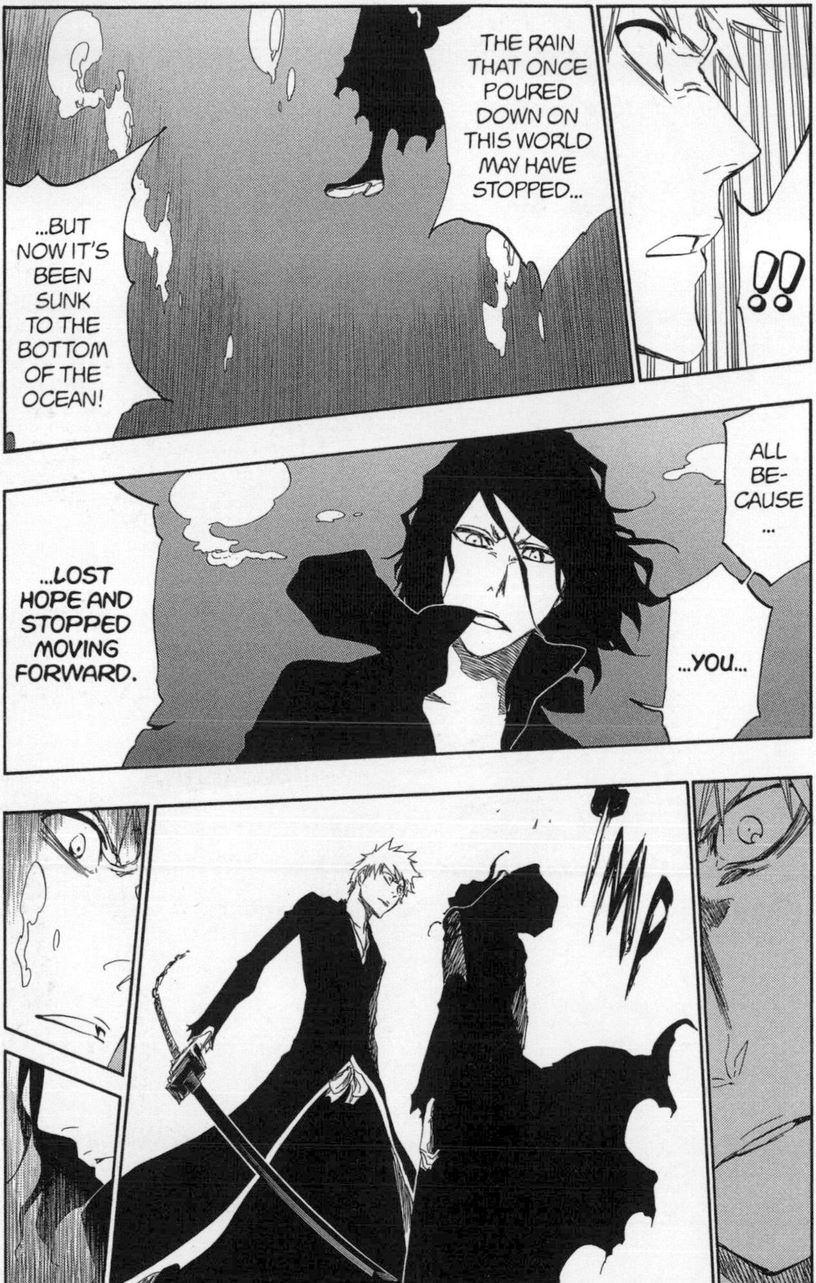
!!
THE RAIN THAT ONCE POURED DOWN ON THIS WORLD MAY HAVE STOPPED...
...BUT NOW IT'S BEEN SUNK TO THE BOTTOM OF THE OCEAN!
ALL BE-CAUSE ...
...YOU...
...LOST HOPE AND STOPPED MOVING FORWARD.
TMP

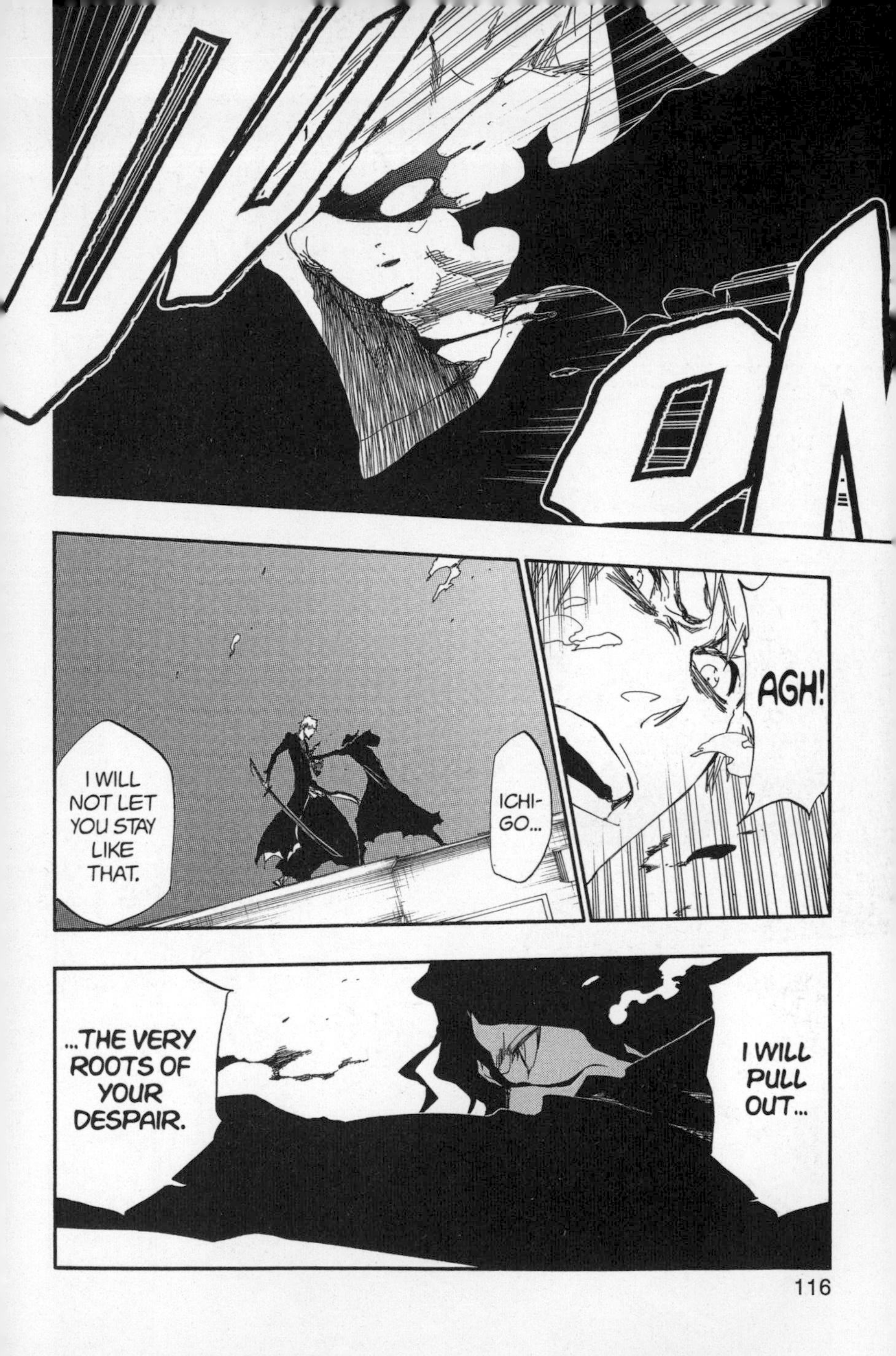
AGH!
ICHI-GO...
I WILL NOT LET YOU STAY LIKE THAT.
I WILL PULL OUT...
...THE VERY ROOTS OF YOUR DESPAIR.

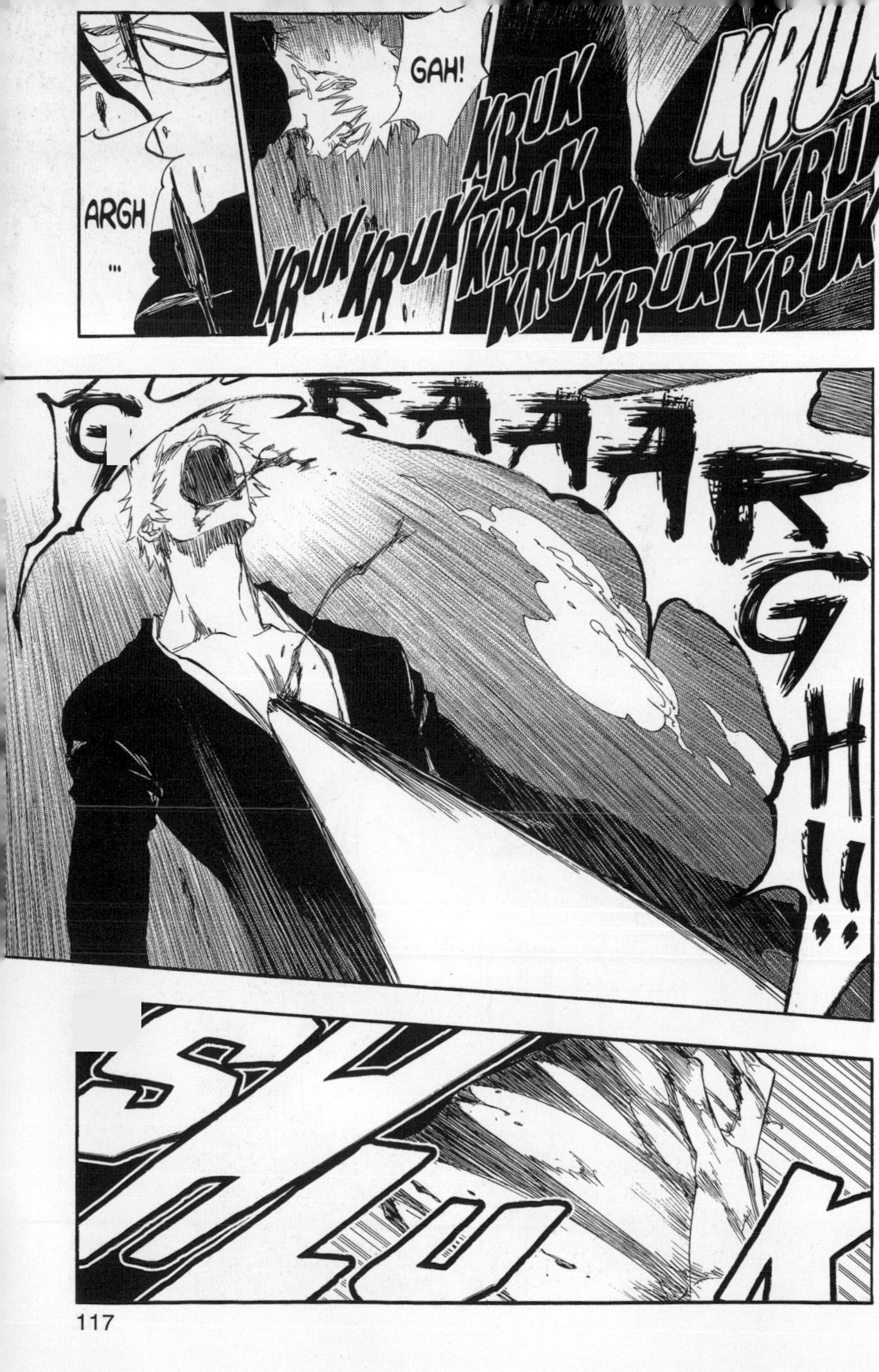
GAH!
KRUK KRUK KRUK KRUK KRUK KRUK KRUK KRUK KRUK
ARGH
...
GRAAARGH!!

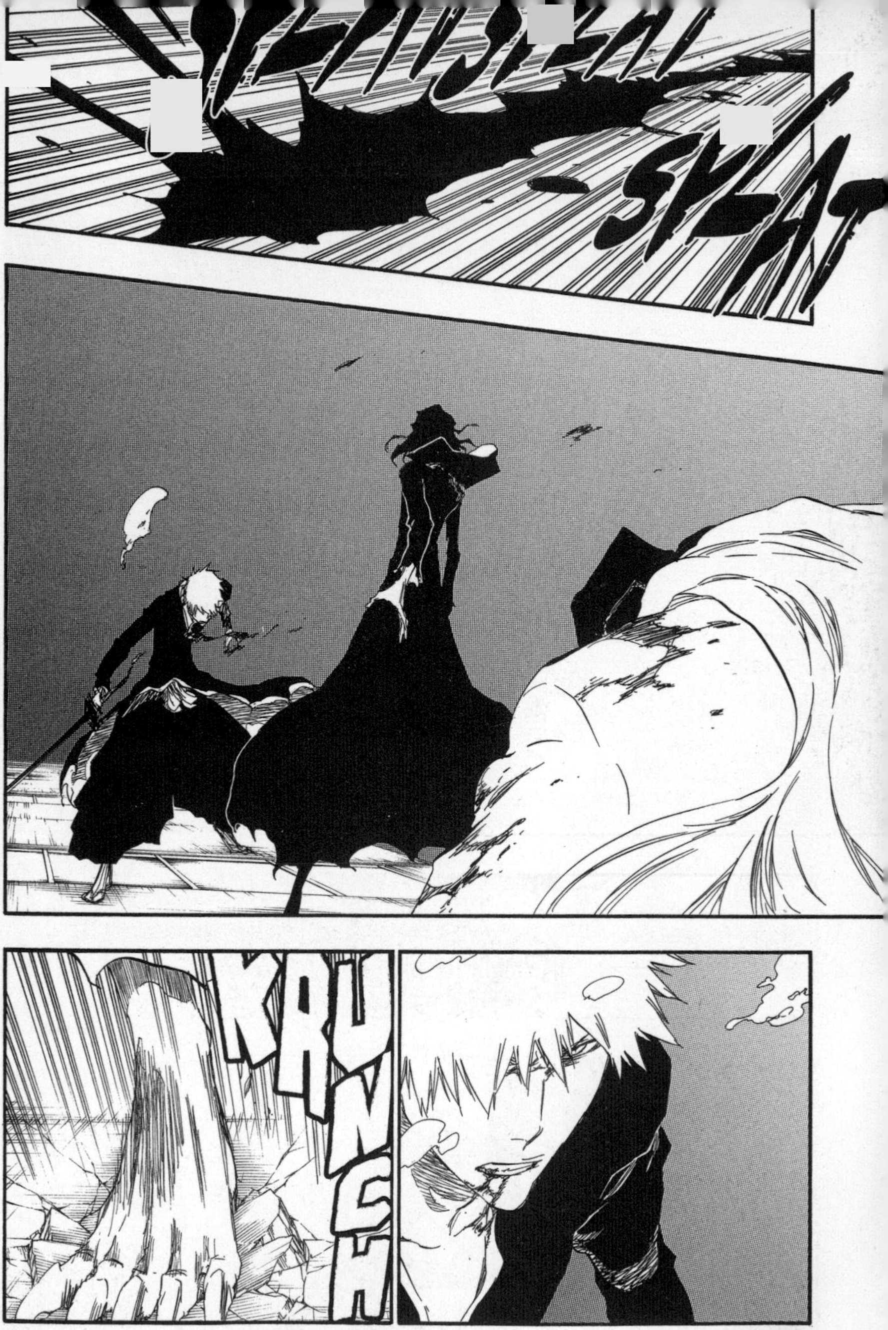
SPLAT
KRUNCH

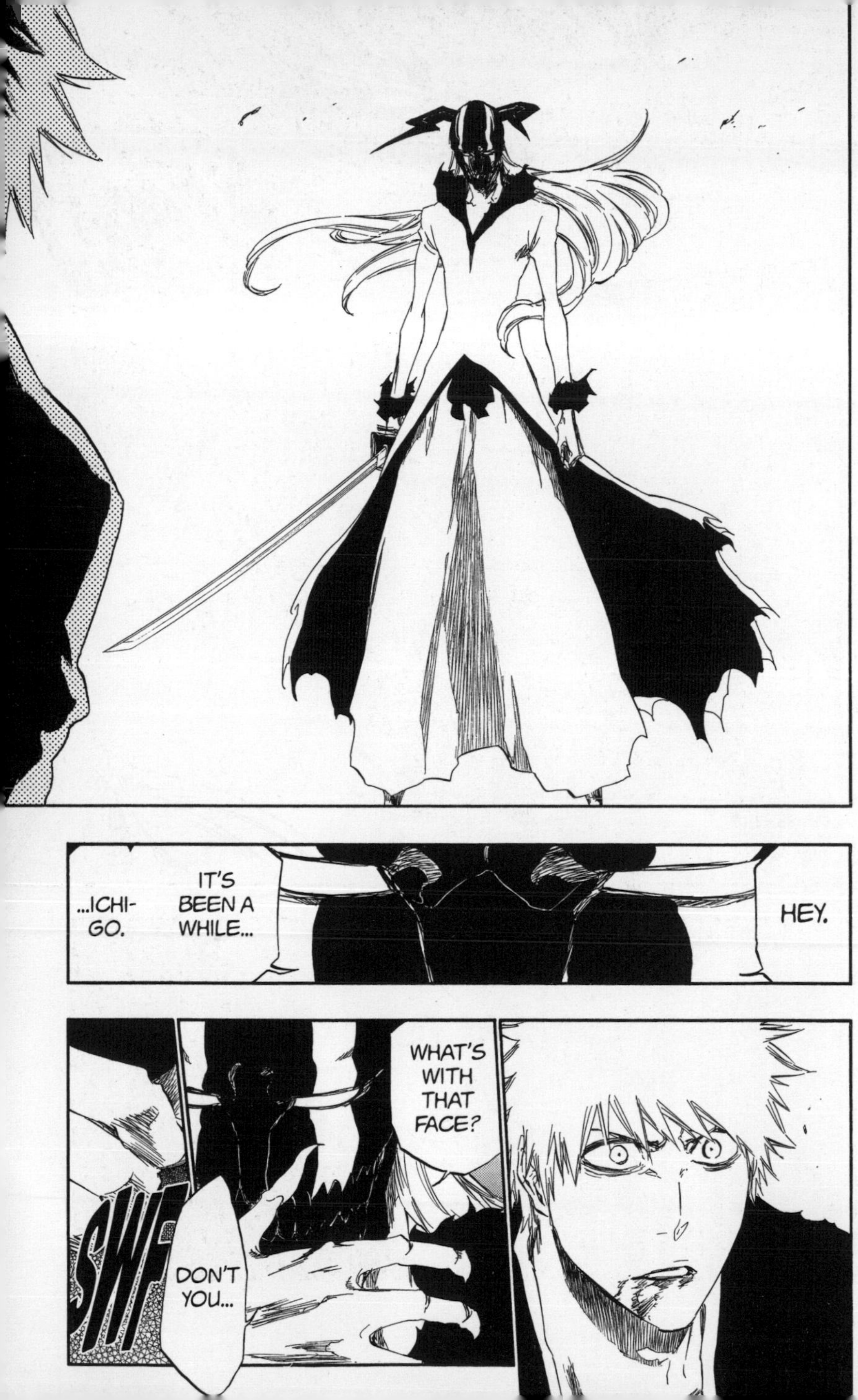
HEY.
IT'S BEEN A WHILE...
...ICHI-GO.
WHAT'S WITH THAT FACE?
DON'T YOU...
SWF

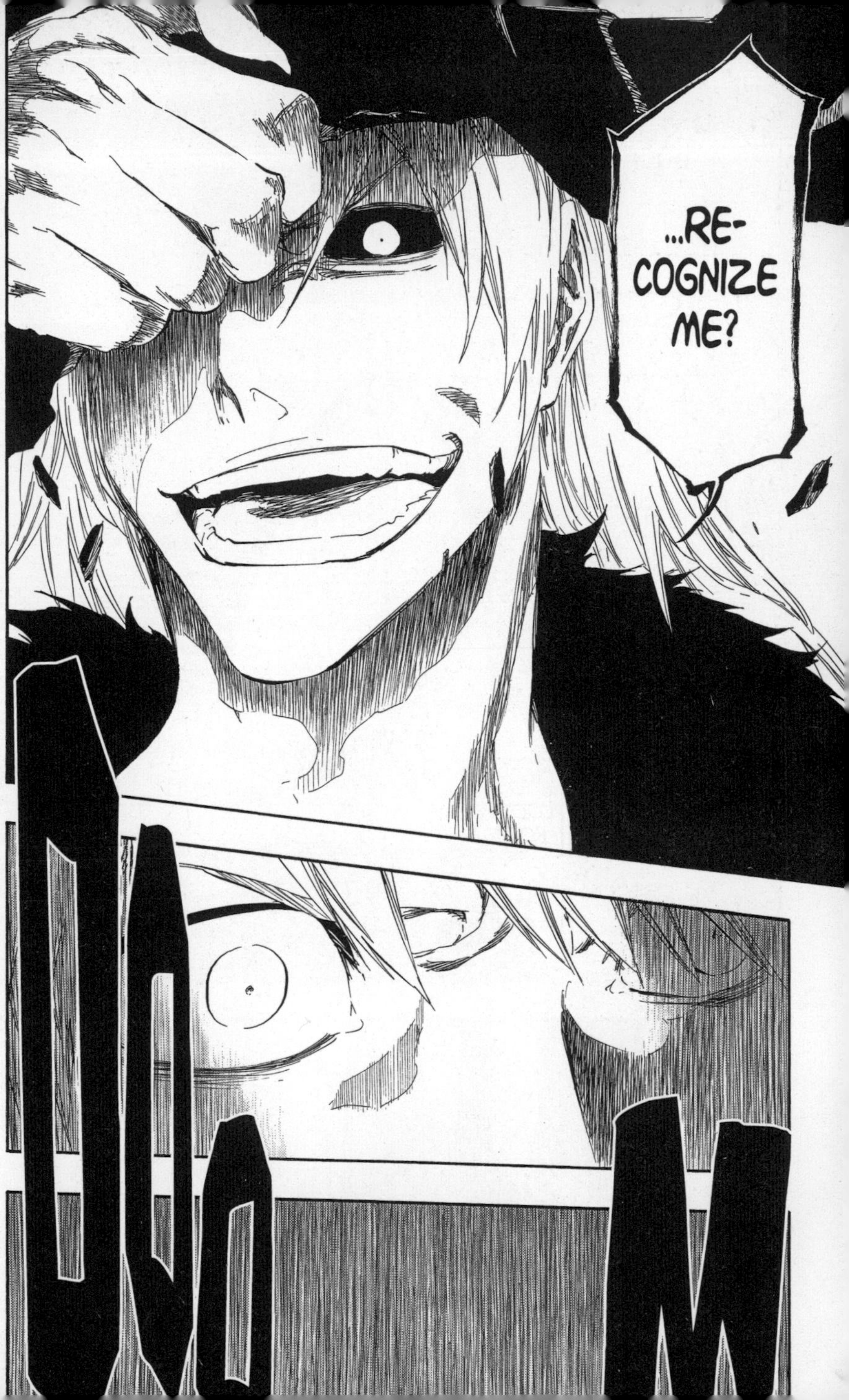
...RE-COGNIZE ME?
DOOM

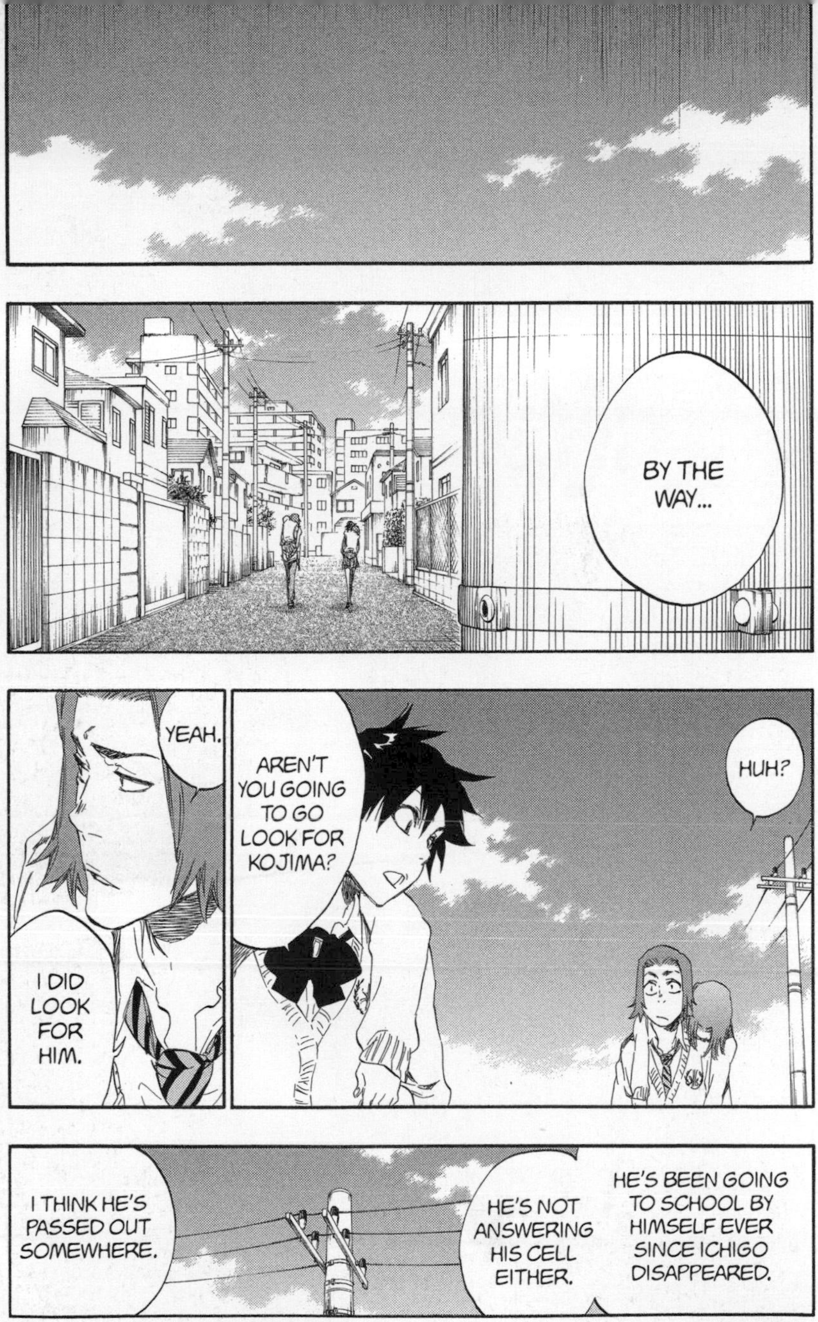
BY THE WAY...
HUH?
AREN'T YOU GOING TO GO LOOK FOR KOJIMA?
YEAH.
I DID LOOK FOR HIM.
HE'S BEEN GOING TO SCHOOL BY HIMSELF EVER SINCE ICHIGO DISAPPEARED.
HE'S NOT ANSWERING HIS CELL EITHER.
I THINK HE'S PASSED OUT SOMEWHERE.

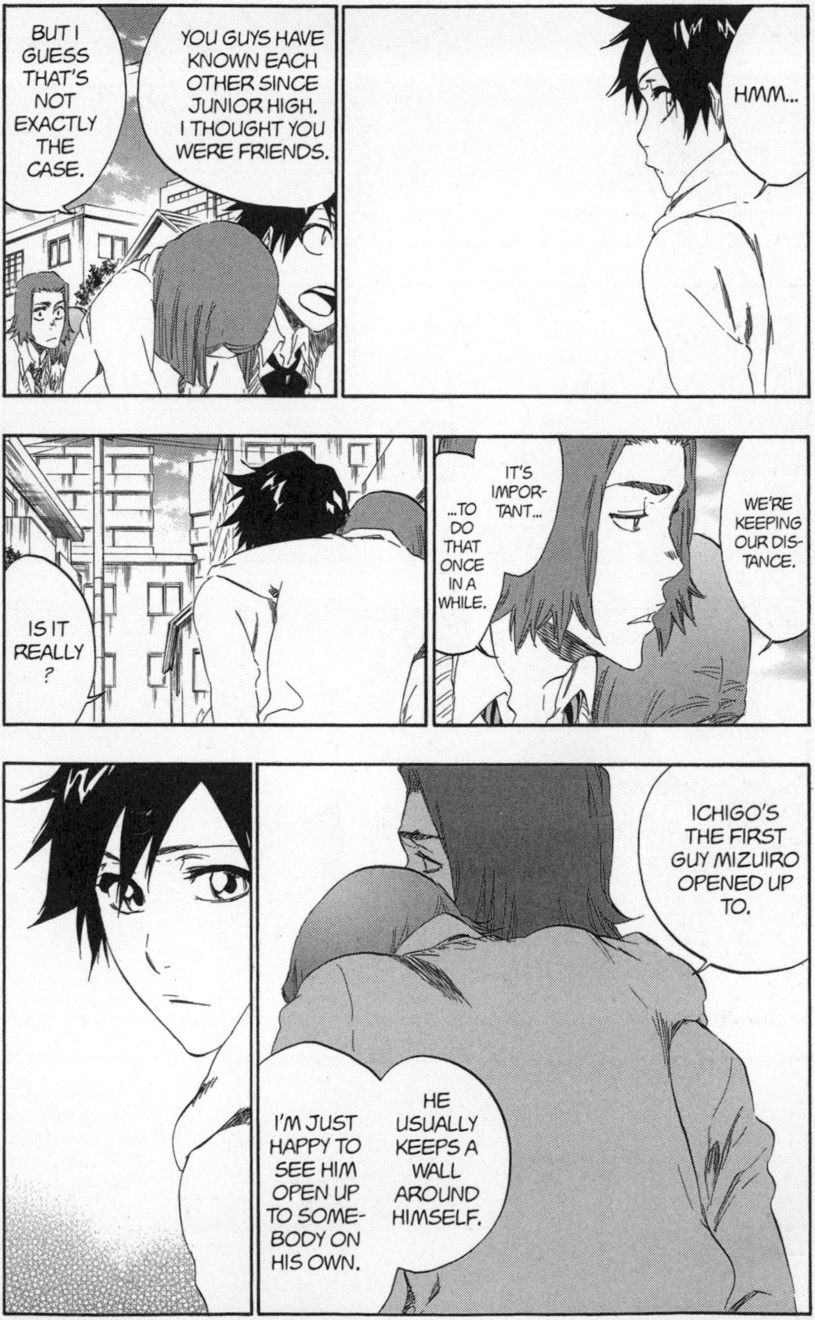
HMM...
YOU GUYS HAVE KNOWN EACH OTHER SINCE JUNIOR HIGH. I THOUGHT YOU WERE FRIENDS.
BUT I GUESS THAT'S NOT EXACTLY THE CASE.
WE'RE KEEPING OUR DISTANCE.
IT'S IMPORTANT...
...TO DO THAT ONCE IN A WHILE.
IS IT REALLY?
ICHIGO'S THE FIRST GUY MIZUIRO OPENED UP TO.
HE USUALLY KEEPS A WALL AROUND HIMSELF.
I'M JUST HAPPY TO SEE HIM OPEN UP TO SOMEBODY ON HIS OWN.

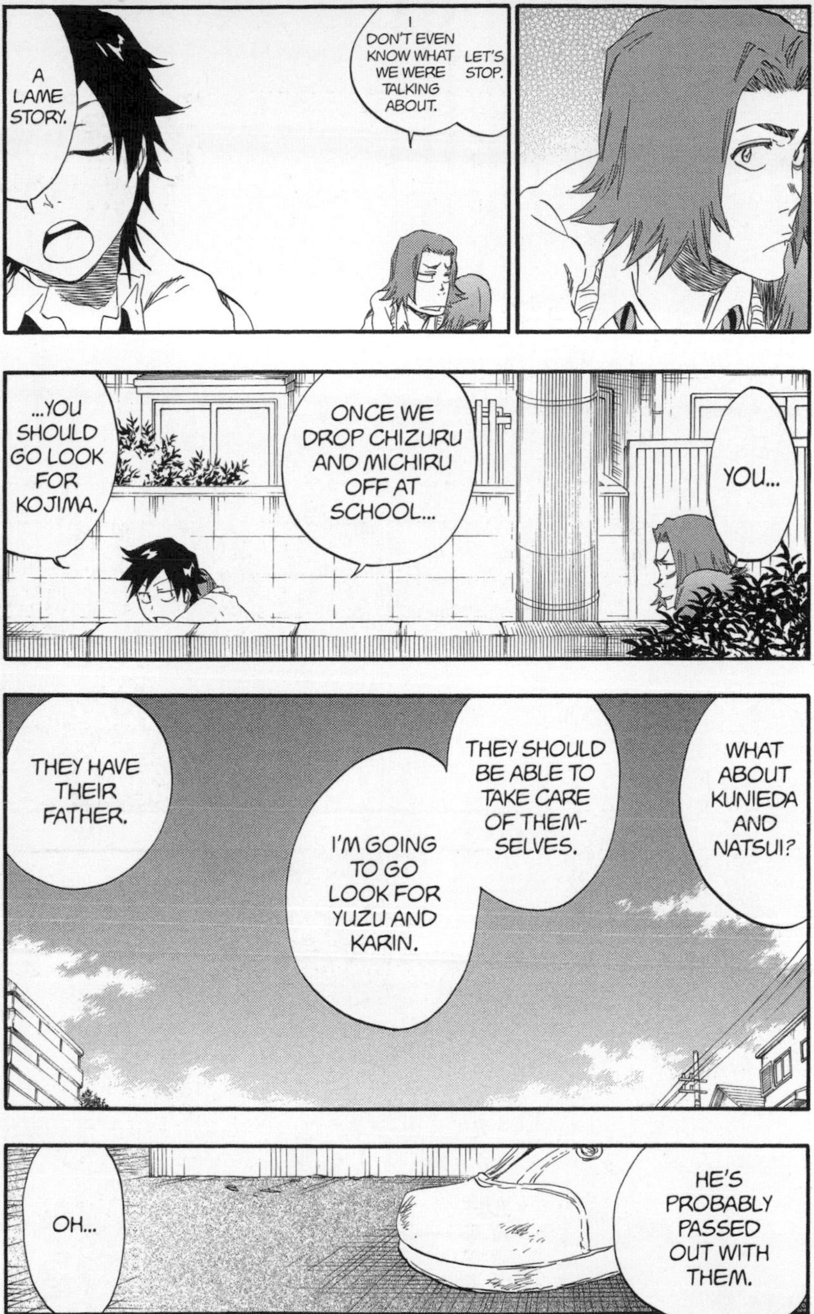
LET'S STOP.
I DON'T EVEN KNOW WHAT WE WERE TALKING ABOUT.
A LAME STORY.
YOU...
ONCE WE DROP CHIZURU AND MICHIRU OFF AT SCHOOL...
...YOU SHOULD GO LOOK FOR KOJIMA.
WHAT ABOUT KUNIEDA AND NATSUI?
THEY SHOULD BE ABLE TO TAKE CARE OF THEM-SELVES.
I'M GOING TO GO LOOK FOR YUZU AND KARIN.
THEY HAVE THEIR FATHER.
HE'S PROBABLY PASSED OUT WITH THEM.
OH...

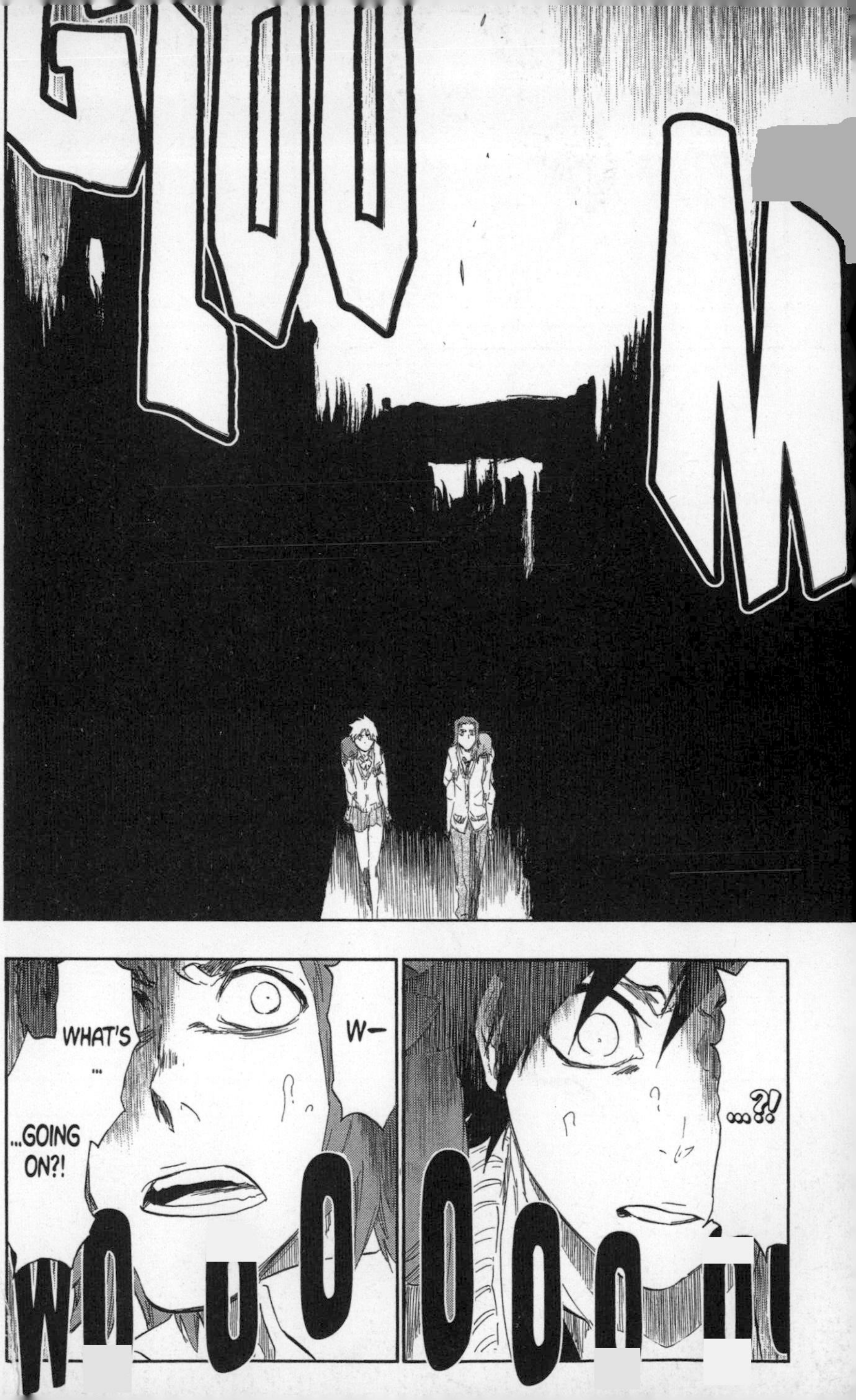
...?!
W-
WHAT'S ...
...GOING ON?!

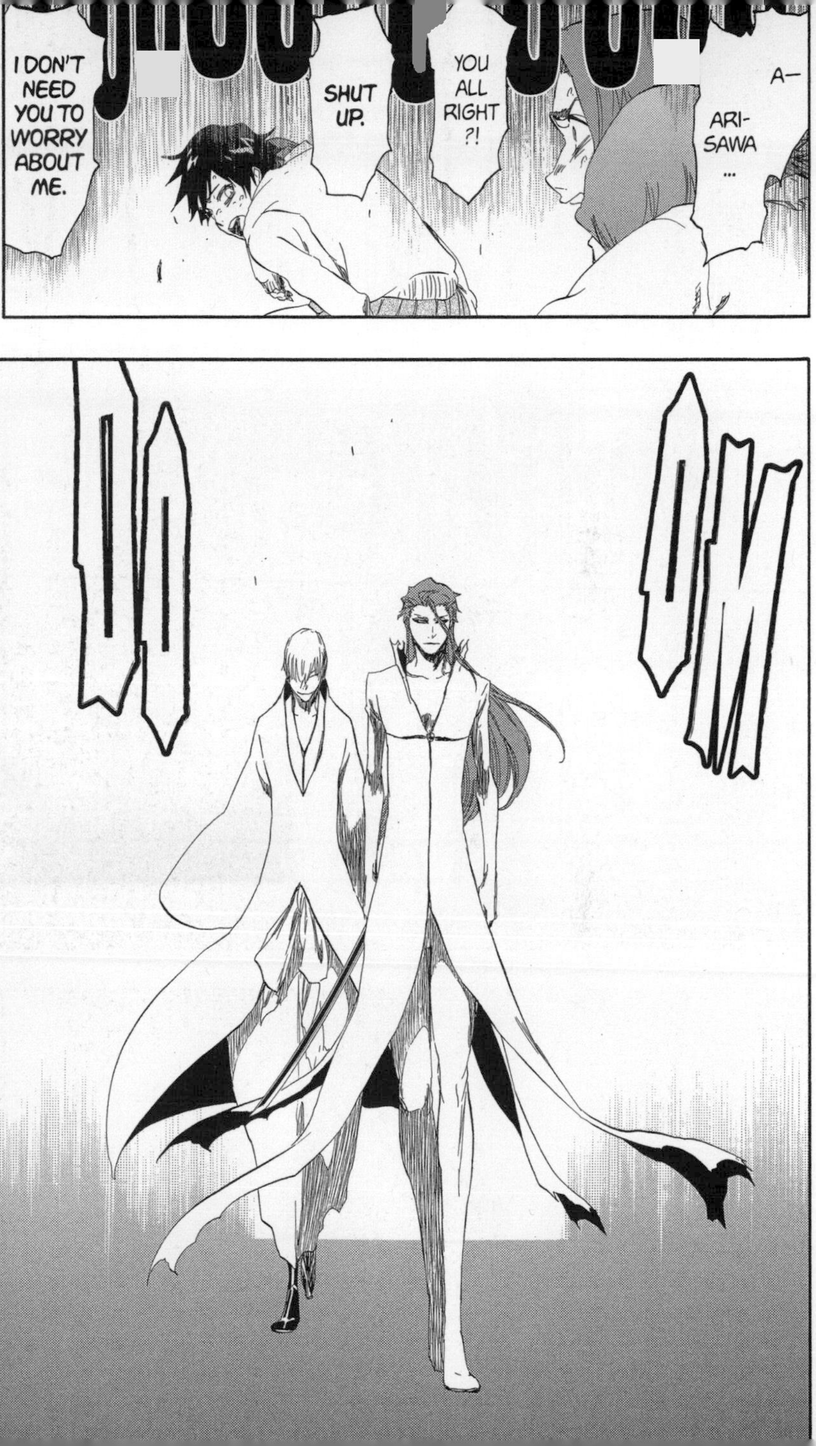
A—
ARI-SAWA...
YOU ALL RIGHT?!
SHUT UP.
I DON'T NEED YOU TO WORRY ABOUT ME.
DOOM

WHO ARE...
...THEY?
ARI-SAWA ...
TUMP
MOST IMPRES-SIVE...
...TO BE ABLE TO MAINTAIN YOUR IDENTITY AT SUCH CLOSE RANGE.

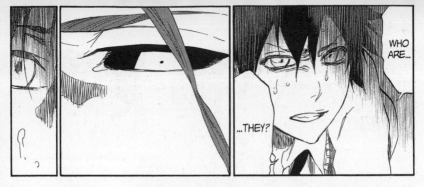

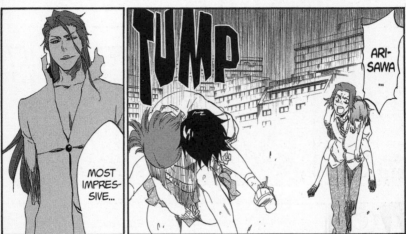

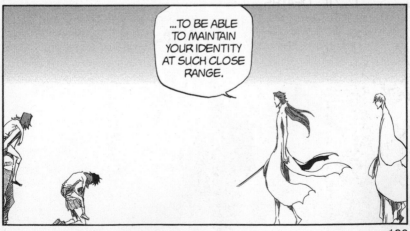

READ THIS WAY

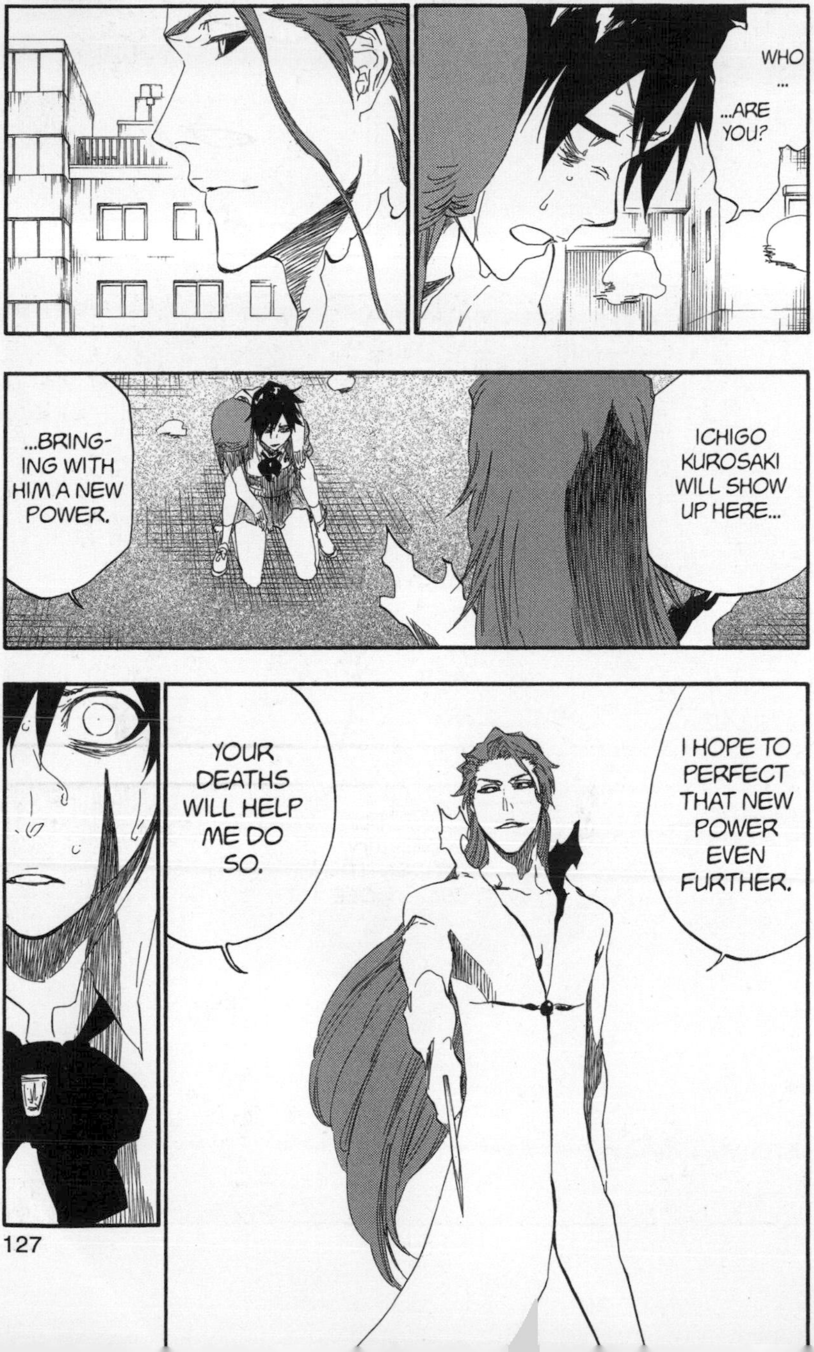
WHO ... ...ARE YOU?
ICHIGO KUROSAKI WILL SHOW UP HERE...
...BRING-ING WITH HIM A NEW POWER.
I HOPE TO PERFECT THAT NEW POWER EVEN FURTHER.
YOUR DEATHS WILL HELP ME DO SO.

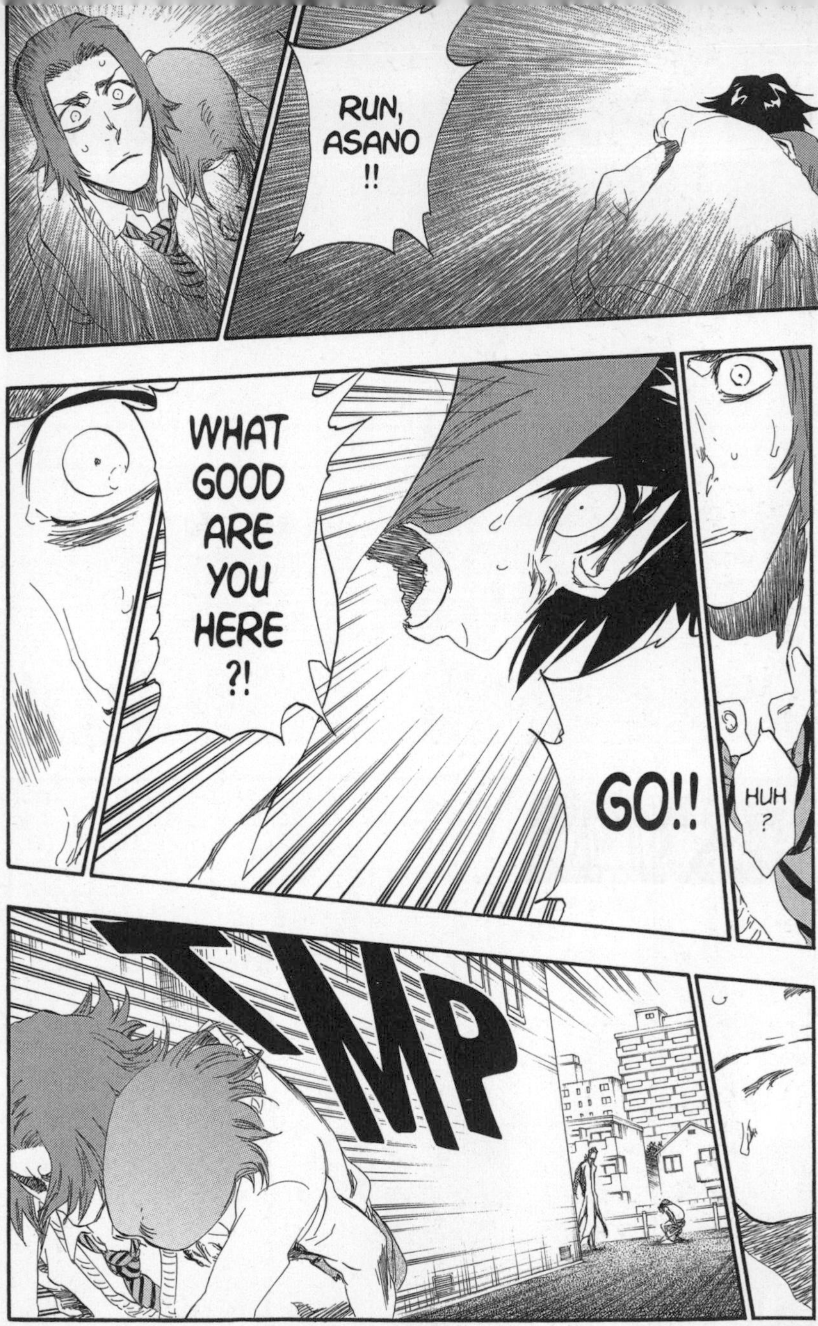
RUN, ASANO !!
HUH ?
WHAT GOOD ARE YOU HERE ?!
GO!!
TMP

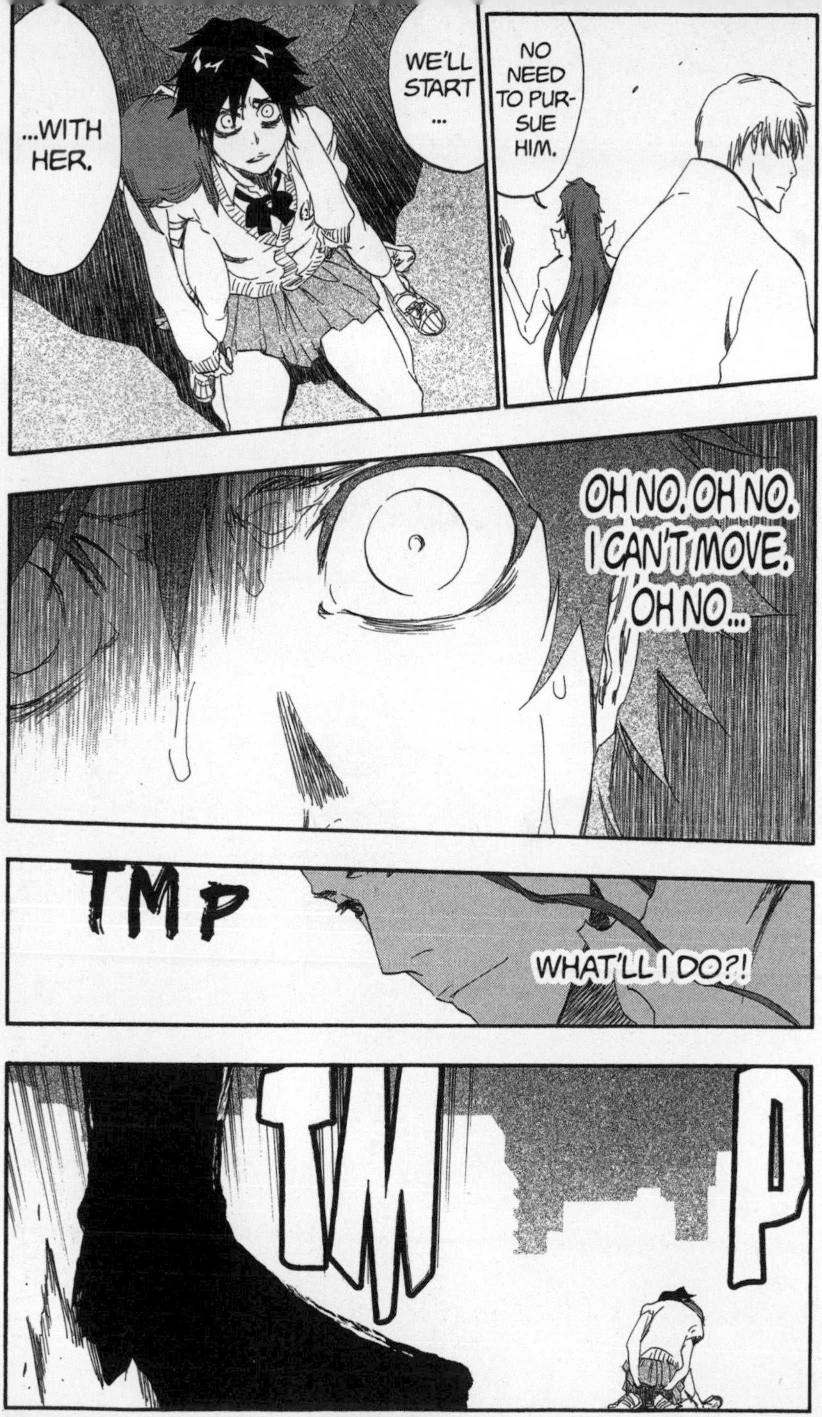
NO NEED TO PUR-SUE HIM.
WE'LL START ...
...WITH HER.
OH NO. OH NO. I CAN'T MOVE. OH NO...
WHAT'LL I DO?!
TMP
TMP

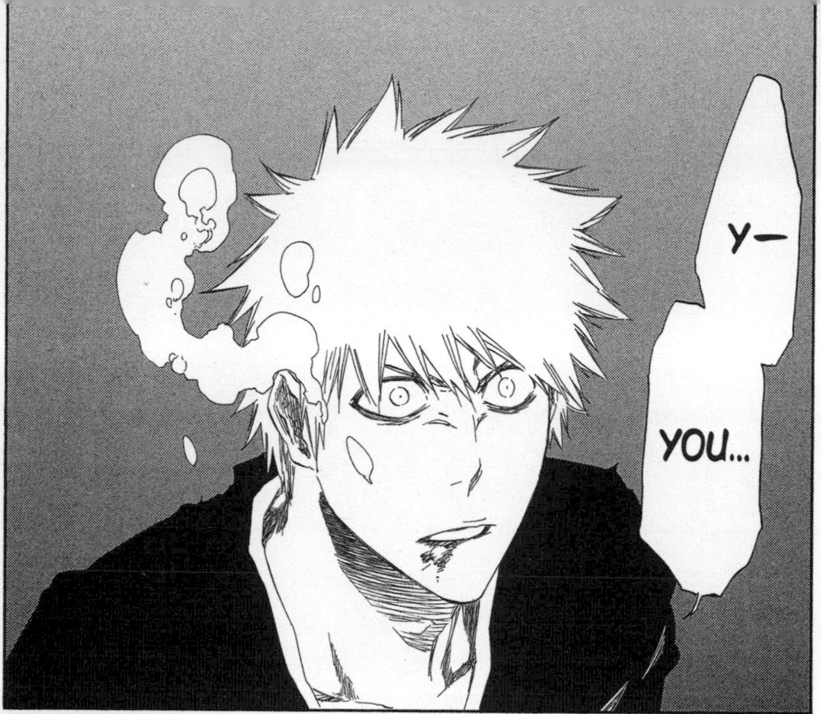
Y—
YOU...

411. DEICIDE 13

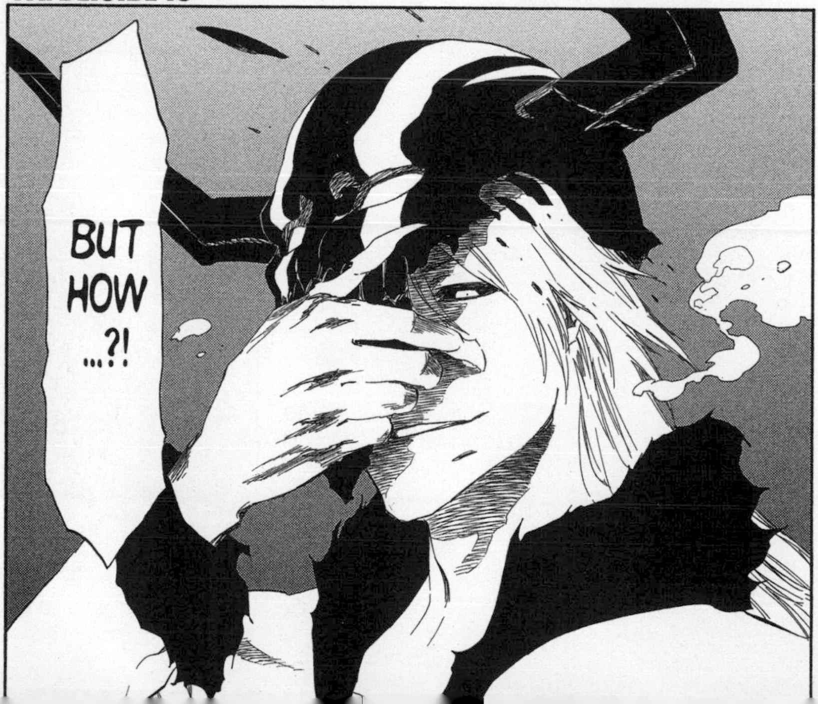
BUT HOW ...?!

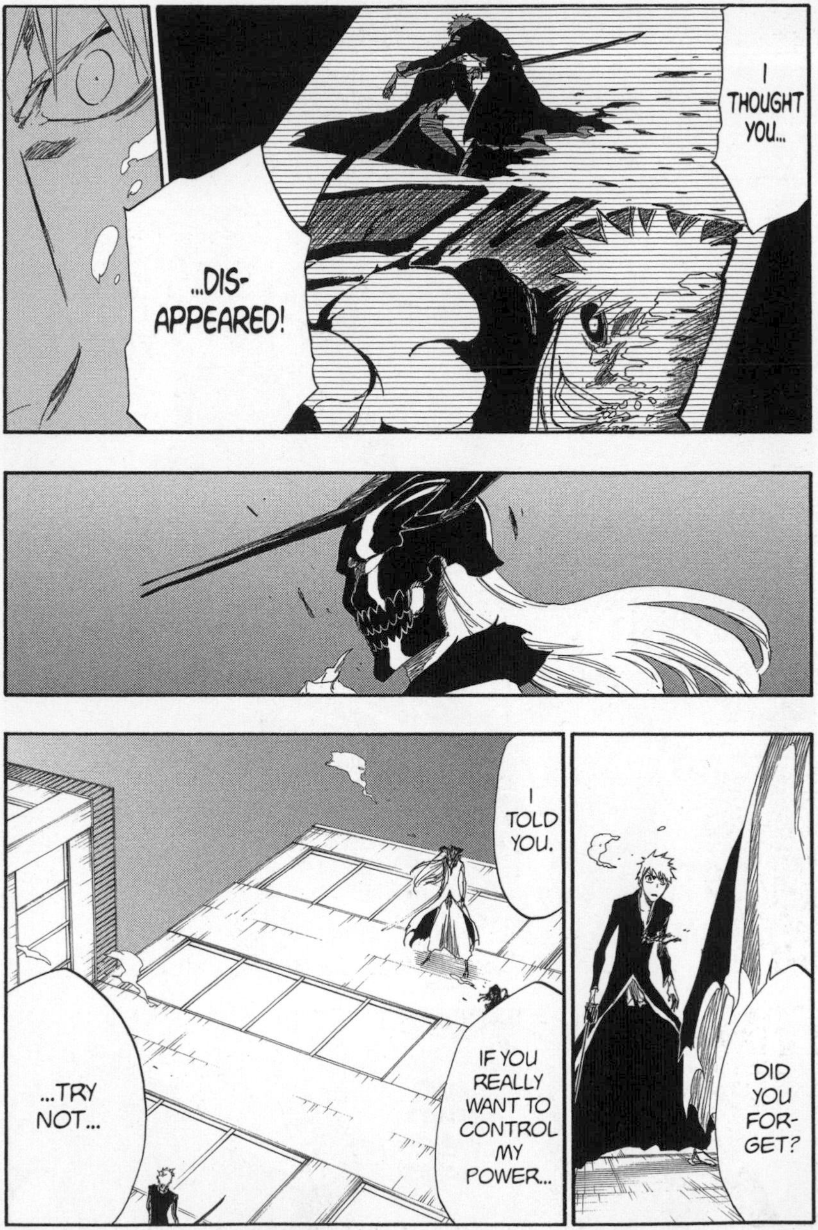
I THOUGHT YOU...
...DIS-APPEARED!
DID YOU FORGET?
I TOLD YOU.
IF YOU REALLY WANT TO CONTROL MY POWER...
...TRY NOT...

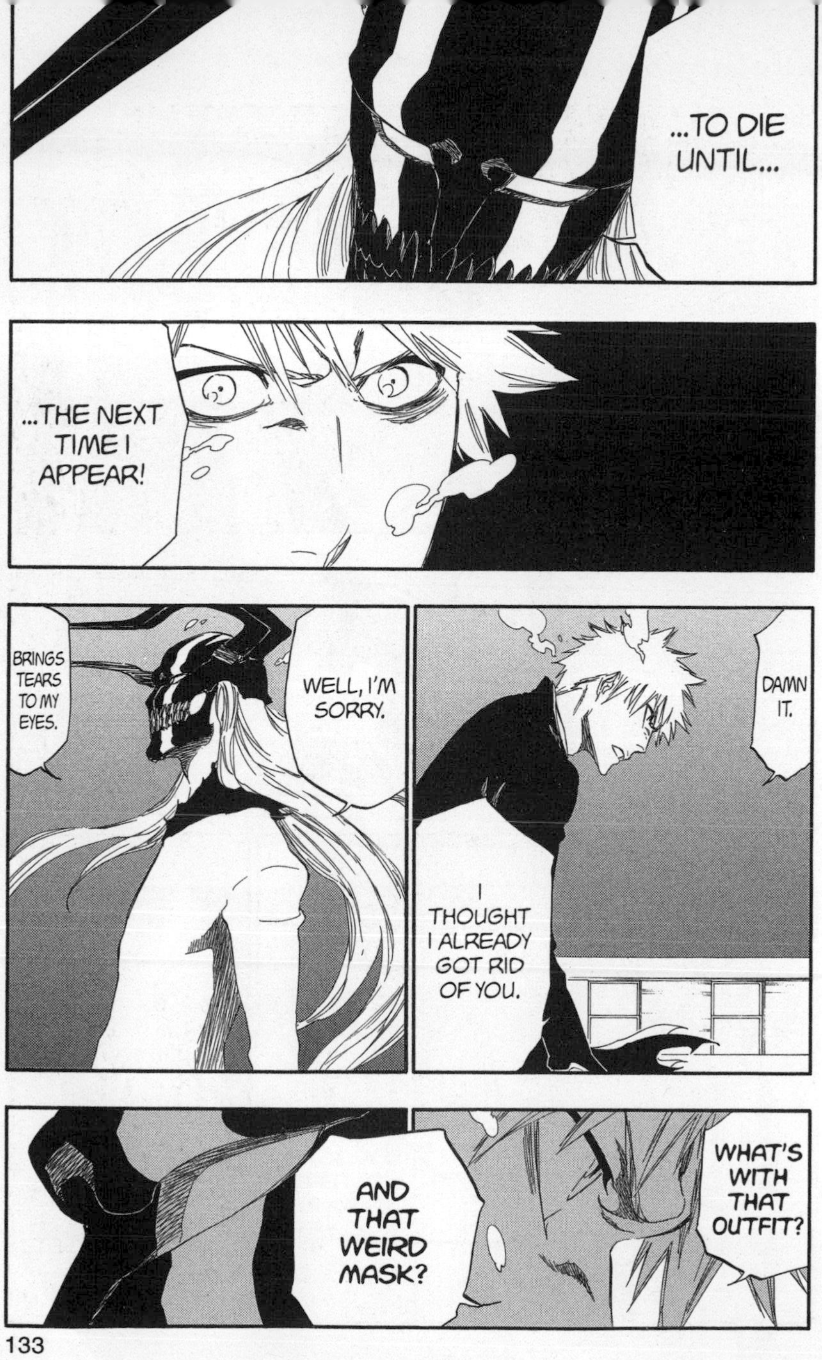
...TO DIE UNTIL...
...THE NEXT TIME I APPEAR!
DAMN IT.
I THOUGHT I ALREADY GOT RID OF YOU.
WELL, I'M SORRY.
BRINGS TEARS TO MY EYES.
WHAT'S WITH THAT OUTFIT?
AND THAT WEIRD MASK?

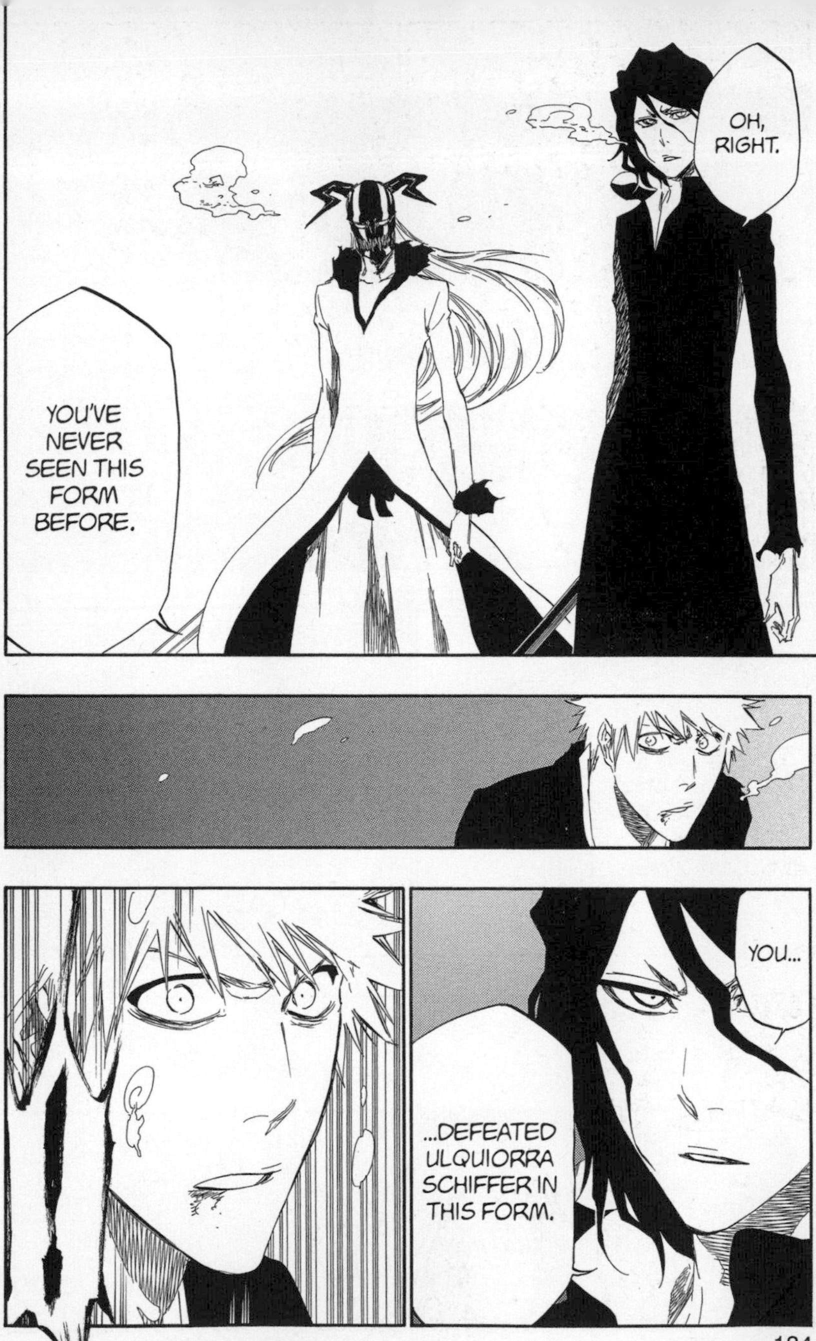
OH, RIGHT.
YOU'VE NEVER SEEN THIS FORM BEFORE.
YOU...
...DEFEATED ULQUIORRA SCHIFFER IN THIS FORM.

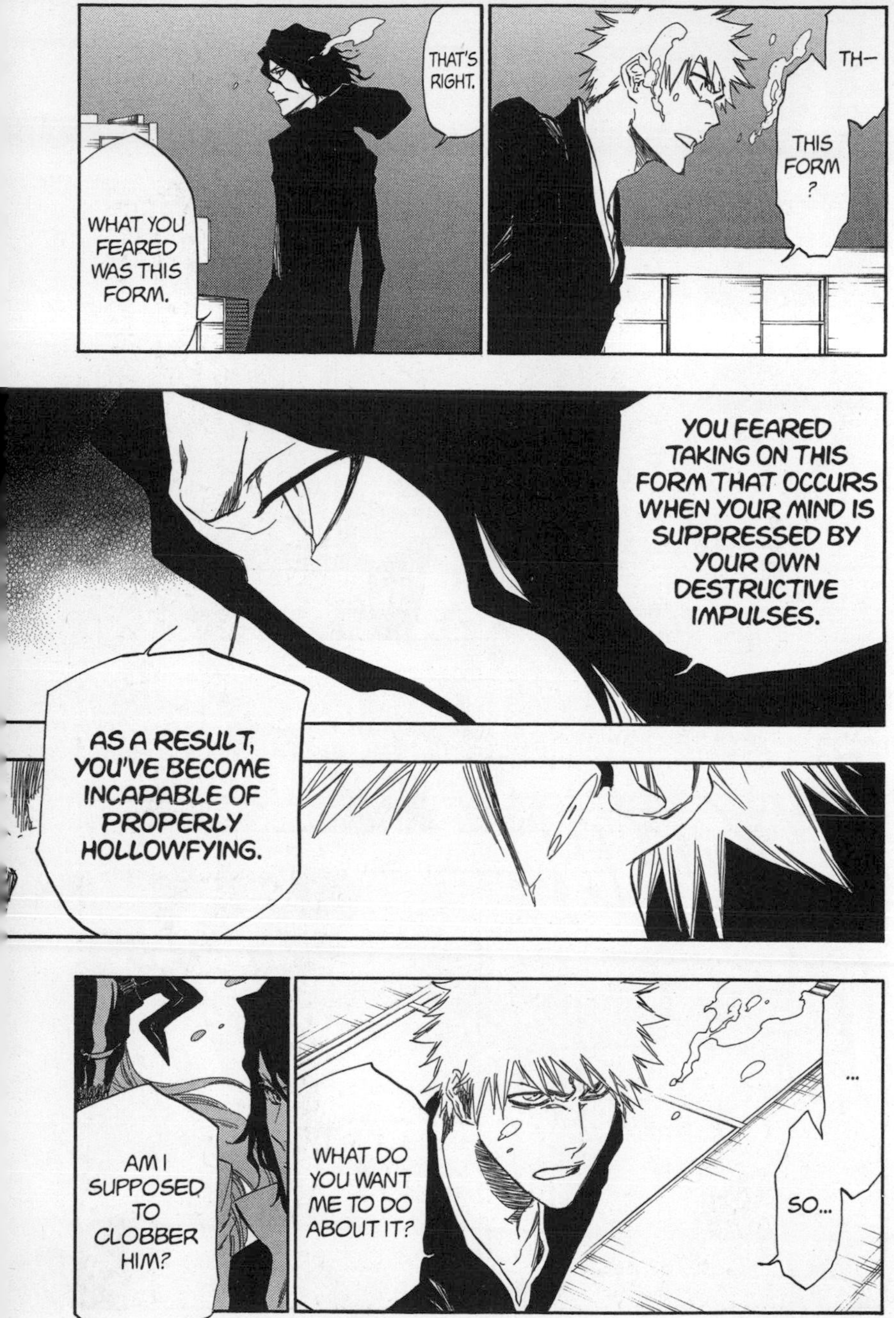
TH—
THIS FORM?
THAT'S RIGHT.
WHAT YOU FEARED WAS THIS FORM.
YOU FEARED TAKING ON THIS FORM THAT OCCURS WHEN YOUR MIND IS SUPPRESSED BY YOUR OWN DESTRUCTIVE IMPULSES.
AS A RESULT, YOU'VE BECOME INCAPABLE OF PROPERLY HOLLOWFYING.
...
SO...
WHAT DO YOU WANT ME TO DO ABOUT IT?
AM I SUPPOSED TO CLOBBER HIM?

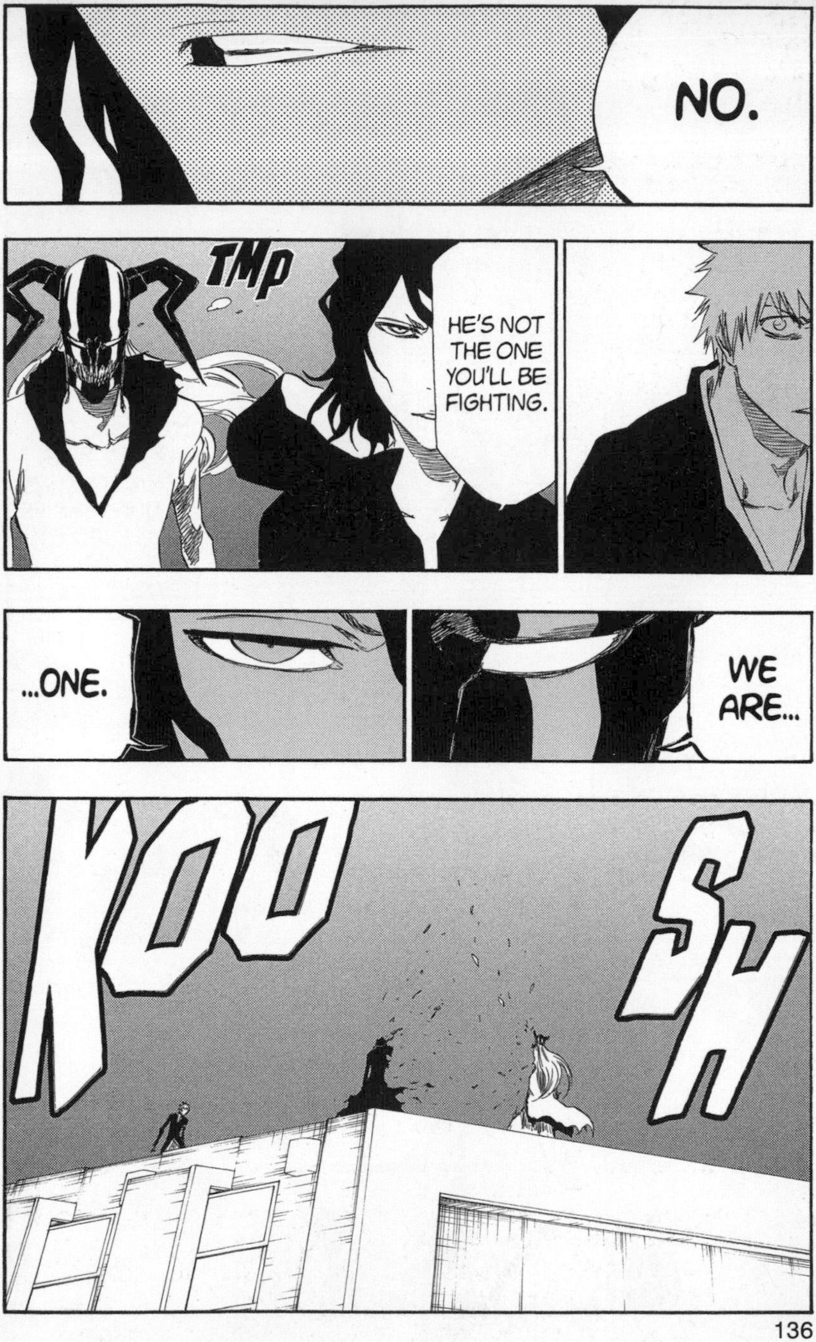
NO.
HE'S NOT THE ONE YOU'LL BE FIGHTING.
TMP
WE ARE...
...ONE.
KOOSH

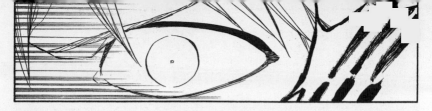

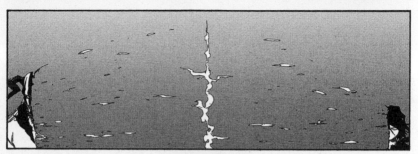

WHAT THE...

...IS THAT ?!

WHAT THE HELL ...

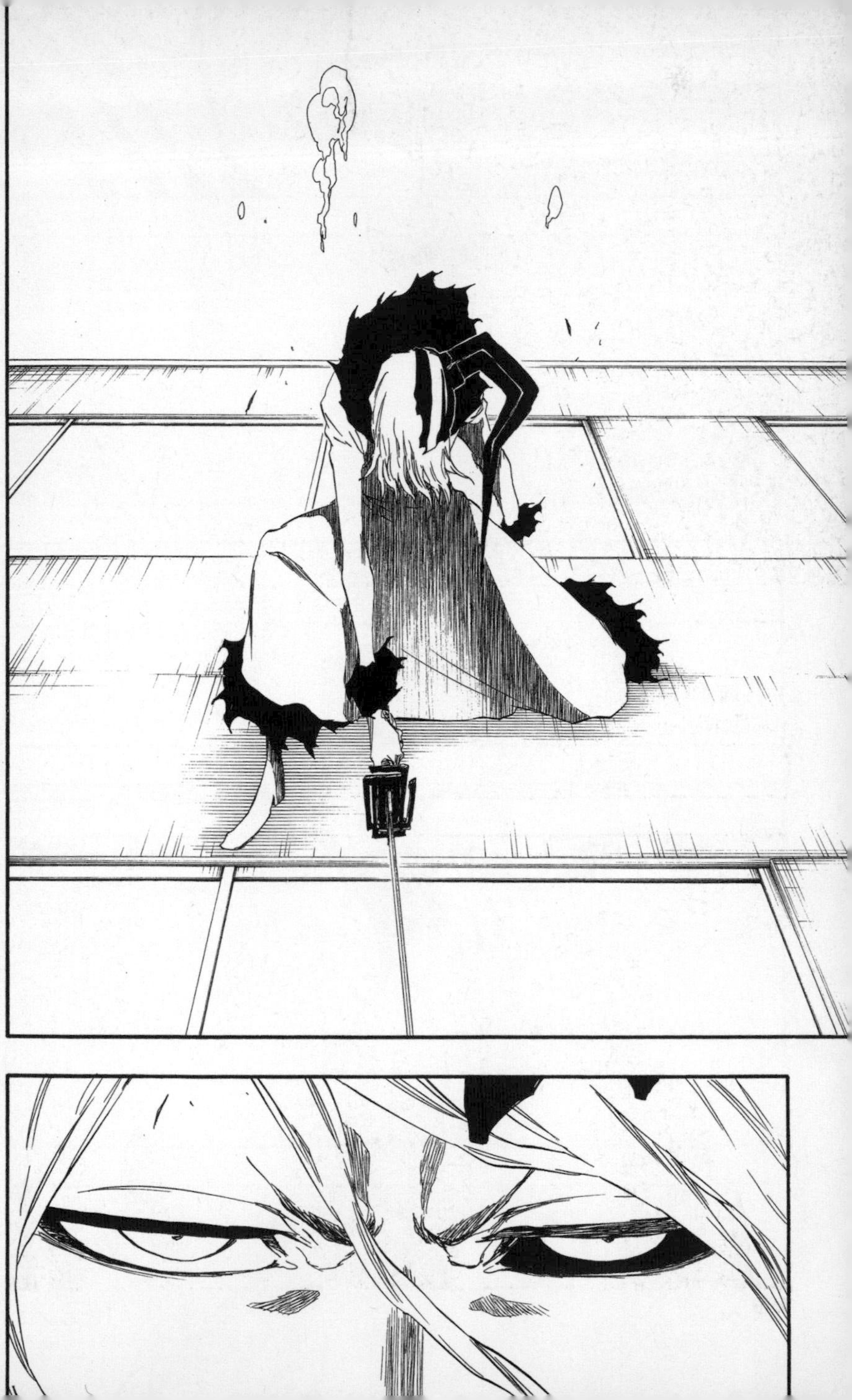

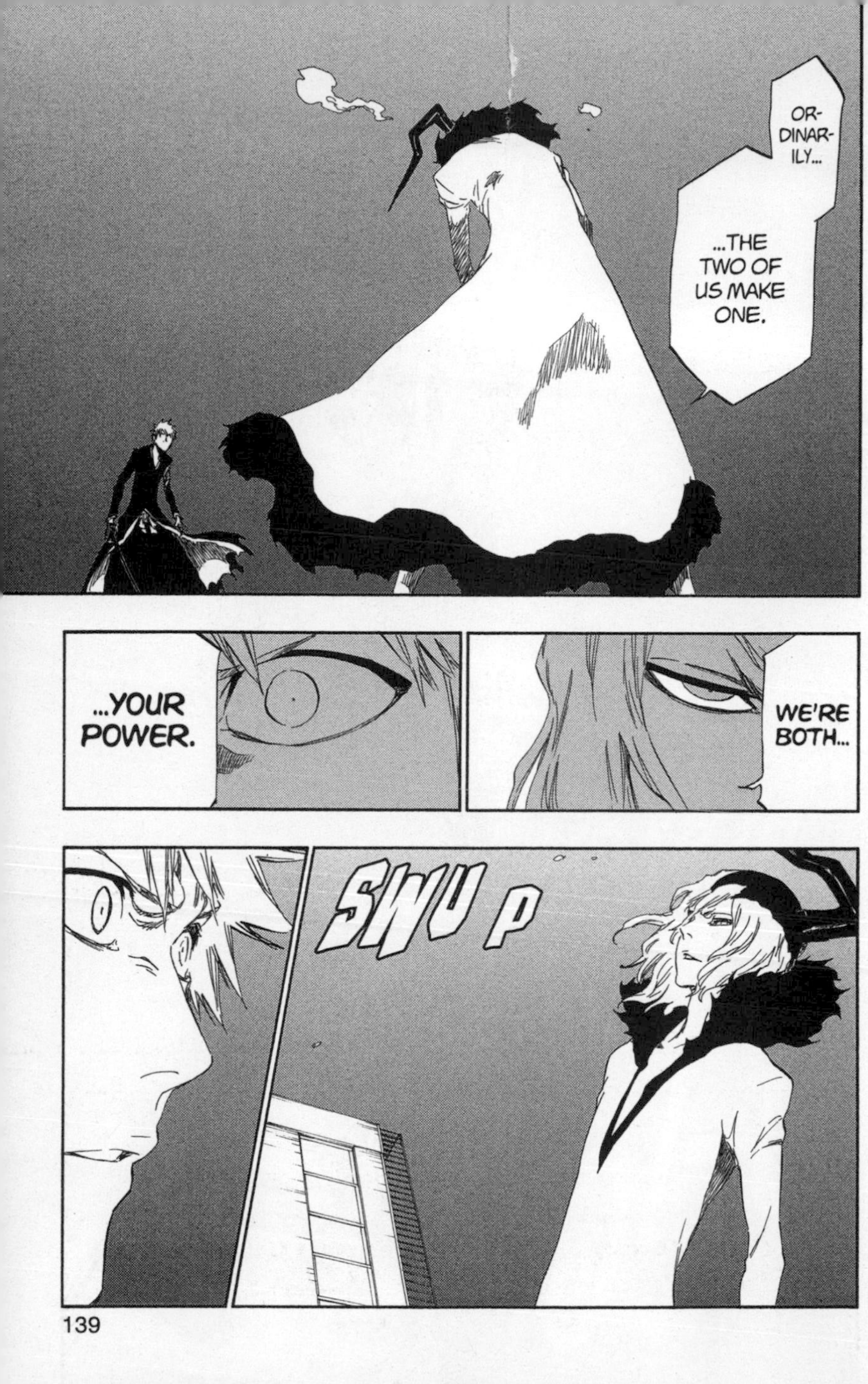
ORDINARILY...
...THE TWO OF US MAKE ONE.
WE'RE BOTH...
...YOUR POWER.
SWUP

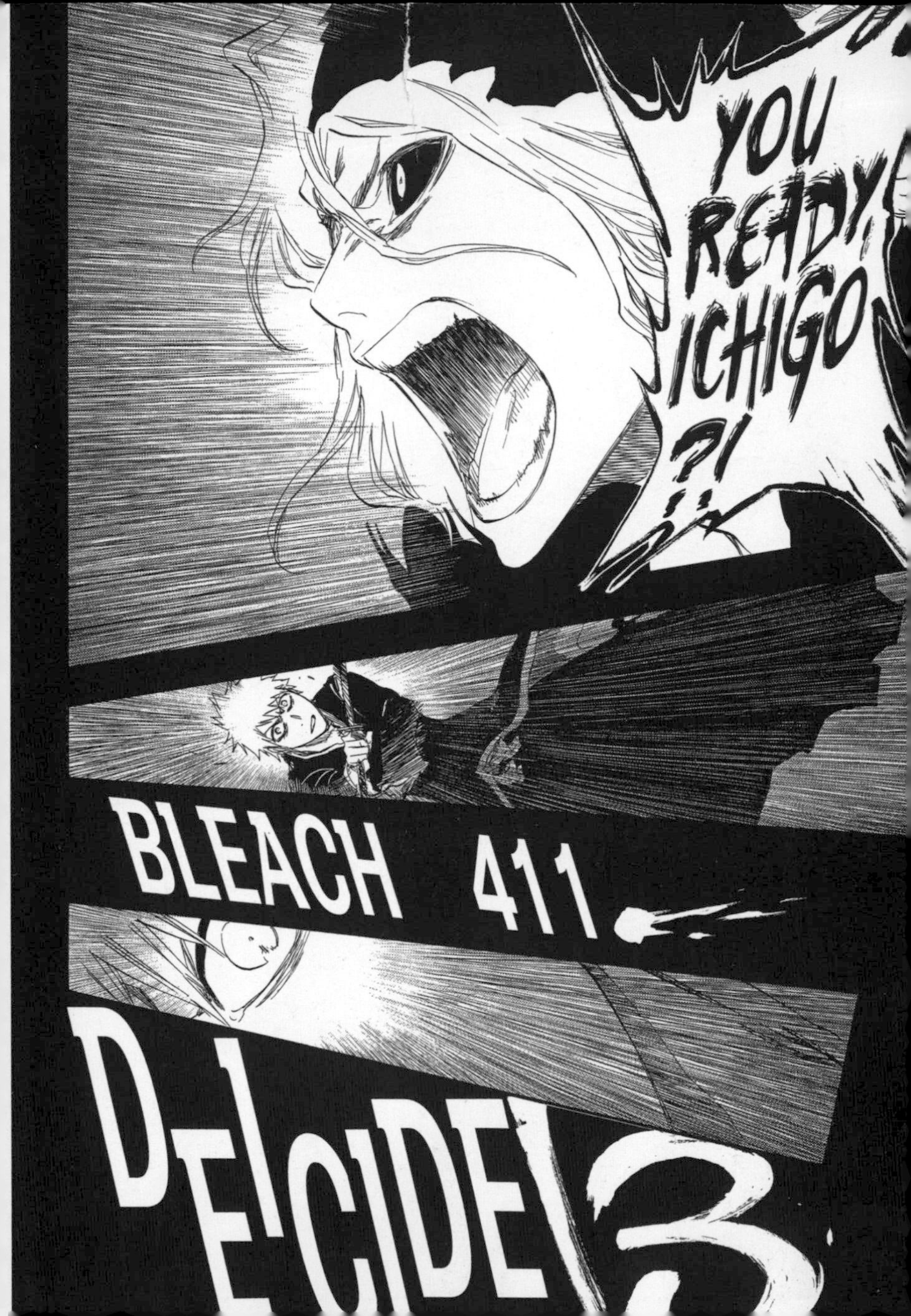
YOU READY, ICHIGO ?!
BLEACH 411.
DEICIDE 3

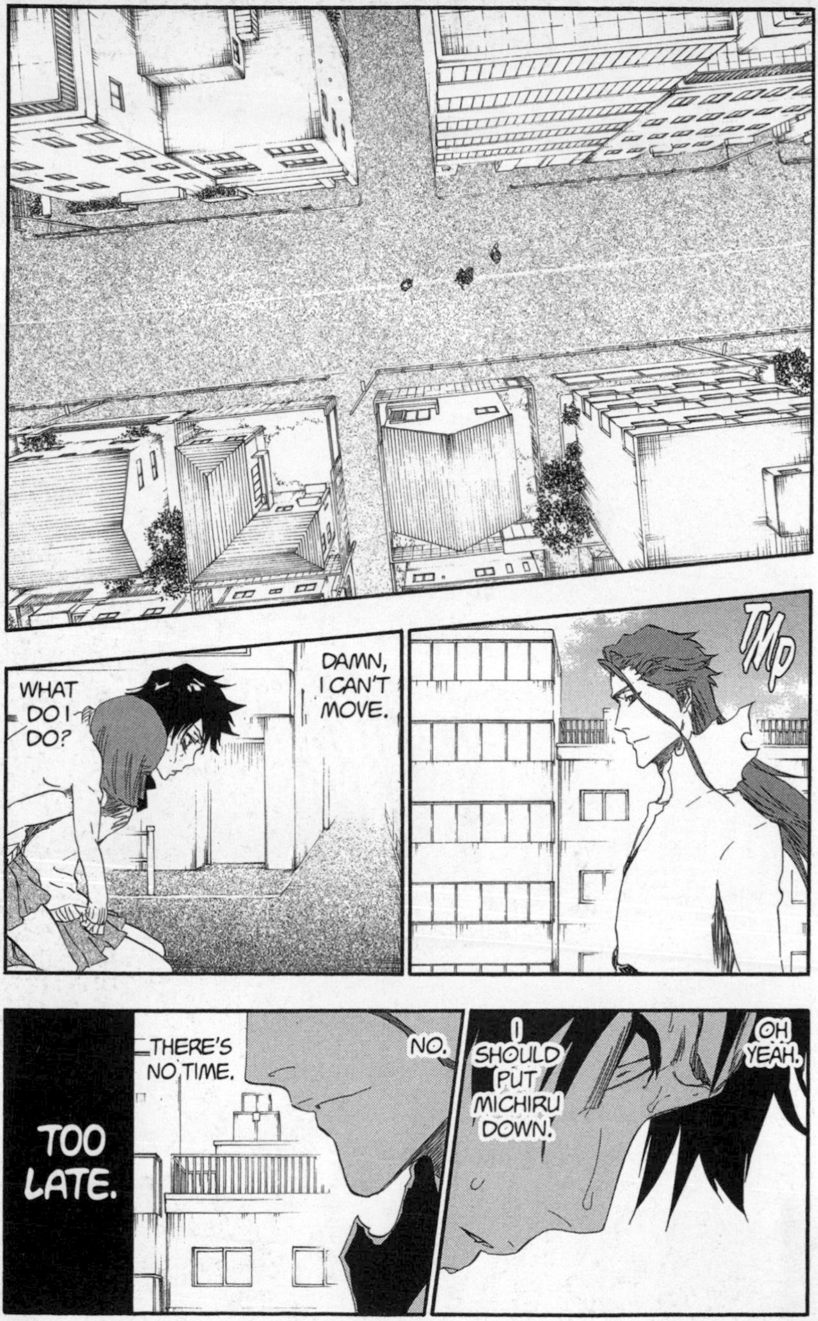
TMP
DAMN, I CAN'T MOVE.
WHAT DO I DO?
OH YEAH.
I SHOULD PUT MICHIRU DOWN.
NO.
THERE'S NO TIME.
TOO LATE.

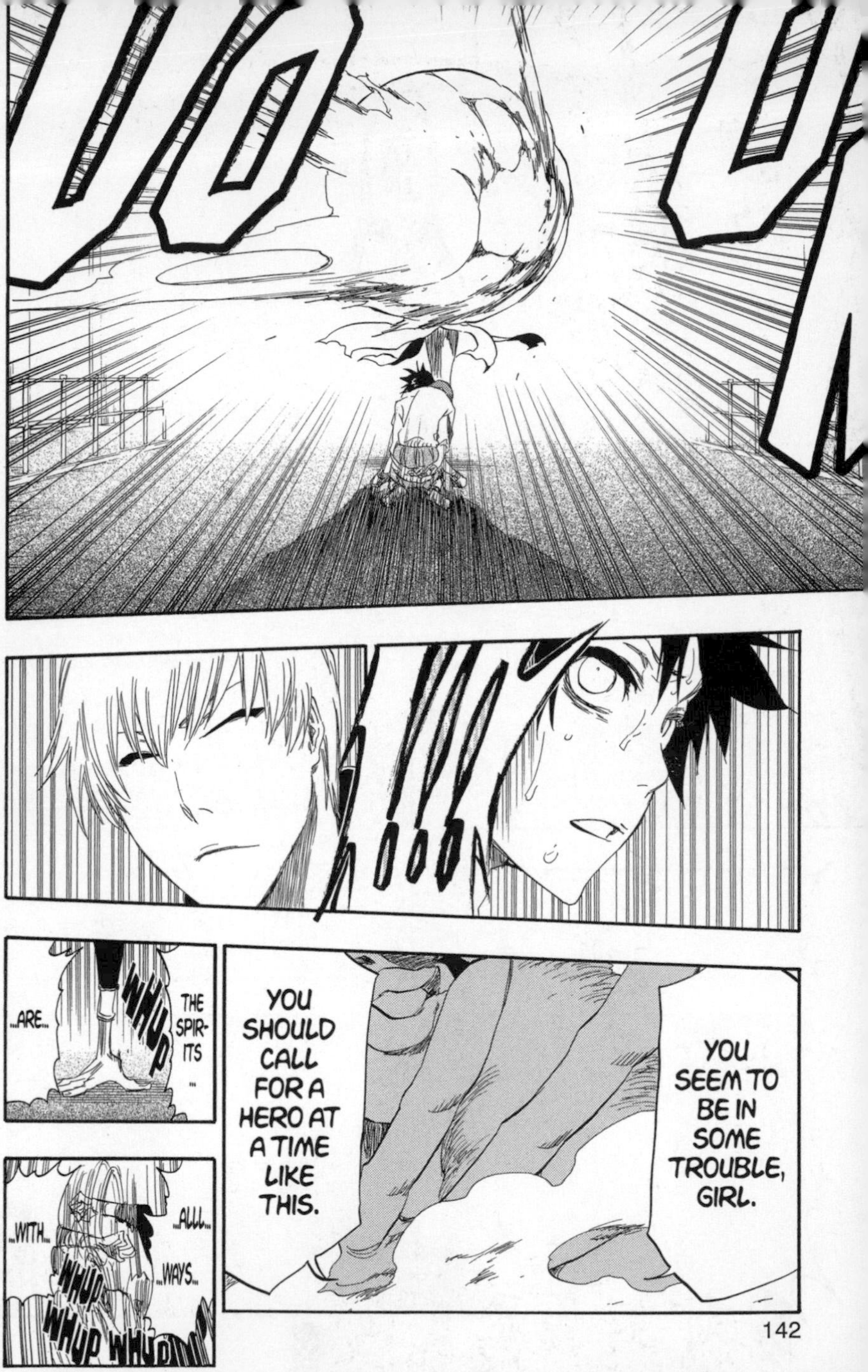
YOU SEEM TO BE IN SOME TROUBLE, GIRL.
YOU SHOULD CALL FOR A HERO AT A TIME LIKE THIS.
THE SPIR-ITS...
WHUP
...ARE...
...ALLL...
...WAYS...
...WITH...
WHUP
WHUP WHUP

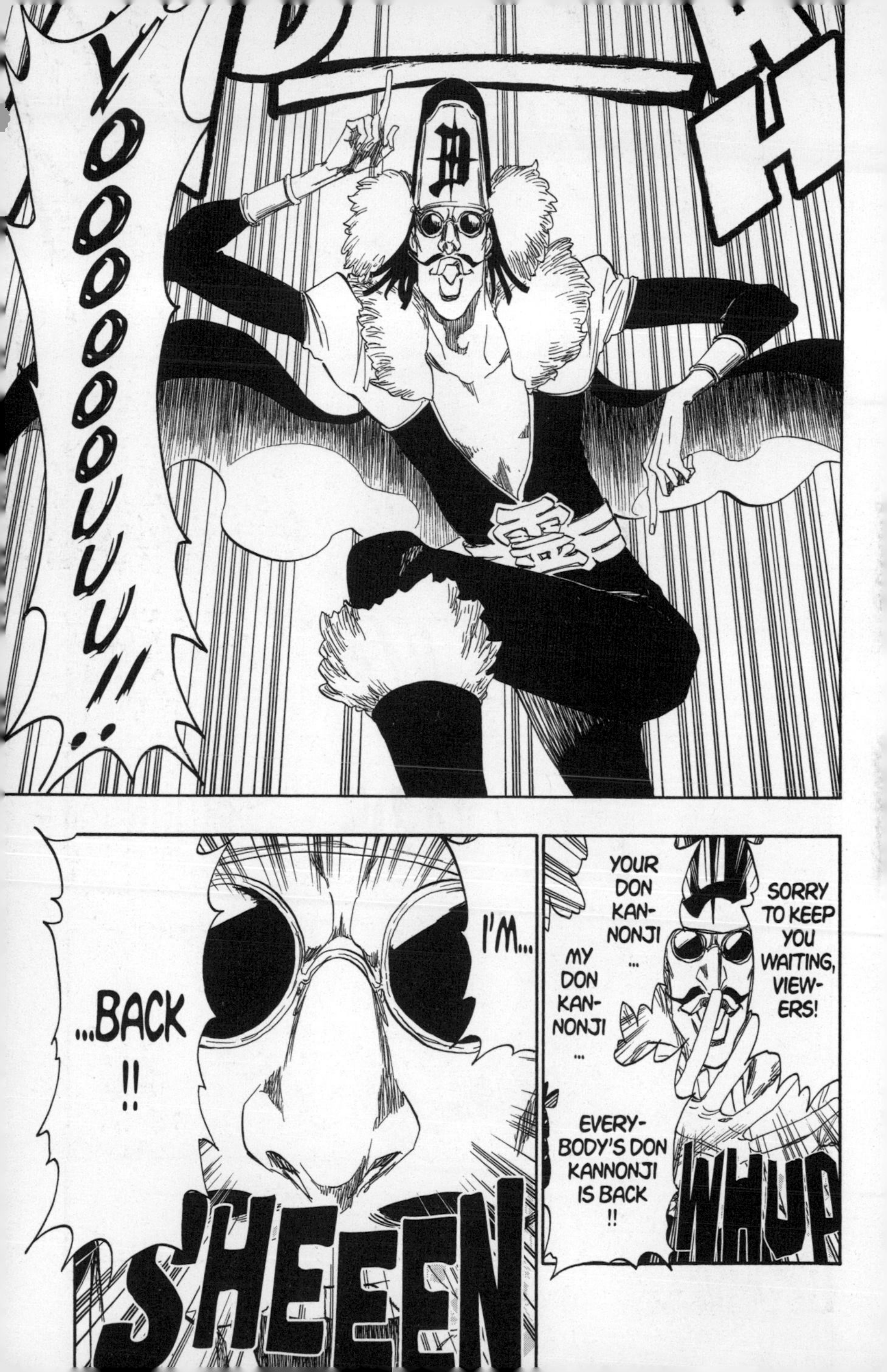
YOOOOOOUUU!!
SORRY TO KEEP YOU WAITING, VIEWERS!
YOUR DON KANNONJI...
MY DON KANNONJI...
EVERYBODY'S DON KANNONJI IS BACK!!
WHUP
I'M...
...BACK!!
SHEEEN

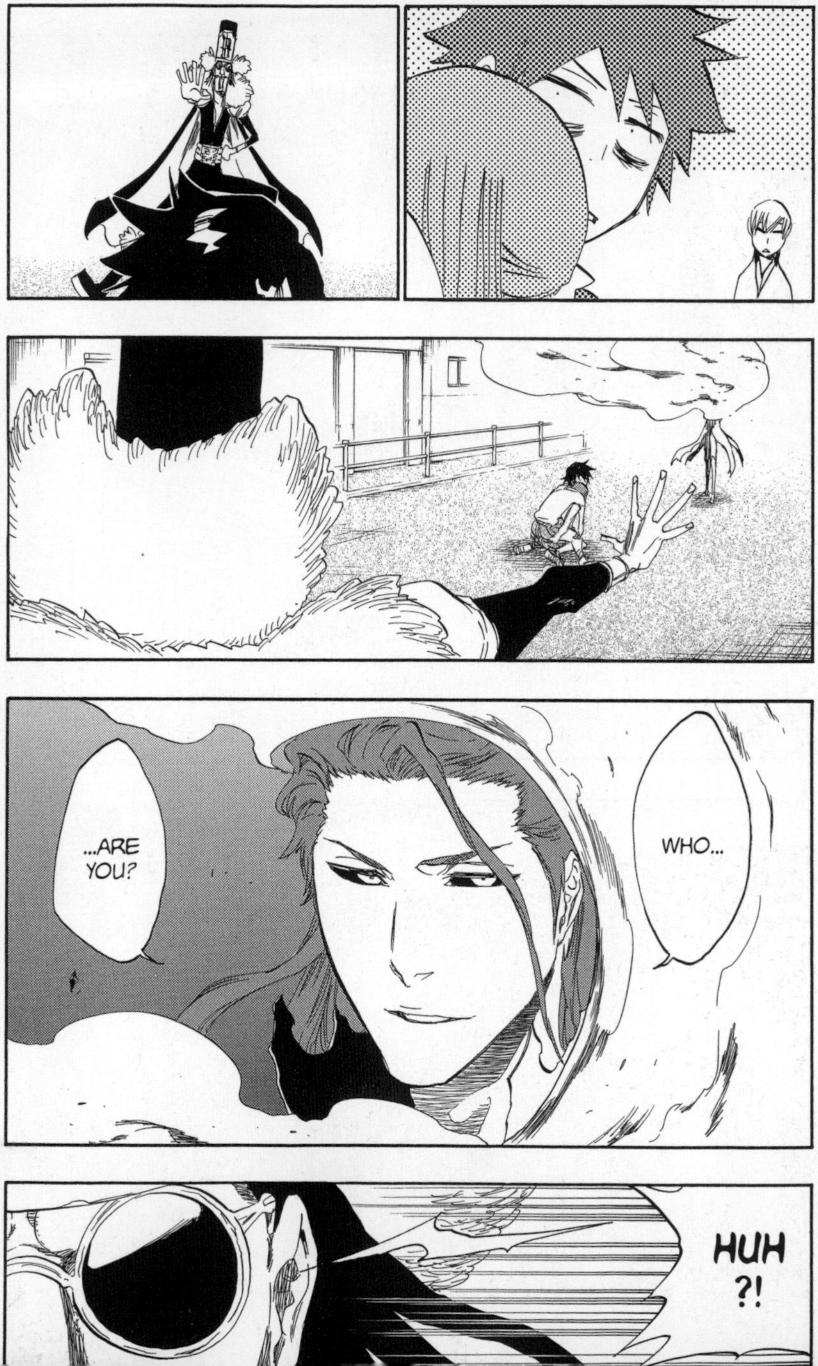
WHO...
...ARE YOU?
HUH ?!

READ THIS WAY

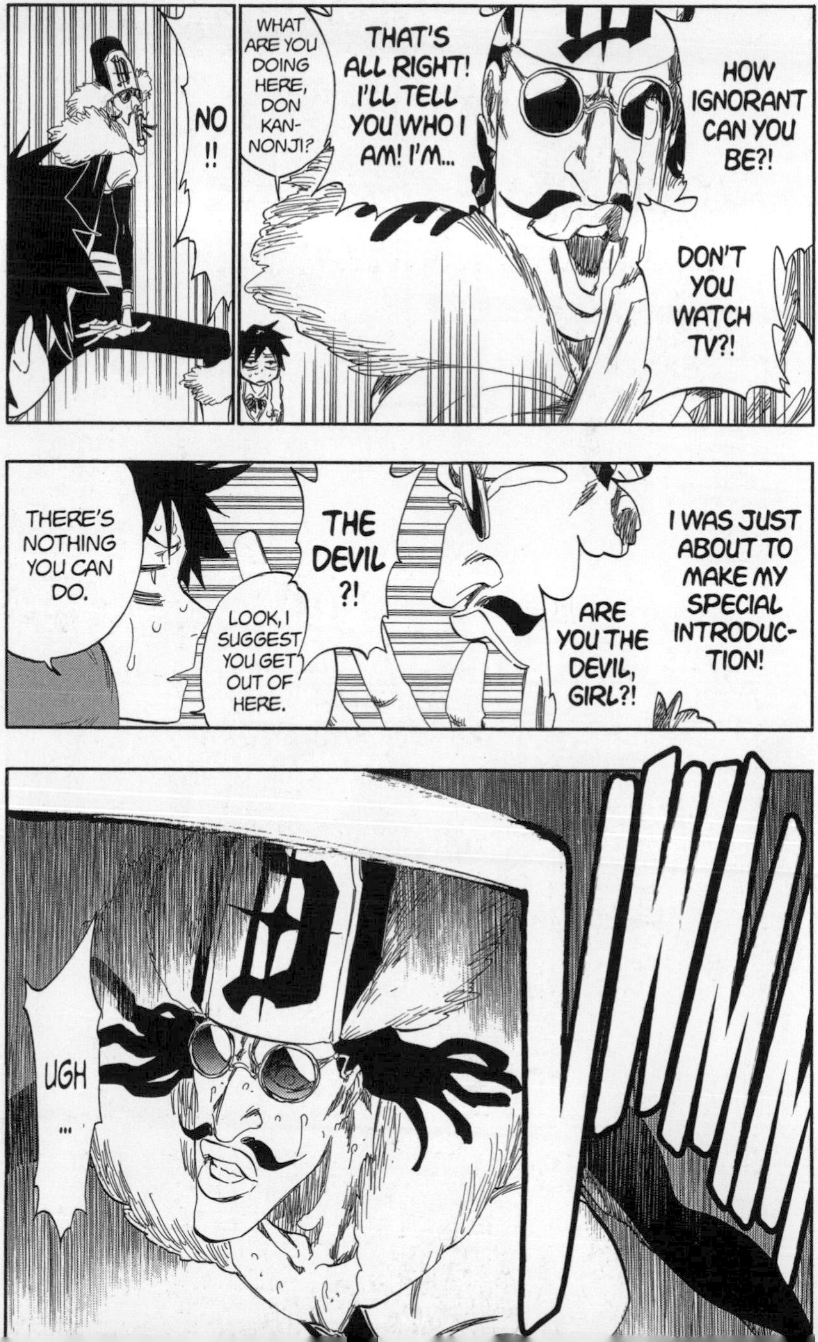
HOW IGNORANT CAN YOU BE?!
DON'T YOU WATCH TV?!
THAT'S ALL RIGHT! I'LL TELL YOU WHO I AM! I'M...
WHAT ARE YOU DOING HERE, DON KAN-NONJI?
NO !!
I WAS JUST ABOUT TO MAKE MY SPECIAL INTRODUC-TION!
ARE YOU THE DEVIL, GIRL?!
THE DEVIL ?!
LOOK, I SUGGEST YOU GET OUT OF HERE.
THERE'S NOTHING YOU CAN DO.
UGH ...

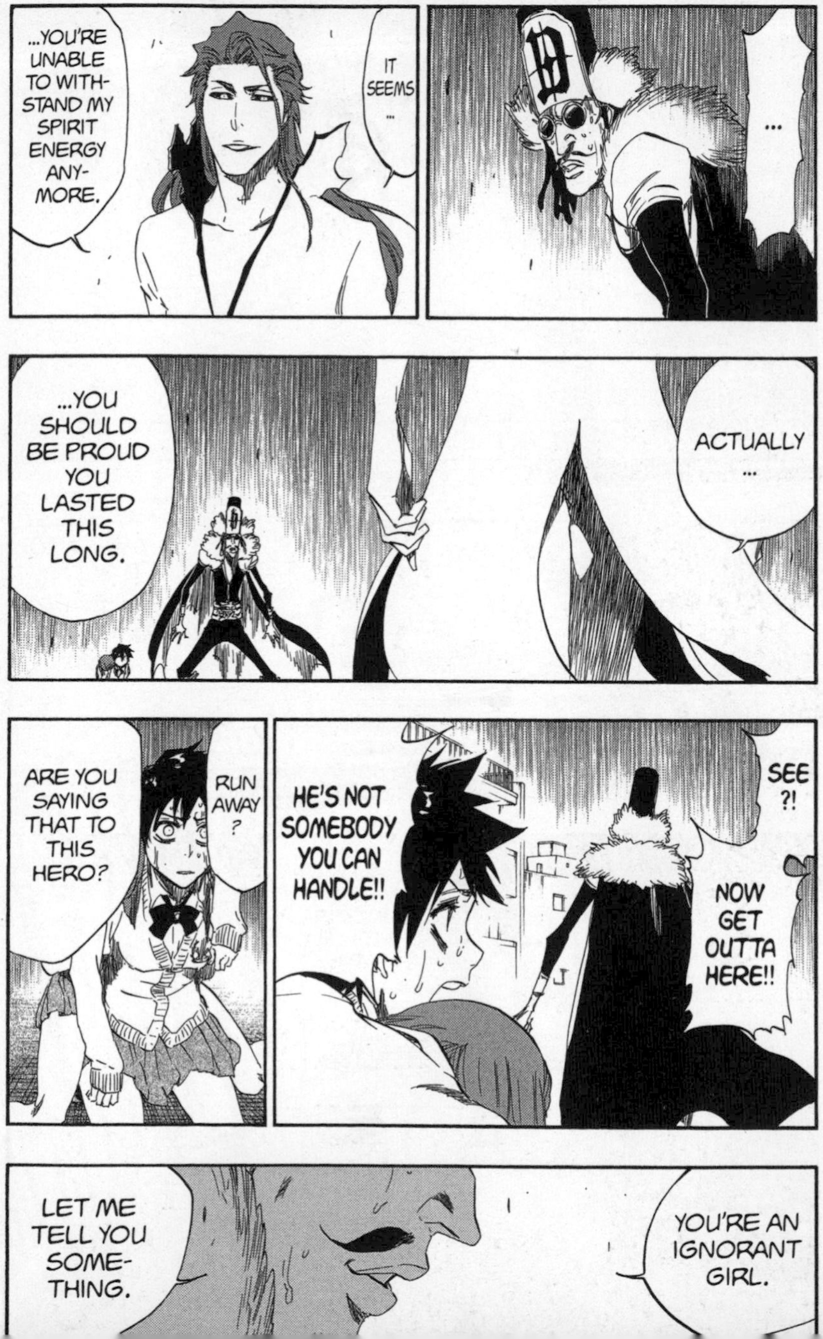
...
IT SEEMS ...
...YOU'RE UNABLE TO WITHSTAND MY SPIRIT ENERGY ANYMORE.
ACTUALLY ...
...YOU SHOULD BE PROUD YOU LASTED THIS LONG.
SEE?!
NOW GET OUTTA HERE!!
HE'S NOT SOMEBODY YOU CAN HANDLE!!
RUN AWAY?
ARE YOU SAYING THAT TO THIS HERO?
YOU'RE AN IGNORANT GIRL.
LET ME TELL YOU SOMETHING.

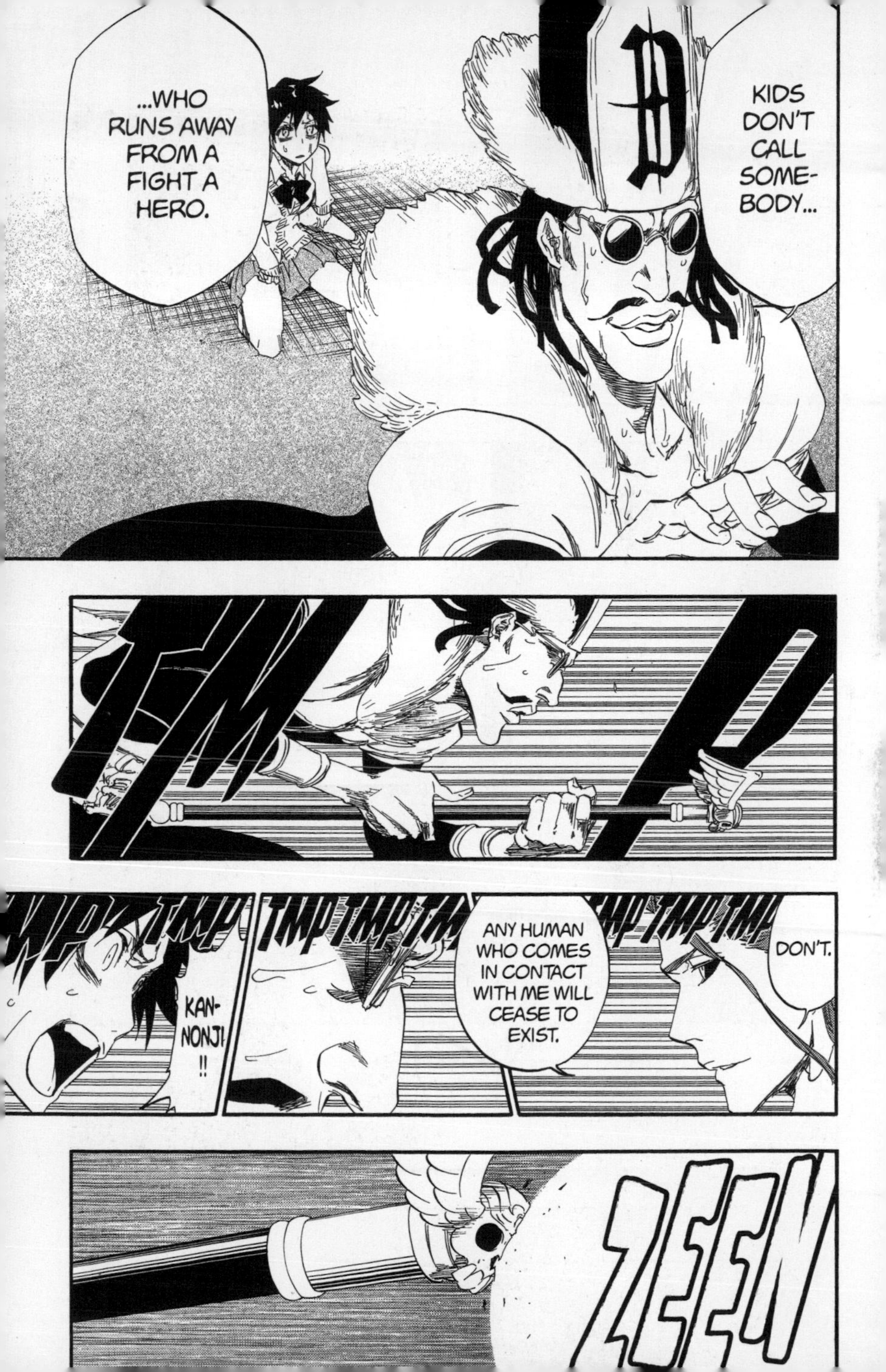
KIDS DON'T CALL SOMEBODY...
...WHO RUNS AWAY FROM A FIGHT A HERO.
TMP
TMP TMP
DON'T.
ANY HUMAN WHO COMES IN CONTACT WITH ME WILL CEASE TO EXIST.
TMP TMP
TMP
KAN-NONJI!!
ZEEN

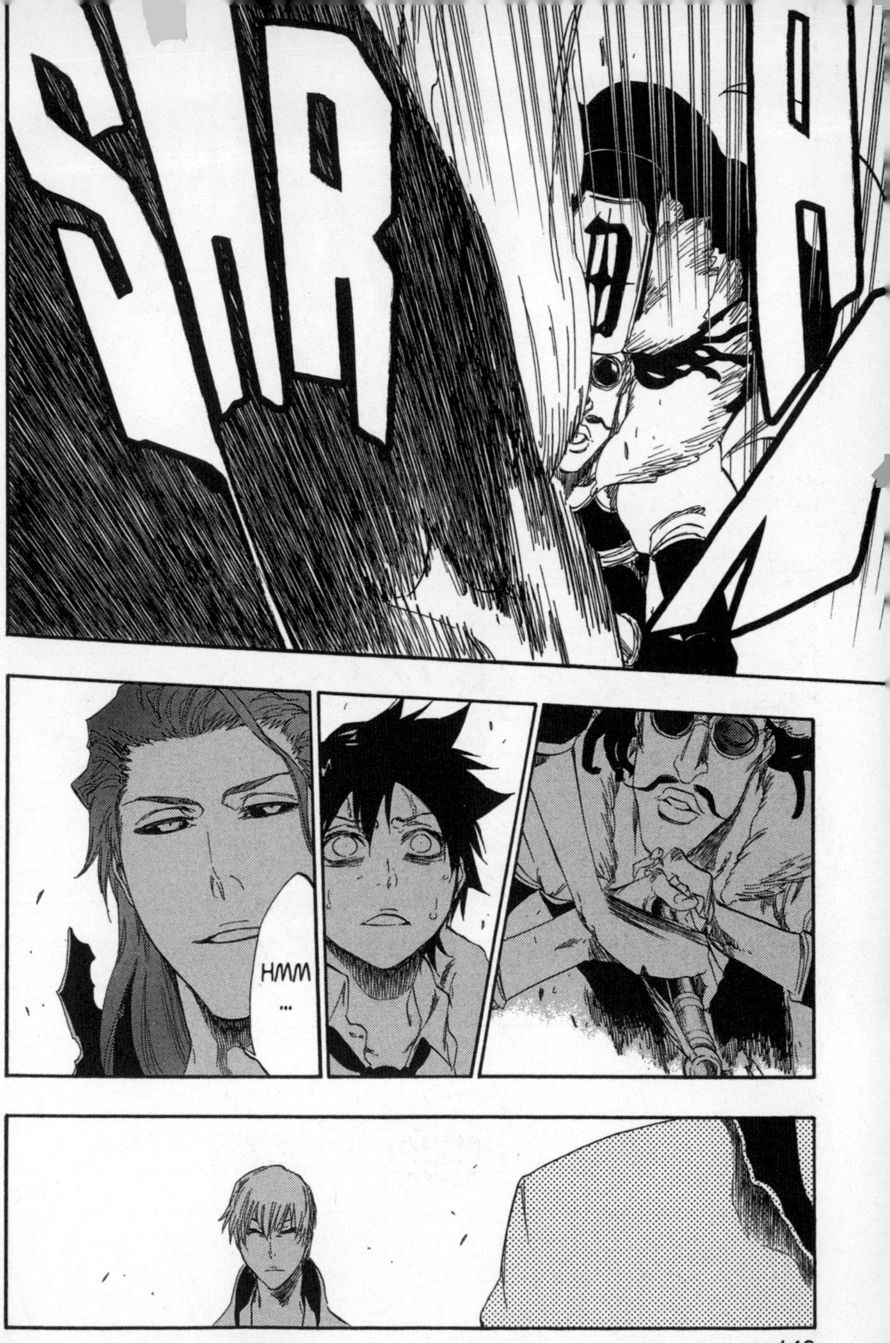
SHRAP
HMM...

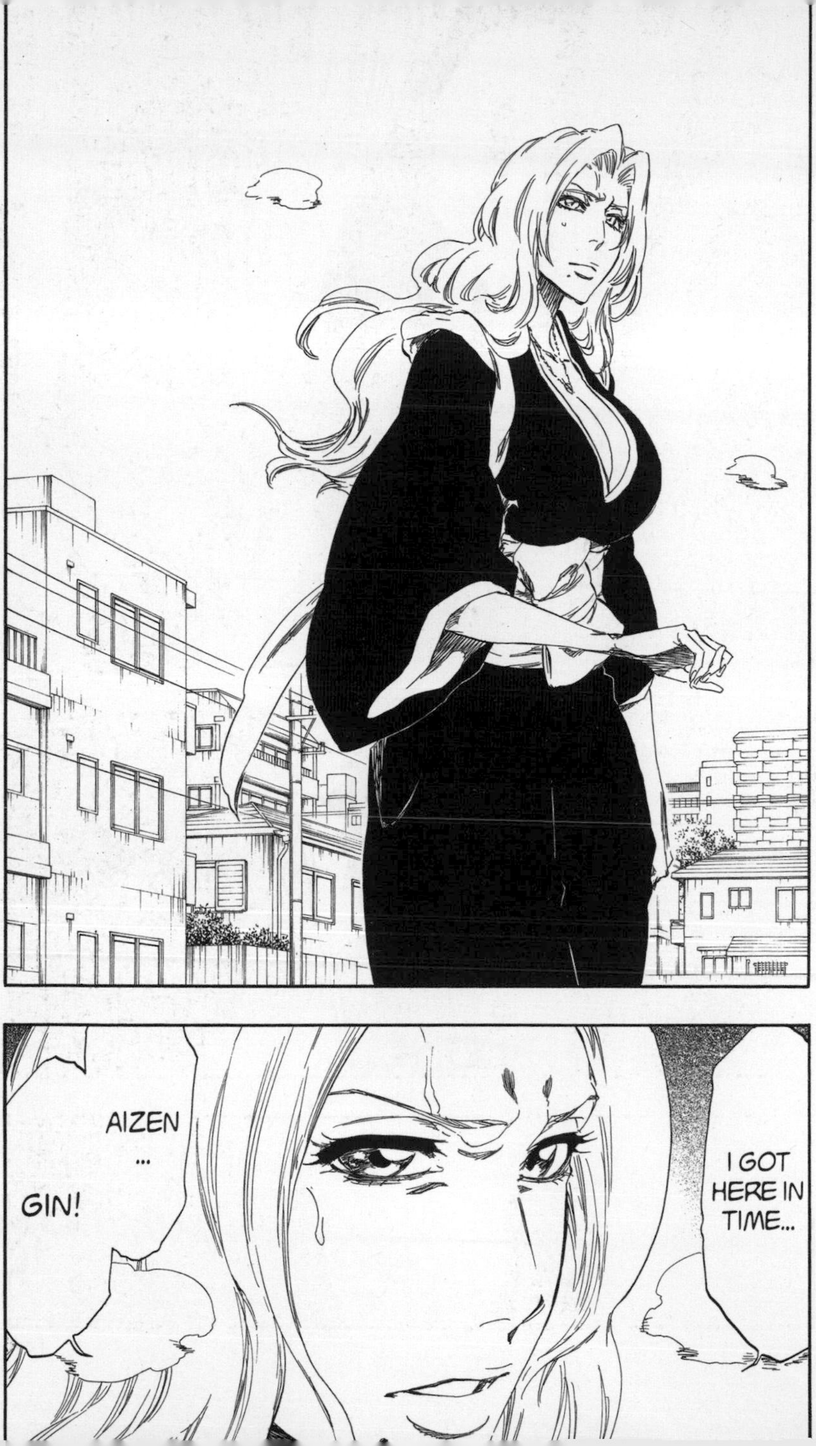
I GOT HERE IN TIME...
AIZEN ... GIN!

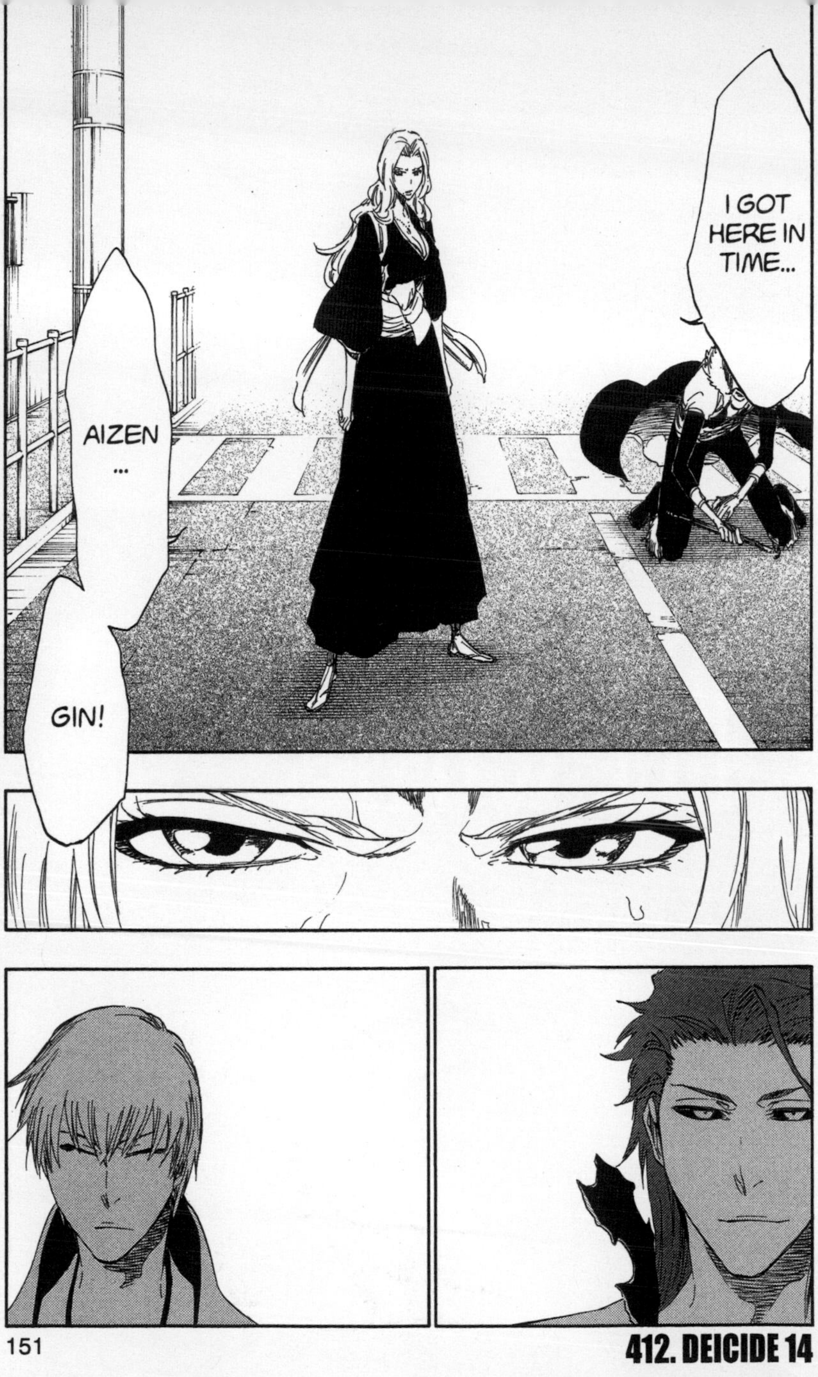
I GOT HERE IN TIME...
AIZEN ...
GIN!

412. DEICIDE 14

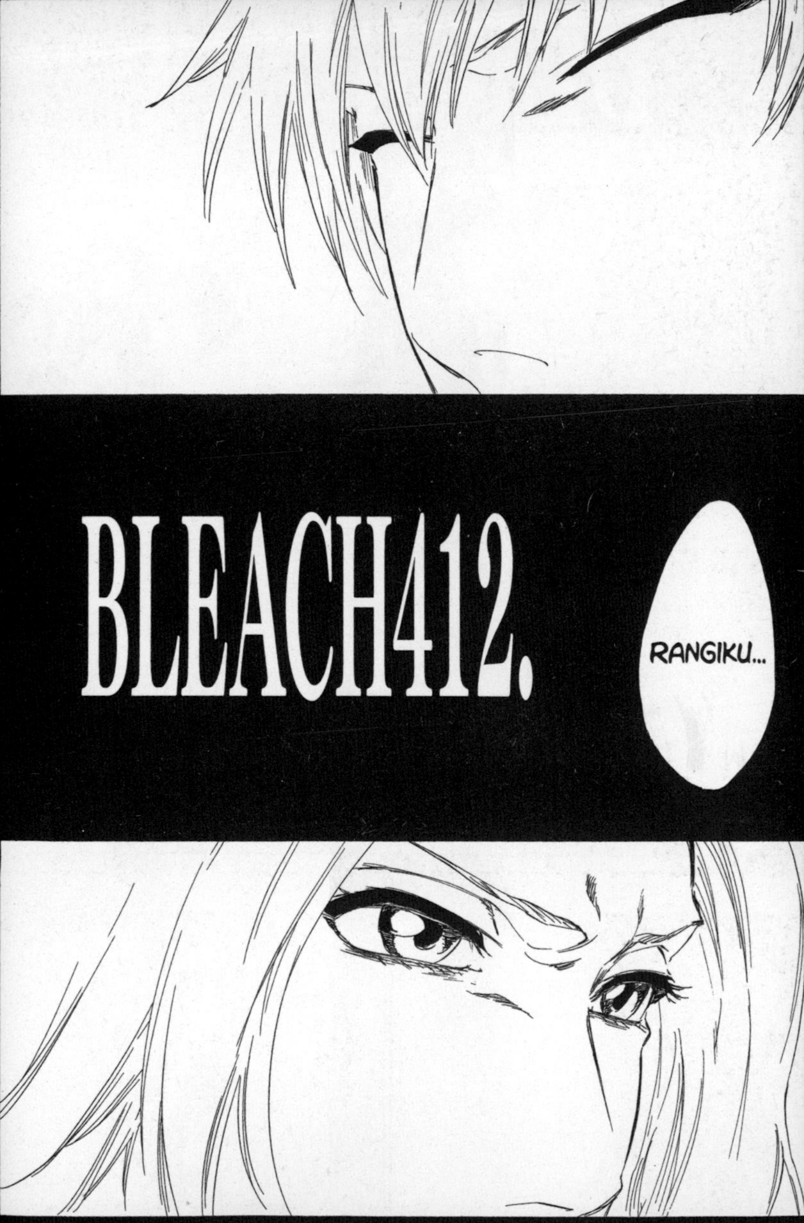
RANGIKU...
BLEACH412.

DEICIDE14

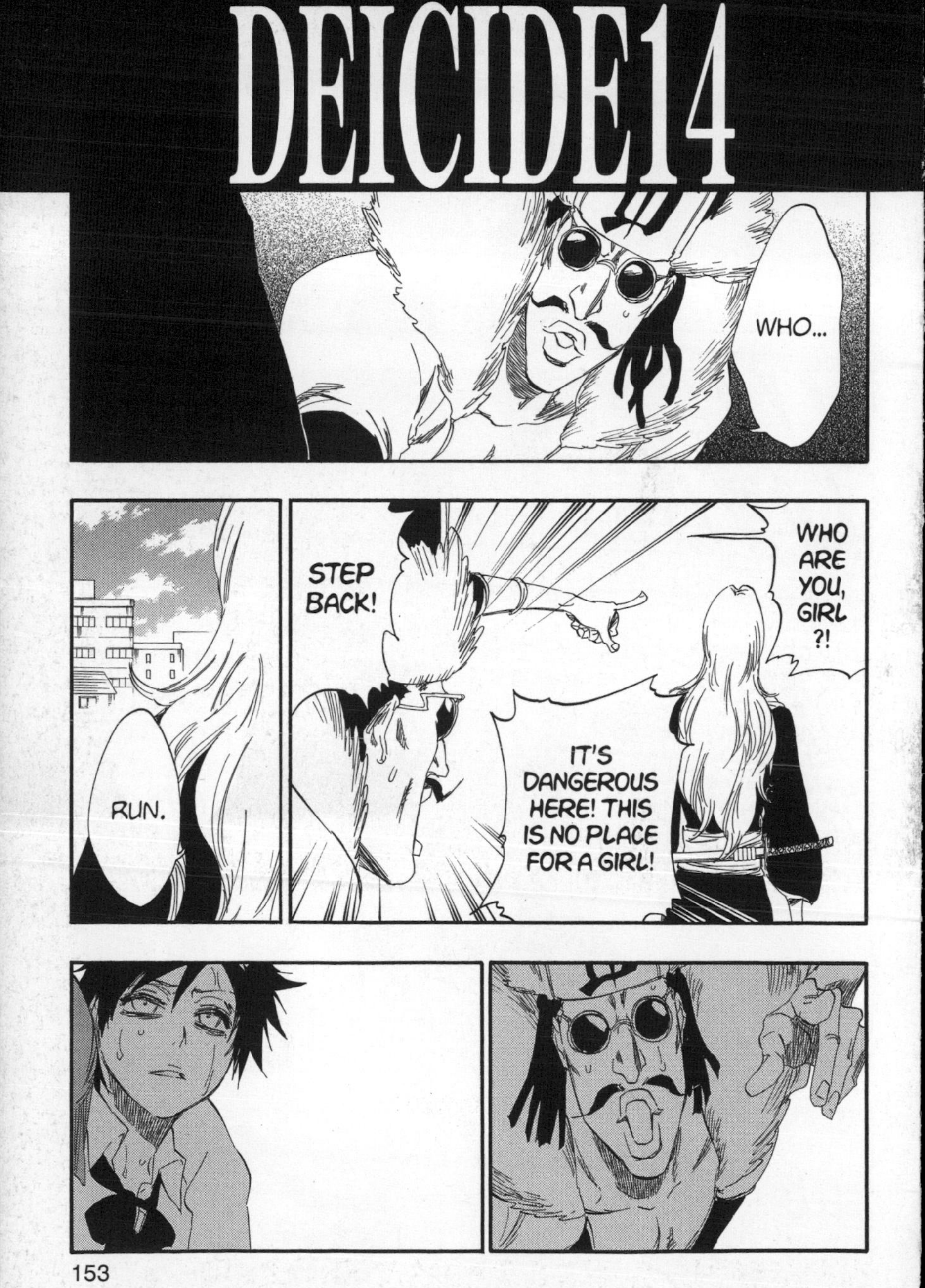
WHO...
WHO ARE YOU, GIRL?!
IT'S DANGEROUS HERE! THIS IS NO PLACE FOR A GIRL!
STEP BACK!
RUN.

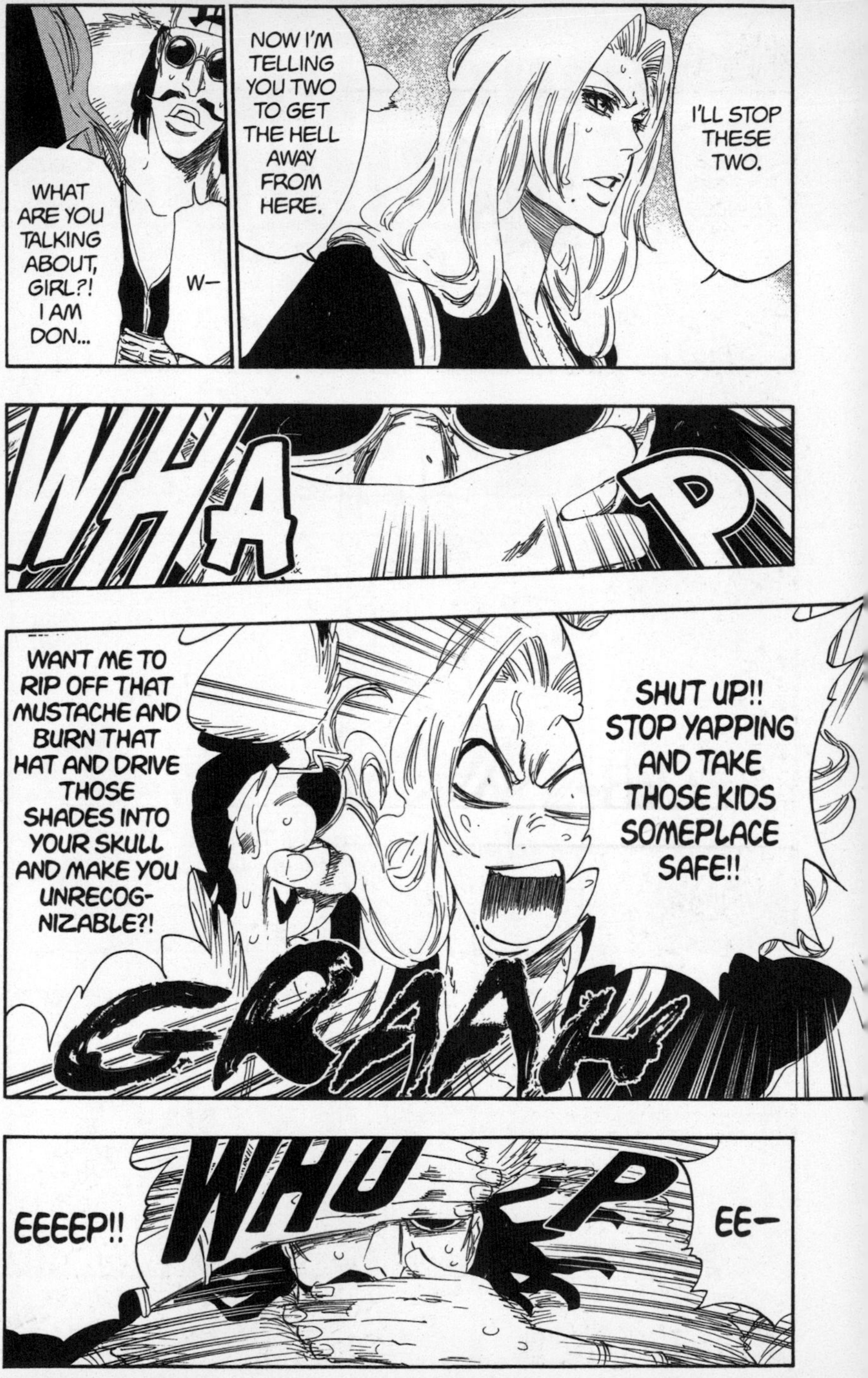
I'LL STOP THESE TWO.
NOW I'M TELLING YOU TWO TO GET THE HELL AWAY FROM HERE.
W—
WHAT ARE YOU TALKING ABOUT, GIRL?! I AM DON...
WHAP
SHUT UP!! STOP YAPPING AND TAKE THOSE KIDS SOMEPLACE SAFE!!
WANT ME TO RIP OFF THAT MUSTACHE AND BURN THAT HAT AND DRIVE THOSE SHADES INTO YOUR SKULL AND MAKE YOU UNRECOG-NIZABLE?!
GRAAH
EE—
EEEEP!!

READ THIS WAY

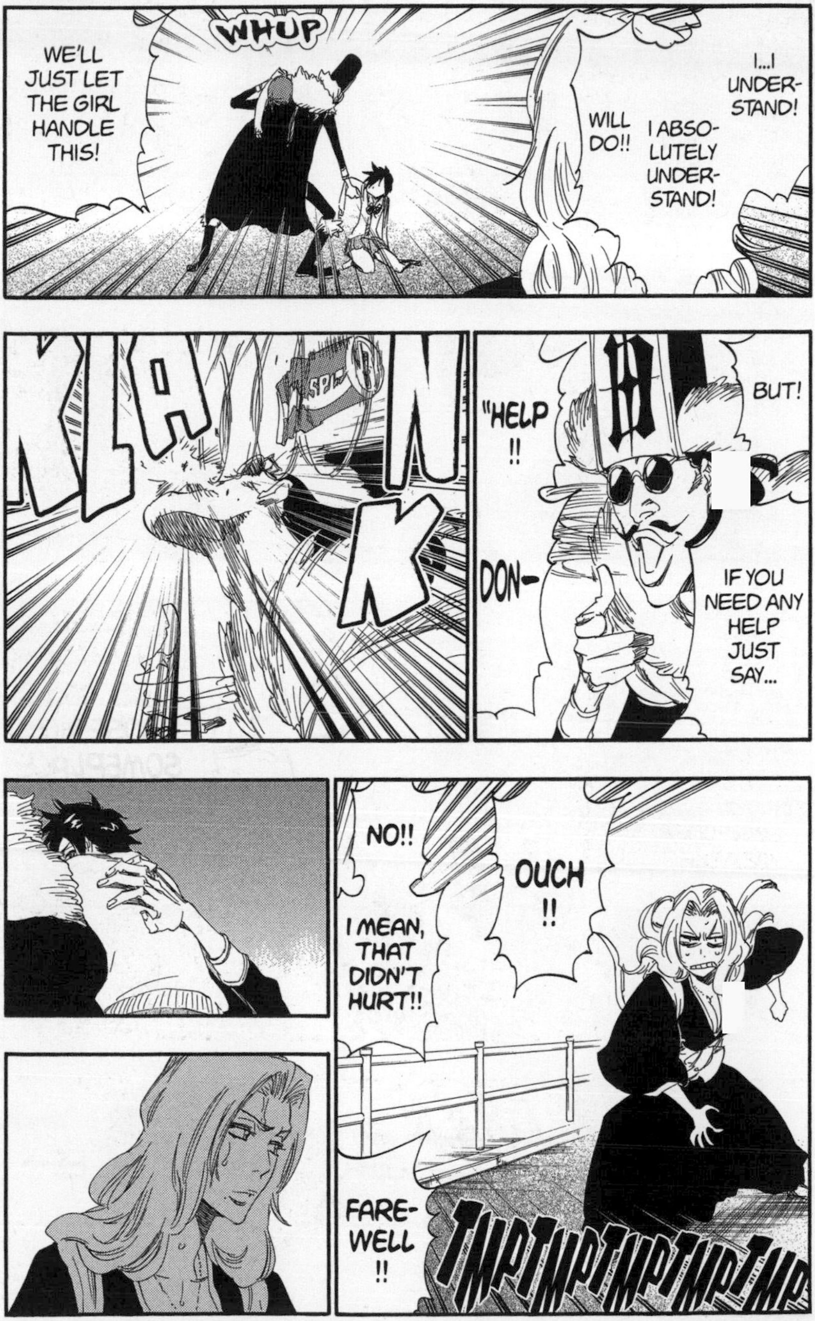
I...I UNDERSTAND!
I ABSOLUTELY UNDERSTAND!
WILL DO!!
WHUP
WE'LL JUST LET THE GIRL HANDLE THIS!
BUT!
IF YOU NEED ANY HELP JUST SAY...
"HELP!!
DON-
NO!!
OUCH!!
I MEAN, THAT DIDN'T HURT!!
FAREWELL!!
TMP TMP TMP TMP TMP

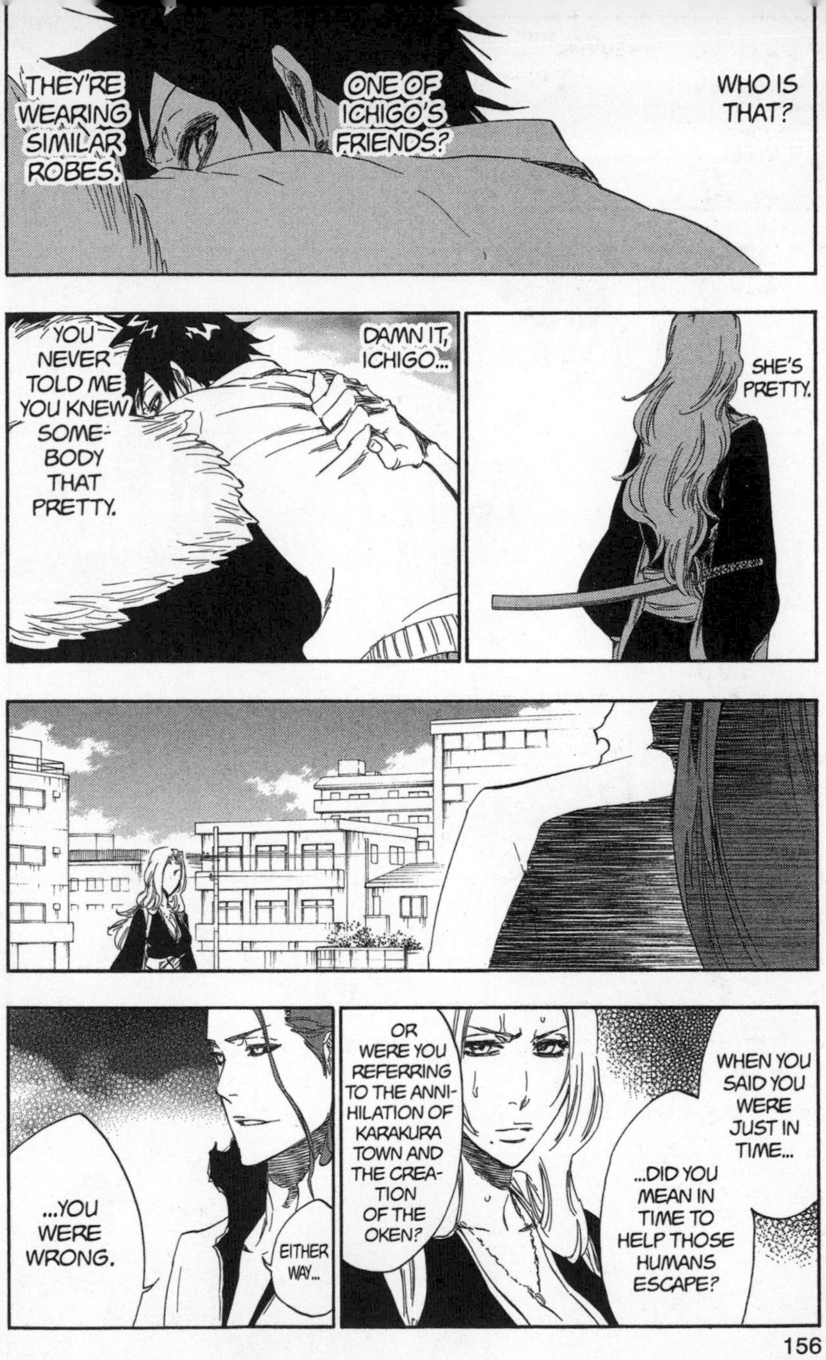
WHO IS THAT?
ONE OF ICHIGO'S FRIENDS?
THEY'RE WEARING SIMILAR ROBES.
SHE'S PRETTY.
DAMN IT, ICHIGO...
YOU NEVER TOLD ME YOU KNEW SOME-BODY THAT PRETTY.
WHEN YOU SAID YOU WERE JUST IN TIME...
...DID YOU MEAN IN TIME TO HELP THOSE HUMANS ESCAPE?
OR WERE YOU REFERRING TO THE ANNI-HILATION OF KARAKURA TOWN AND THE CREA-TION OF THE OKEN?
EITHER WAY...
...YOU WERE WRONG.

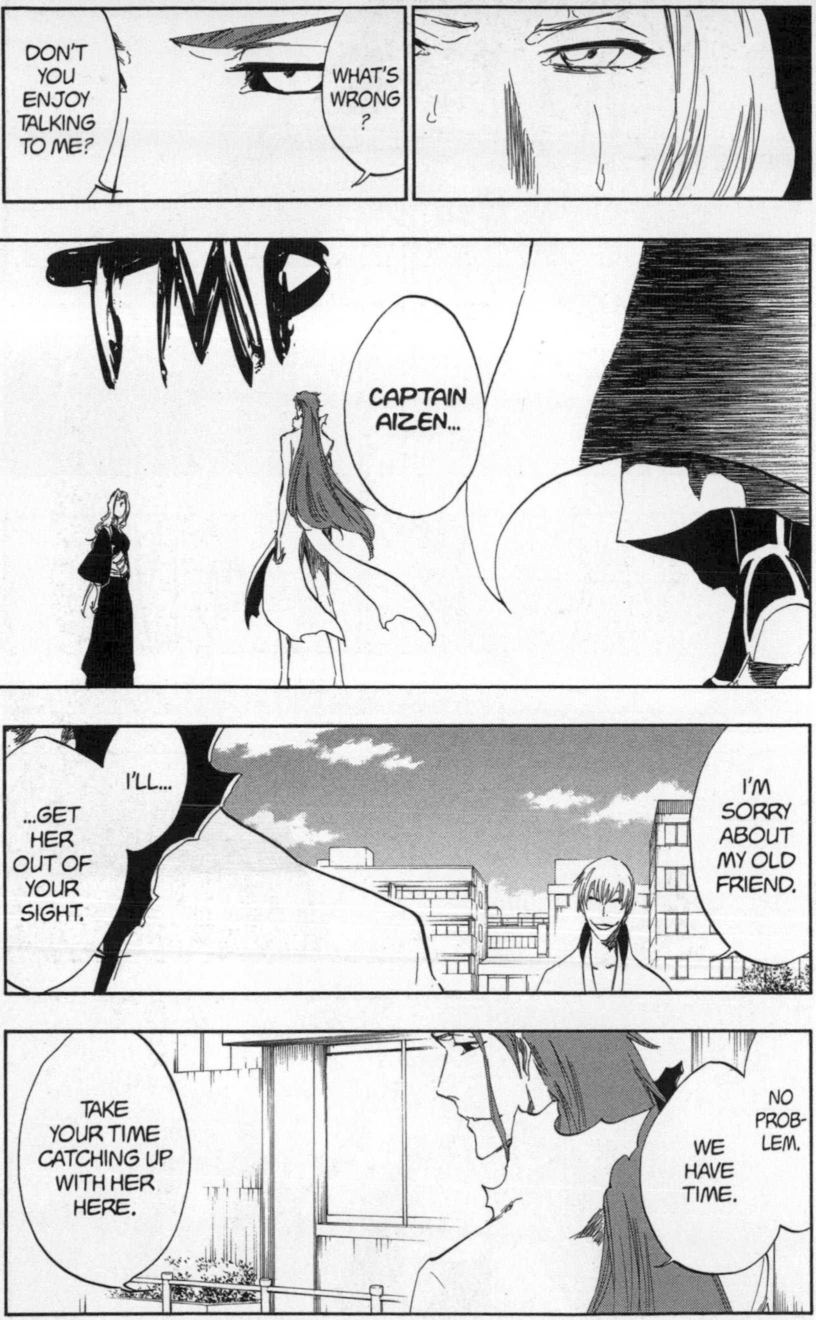
WHAT'S WRONG?
DON'T YOU ENJOY TALKING TO ME?
TMP
CAPTAIN AIZEN...
I'M SORRY ABOUT MY OLD FRIEND.
I'LL...
...GET HER OUT OF YOUR SIGHT.
NO PROBLEM.
WE HAVE TIME.
TAKE YOUR TIME CATCHING UP WITH HER HERE.

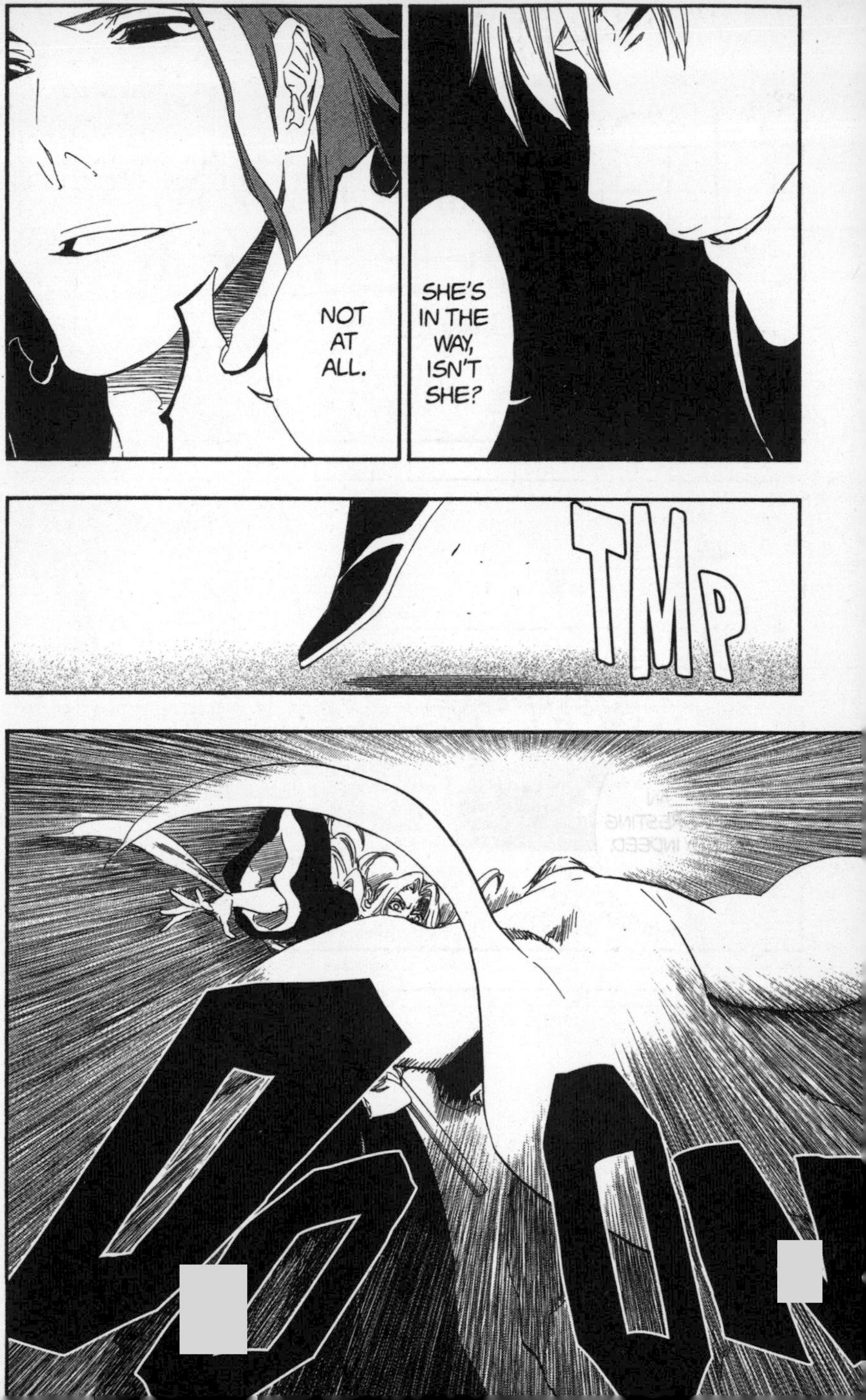
SHE'S IN THE WAY, ISN'T SHE?
NOT AT ALL.
TMP

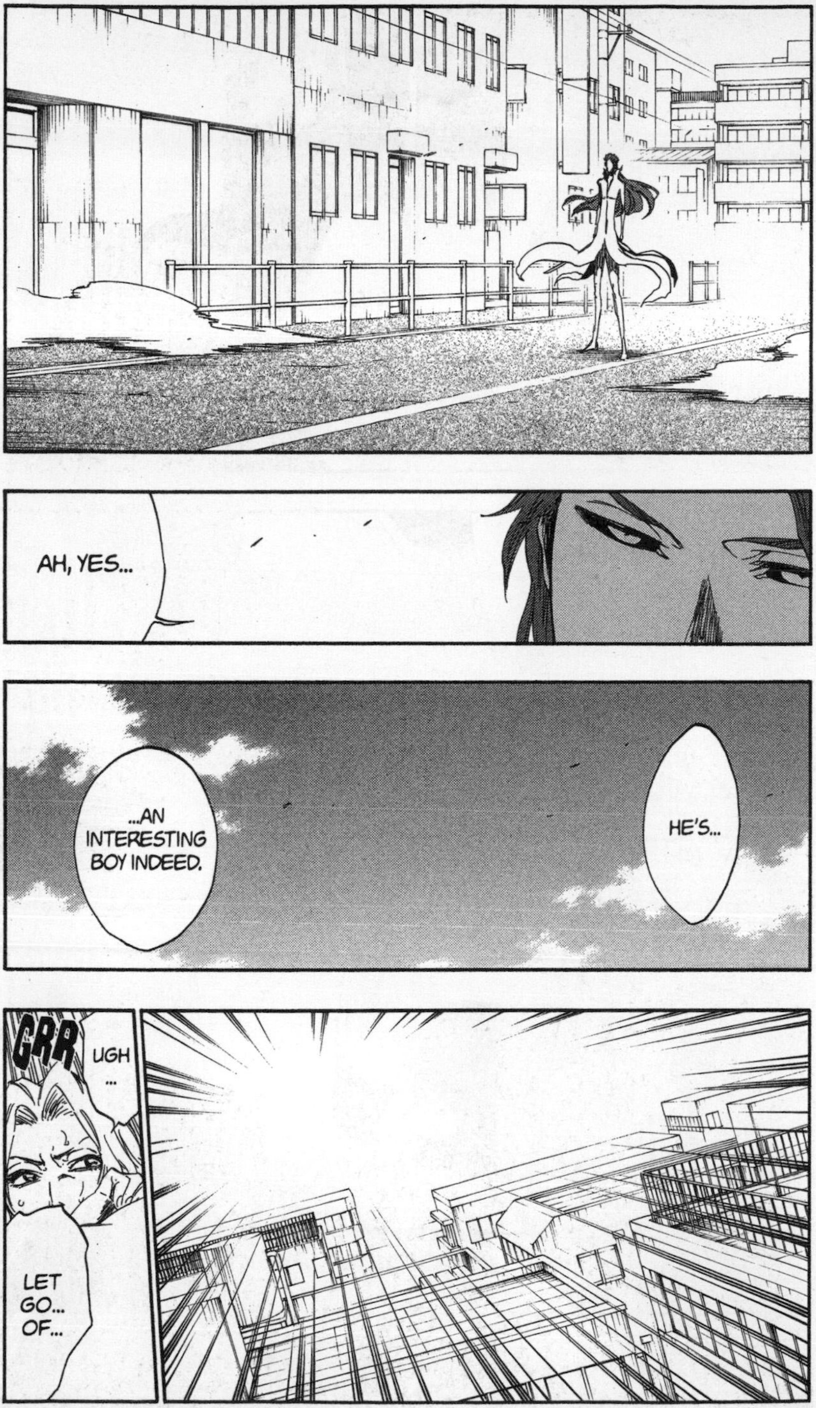
AH, YES...
HE'S...
...AN INTERESTING BOY INDEED.
GRR
UGH ...
LET GO... OF...

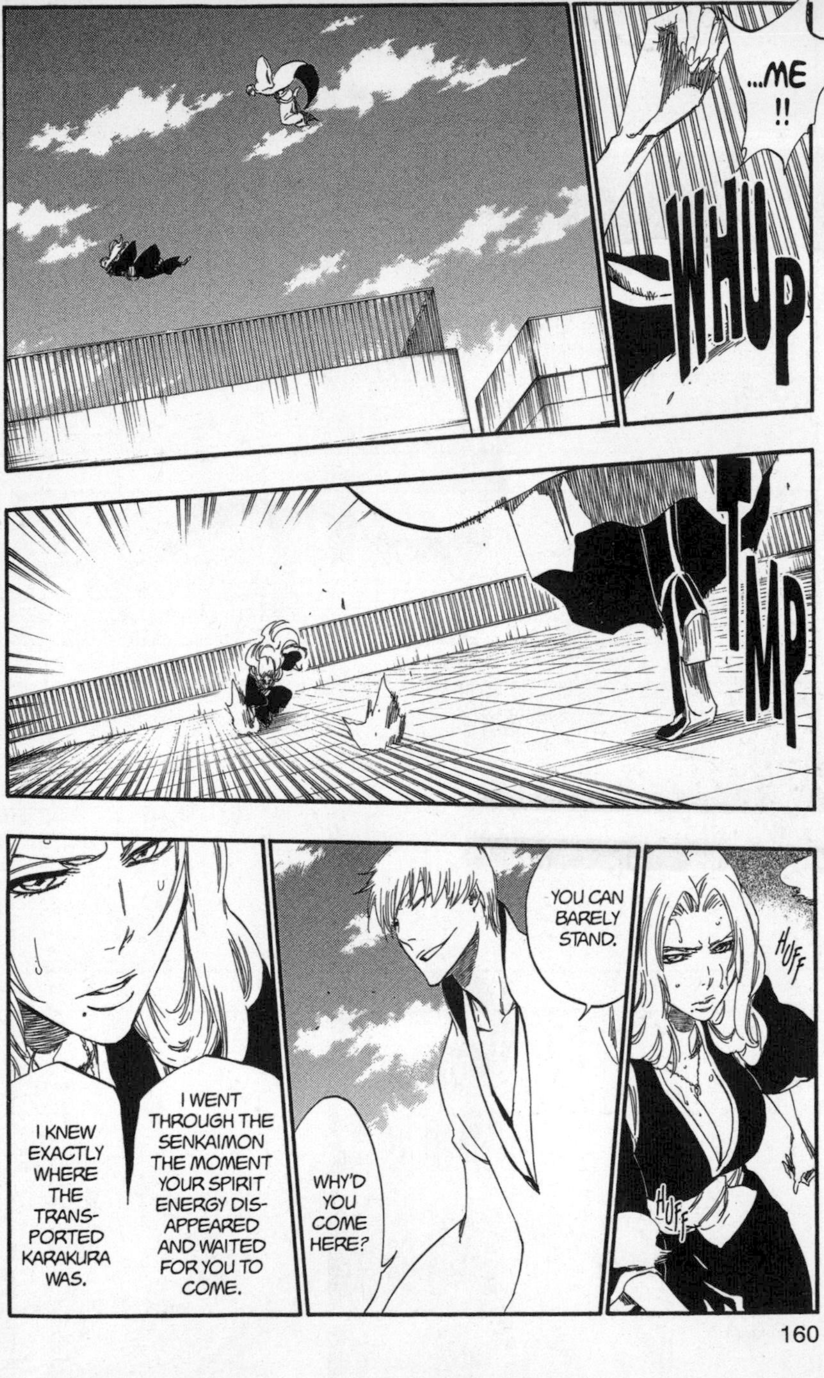
...ME !!
WHUP
TMP
YOU CAN BARELY STAND.
HUFF
HUFF
WHY'D YOU COME HERE?
I WENT THROUGH THE SENKAIMON THE MOMENT YOUR SPIRIT ENERGY DIS-APPEARED AND WAITED FOR YOU TO COME.
I KNEW EXACTLY WHERE THE TRANS-PORTED KARAKURA WAS.

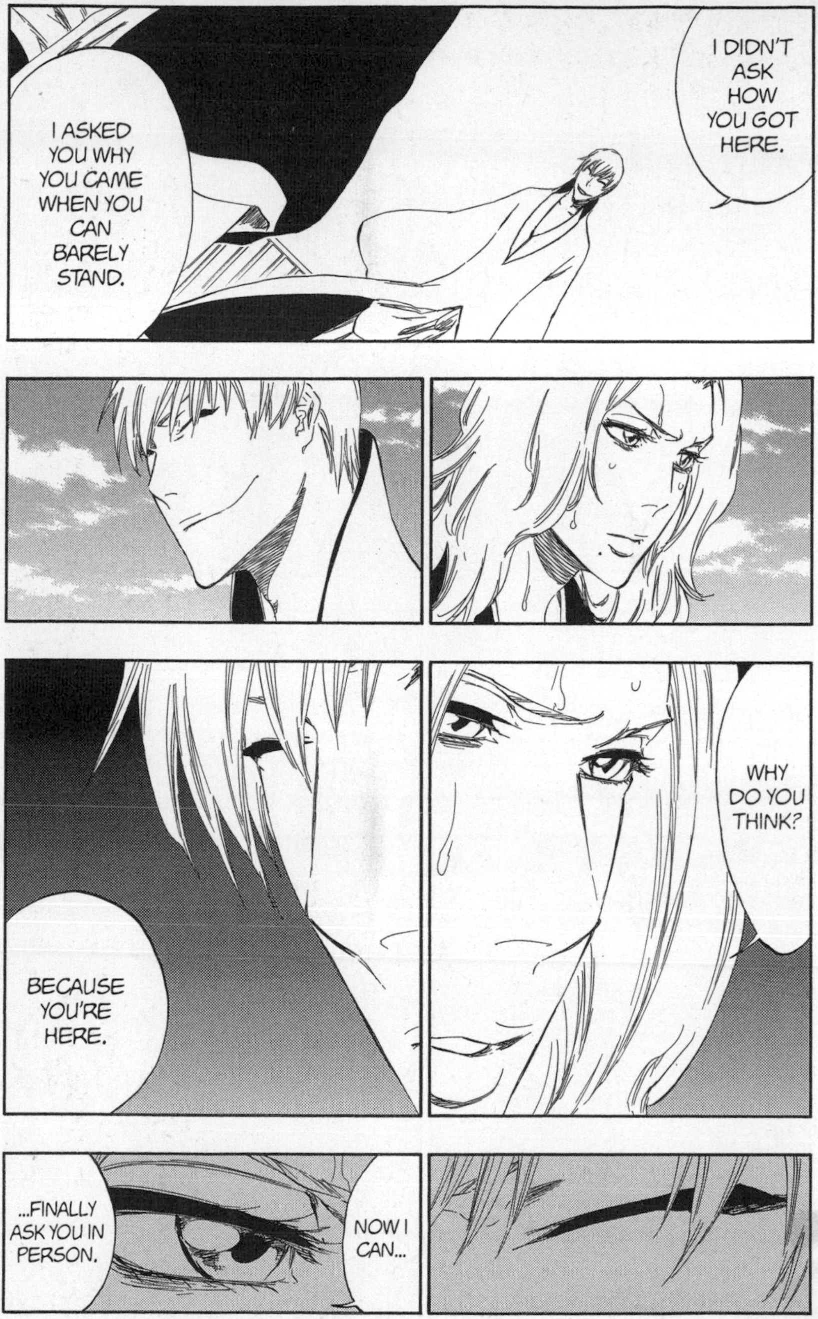
I DIDN'T ASK HOW YOU GOT HERE.
I ASKED YOU WHY YOU CAME WHEN YOU CAN BARELY STAND.
WHY DO YOU THINK?
BECAUSE YOU'RE HERE.
NOW I CAN...
...FINALLY ASK YOU IN PERSON.

...CHOOSE TO SERVE AIZEN?

WHY DID YOU ...

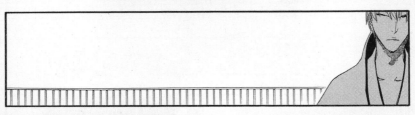

ARE YOU ...

...SERI-OUS?

WHY DID YOU BETRAY KIRA WHO TRUSTED YOU SO COMPLETE-LY?

WHY ?

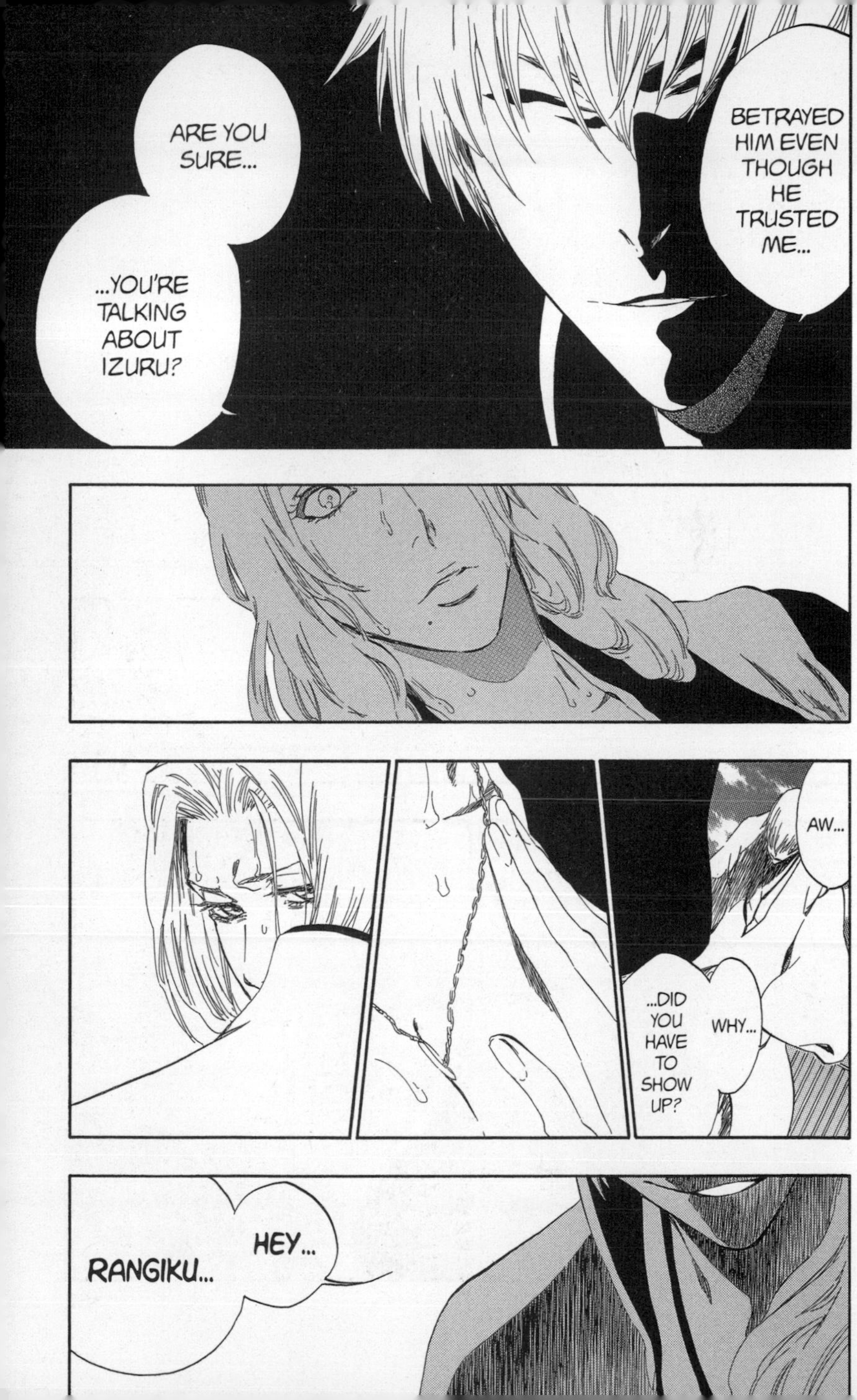
BETRAYED HIM EVEN THOUGH HE TRUSTED ME...
ARE YOU SURE...
...YOU'RE TALKING ABOUT IZURU?
AW...
WHY...
...DID YOU HAVE TO SHOW UP?
HEY...
RANGIKU...

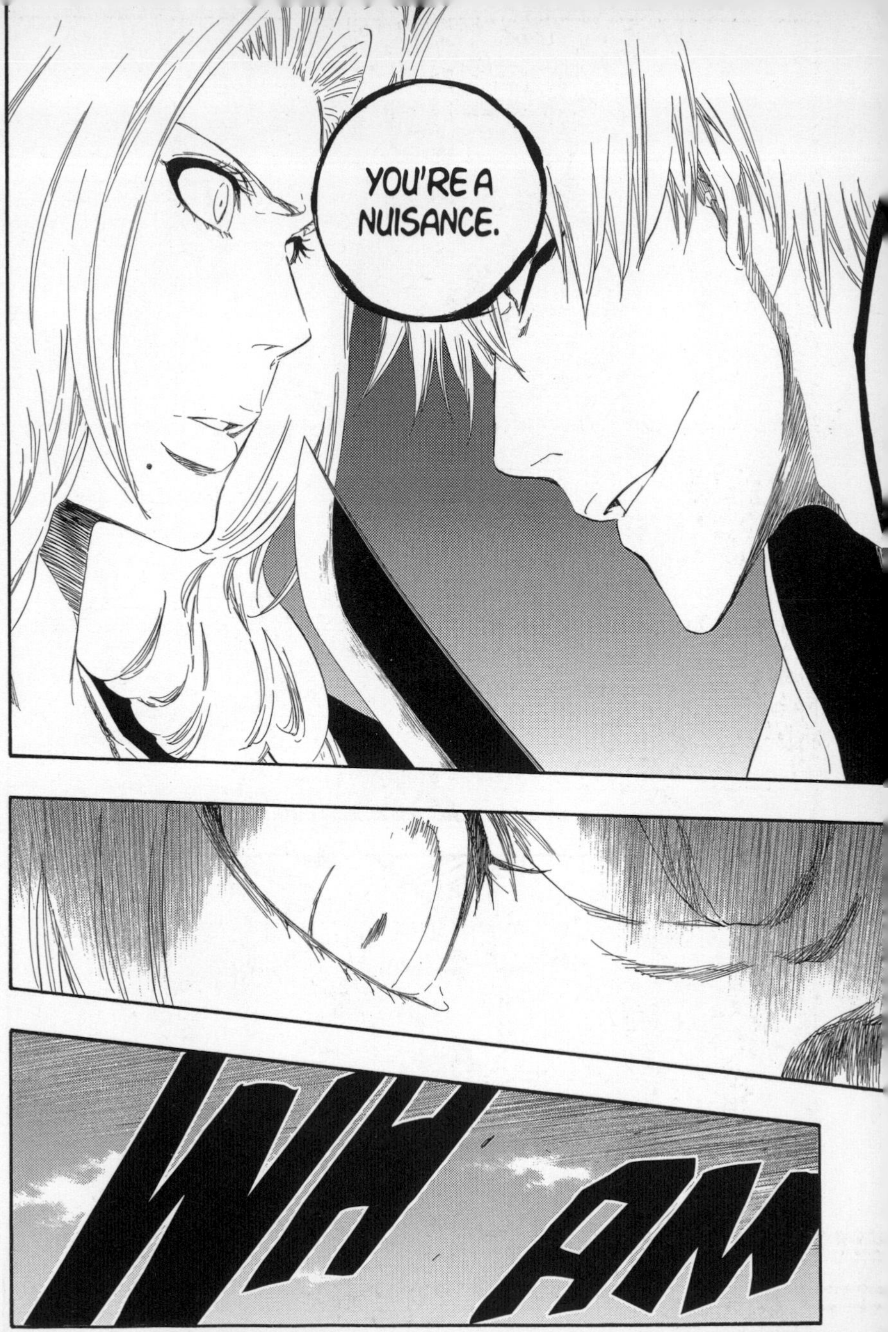
YOU'RE A NUISANCE.
WHAM

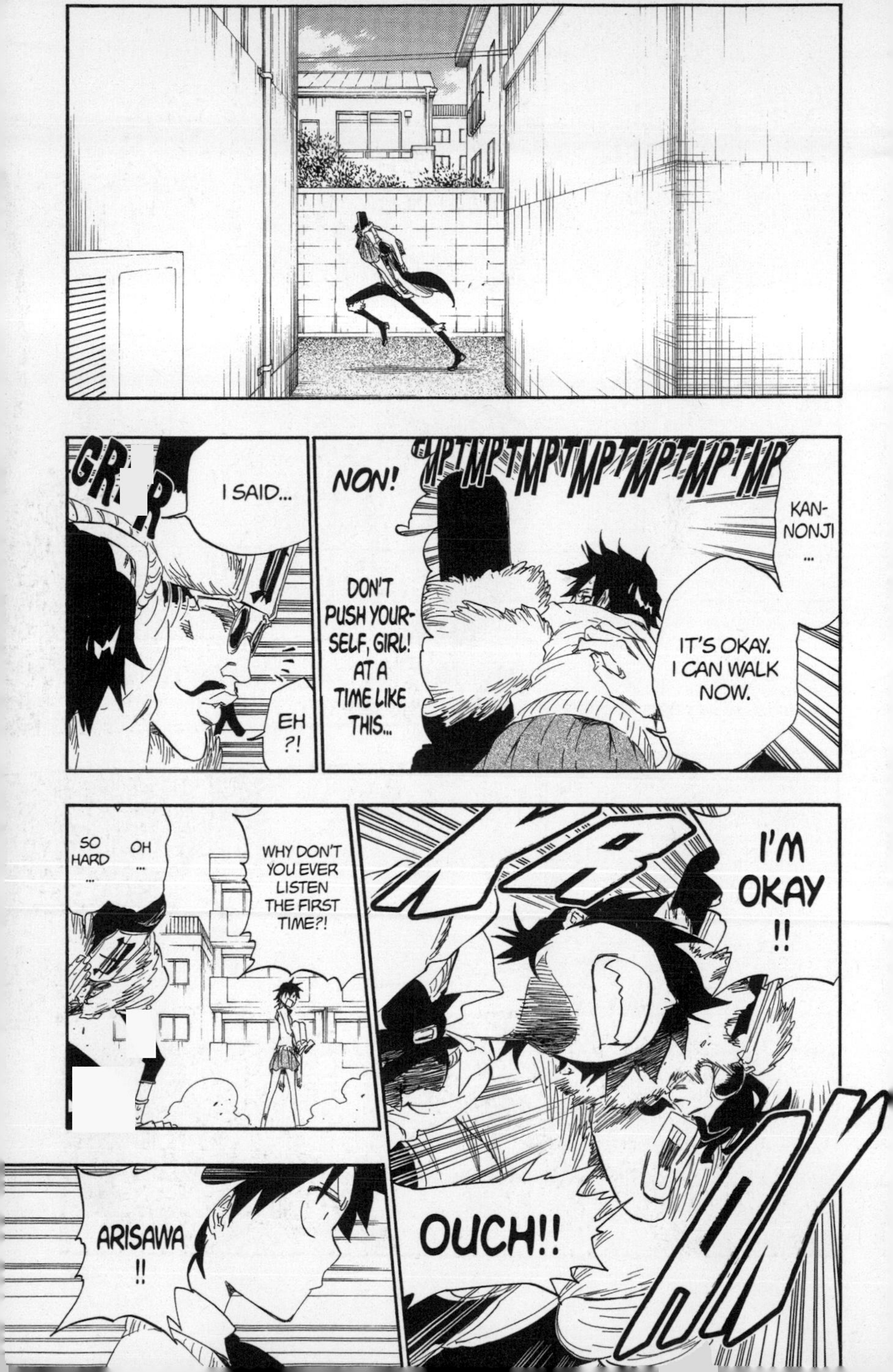
KAN-NONJI...
IT'S OKAY. I CAN WALK NOW.
NON!
DON'T PUSH YOUR-SELF, GIRL! AT A TIME LIKE THIS...
I SAID...
EH?!
I'M OKAY!!
OUCH!!
WHY DON'T YOU EVER LISTEN THE FIRST TIME?!
OH...
SO HARD...
ARISAWA!!

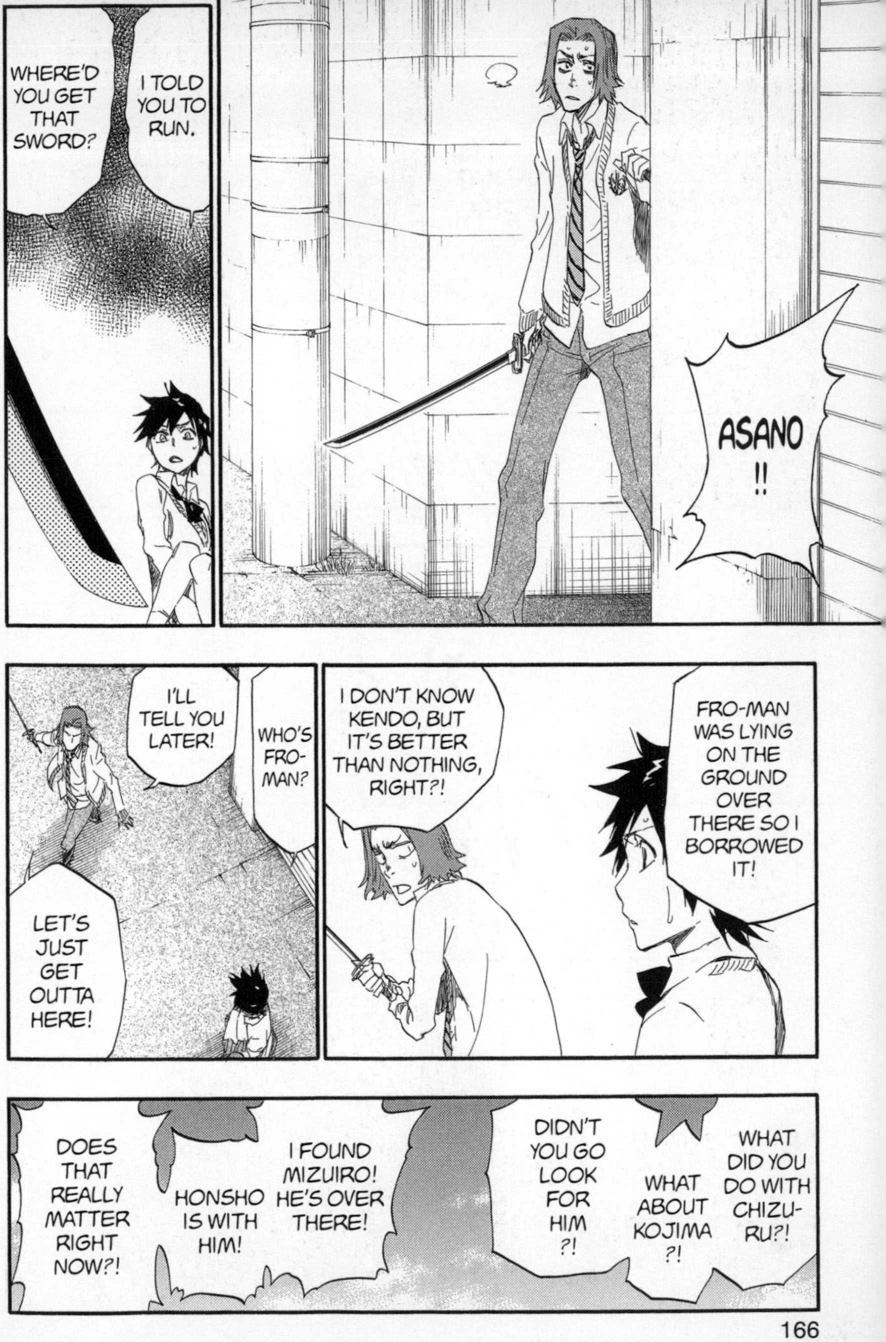
ASANO !!
I TOLD YOU TO RUN.
WHERE'D YOU GET THAT SWORD?
FRO-MAN WAS LYING ON THE GROUND OVER THERE SO I BORROWED IT!
I DON'T KNOW KENDO, BUT IT'S BETTER THAN NOTHING, RIGHT?!
WHO'S FRO-MAN?
I'LL TELL YOU LATER!
LET'S JUST GET OUTTA HERE!
WHAT DID YOU DO WITH CHIZU-RU?!
WHAT ABOUT KOJIMA ?!
DIDN'T YOU GO LOOK FOR HIM ?!
I FOUND MIZUIRO! HE'S OVER THERE!
HONSHO IS WITH HIM!
DOES THAT REALLY MATTER RIGHT NOW?!

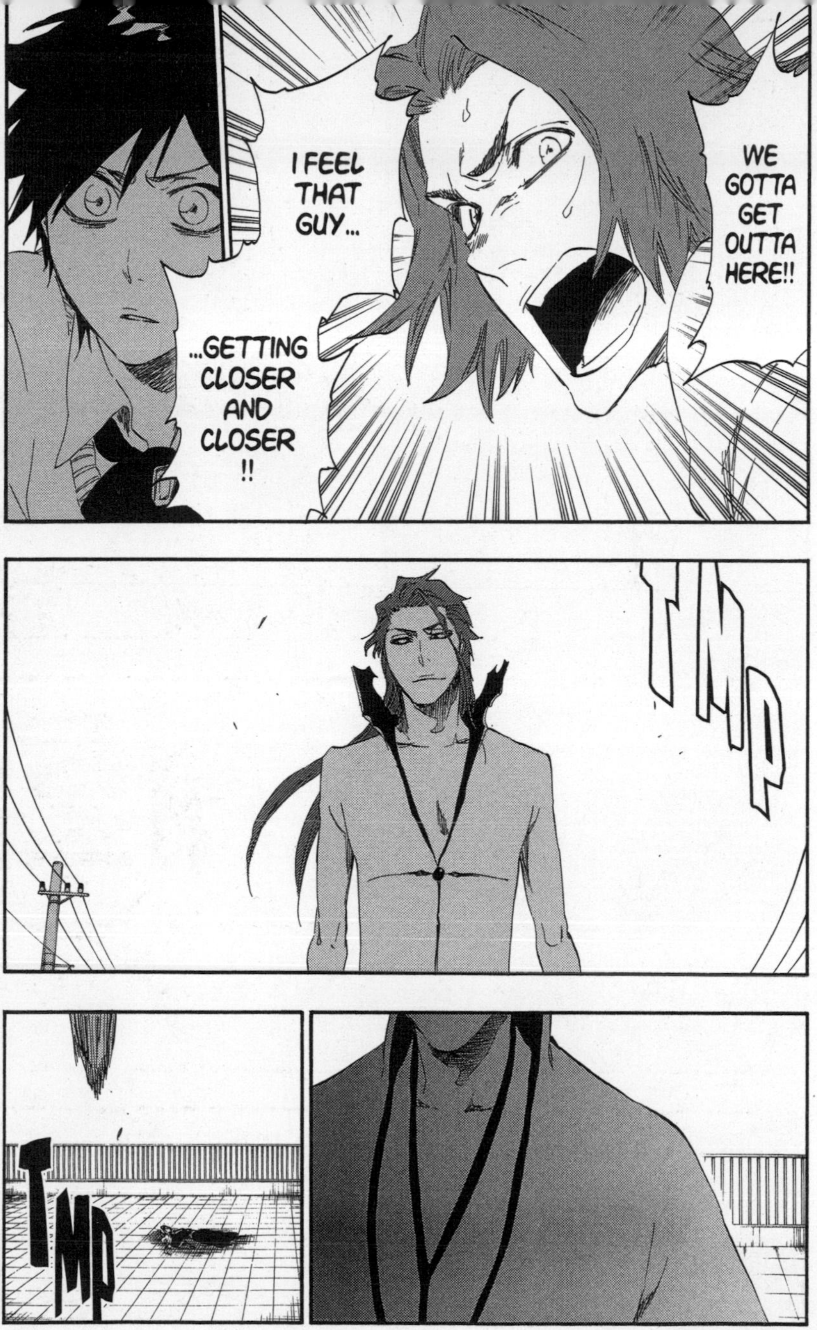
WE GOTTA GET OUTTA HERE!!
I FEEL THAT GUY...
...GETTING CLOSER AND CLOSER !!
TMP
TMP

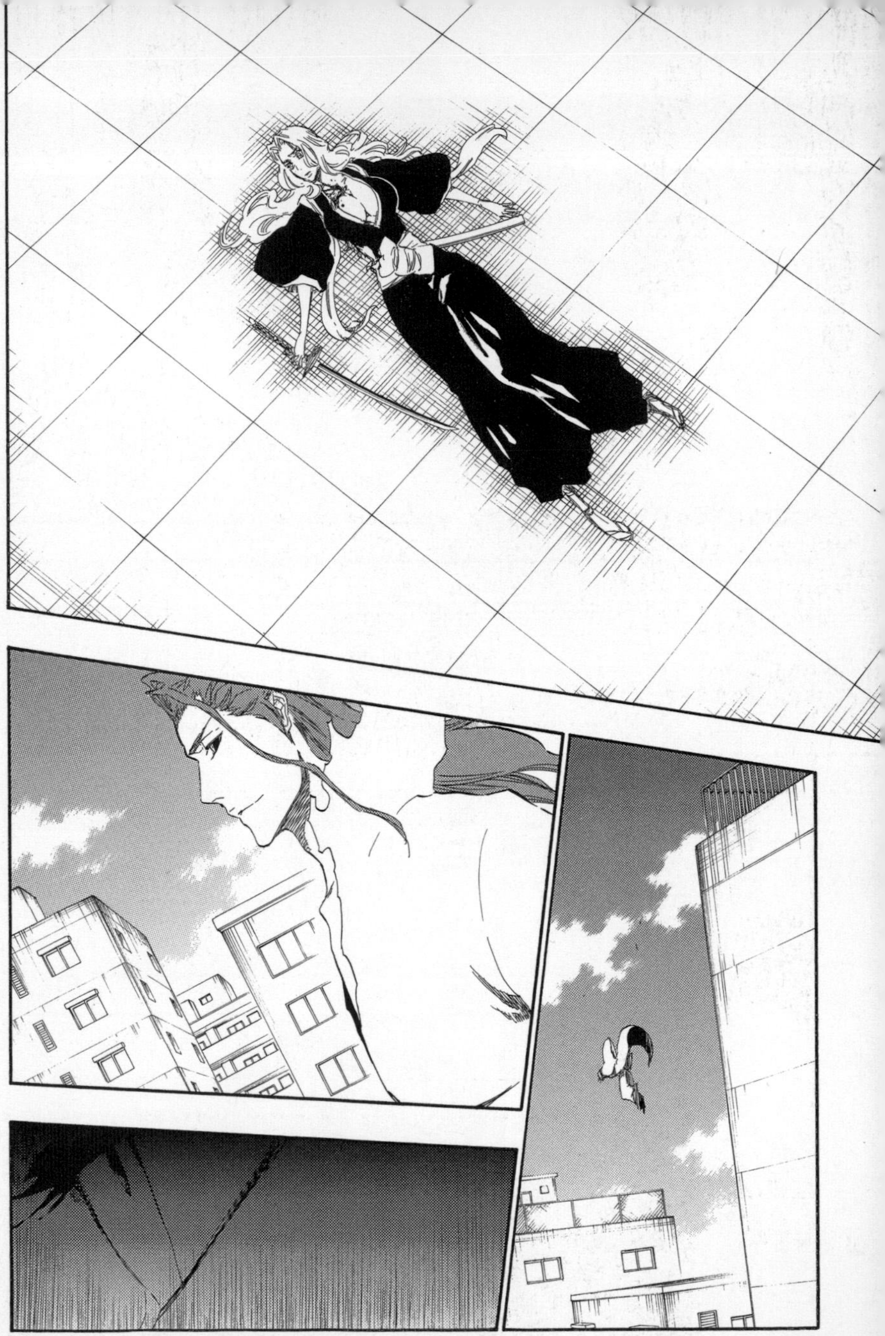

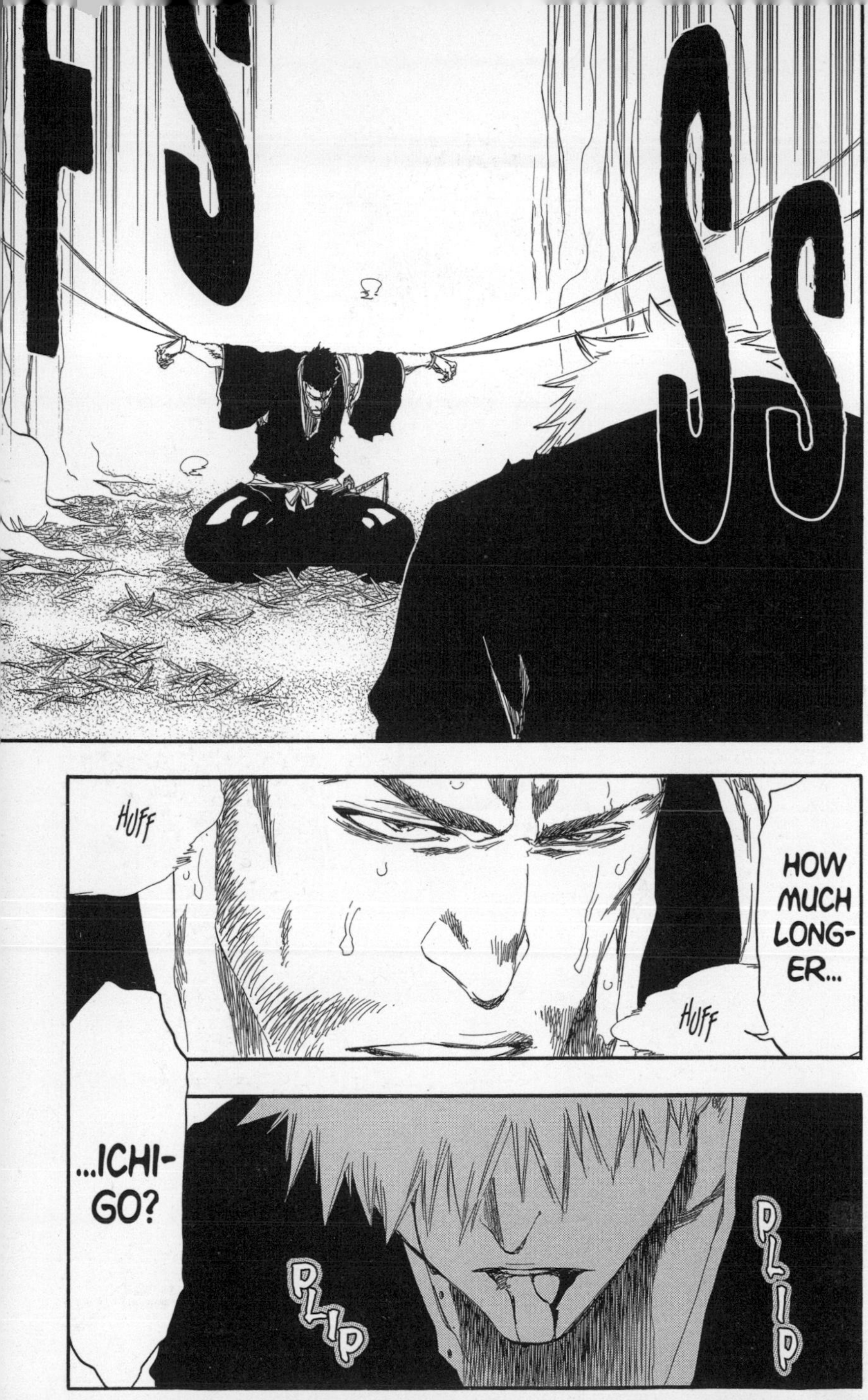
FSSS
HOW MUCH LONGER...
HUFF
HUFF
PLIP
...ICHIGO?
PLIP

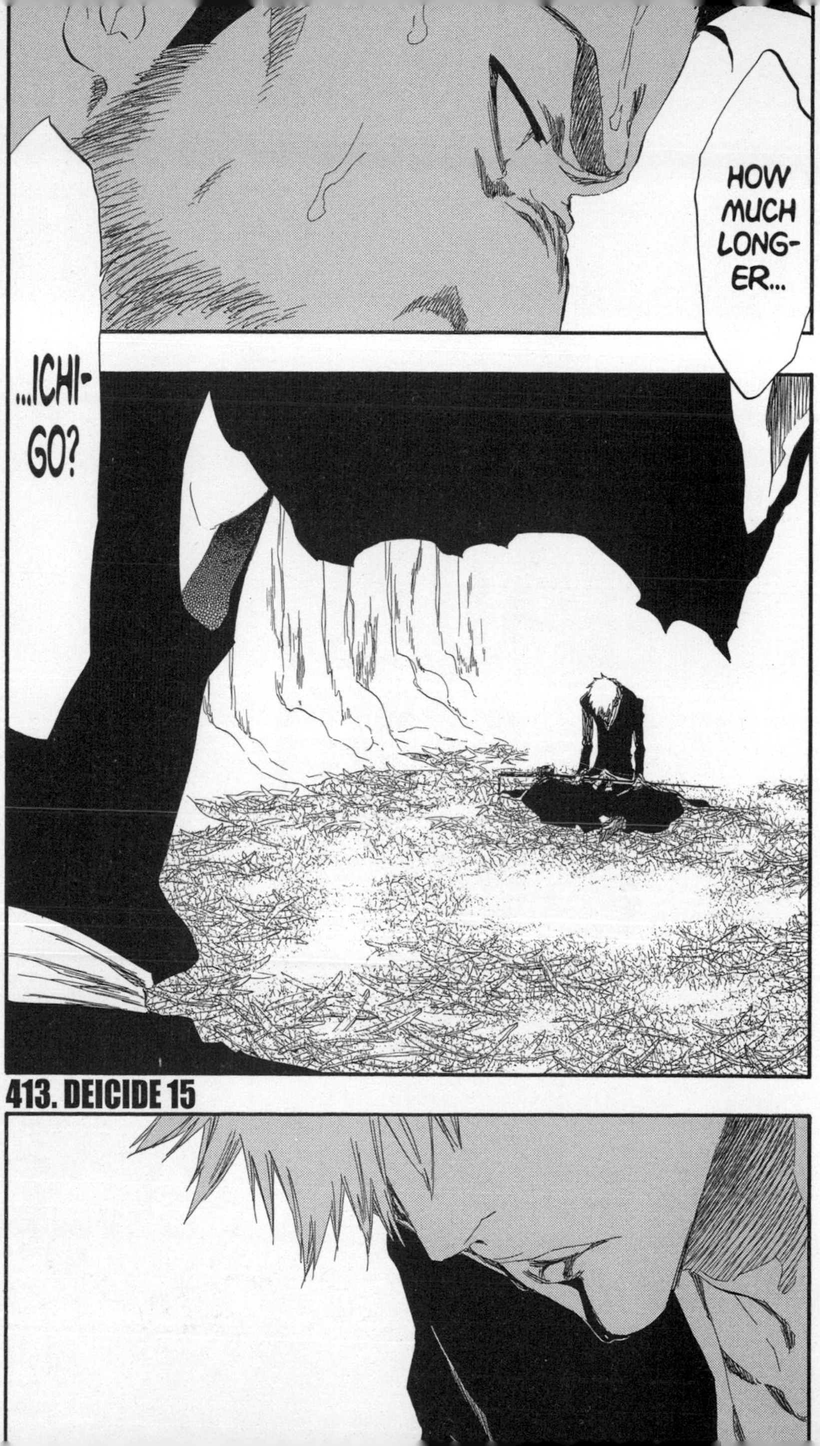
HOW MUCH LONG-ER...
...ICHI-GO?
413. DEICIDE 15

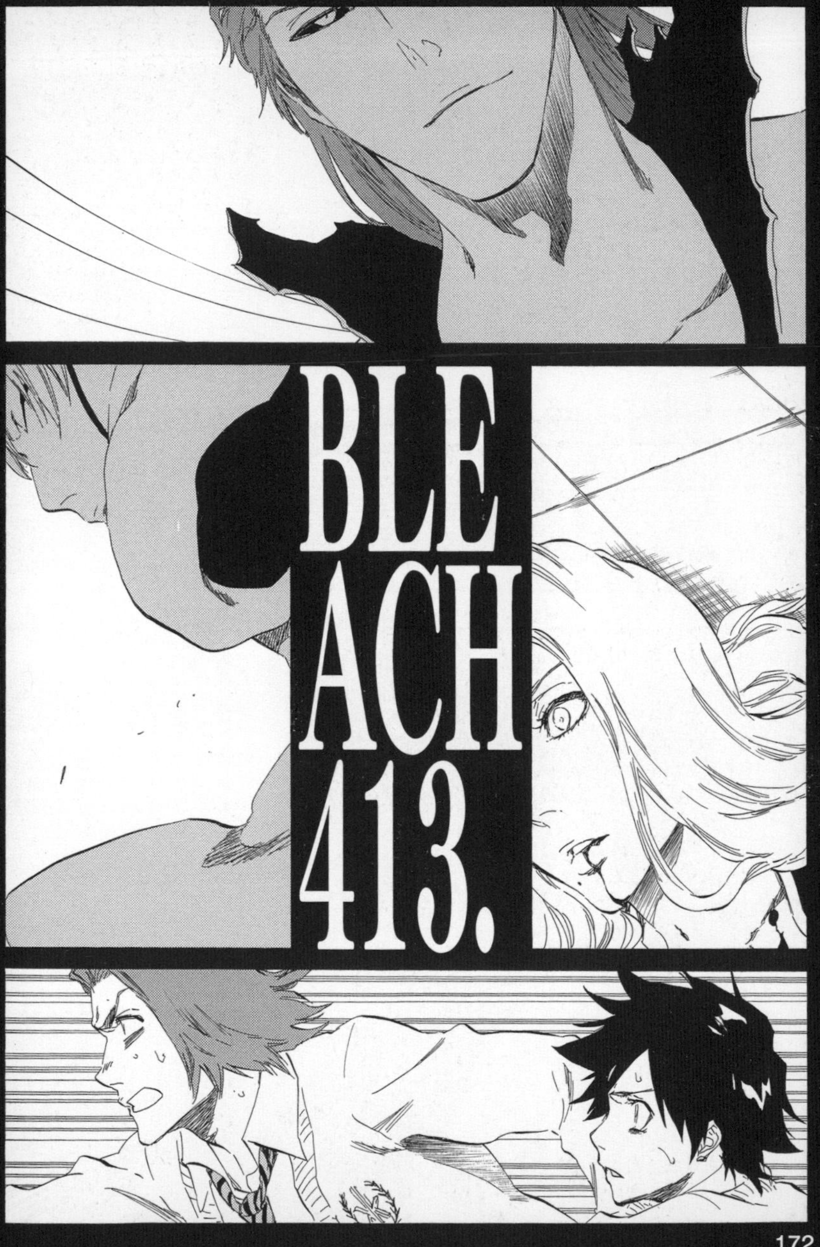
BLEACH 413.

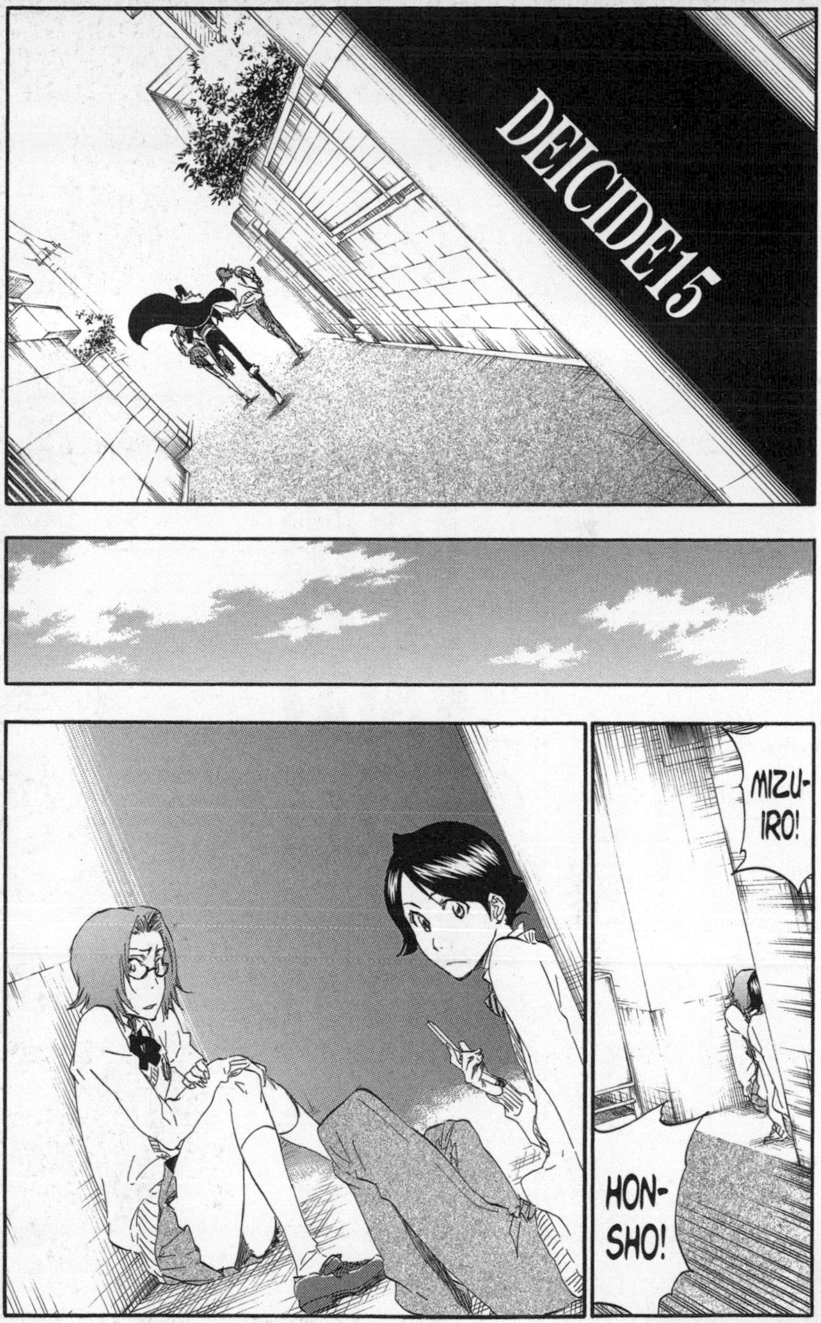
DEICIDE15
MIZU-IRO!
HON-SHO!

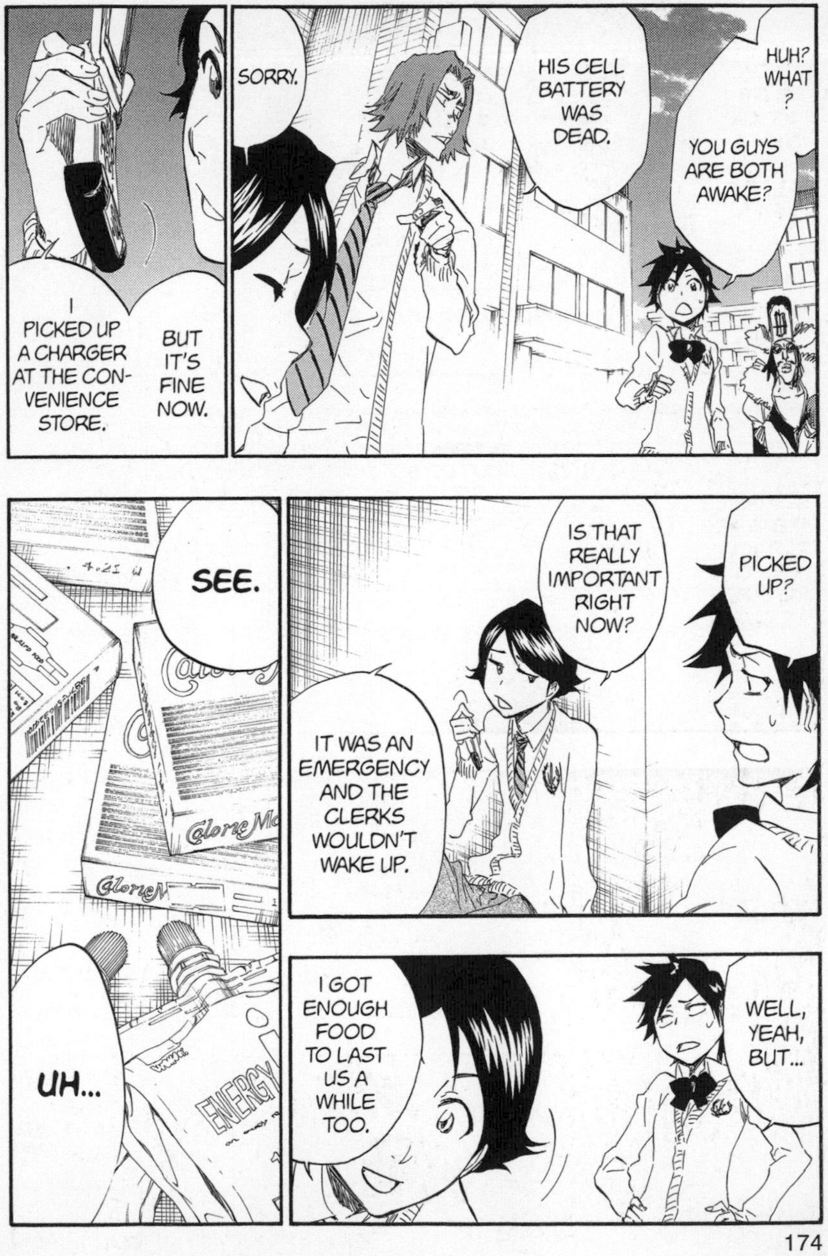
HUH? WHAT? YOU GUYS ARE BOTH AWAKE?
HIS CELL BATTERY WAS DEAD.
SORRY.
BUT IT'S FINE NOW.
I PICKED UP A CHARGER AT THE CON-VENIENCE STORE.
PICKED UP?
IS THAT REALLY IMPORTANT RIGHT NOW?
IT WAS AN EMERGENCY AND THE CLERKS WOULDN'T WAKE UP.
WELL, YEAH, BUT...
I GOT ENOUGH FOOD TO LAST US A WHILE TOO.
SEE.
UH...

READ THIS WAY

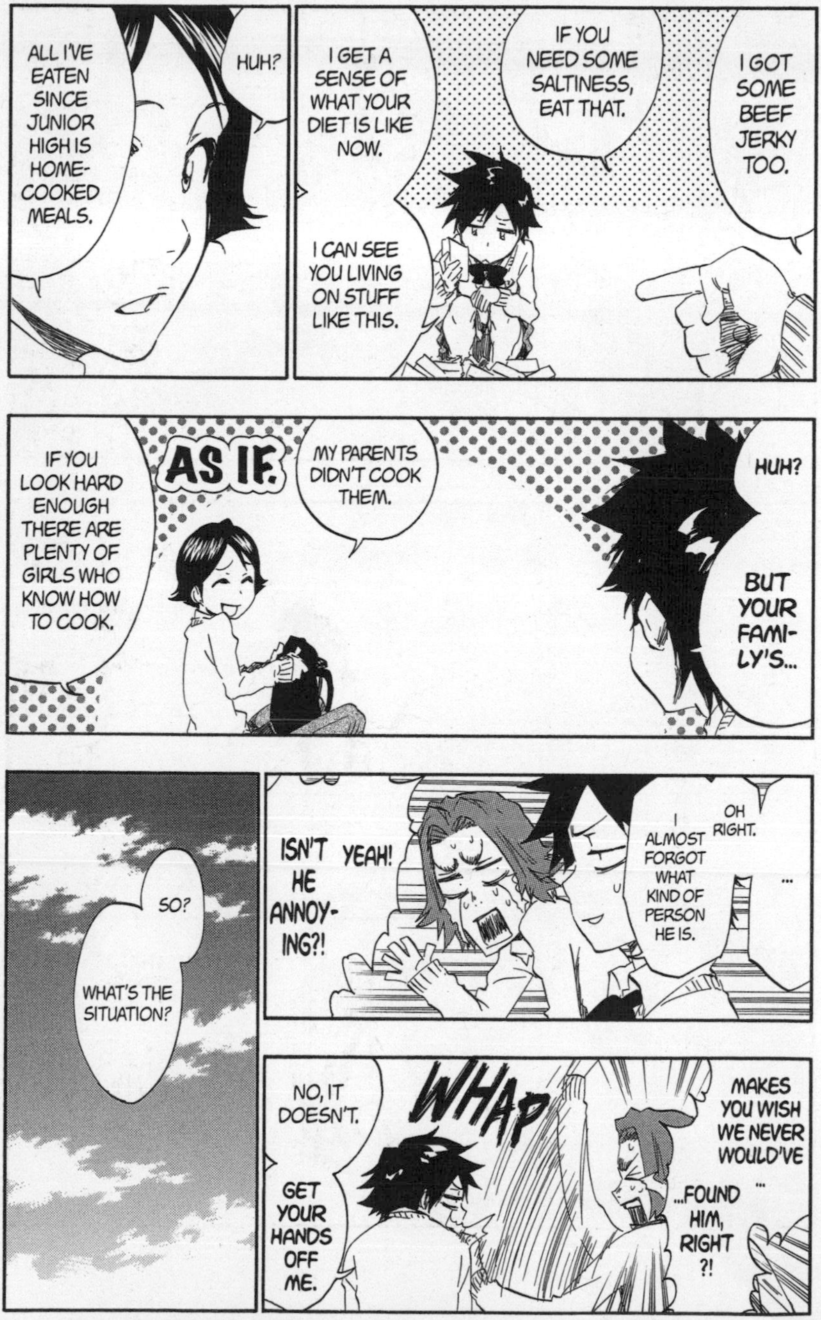
I GOT SOME BEEF JERKY TOO.
IF YOU NEED SOME SALTINESS, EAT THAT.
I GET A SENSE OF WHAT YOUR DIET IS LIKE NOW.
I CAN SEE YOU LIVING ON STUFF LIKE THIS.
HUH?
ALL I'VE EATEN SINCE JUNIOR HIGH IS HOME-COOKED MEALS.
HUH?
BUT YOUR FAMILY'S...
MY PARENTS DIDN'T COOK THEM.
AS IF.
IF YOU LOOK HARD ENOUGH THERE ARE PLENTY OF GIRLS WHO KNOW HOW TO COOK.
OH RIGHT.
...
I ALMOST FORGOT WHAT KIND OF PERSON HE IS.
YEAH!
ISN'T HE ANNOYING?!
MAKES YOU WISH WE NEVER WOULD'VE...
...FOUND HIM, RIGHT?!
WHAP
NO, IT DOESN'T.
GET YOUR HANDS OFF ME.
SO?
WHAT'S THE SITUATION?

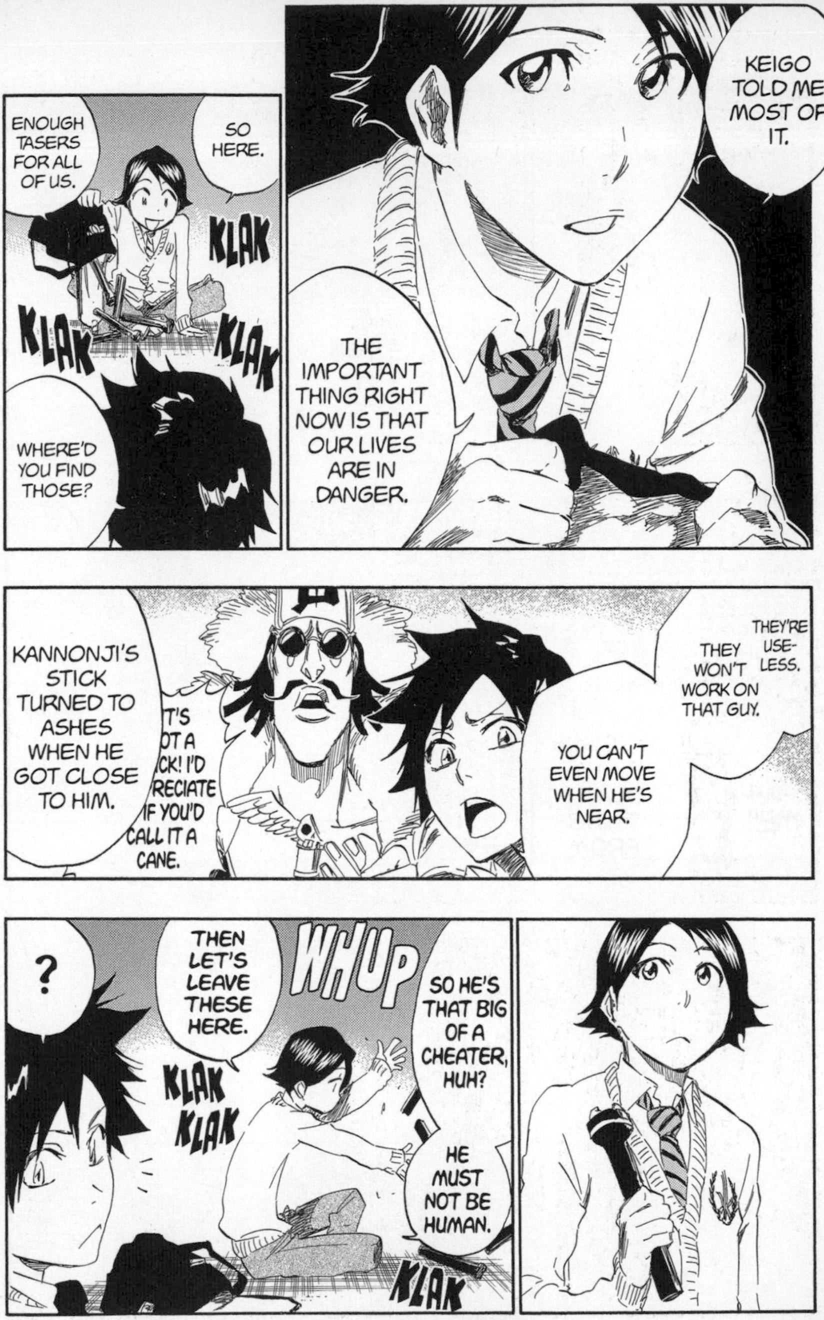
KEIGO TOLD ME MOST OF IT.
THE IMPORTANT THING RIGHT NOW IS THAT OUR LIVES ARE IN DANGER.
SO HERE.
ENOUGH TASERS FOR ALL OF US.
KLAK
KLAK
KLAK
WHERE'D YOU FIND THOSE?
THEY'RE USELESS.
THEY WON'T WORK ON THAT GUY.
YOU CAN'T EVEN MOVE WHEN HE'S NEAR.
KANNONJI'S STICK TURNED TO ASHES WHEN HE GOT CLOSE TO HIM.
T'S OT A CK! I'D RECIATE IF YOU'D CALL IT A CANE.
SO HE'S THAT BIG OF A CHEATER, HUH?
WHUP
THEN LET'S LEAVE THESE HERE.
?
KLAK KLAK
HE MUST NOT BE HUMAN.
KLAK

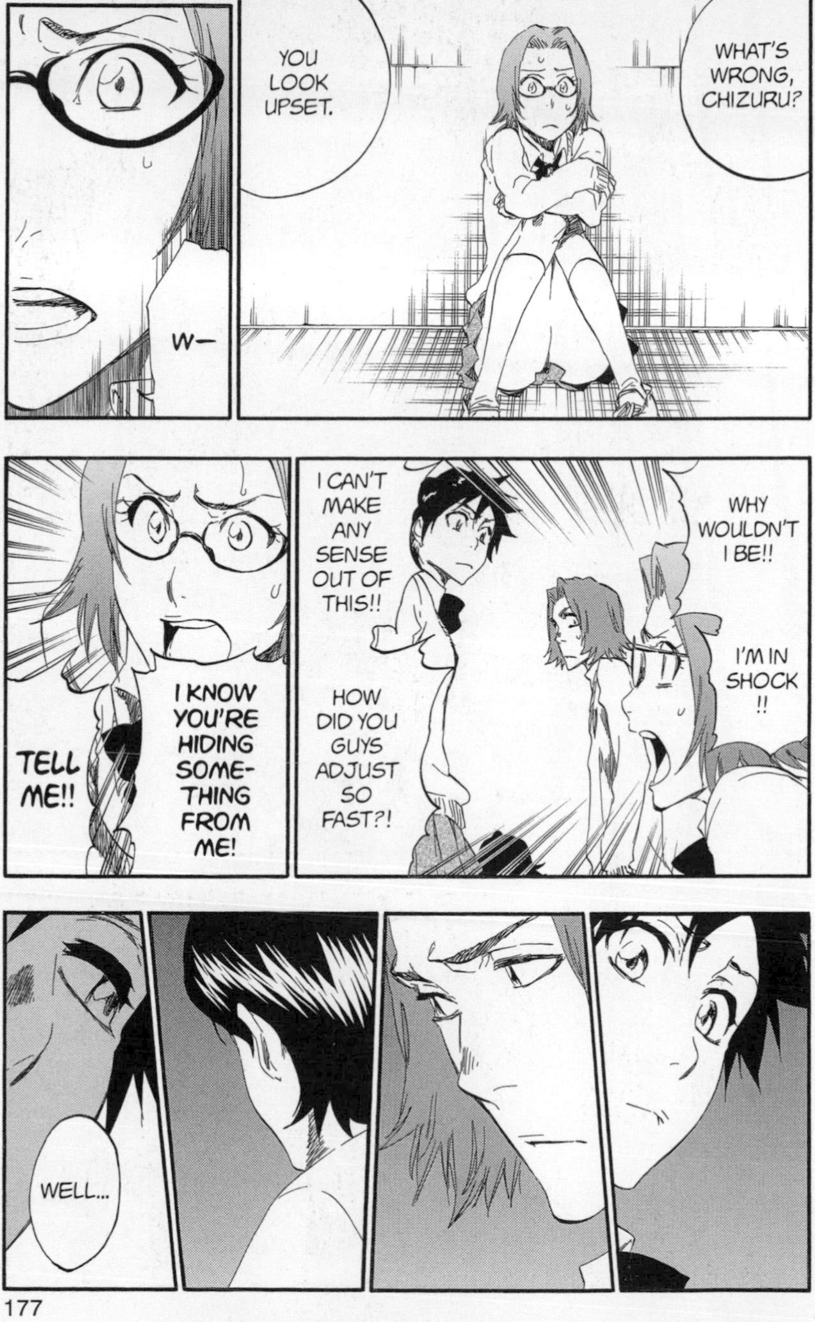
WHAT'S WRONG, CHIZURU?
YOU LOOK UPSET.
W—
WHY WOULDN'T I BE!!
I'M IN SHOCK !!
I CAN'T MAKE ANY SENSE OUT OF THIS!!
HOW DID YOU GUYS ADJUST SO FAST?!
I KNOW YOU'RE HIDING SOME-THING FROM ME!
TELL ME!!
WELL...

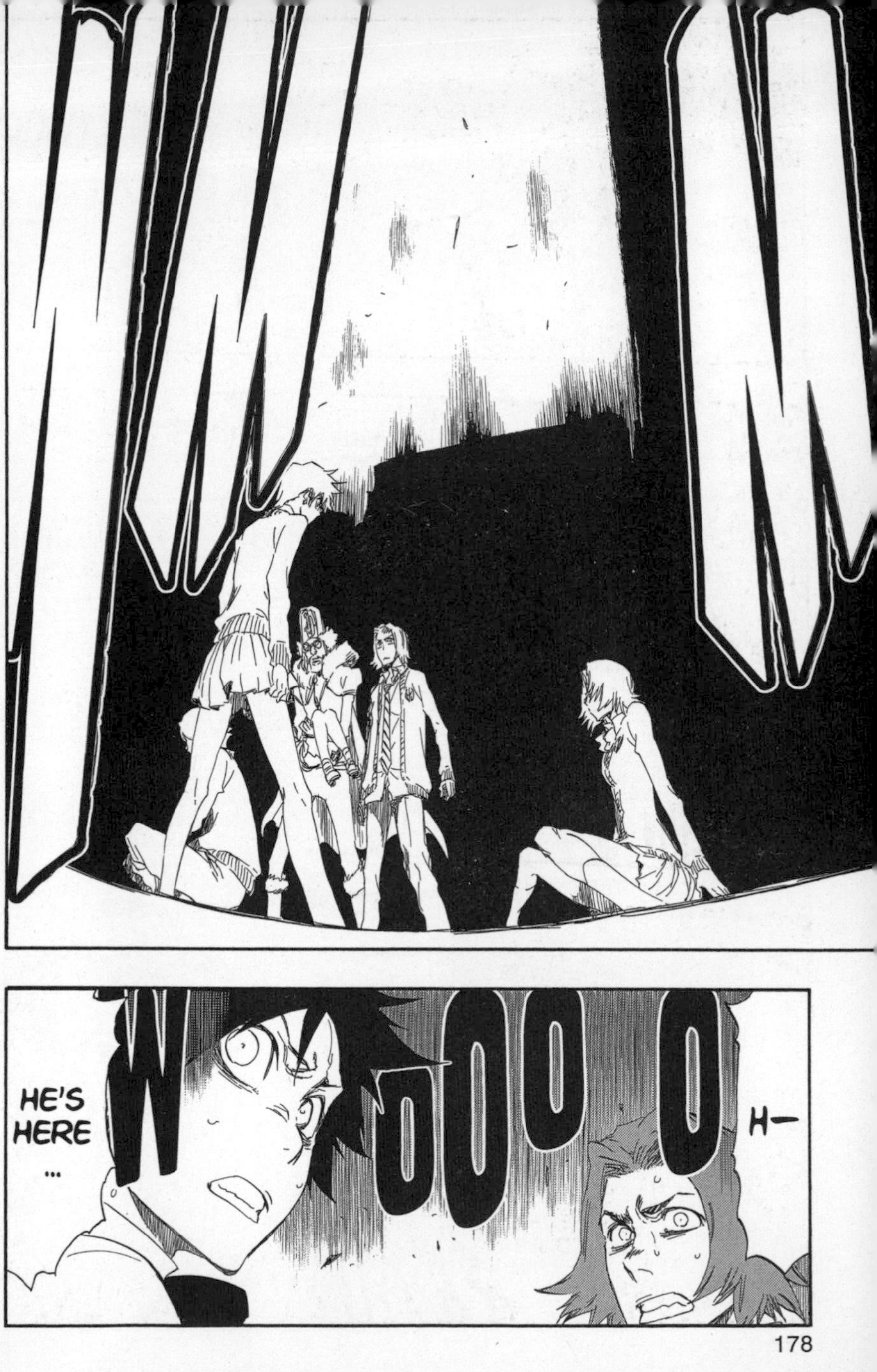
H—
HE'S HERE ...

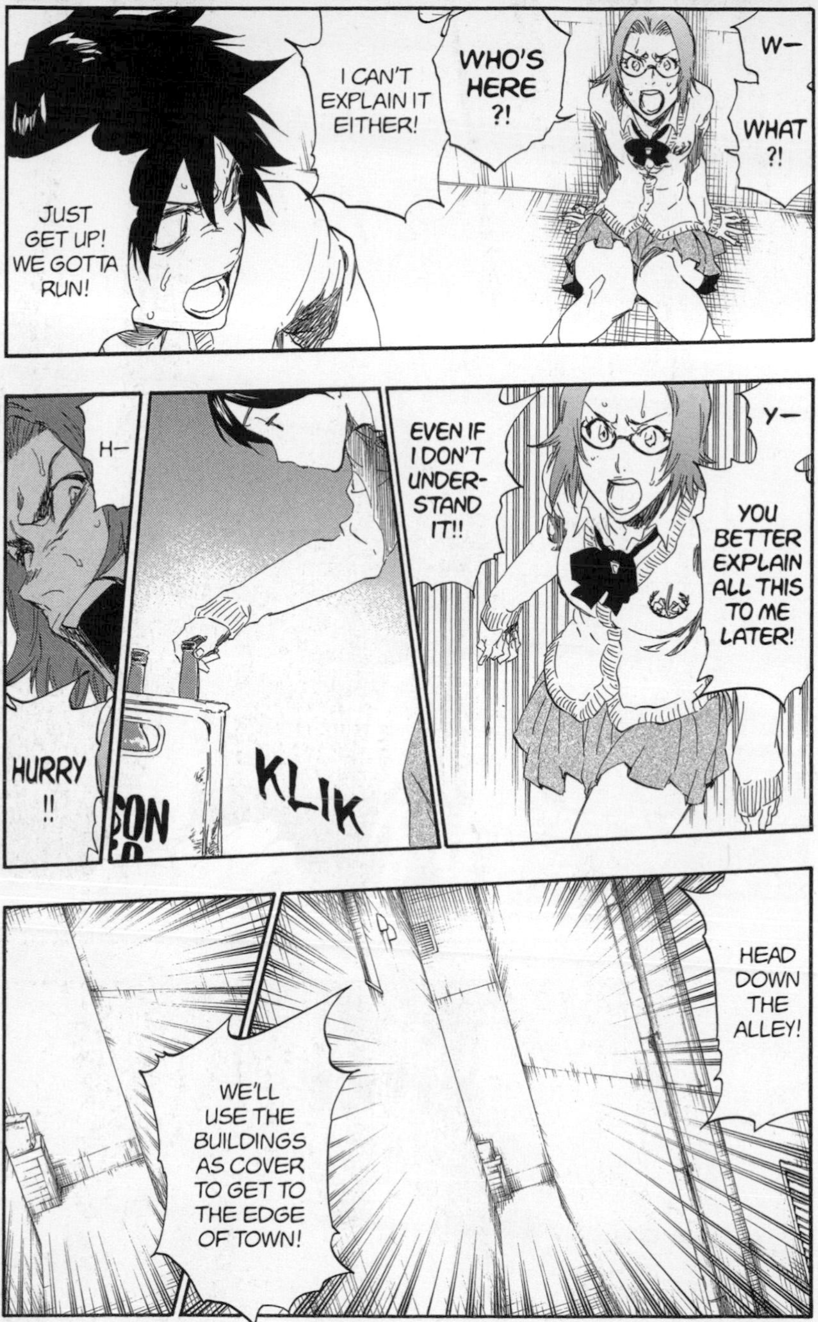
W—
WHAT?!
WHO'S HERE?!
I CAN'T EXPLAIN IT EITHER!
JUST GET UP! WE GOTTA RUN!
Y—
YOU BETTER EXPLAIN ALL THIS TO ME LATER!
EVEN IF I DON'T UNDER-STAND IT!!
KLIK
H—
HURRY!!
HEAD DOWN THE ALLEY!
WE'LL USE THE BUILDINGS AS COVER TO GET TO THE EDGE OF TOWN!

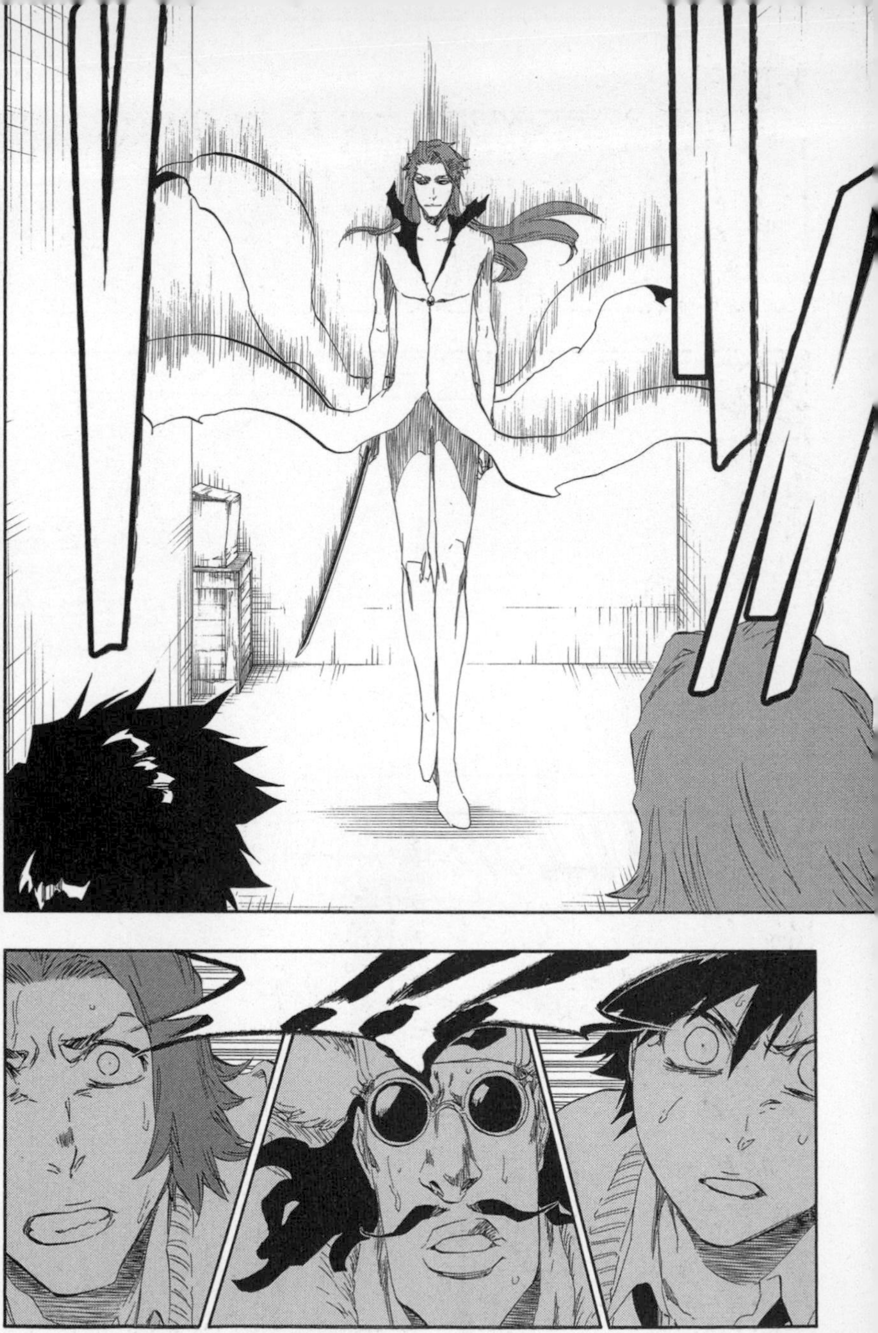

READ THIS WAY

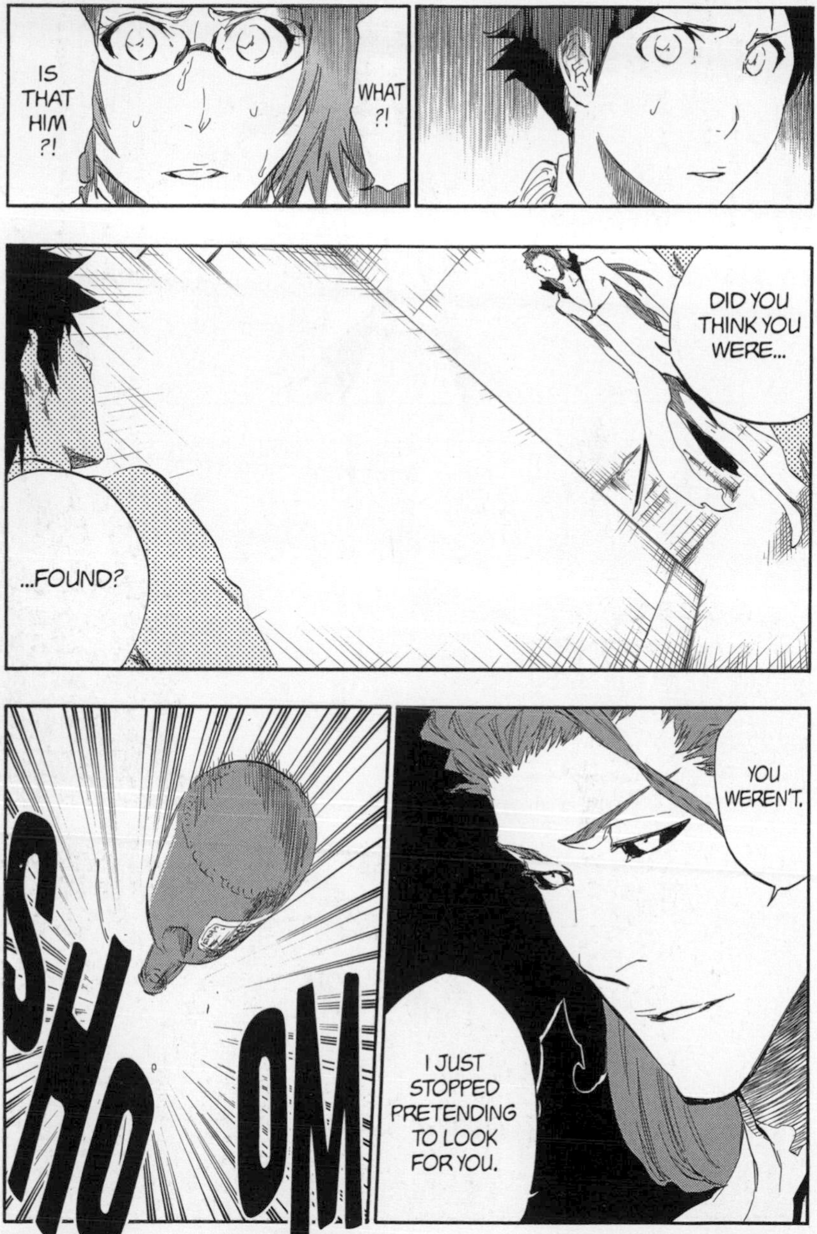
WHAT ?!
IS THAT HIM ?!
DID YOU THINK YOU WERE...
...FOUND?
YOU WEREN'T.
I JUST STOPPED PRETENDING TO LOOK FOR YOU.
SHOOM

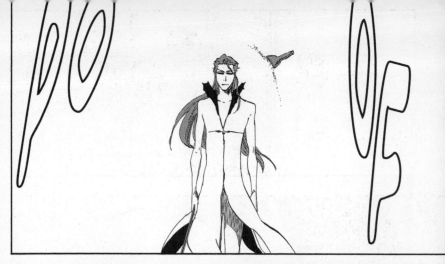

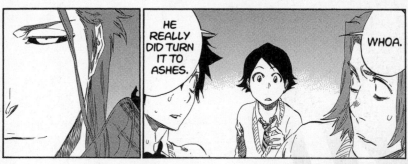

POOF
WHOA.
HE REALLY DID TURN IT TO ASHES.
THEN... HOW ABOUT THIS.
SNAP
KLUNK
FSHHHHHHHH

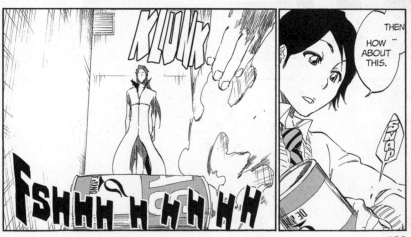

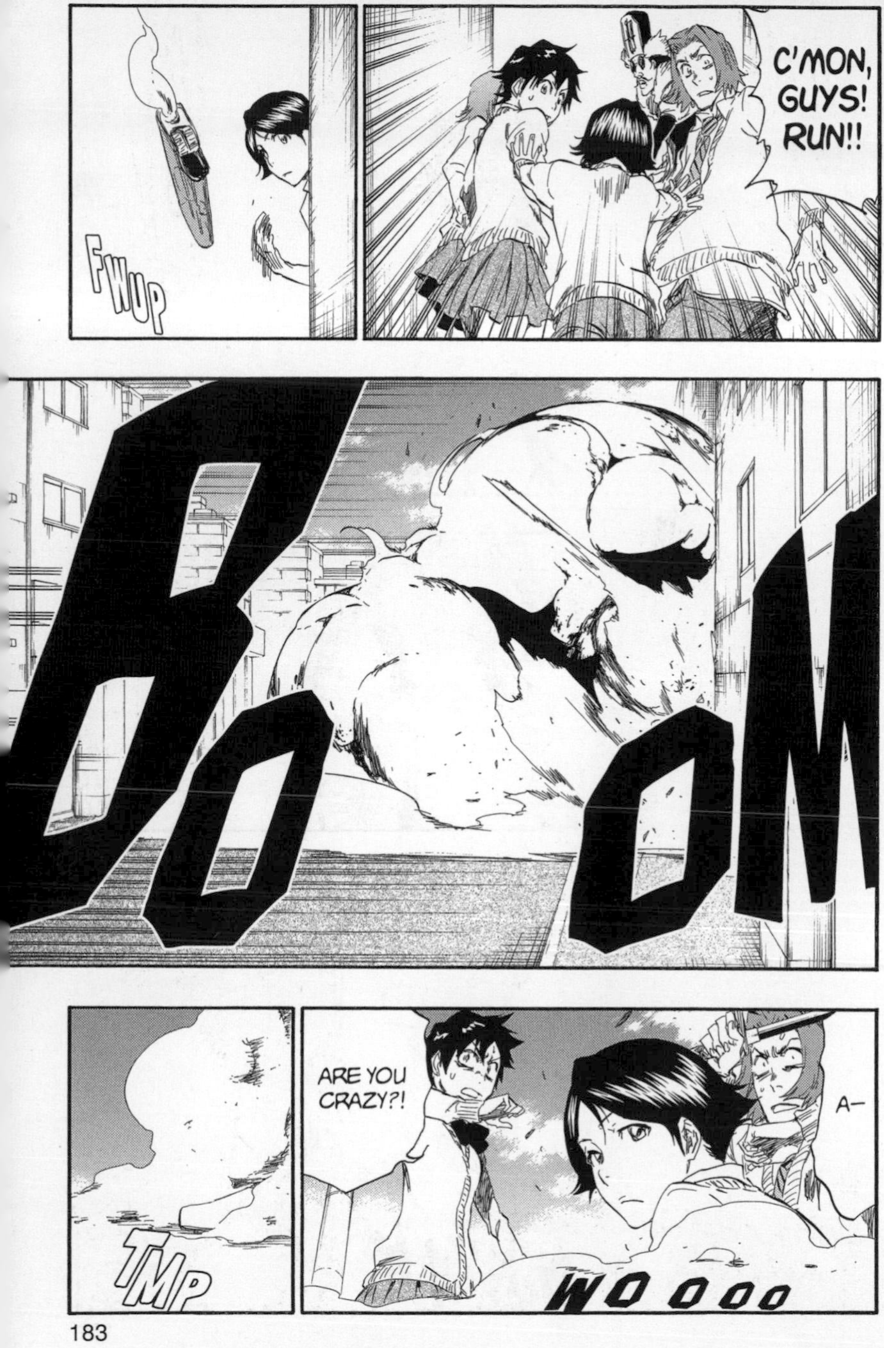
C'MON, GUYS! RUN!!
FWUP
BOOM
A—
ARE YOU CRAZY?!
WO O O O
TMP

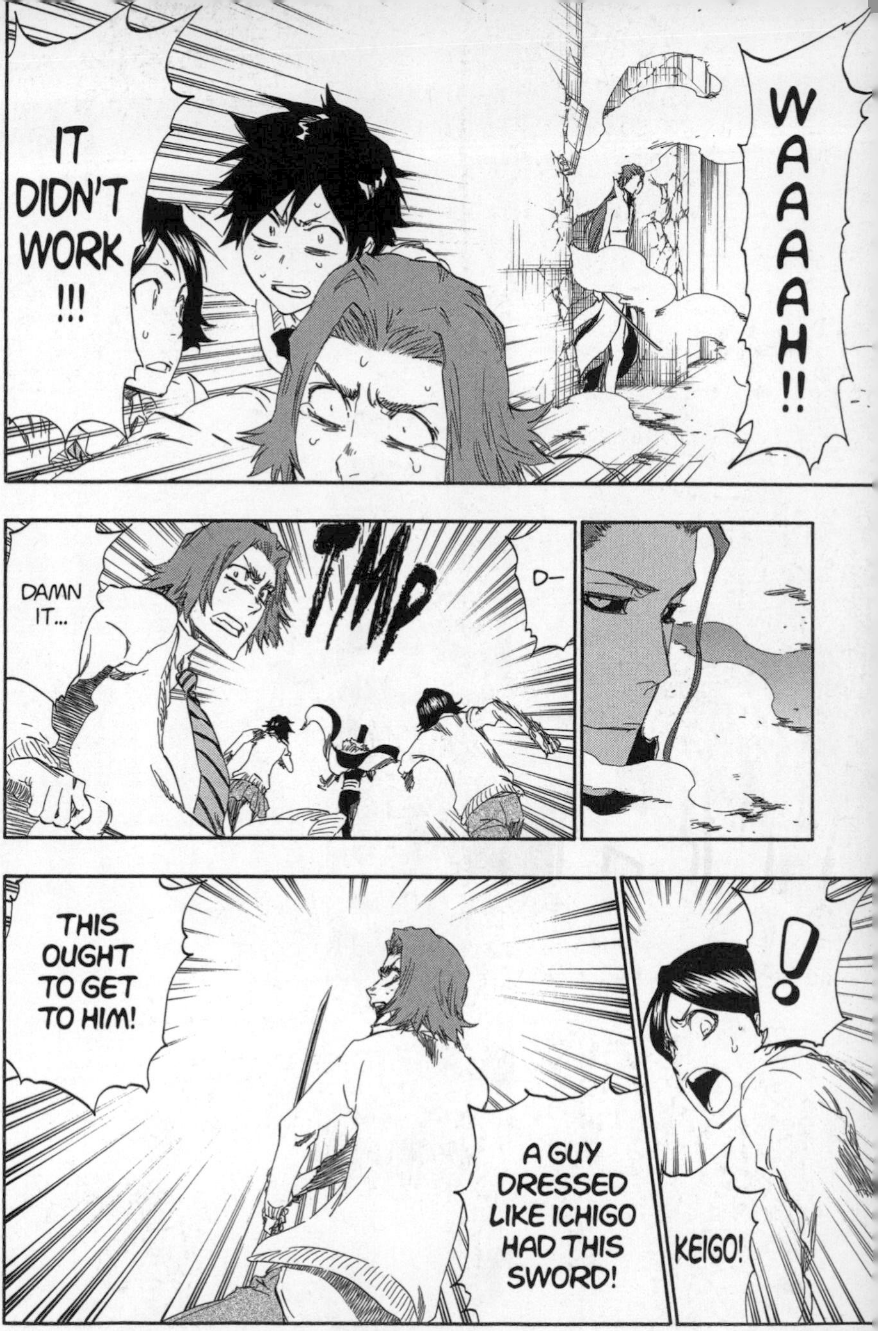
WAAAAAH!!
IT DIDN'T WORK !!!
D—
TMP
DAMN IT...
!
KEIGO!
A GUY DRESSED LIKE ICHIGO HAD THIS SWORD!
THIS OUGHT TO GET TO HIM!

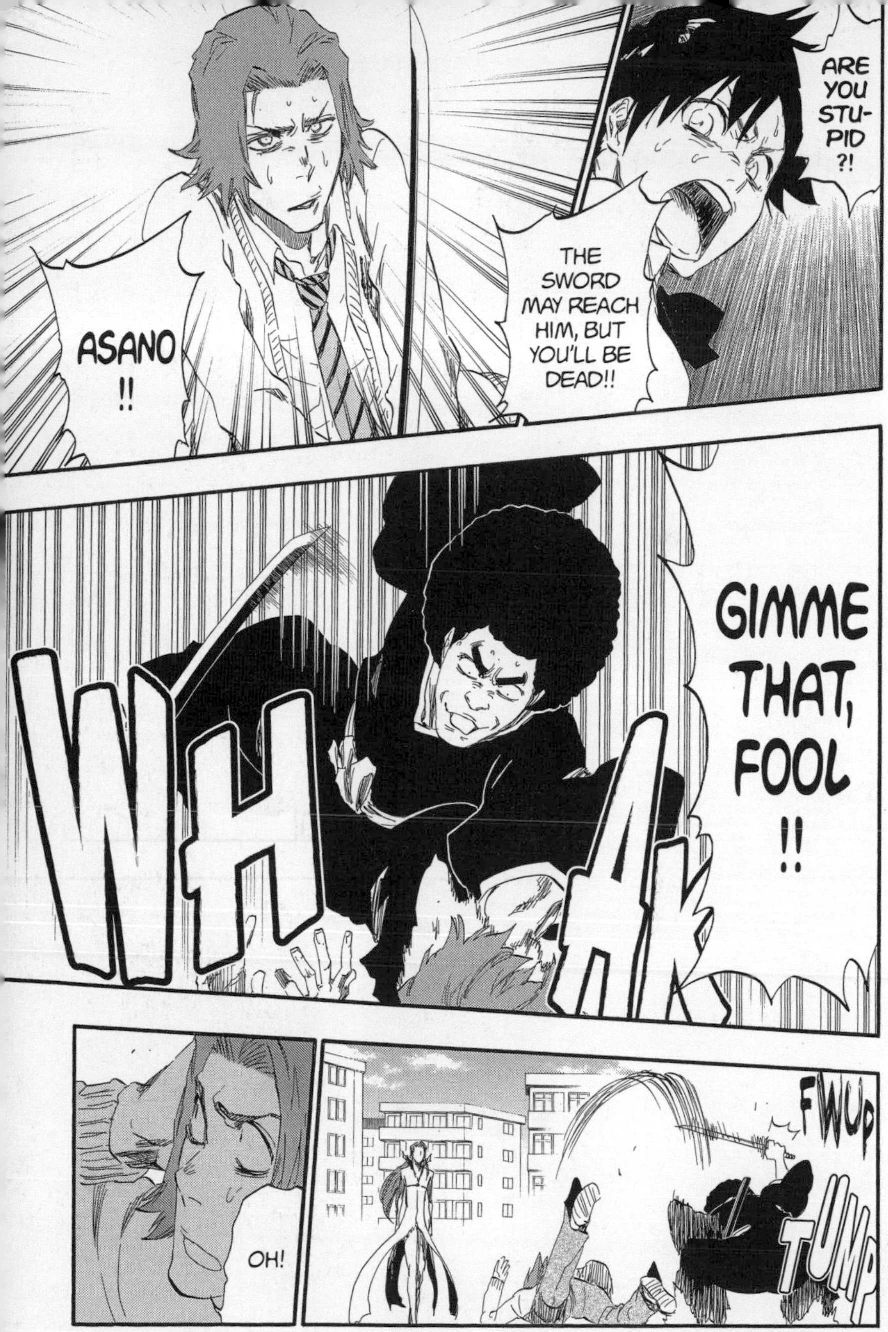
ARE YOU STU-PID?!
THE SWORD MAY REACH HIM, BUT YOU'LL BE DEAD!!
ASANO!!
GIMME THAT, FOOL!!
WHA
FWUP
TUMP
OH!

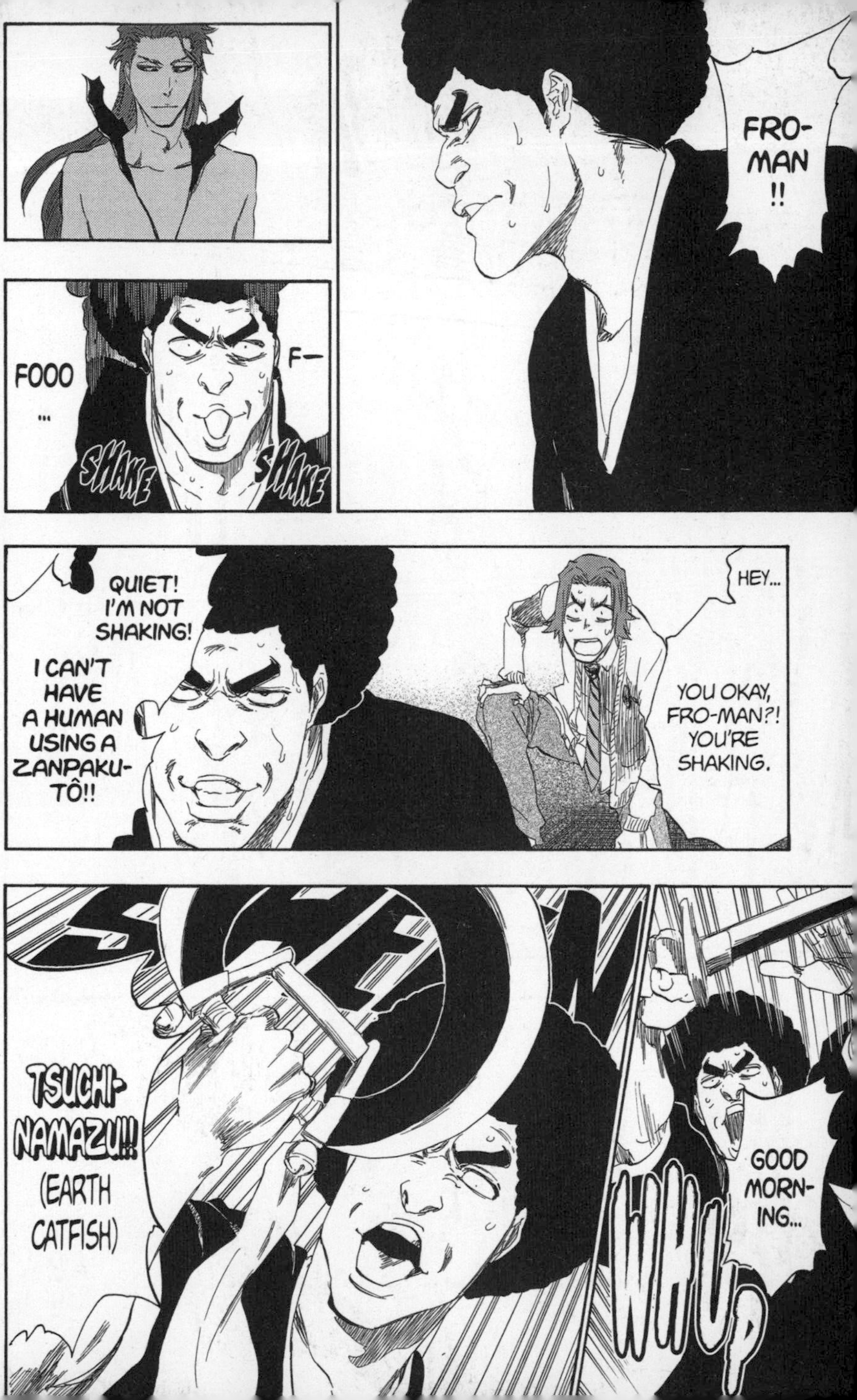
FRO-MAN !!
F—
FOOO ...
SHAKE
SHAKE
HEY...
YOU OKAY, FRO-MAN?! YOU'RE SHAKING.
QUIET! I'M NOT SHAKING!
I CAN'T HAVE A HUMAN USING A ZANPAKU-TÔ!!
GOOD MORN-ING...
WHUP
TSUCHI-NAMAZU!!!
(EARTH CATFISH)

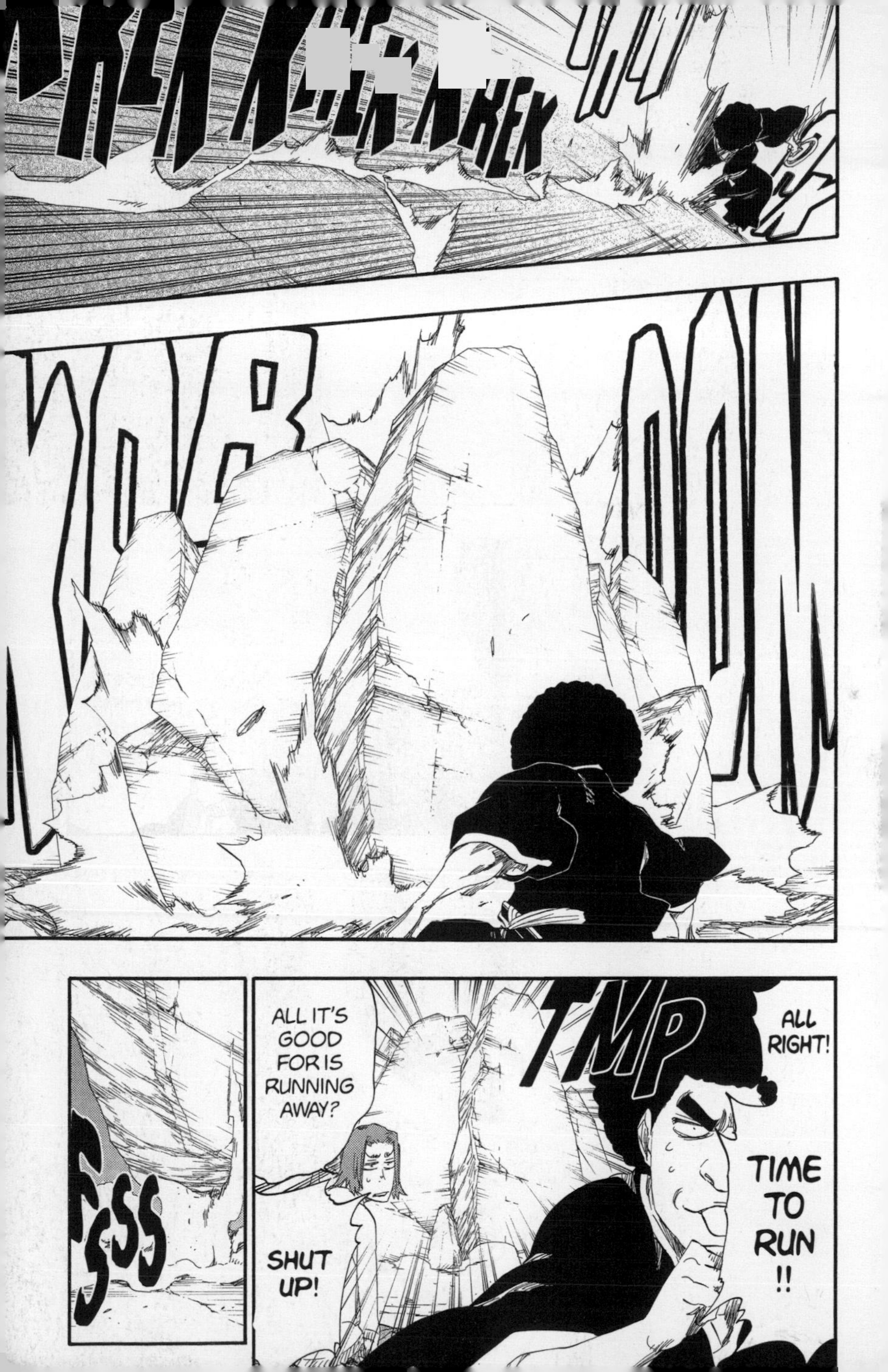
ALL RIGHT!
TMP
TIME TO RUN !!
ALL IT'S GOOD FOR IS RUNNING AWAY?
SHUT UP!

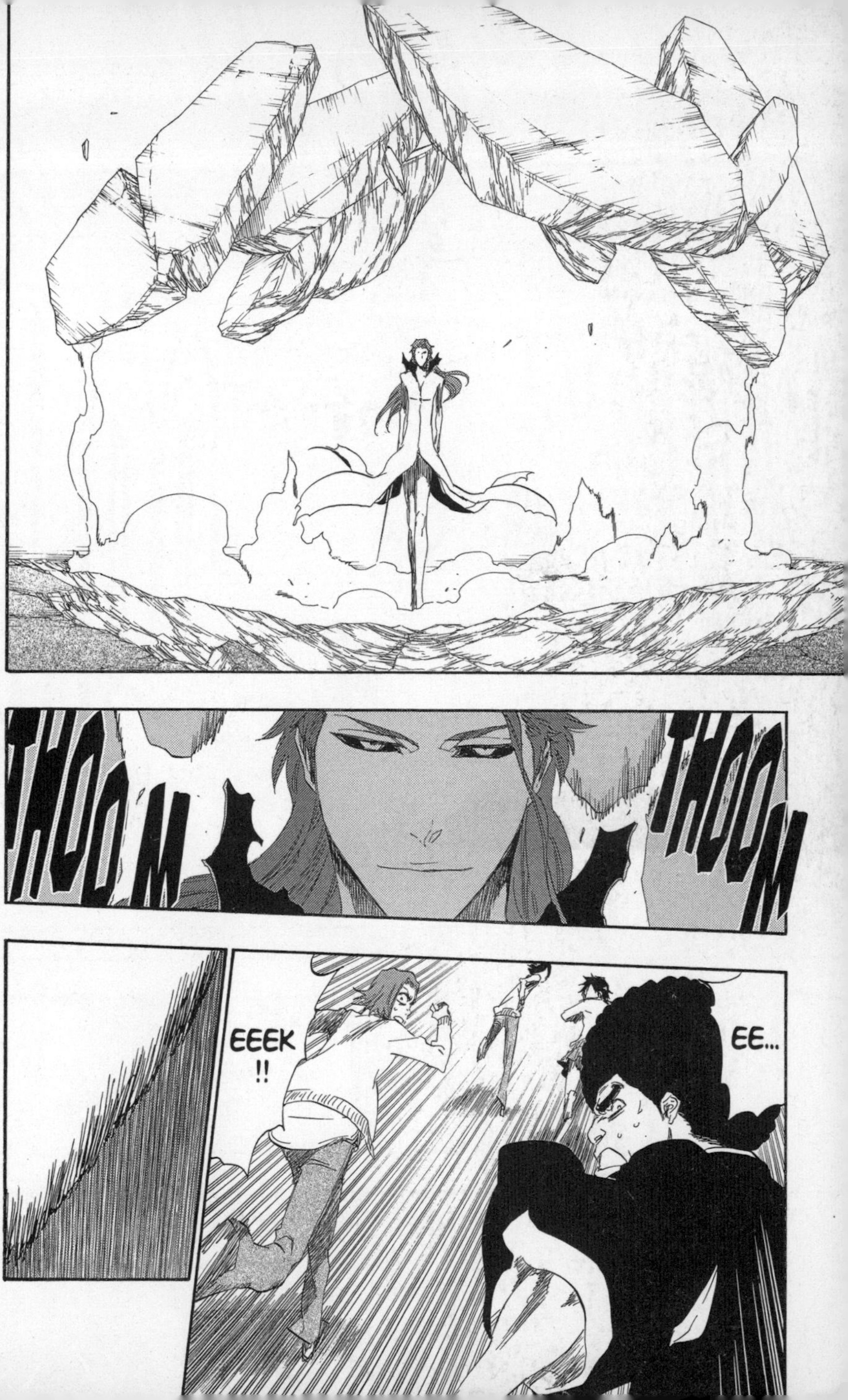
THOOM
THOOM
EE...
EEEK !!

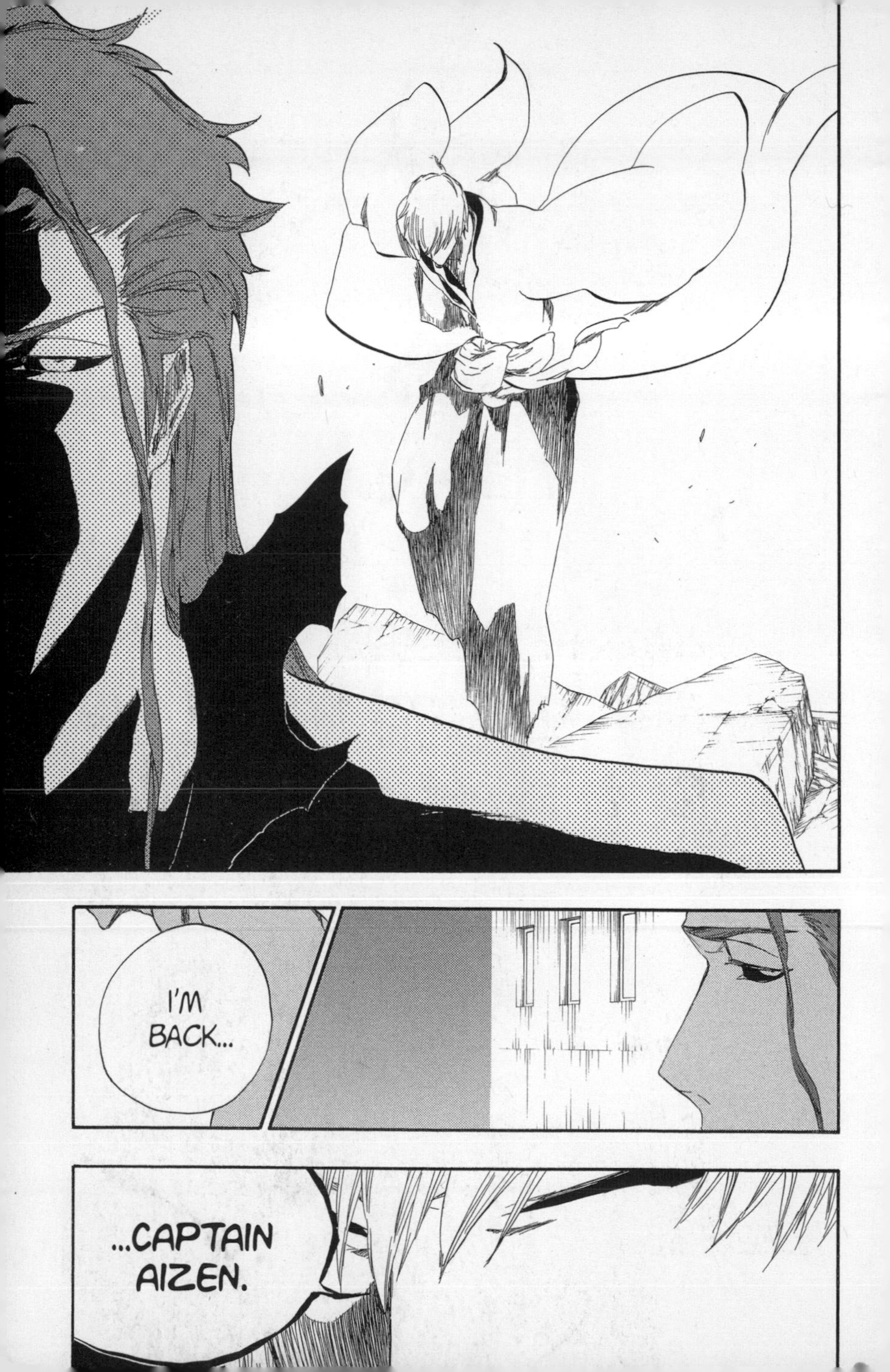
I'M BACK...
...CAPTAIN AIZEN.

CONTI
NUED
IN
BLEACH
48

Next Volume Preview

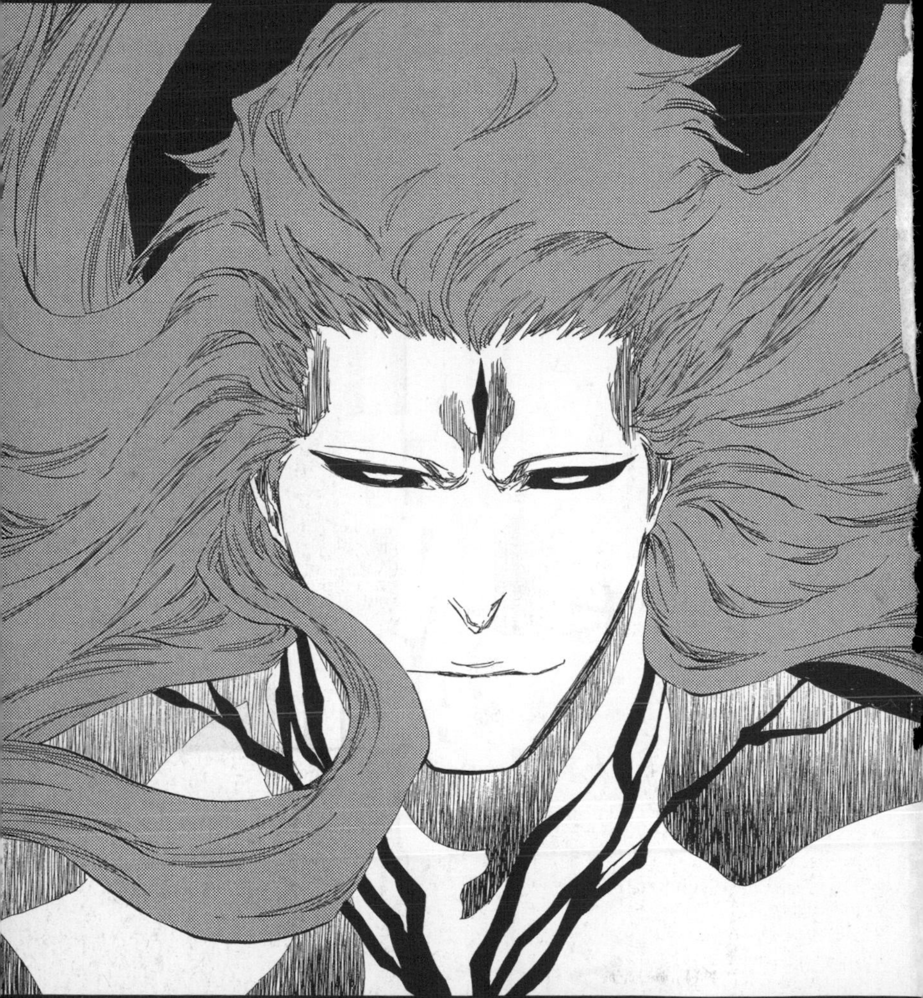

As Aizen prepares to destroy Karakura Town, Gin starts acting strangely. What is behind Gin's hidden ambition? And when Ichigo returns from mastering the final Getsuga Tensho technique, what will be left of his beloved hometown...?

You're Reading in the Wrong Direction!!

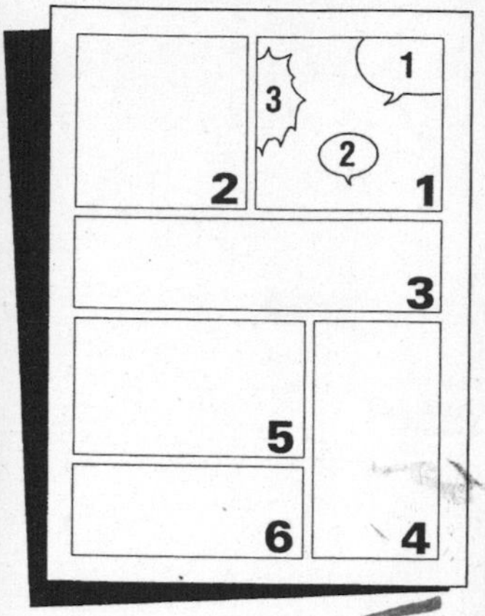
1
3
2
1
2
3
4
5
6

Whoops! Guess what? You're starting at the wrong end of the comic!

...It's true! In keeping with the original Japanese format, **Bleach** is meant to be read from right to left, starting in the upper-right corner.

Unlike English, which is read from left to right, Japanese is read from right to left, meaning that action, sound effects and word-balloon order are completely reversed... something which can make readers unfamiliar with Japanese feel pretty backwards themselves. For this reason, manga or Japanese comics published in the U.S. in English have sometimes been published "flopped"—that is, printed in exact reverse order, as though seen from the other side of a mirror.

By flopping pages, U.S. publishers can avoid confusing readers, but the compromise is not without its downside. For one thing, a character in a flopped manga series who once wore in the original Japanese version a T-shirt emblazoned with "M A Y" (as in "the merry month of") now wears one which reads "Y A M"! Additionally, many manga creators in Japan are themselves unhappy with the process, as some feel the mirror-imaging of their art skews their original intentions.

We are proud to bring you Tite Kubo's **Bleach** in the original unflopped format. For now, though, turn to the other side of the book and let the adventure begin...!

—Editor

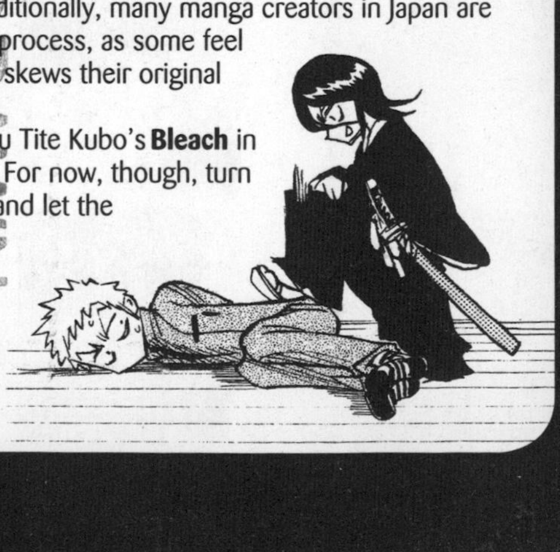